P9-DXM-621

This is the last page.

BEASTARS reads from right to left to preserve the orientation of the original Japanese artwork.

TOKYO GHOUL

C O M P L E T E   B O X   S E T

STORY AND ART BY **SUI ISHIDA**

KEN KANEKI is an ordinary college student until a violent encounter turns him into the first half-human, half-Ghoul hybrid. Trapped between two worlds, he must survive Ghoul turf wars, learn more about Ghoul society and master his new powers.

[Box set collects all fourteen volumes of the original *Tokyo Ghoul* series. Includes an exclusive double-sided poster.]

COLLECT THE COMPLETE SERIES

TOKYO GHOUL © 2011 by Sui Ishida/SHUEISHA Inc.

CHILDREN OF THE WHALES

In this postapocalyptic fantasy, a sea of sand swallows everything but the past.

In an endless sea of sand drifts the Mud Whale, a floating island city of clay and magic. In its chambers a small community clings to survival, cut off from its own history by the shadows of the past.

viz.com

RATED T+ OLDER TEEN

© 2013 ABI UMEDA (AKITASHOTEN)

MURDERED AGAIN AND AGAIN,
ONE GIRL ALWAYS
COMES BACK FOR
MORE...

The complete classic
horror series, now
available in a single
deluxe volume.

TOMIE

Story and Art by JUNJI ITO

NO USE ESCAPING

TOMIE

JUNJI ITO

TOMIE

VIZ SIGNATURE

viz media
viz.com

© Junji Ito/Asahi Shimbun Publications Inc.

COMING IN VOLUME 2...

Dwarf rabbit Haru's odd behavior causes wolf Legoshi to flee. He then learns that the school's drama club recruits new students to help them with their inner demons. What does the drama club's star actor, red deer Louis, wrestle with...? Before Legoshi can figure it out, Louis pressures him to face not only his own weaknesses but also his strengths. Legoshi's character is put to the test when his onstage fight choreography with tiger Bill turns all too real. Has someone broken the school rules? And could the battle between Legoshi and Bill involve...rabbits?

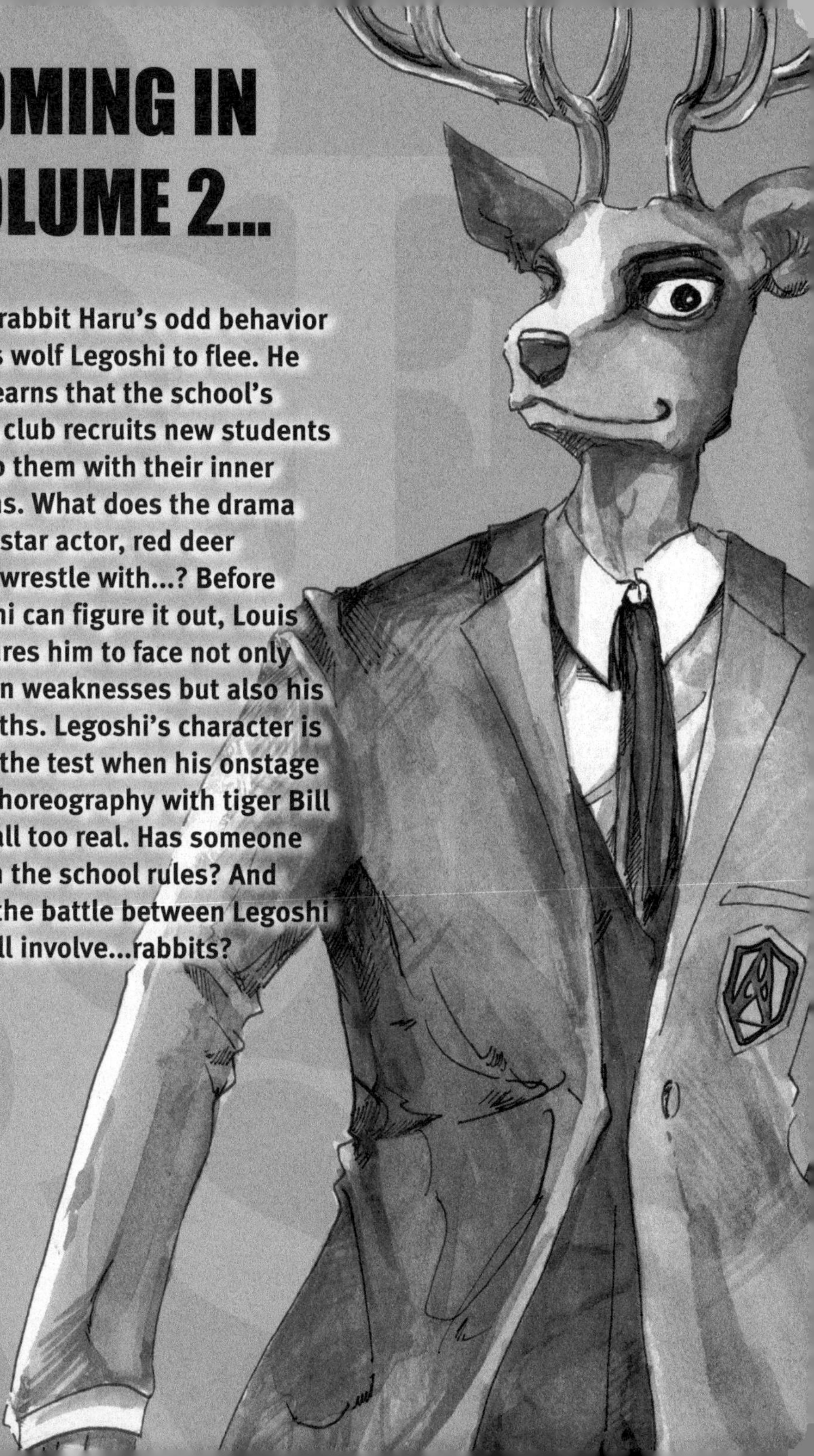

BEASTARS
VOL. 1
VIZ Signature Edition

Story & Art by
Paru Itagaki

Translation/Tomoko Kimura
English Adaptation/Annette Roman
Touch-Up Art & Lettering/Susan Daigle-Leach
Cover & Interior Design/Yukiko Whitley
Editor/Annette Roman

BEASTARS Volume 1
© 2017 PARU ITAGAKI
All rights reserved.
First published in 2017 by Akita Publishing Co., Ltd., Tokyo
English translation rights arranged with AKITA PUBLISHING CO., LTD. through
Tuttle-Mori Agency, Inc., Tokyo

The stories, characters and incidents mentioned in this publication are entirely
fictional.

No portion of this book may be reproduced or transmitted in any form or by any
means without written permission from the copyright holders.

Printed in the U.S.A.

Published by VIZ Media, LLC
P.O. Box 77010
San Francisco, CA 94107

10 9 8 7 6 5 4 3 2 1
First printing, July 2019

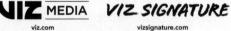

VIZ MEDIA   VIZ SIGNATURE
viz.com   vizsignature.com

PARENTAL ADVISORY
BEASTARS is rated T+ and is recommended
for ages 16 and up. It contains adult themes,
sexual situations and violence.

BEASTARS

BEASTARS

Volume 1

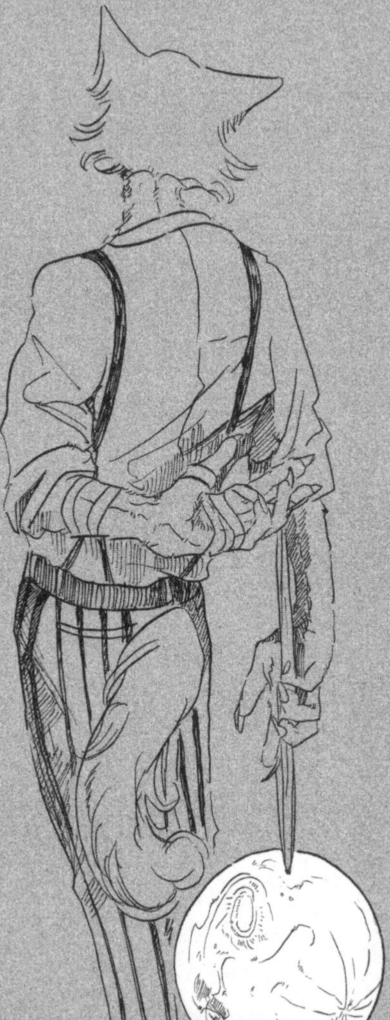

Story & Art by

Paru Itagaki

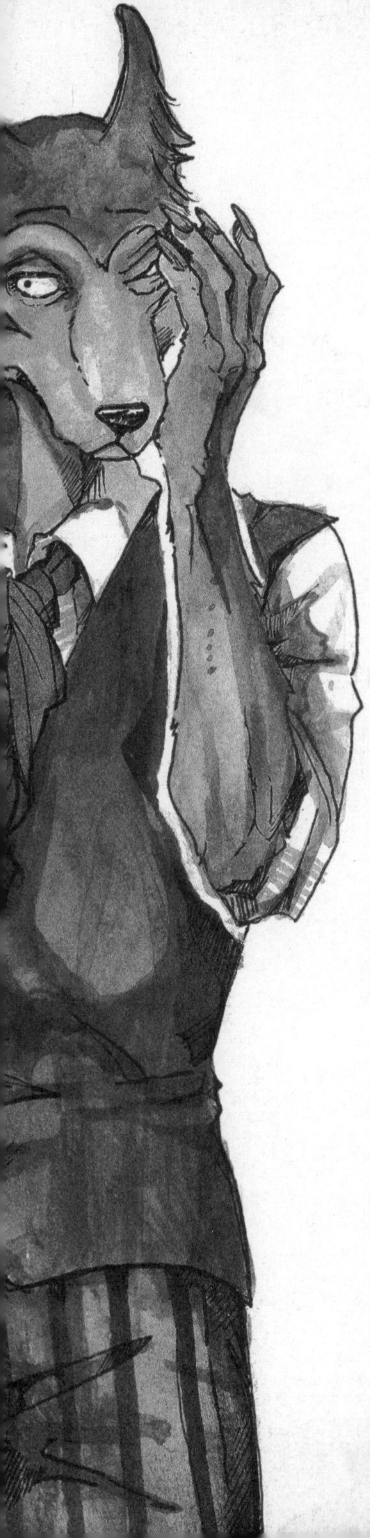

BEASTARS
Volume 1

CONTENTS

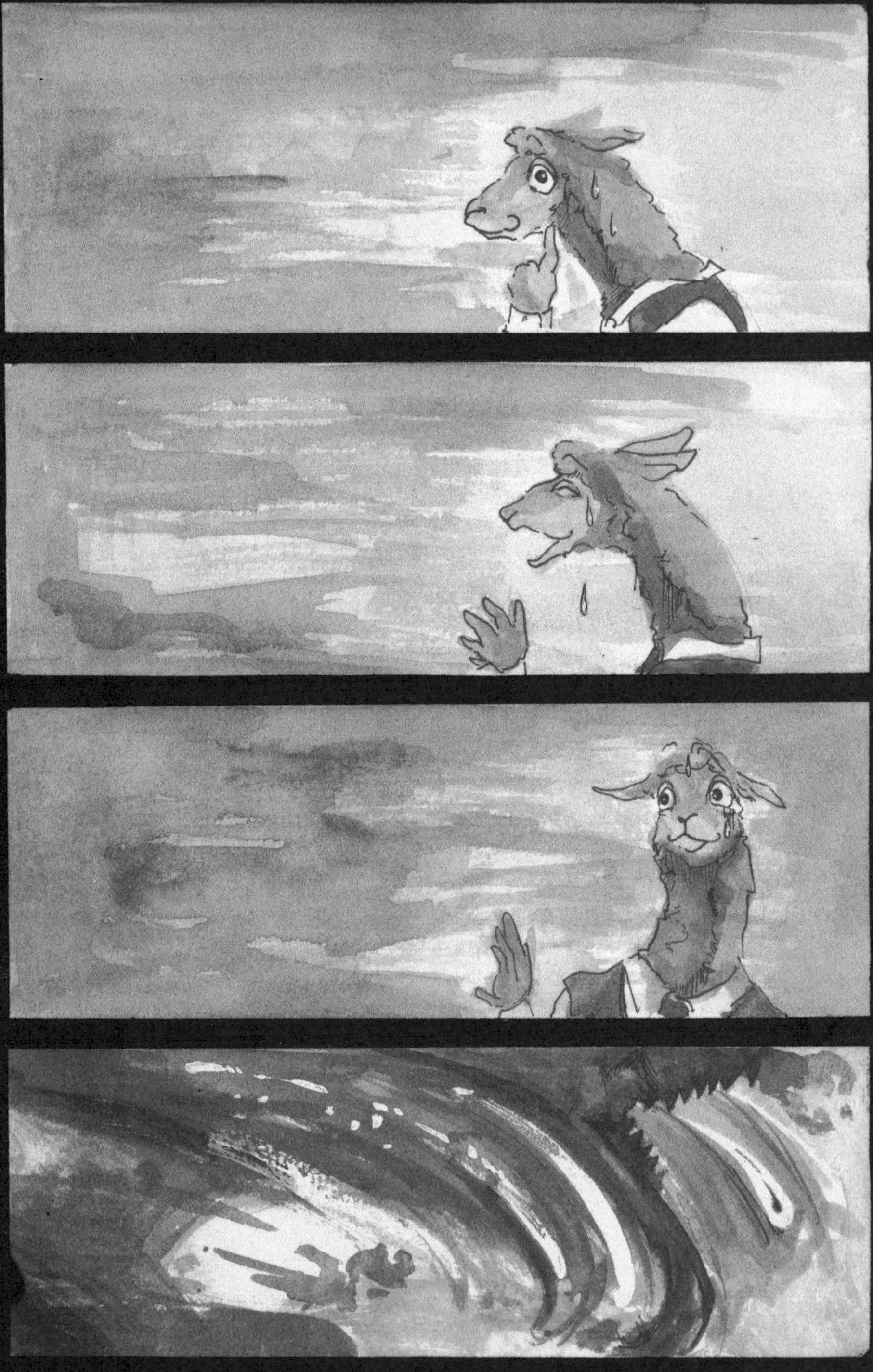

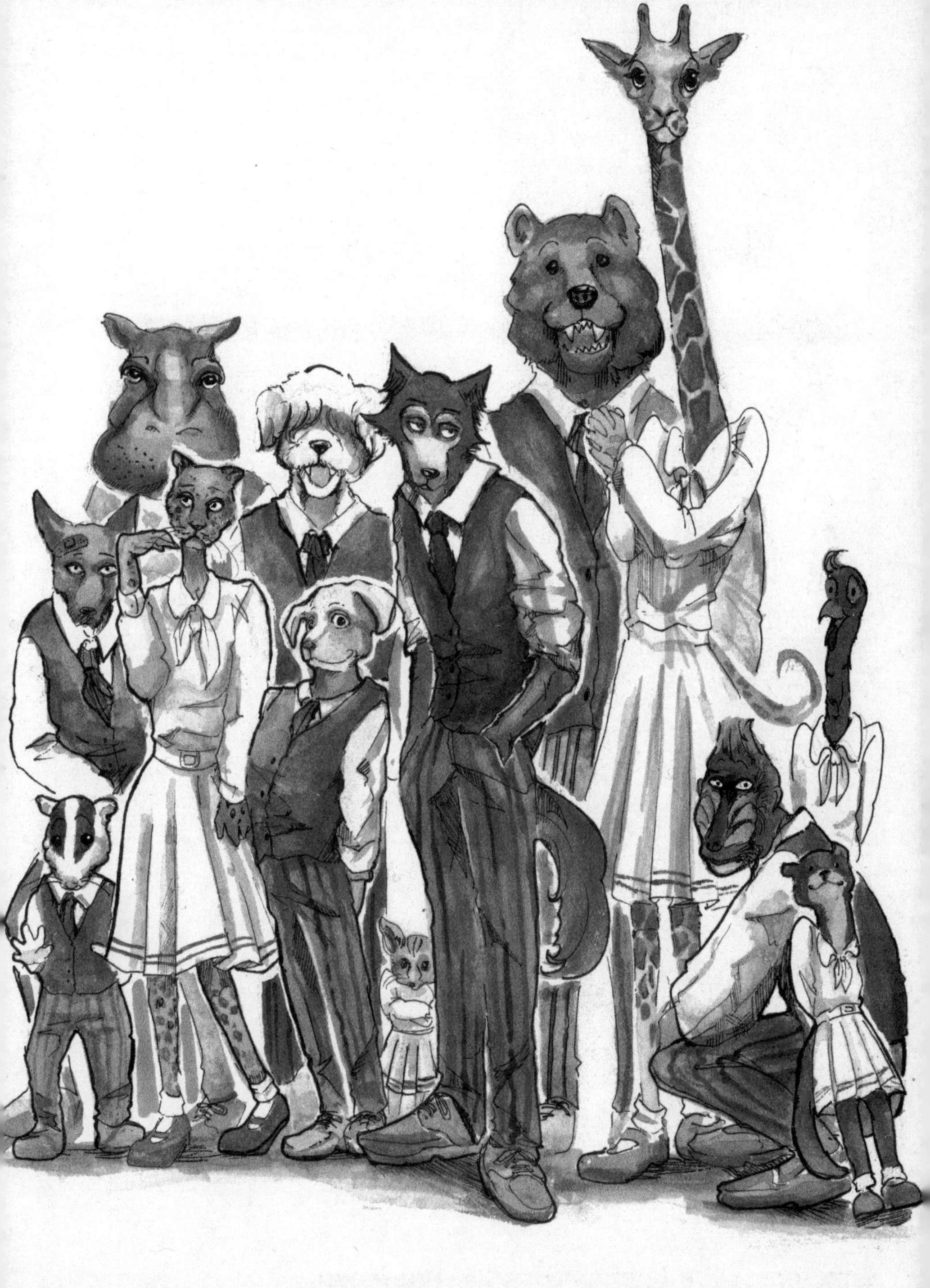

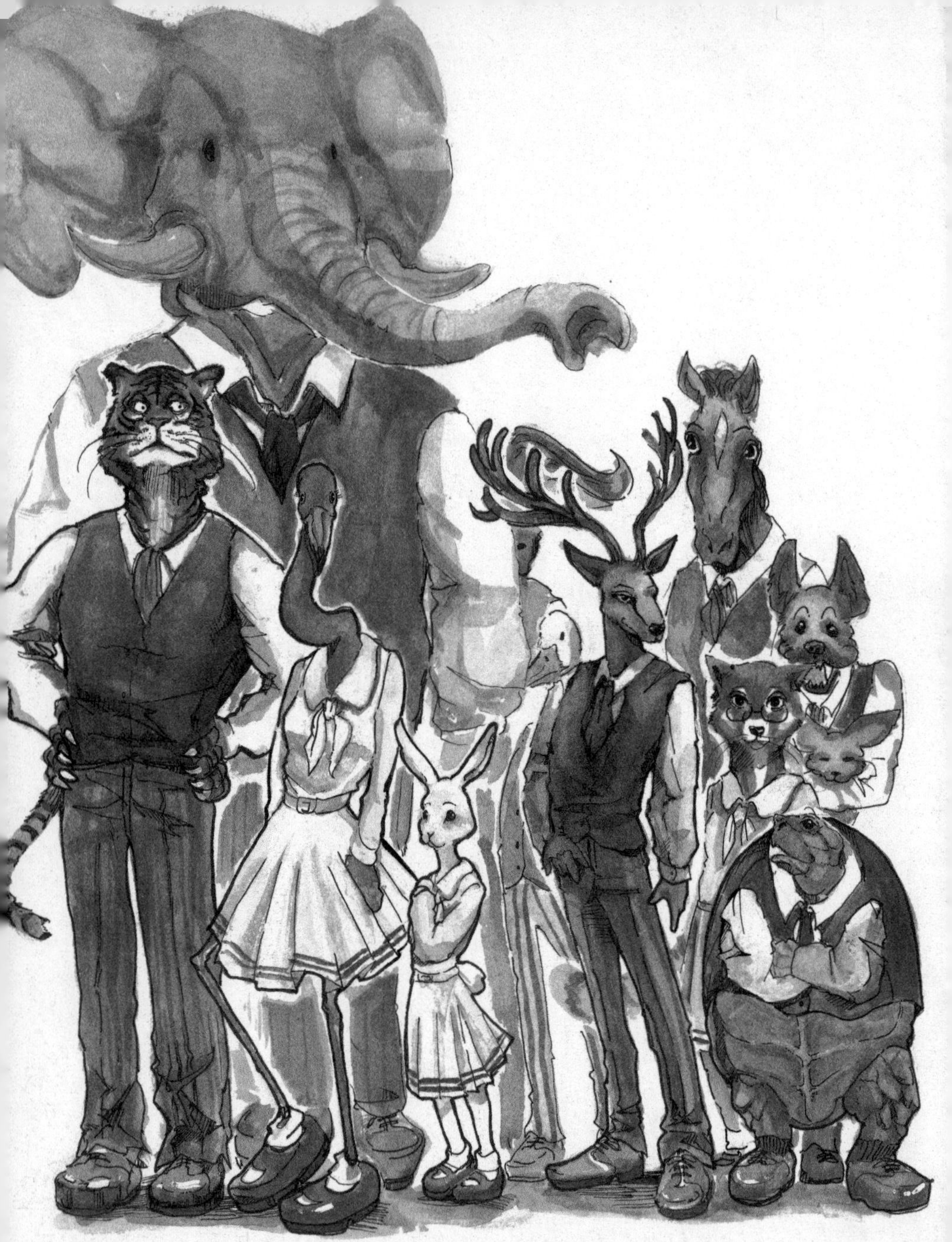

Chapter 1: Introduction upon the Full Moon

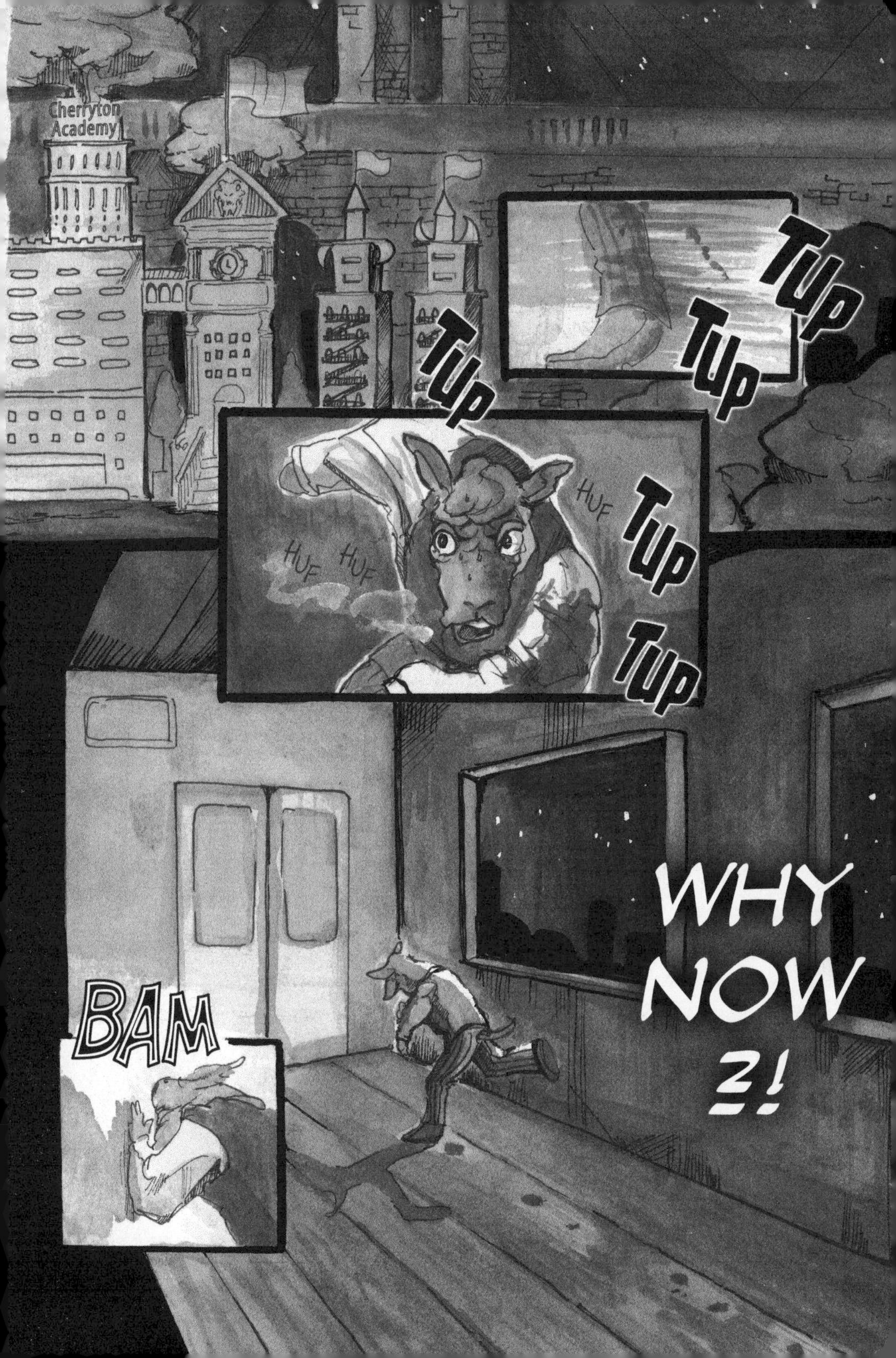

Cherryton Academy
TUP TUP
TUP
HUF
HUF HUF
TUP TUP
WHY NOW ?!
BAM

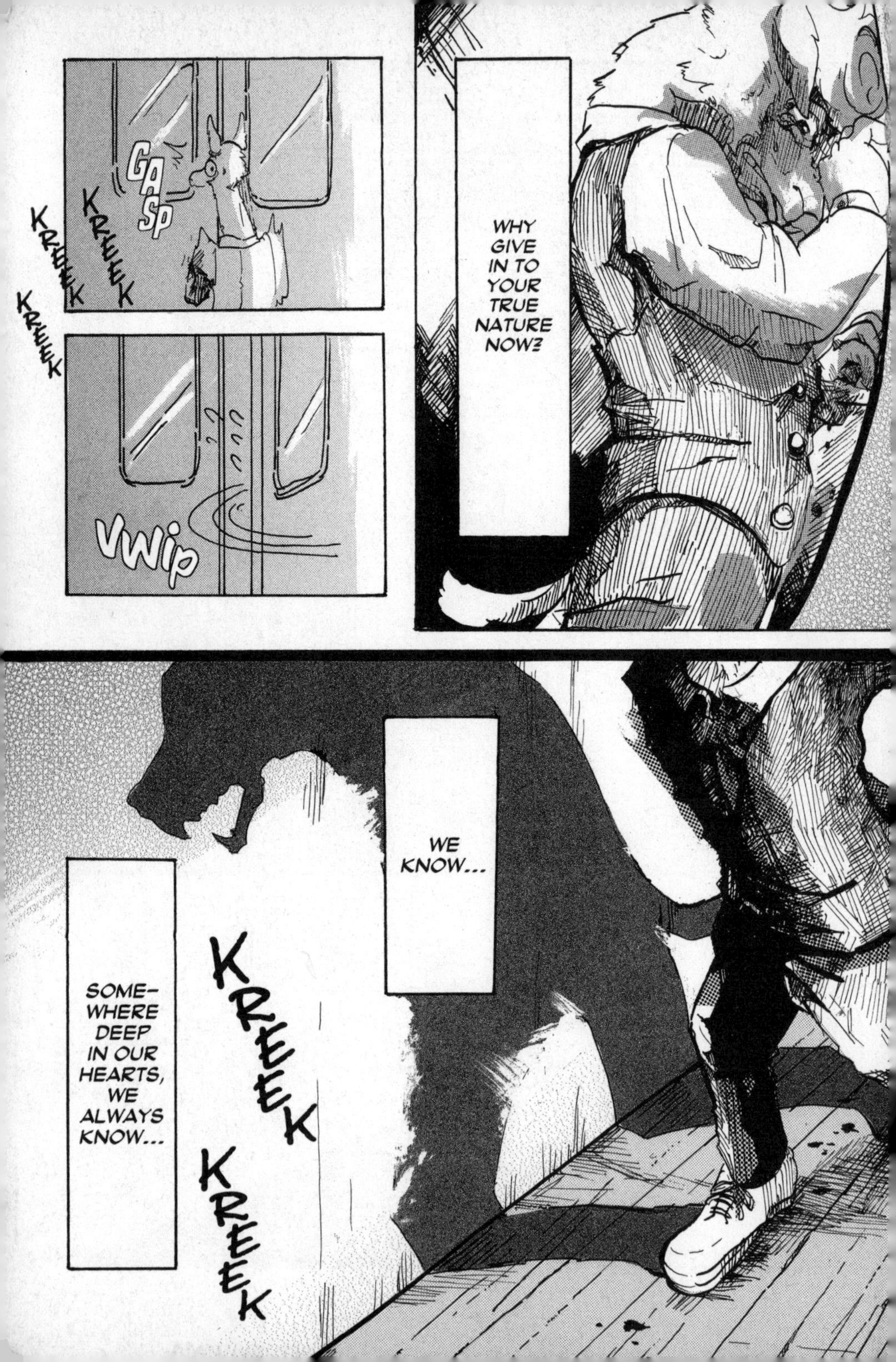
WHY GIVE IN TO YOUR TRUE NATURE NOW?
GASP
KREEK
KREEK
KREEK
VWIP
WE KNOW...
KREEK
KREEK
SOMEWHERE DEEP IN OUR HEARTS, WE ALWAYS KNOW...

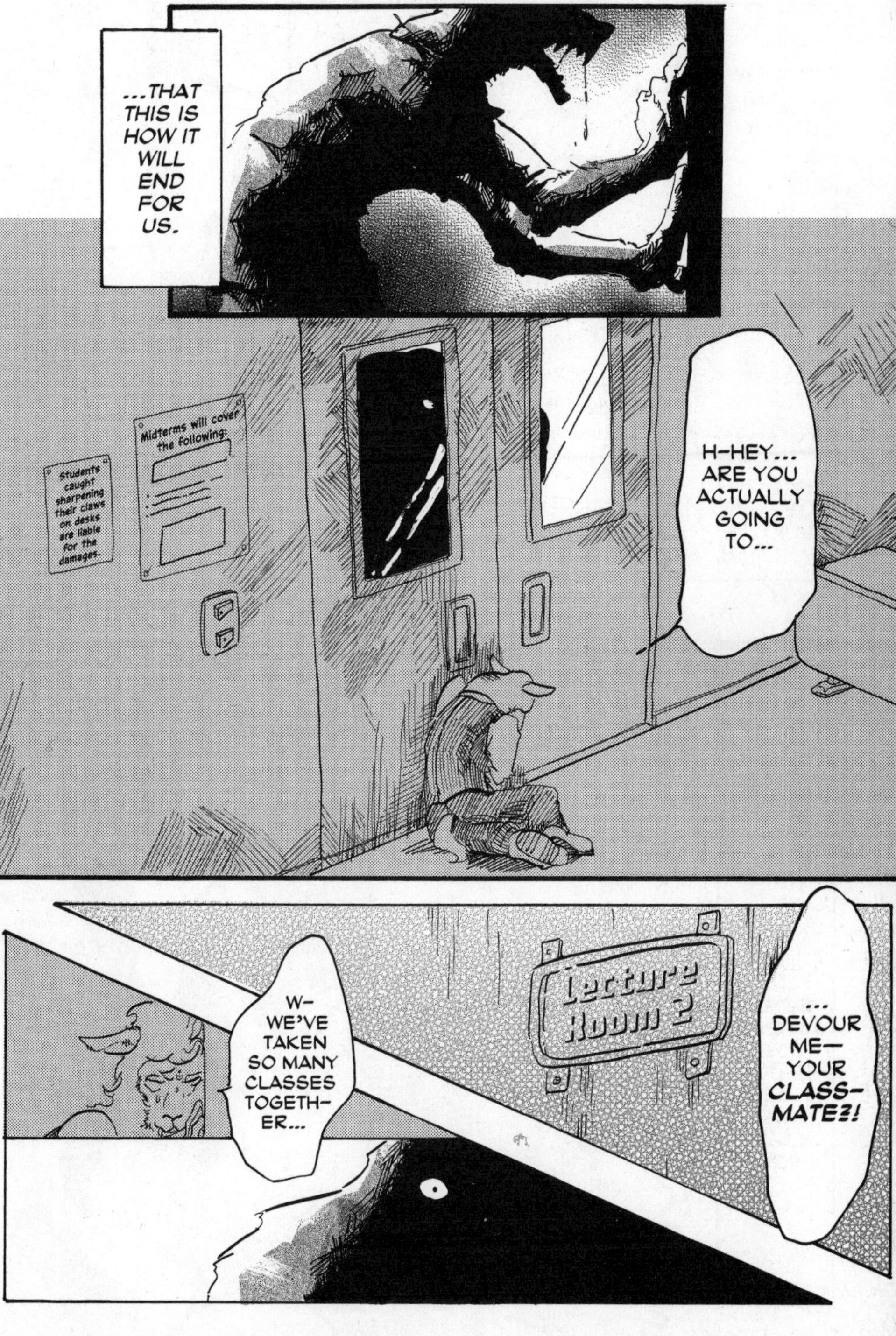
...THAT THIS IS HOW IT WILL END FOR US.
H-HEY... ARE YOU ACTUALLY GOING TO...
Midterms will cover the following:
Students caught sharpening their claws on desks are liable for the damages.
... DEVOUR ME— YOUR CLASS-MATE?!
Lecture Room 2
W— WE'VE TAKEN SO MANY CLASSES TOGETH-ER...

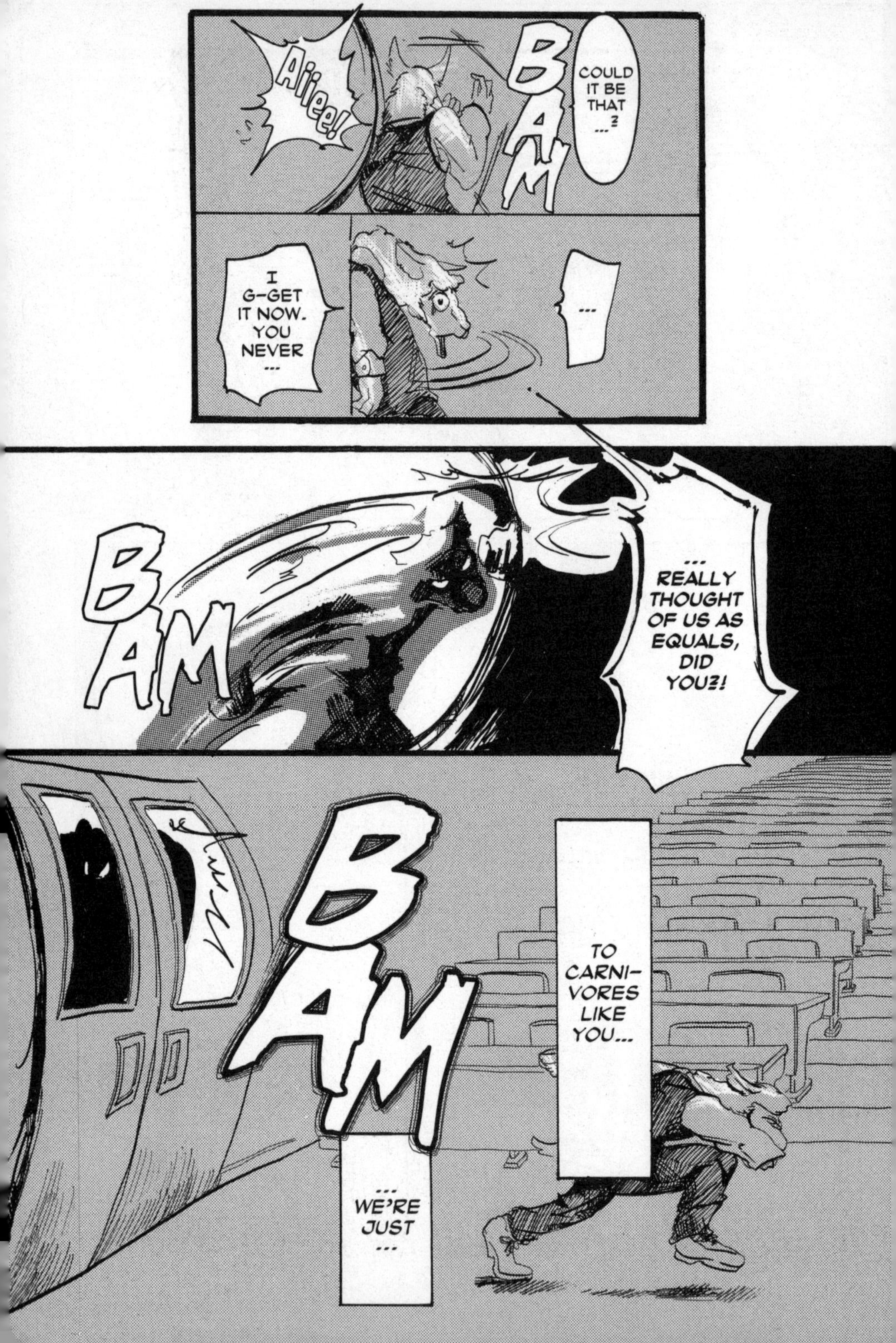
COULD IT BE THAT ...?
BAM
Aiiee!
...
I G-GET IT NOW. YOU NEVER ...
... REALLY THOUGHT OF US AS EQUALS, DID YOU?!
BAM
TO CARNI-VORES LIKE YOU...
BAM
... WE'RE JUST ...

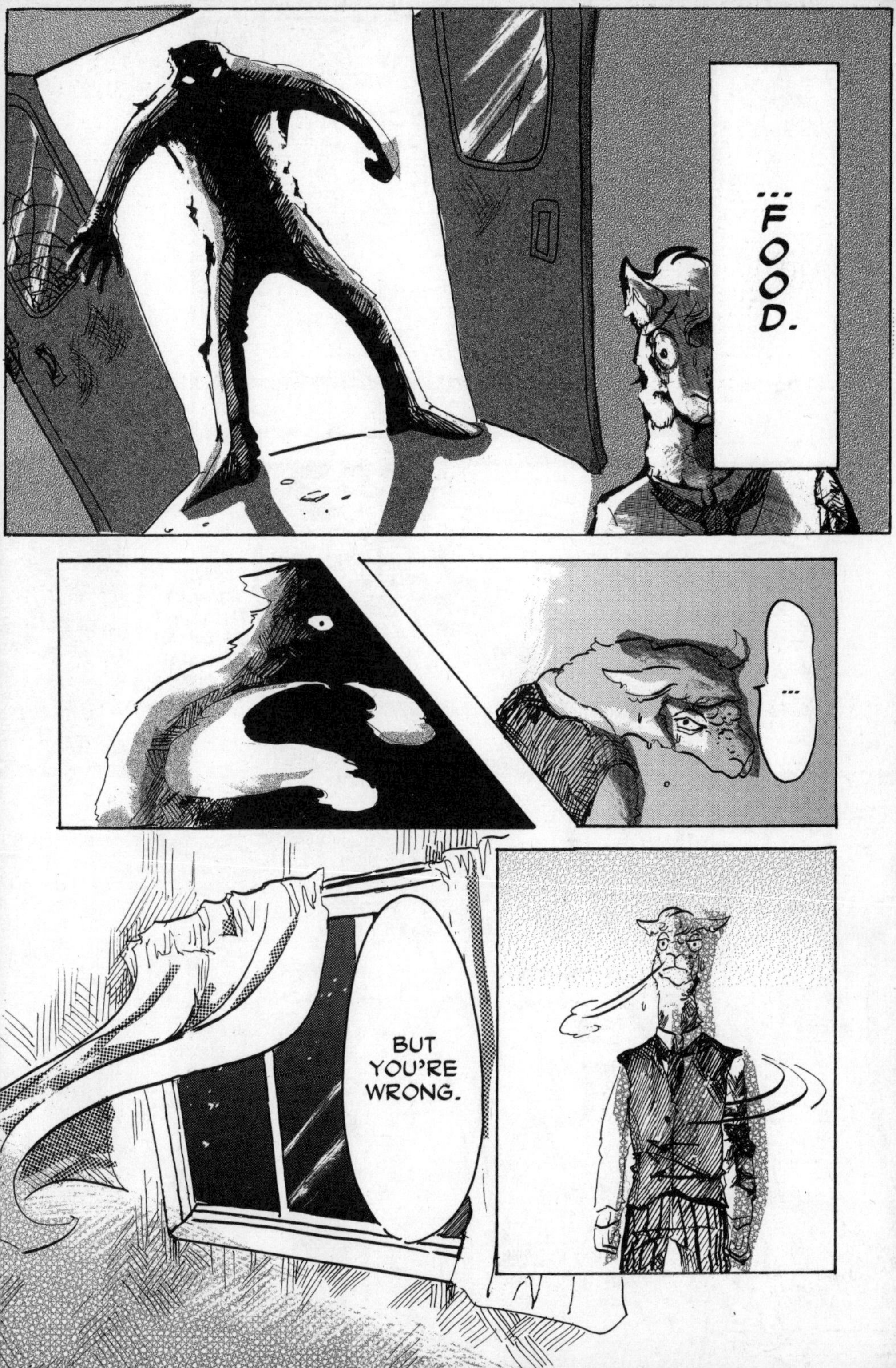
...FOOD.
...
BUT YOU'RE WRONG.

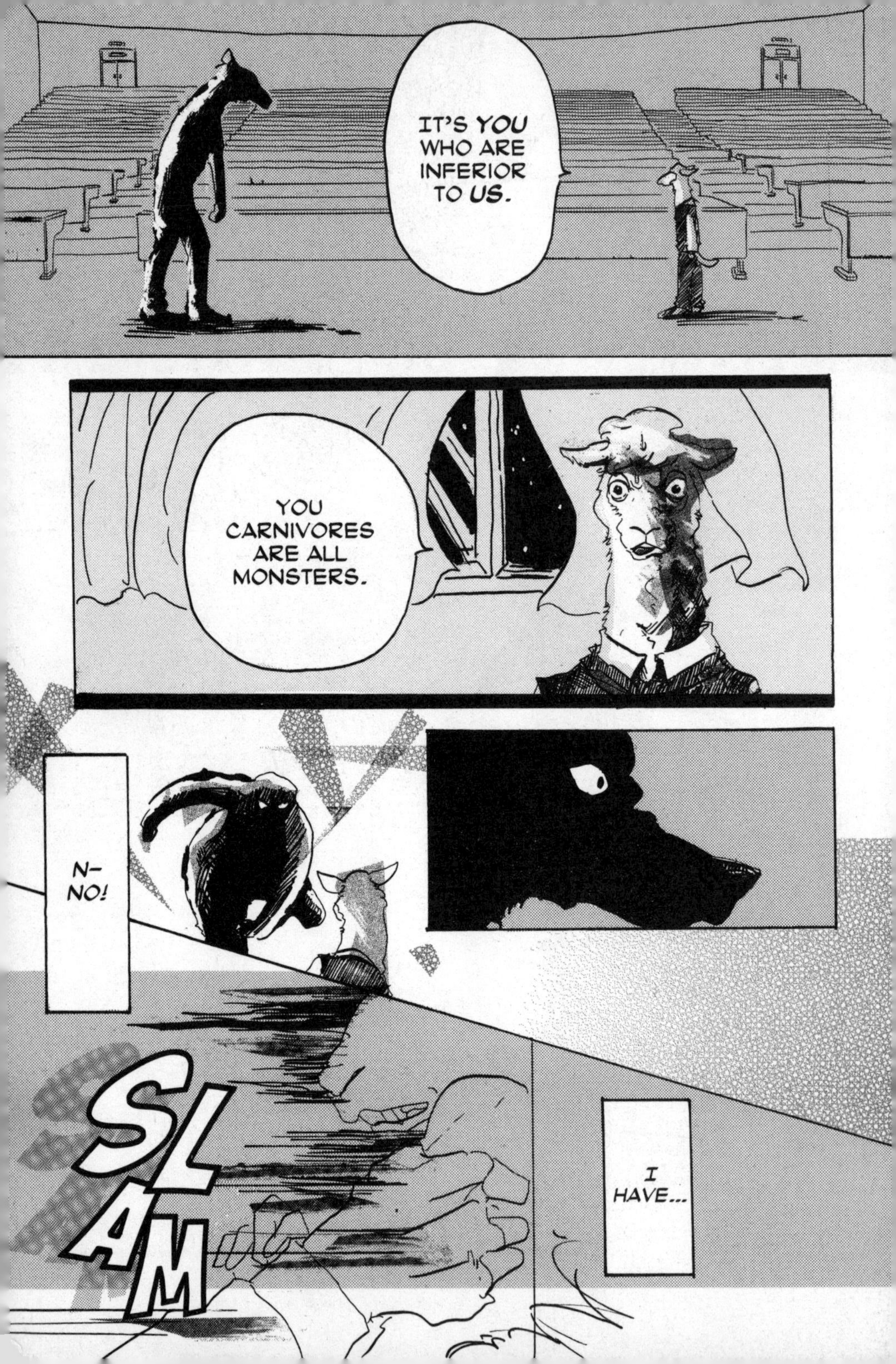
IT'S YOU WHO ARE INFERIOR TO US.
YOU CARNIVORES ARE ALL MONSTERS.
N- NO!
I HAVE...
SLAM

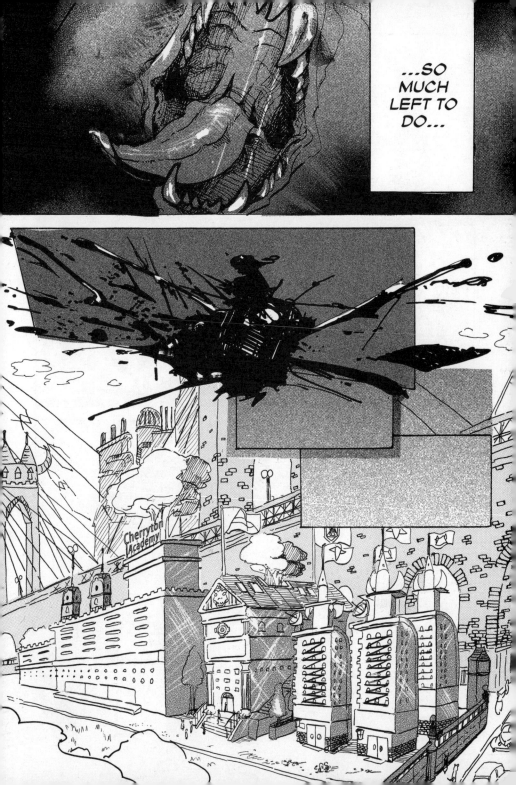

...SO MUCH LEFT TO DO...

Cherryton Academy

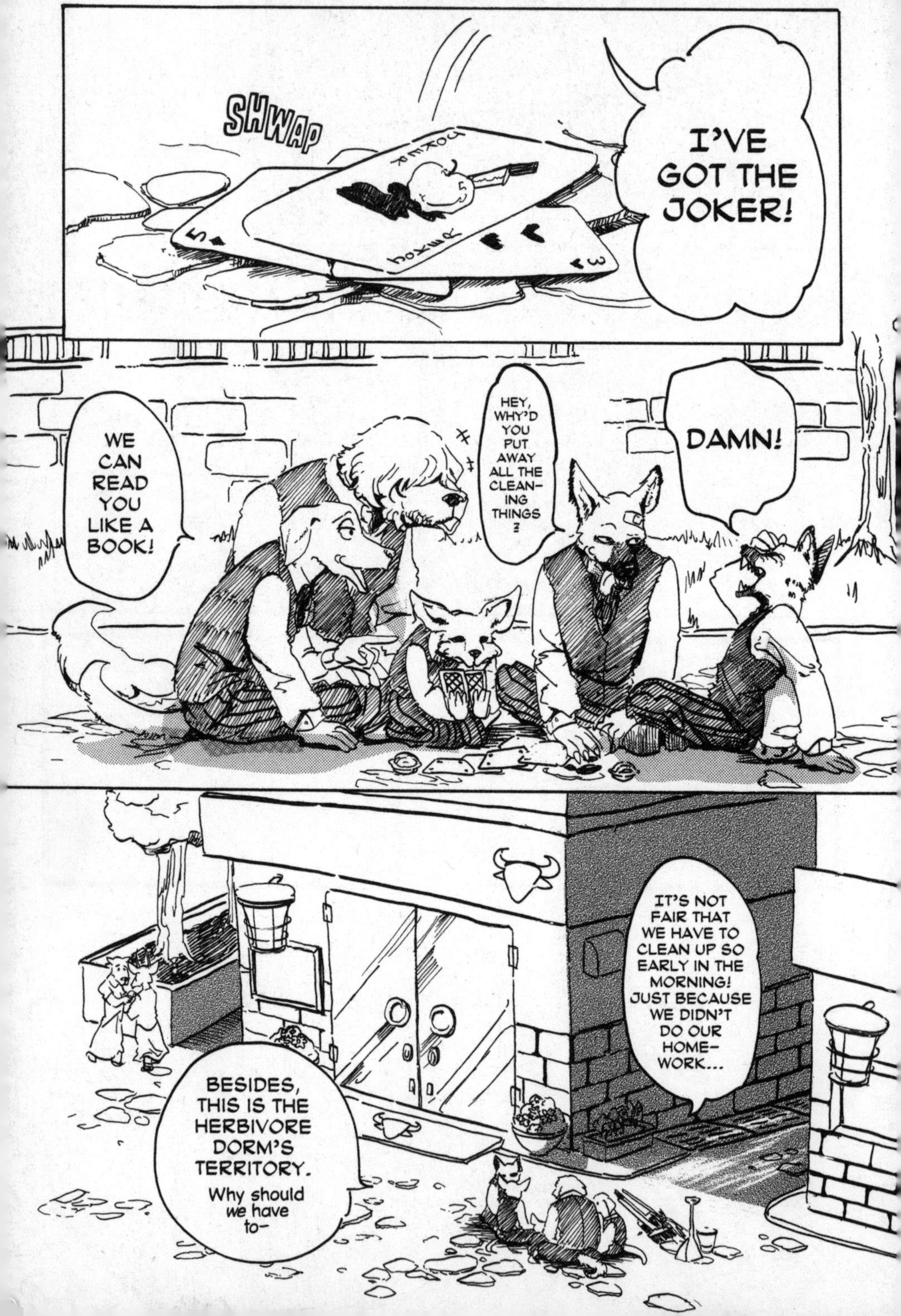
I'VE GOT THE JOKER!
SHWAP
DAMN!
HEY, WHY'D YOU PUT AWAY ALL THE CLEAN-ING THINGS?
WE CAN READ YOU LIKE A BOOK!
IT'S NOT FAIR THAT WE HAVE TO CLEAN UP SO EARLY IN THE MORNING! JUST BECAUSE WE DIDN'T DO OUR HOME-WORK...
BESIDES, THIS IS THE HERBIVORE DORM'S TERRITORY.
Why should we have to-

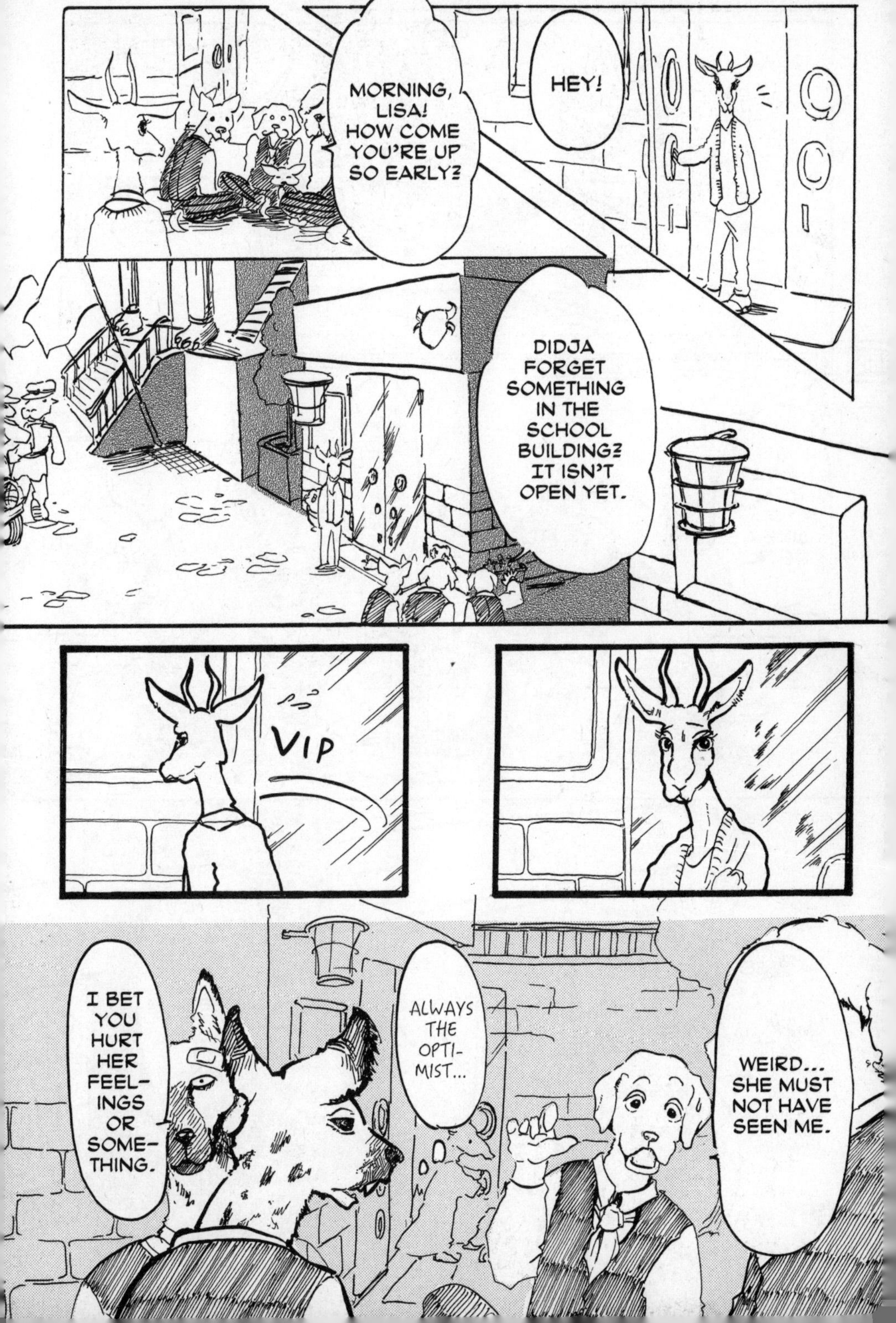
HEY!
MORNING, LISA! HOW COME YOU'RE UP SO EARLY?
DIDJA FORGET SOMETHING IN THE SCHOOL BUILDING? IT ISN'T OPEN YET.
VIP
WEIRD... SHE MUST NOT HAVE SEEN ME.
ALWAYS THE OPTI-MIST...
I BET YOU HURT HER FEEL-INGS OR SOME-THING.

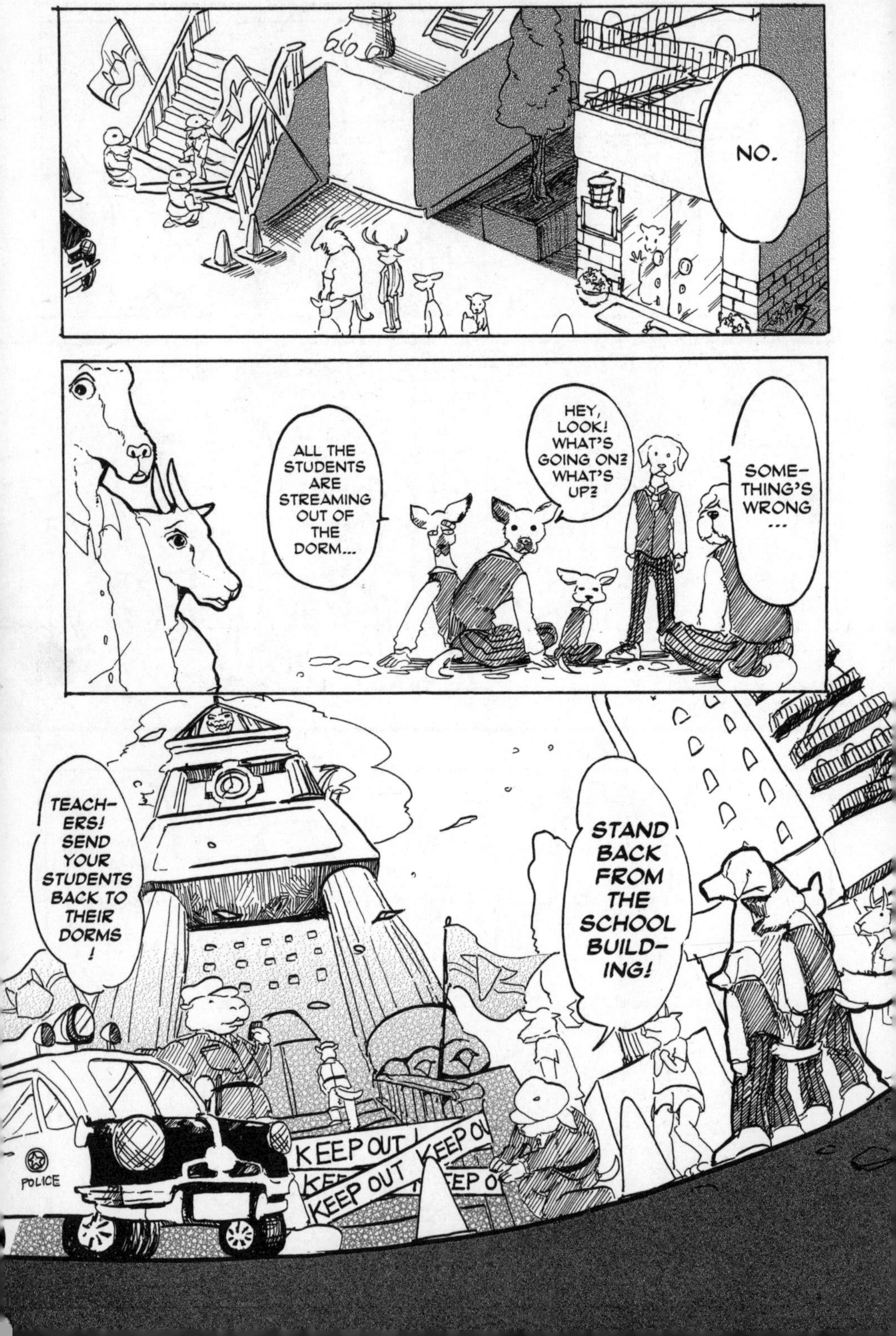
NO.
SOMETHING'S WRONG...
HEY, LOOK! WHAT'S GOING ON? WHAT'S UP?
ALL THE STUDENTS ARE STREAMING OUT OF THE DORM...
STAND BACK FROM THE SCHOOL BUILDING!
TEACHERS! SEND YOUR STUDENTS BACK TO THEIR DORMS!
KEEP OUT
KEEP OUT
POLICE

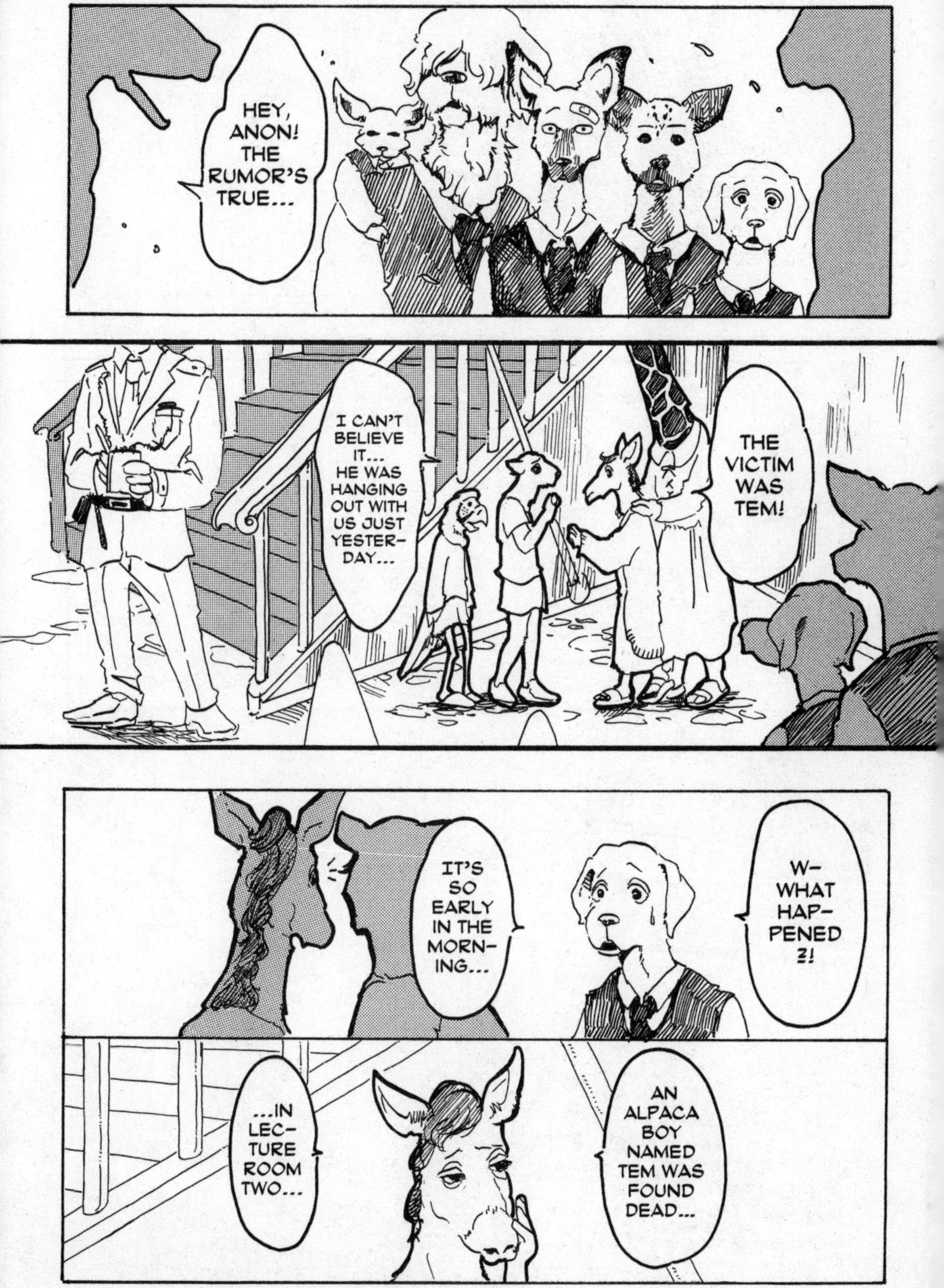
HEY, ANON! THE RUMOR'S TRUE...
THE VICTIM WAS TEM!
I CAN'T BELIEVE IT... HE WAS HANGING OUT WITH US JUST YESTERDAY...
W-WHAT HAPPENED?!
IT'S SO EARLY IN THE MORNING...
AN ALPACA BOY NAMED TEM WAS FOUND DEAD...
...IN LECTURE ROOM TWO...

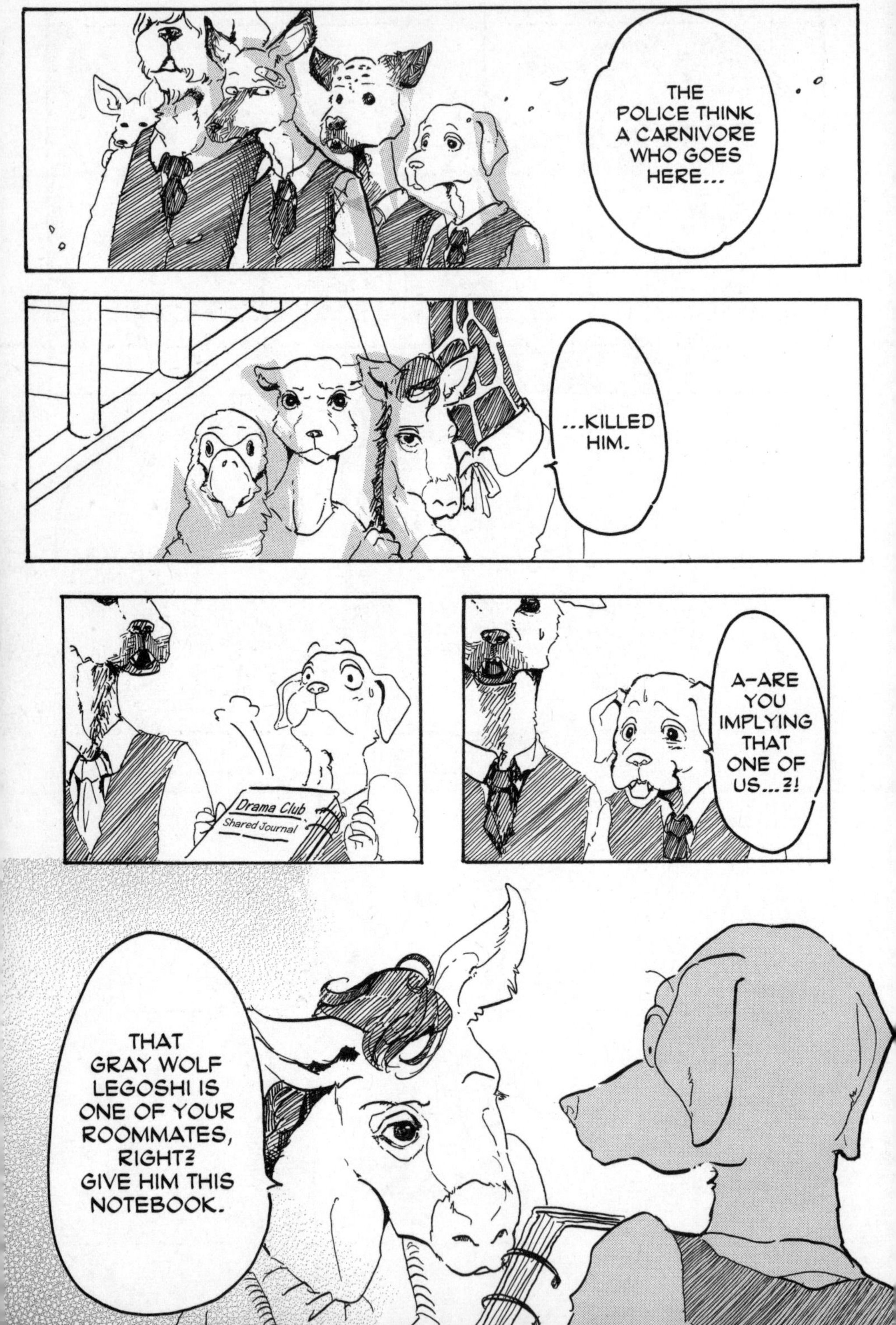
THE POLICE THINK A CARNIVORE WHO GOES HERE...
...KILLED HIM.
A-ARE YOU IMPLYING THAT ONE OF US...?!
Drama Club
Shared Journal
THAT GRAY WOLF LEGOSHI IS ONE OF YOUR ROOMMATES, RIGHT? GIVE HIM THIS NOTEBOOK.

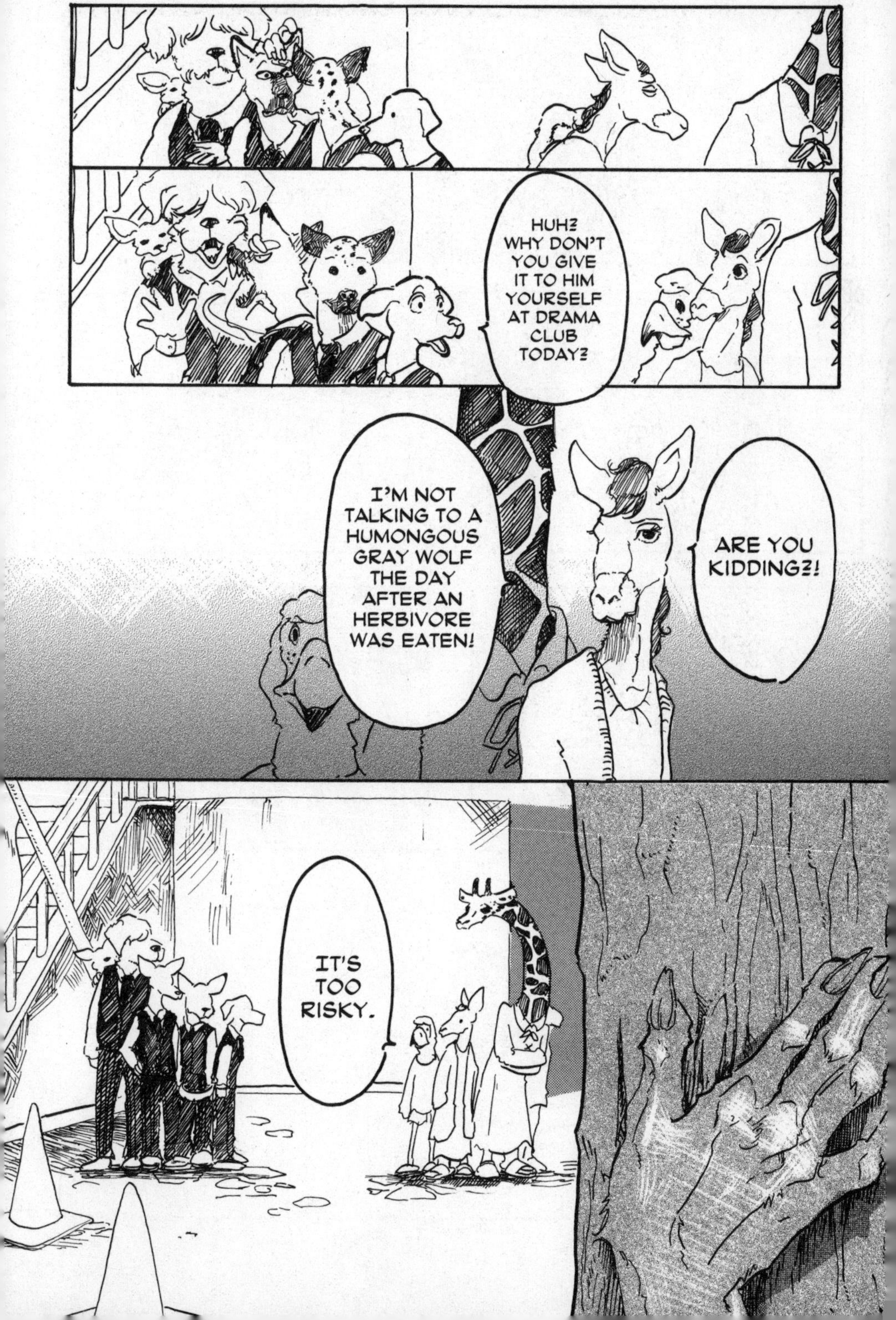
HUH? WHY DON'T YOU GIVE IT TO HIM YOURSELF AT DRAMA CLUB TODAY?
ARE YOU KIDDING?!
I'M NOT TALKING TO A HUMONGOUS GRAY WOLF THE DAY AFTER AN HERBIVORE WAS EATEN!
IT'S TOO RISKY.

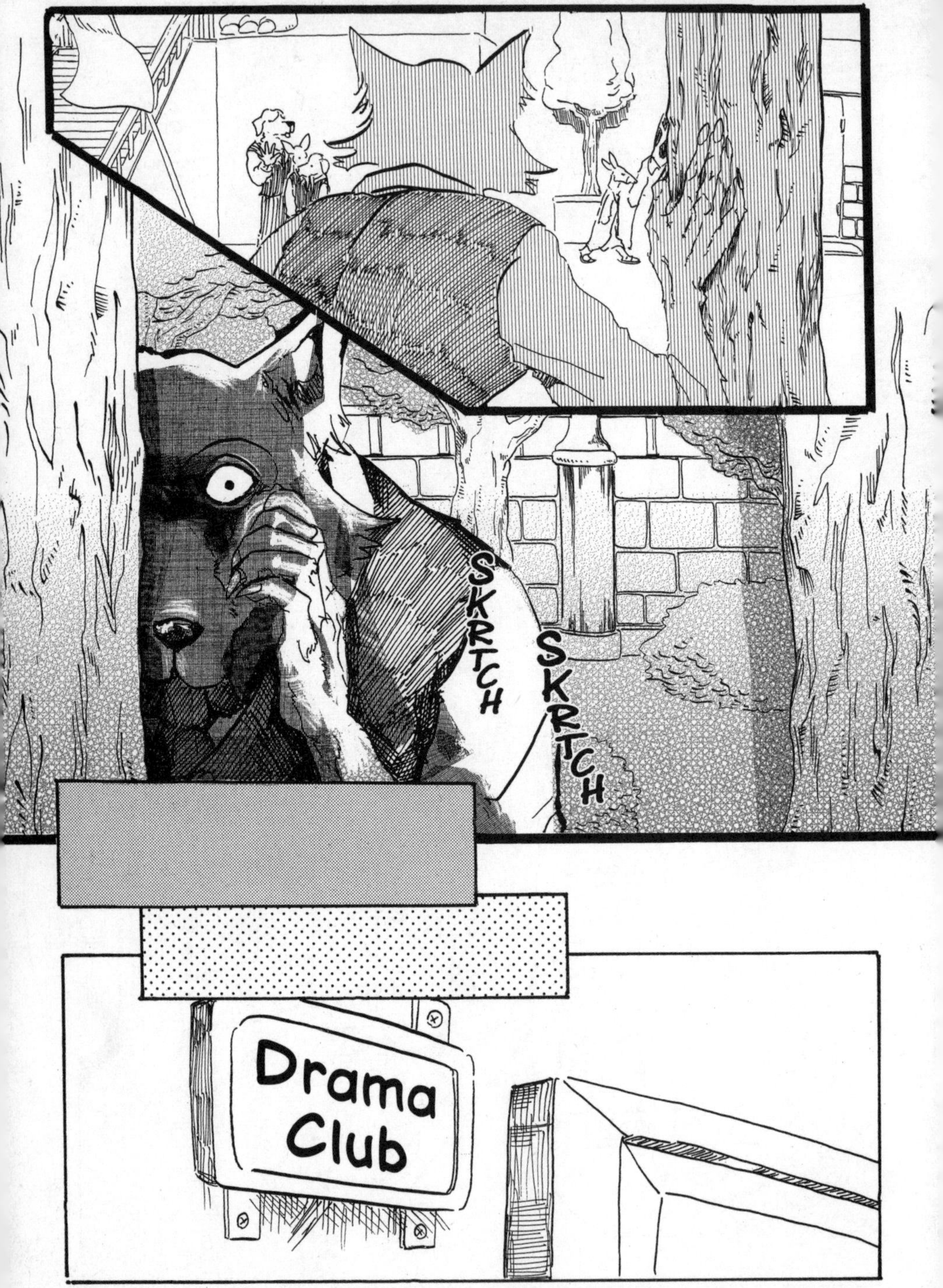
SKRTCH
SKRTCH
Drama Club

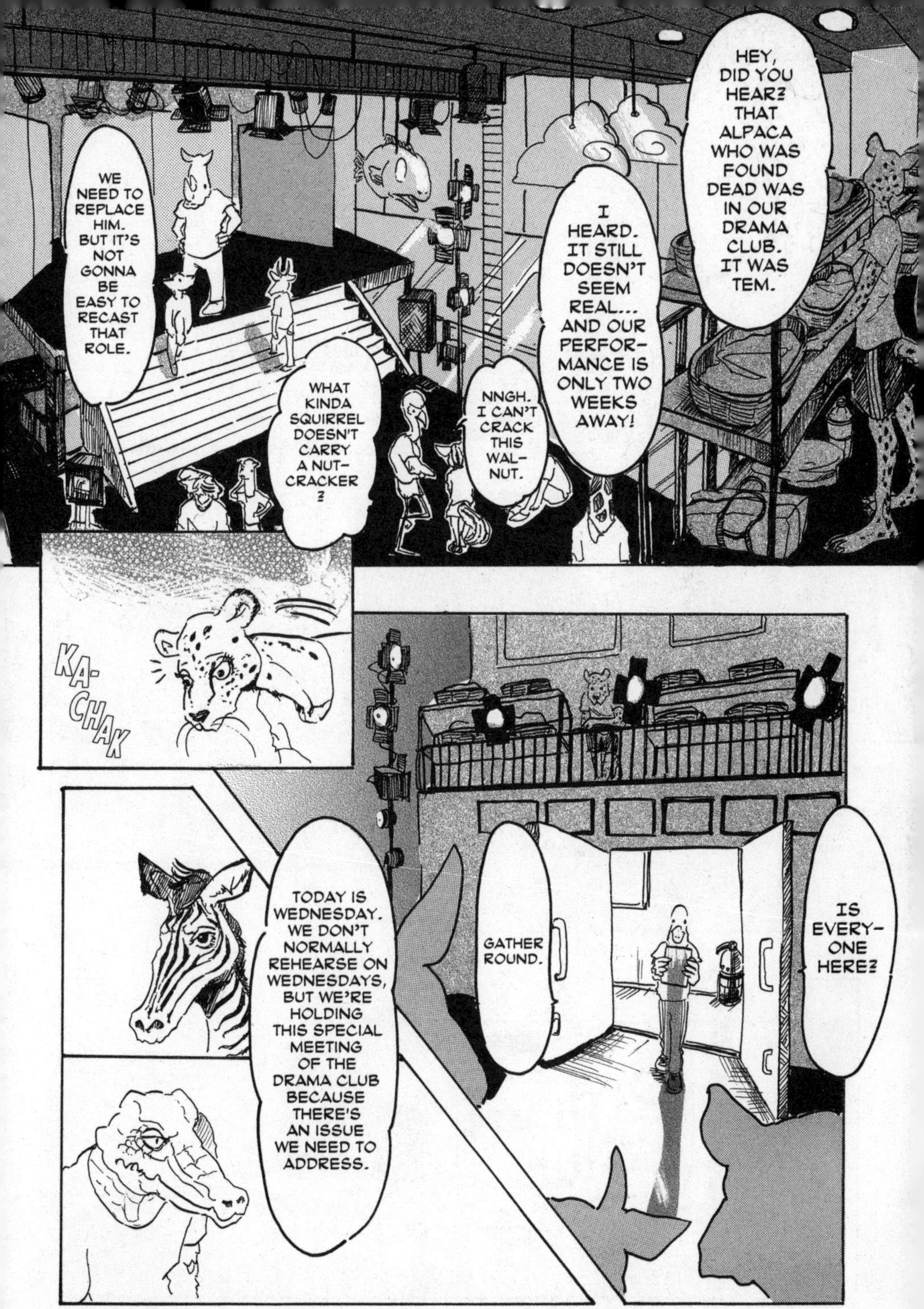
HEY, DID YOU HEAR? THAT ALPACA WHO WAS FOUND DEAD WAS IN OUR DRAMA CLUB. IT WAS TEM.
I HEARD. IT STILL DOESN'T SEEM REAL... AND OUR PERFORMANCE IS ONLY TWO WEEKS AWAY!
NNGH. I CAN'T CRACK THIS WALNUT.
WHAT KINDA SQUIRREL DOESN'T CARRY A NUTCRACKER?
WE NEED TO REPLACE HIM. BUT IT'S NOT GONNA BE EASY TO RECAST THAT ROLE.
IS EVERYONE HERE?
GATHER ROUND.
KA-CHAK
TODAY IS WEDNESDAY. WE DON'T NORMALLY REHEARSE ON WEDNESDAYS, BUT WE'RE HOLDING THIS SPECIAL MEETING OF THE DRAMA CLUB BECAUSE THERE'S AN ISSUE WE NEED TO ADDRESS.

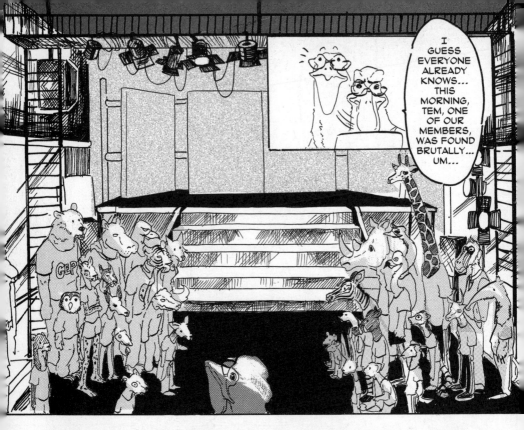

I GUESS EVERYONE ALREADY KNOWS... THIS MORNING, TEM, ONE OF OUR MEMBERS, WAS FOUND BRUTALLY... UM...

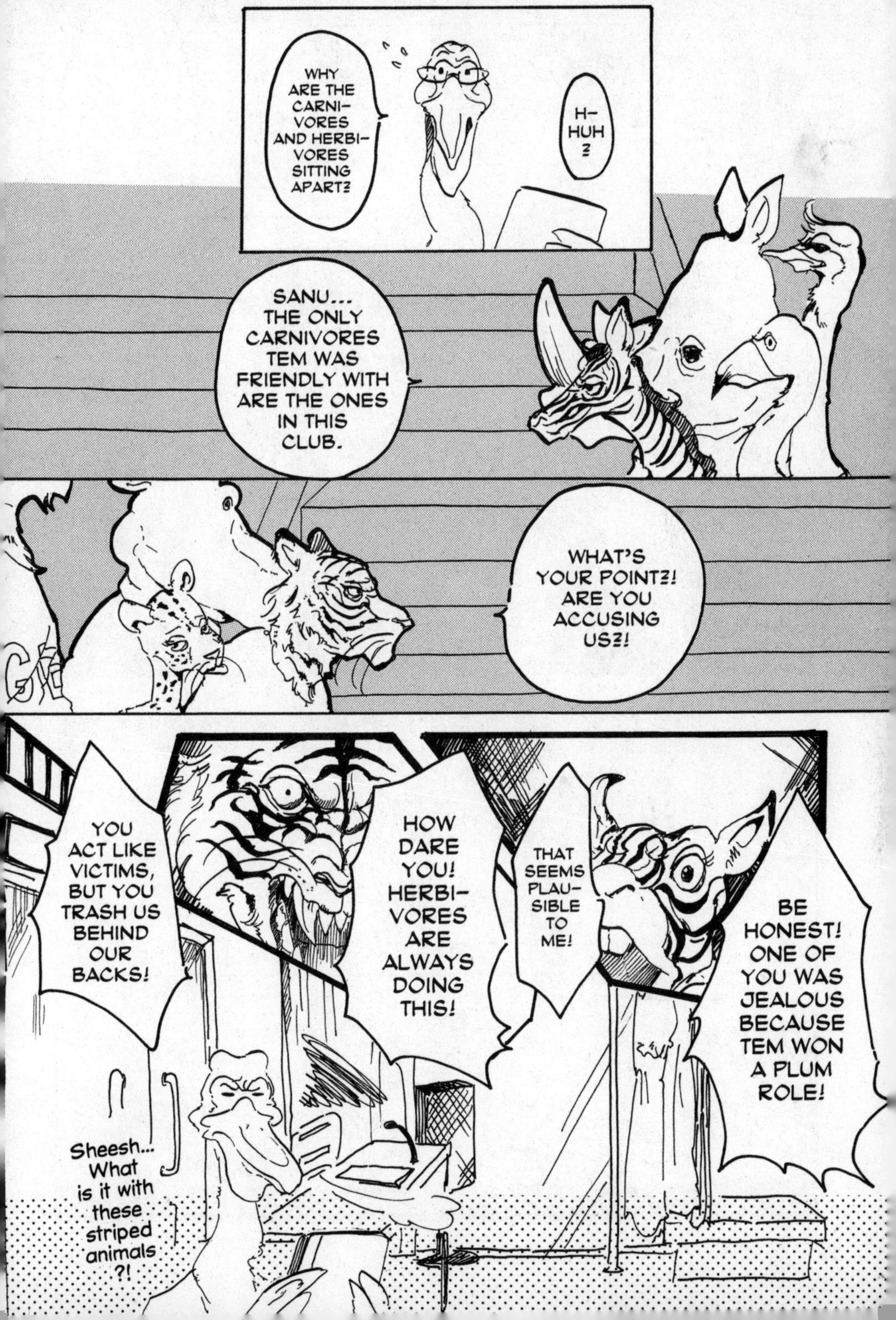
H-HUH?
WHY ARE THE CARNIVORES AND HERBIVORES SITTING APART?
SANU... THE ONLY CARNIVORES TEM WAS FRIENDLY WITH ARE THE ONES IN THIS CLUB.
WHAT'S YOUR POINT?! ARE YOU ACCUSING US?!
BE HONEST! ONE OF YOU WAS JEALOUS BECAUSE TEM WON A PLUM ROLE!
THAT SEEMS PLAUSIBLE TO ME!
HOW DARE YOU! HERBIVORES ARE ALWAYS DOING THIS!
YOU ACT LIKE VICTIMS, BUT YOU TRASH US BEHIND OUR BACKS!
Sheesh... What is it with these striped animals?!

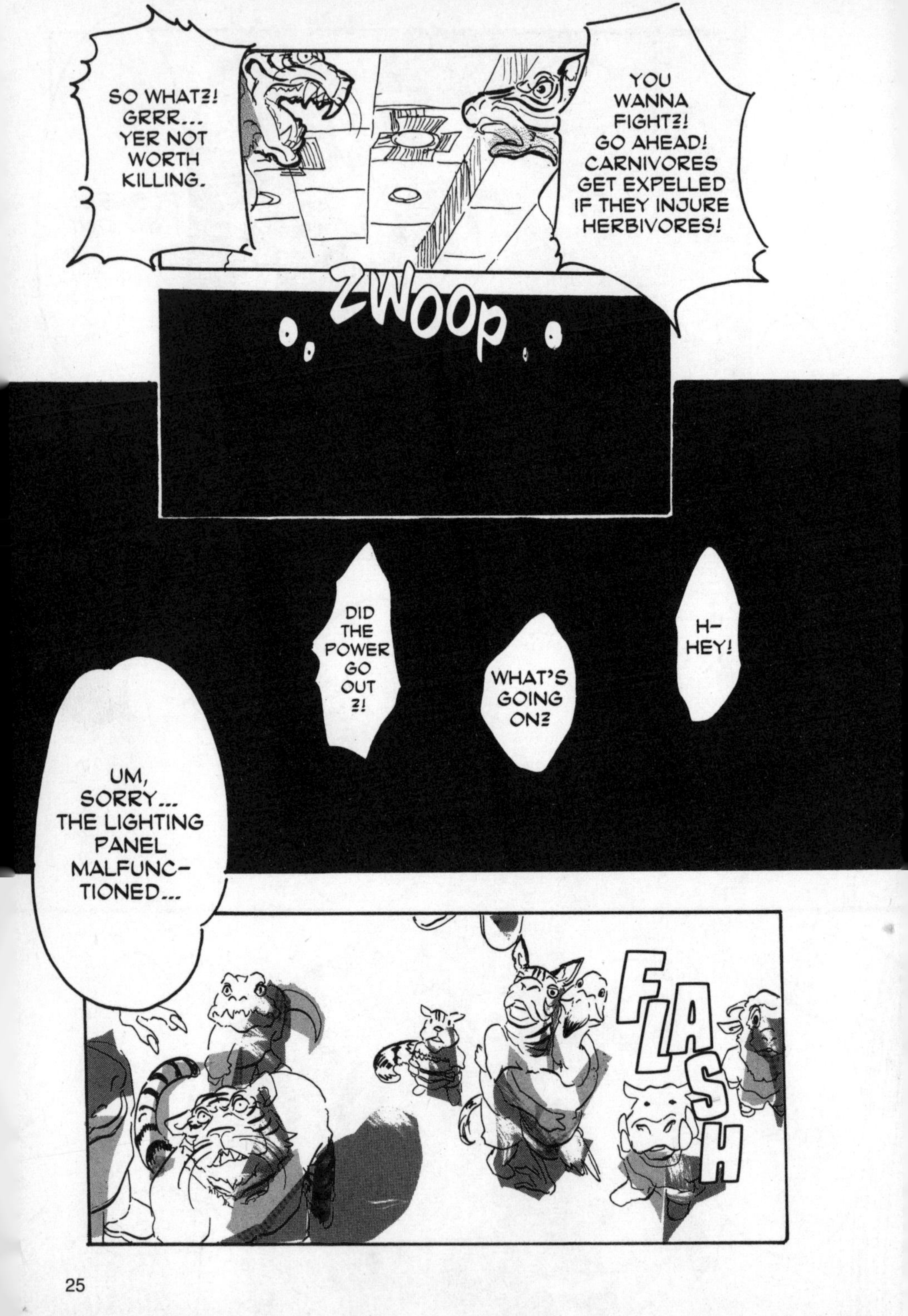
YOU WANNA FIGHT?! GO AHEAD! CARNIVORES GET EXPELLED IF THEY INJURE HERBIVORES!
SO WHAT?! GRRR... YER NOT WORTH KILLING.
ZWOOP
H-HEY!
WHAT'S GOING ON?
DID THE POWER GO OUT?!
UM, SORRY... THE LIGHTING PANEL MALFUNCTIONED...
FLASH

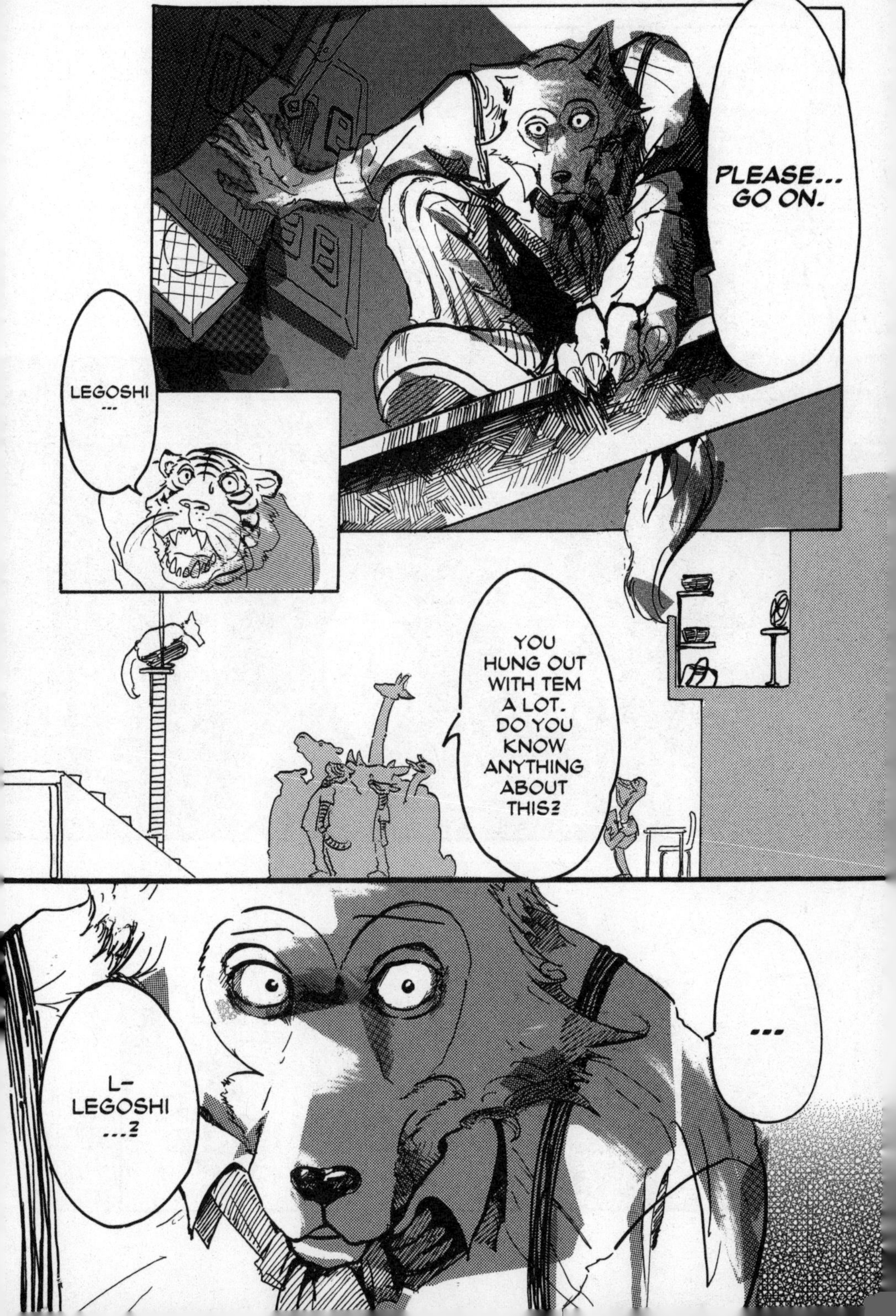
PLEASE... GO ON.
LEGOSHI...
YOU HUNG OUT WITH TEM A LOT. DO YOU KNOW ANYTHING ABOUT THIS?
...
L-LEGOSHI...?

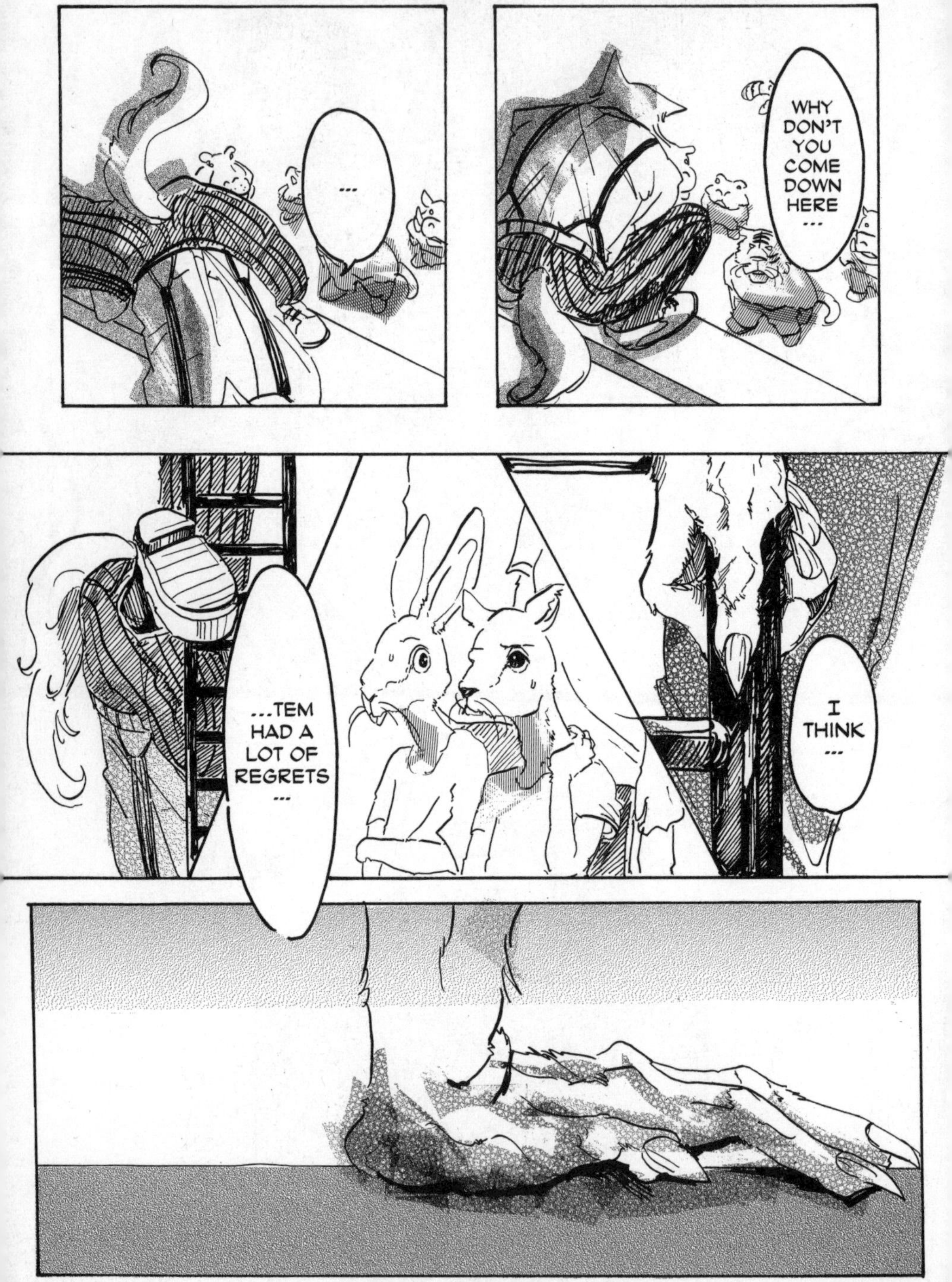
WHY DON'T YOU COME DOWN HERE ...
...
I THINK ...
...TEM HAD A LOT OF REGRETS ...

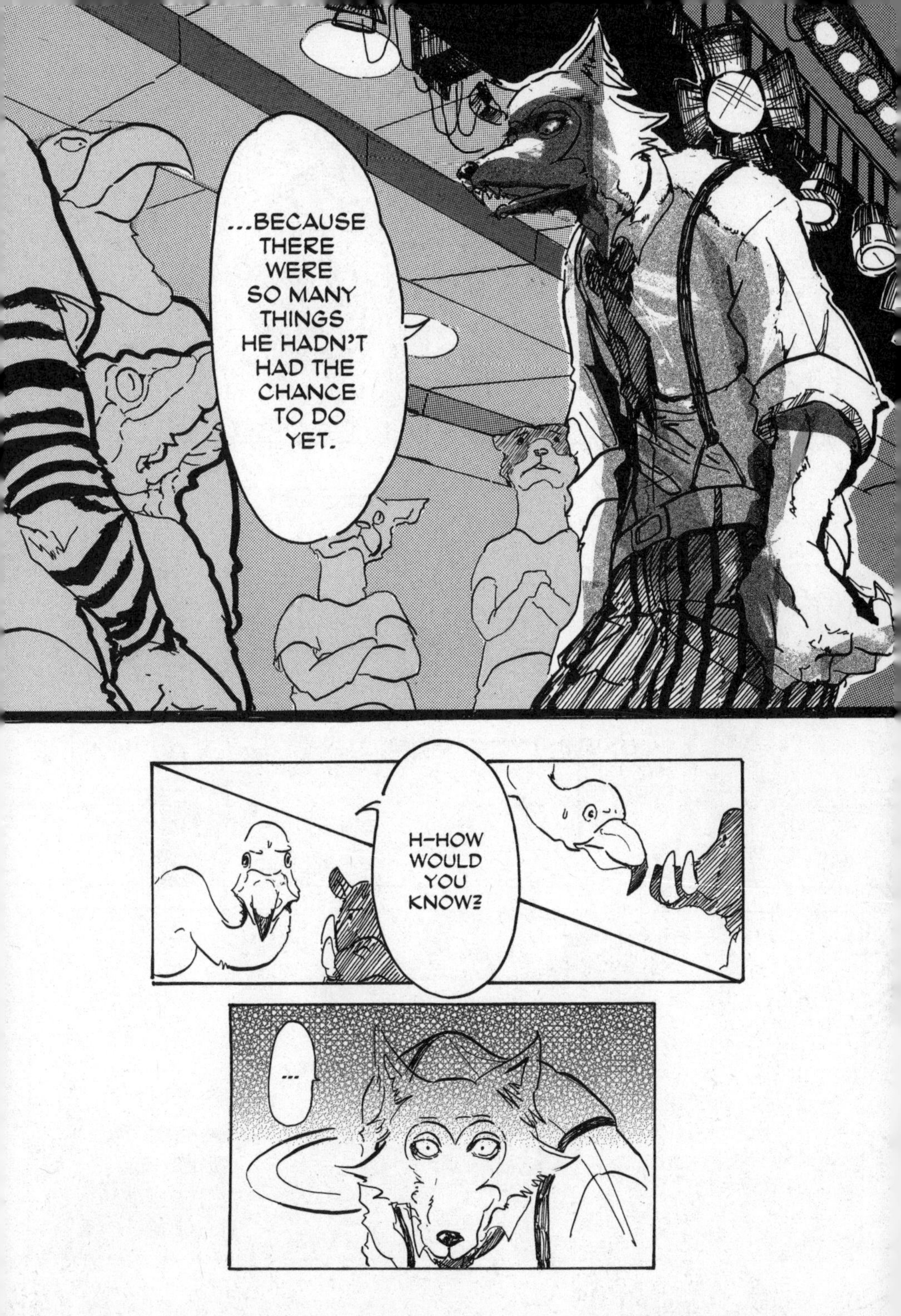
...BECAUSE THERE WERE SO MANY THINGS HE HADN'T HAD THE CHANCE TO DO YET.
H-HOW WOULD YOU KNOW?
...

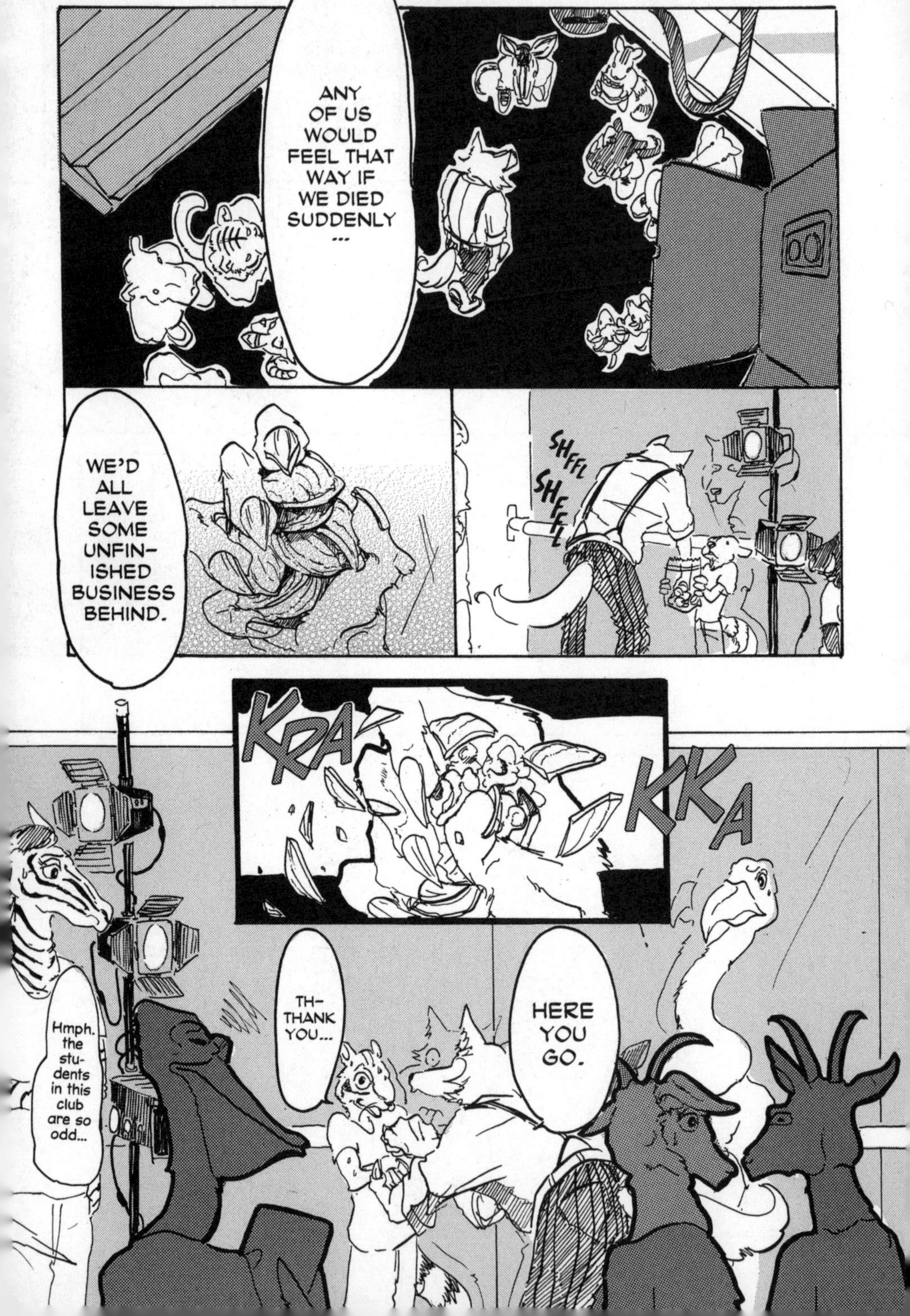
ANY OF US WOULD FEEL THAT WAY IF WE DIED SUDDENLY...
SHFFL SHFFL
WE'D ALL LEAVE SOME UNFIN-ISHED BUSINESS BEHIND.
KRAKKA
HERE YOU GO.
TH-THANK YOU...
Hmph. the stu-dents in this club are so odd...

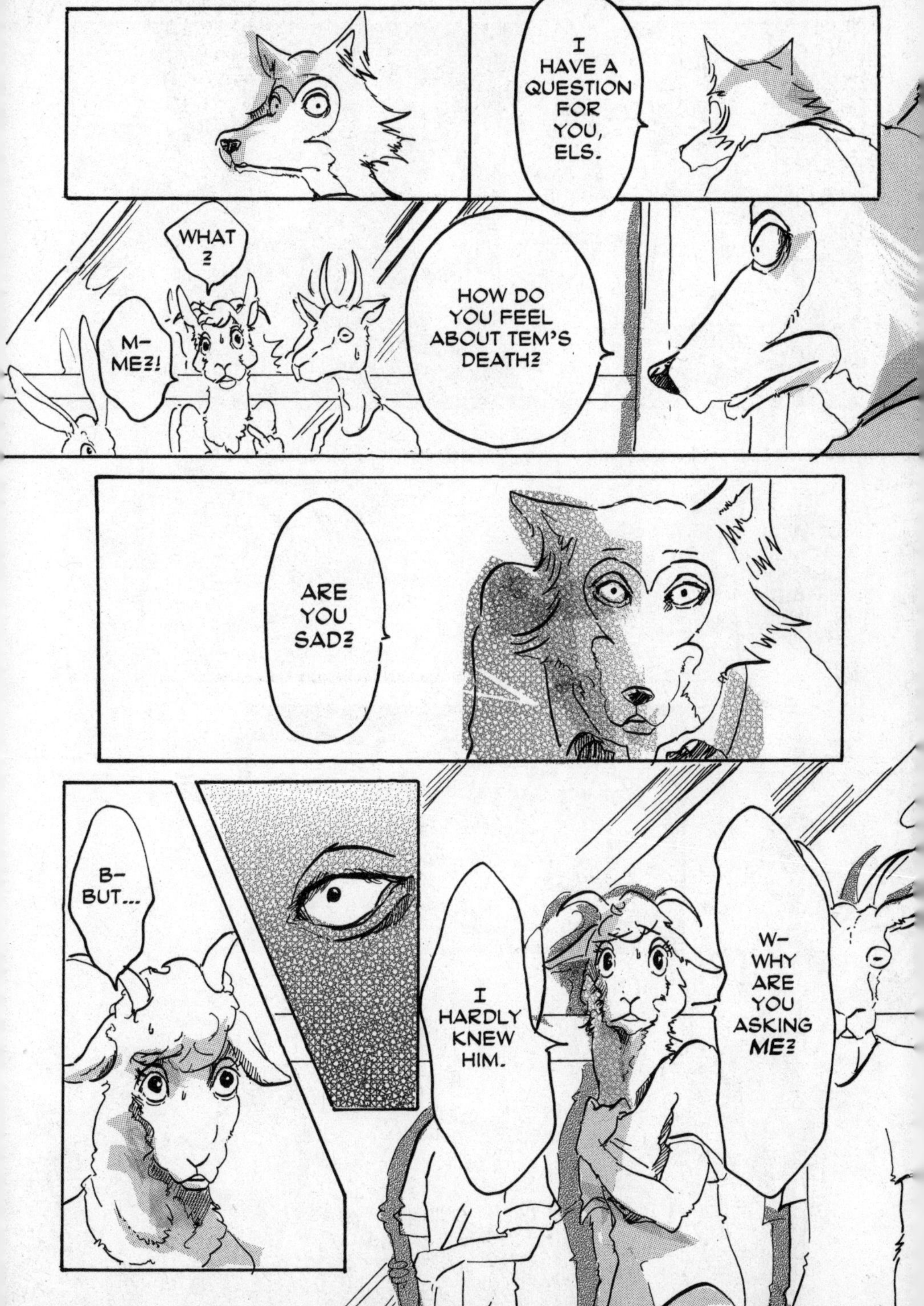
I HAVE A QUESTION FOR YOU, ELS.
HOW DO YOU FEEL ABOUT TEM'S DEATH?
WHAT?
M-ME?!
ARE YOU SAD?
W-WHY ARE YOU ASKING *ME*?
I HARDLY KNEW HIM.
B-BUT...

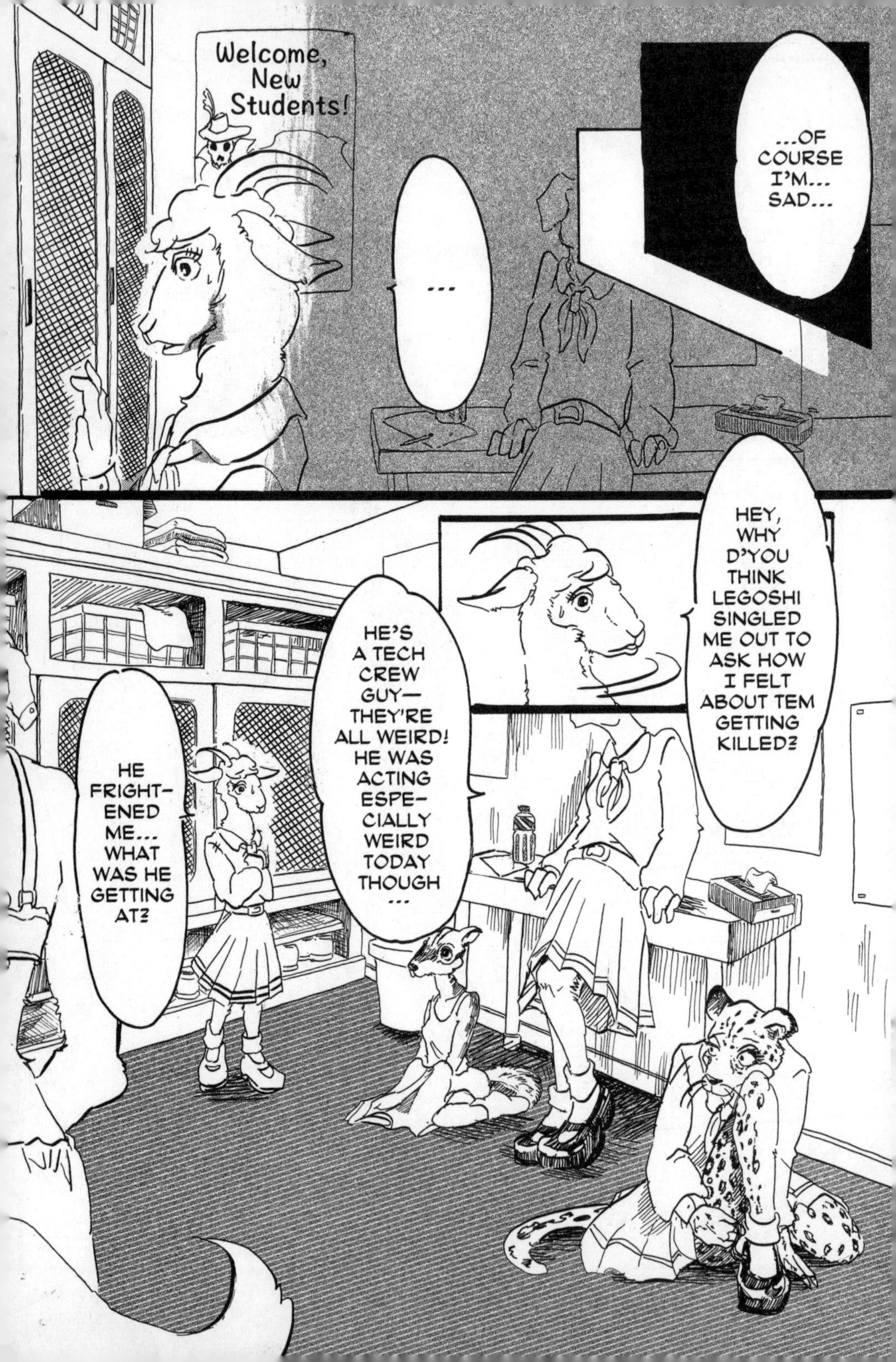
...OF COURSE I'M... SAD...
...
Welcome, New Students!
HEY, WHY D'YOU THINK LEGOSHI SINGLED ME OUT TO ASK HOW I FELT ABOUT TEM GETTING KILLED?
HE'S A TECH CREW GUY— THEY'RE ALL WEIRD! HE WAS ACTING ESPECIALLY WEIRD TODAY THOUGH ...
HE FRIGHTENED ME... WHAT WAS HE GETTING AT?

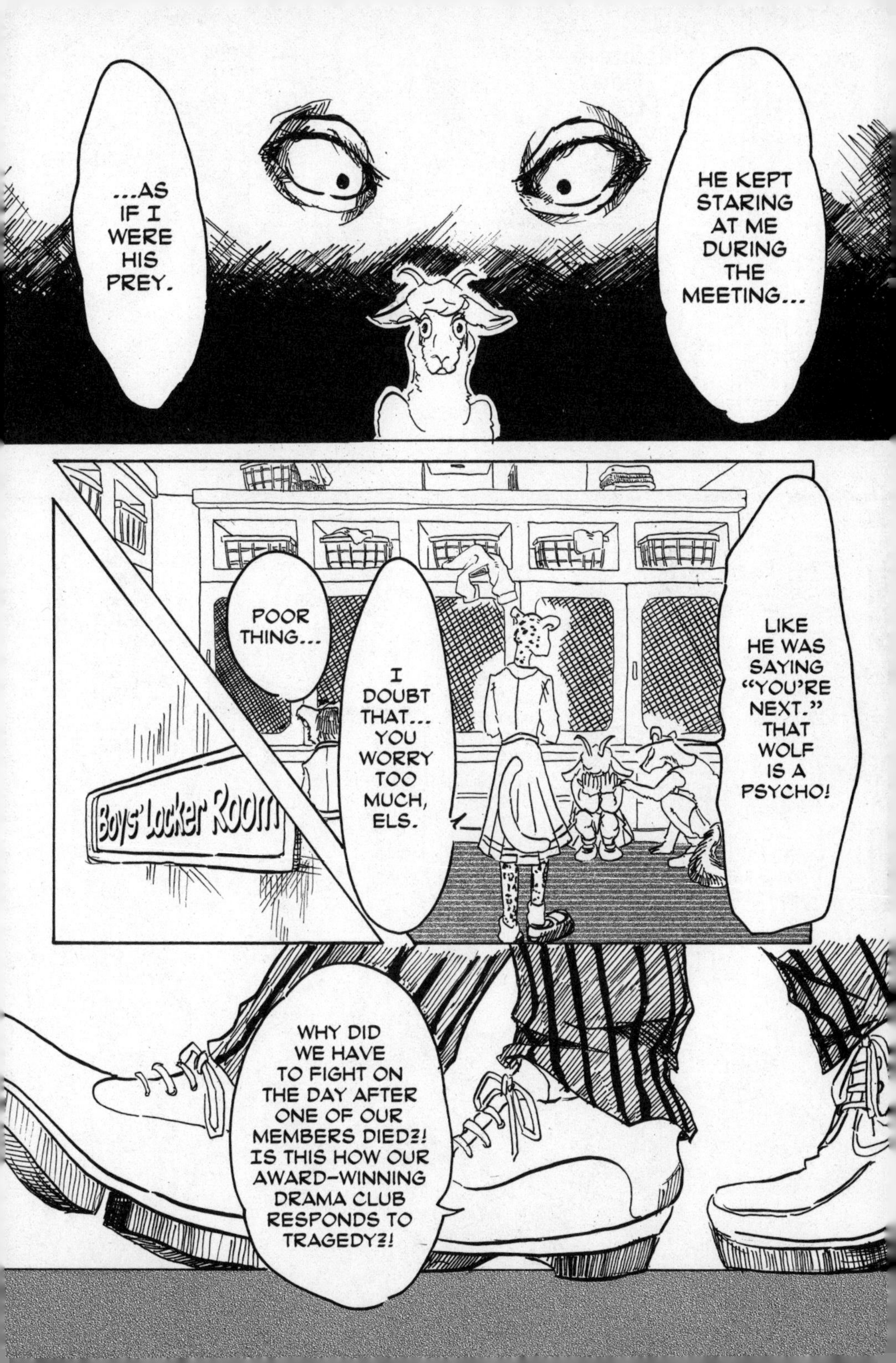
HE KEPT STARING AT ME DURING THE MEETING...
...AS IF I WERE HIS PREY.
LIKE HE WAS SAYING "YOU'RE NEXT." THAT WOLF IS A PSYCHO!
I DOUBT THAT... YOU WORRY TOO MUCH, ELS.
POOR THING...
Boys' Locker Room
WHY DID WE HAVE TO FIGHT ON THE DAY AFTER ONE OF OUR MEMBERS DIED?! IS THIS HOW OUR AWARD-WINNING DRAMA CLUB RESPONDS TO TRAGEDY?!

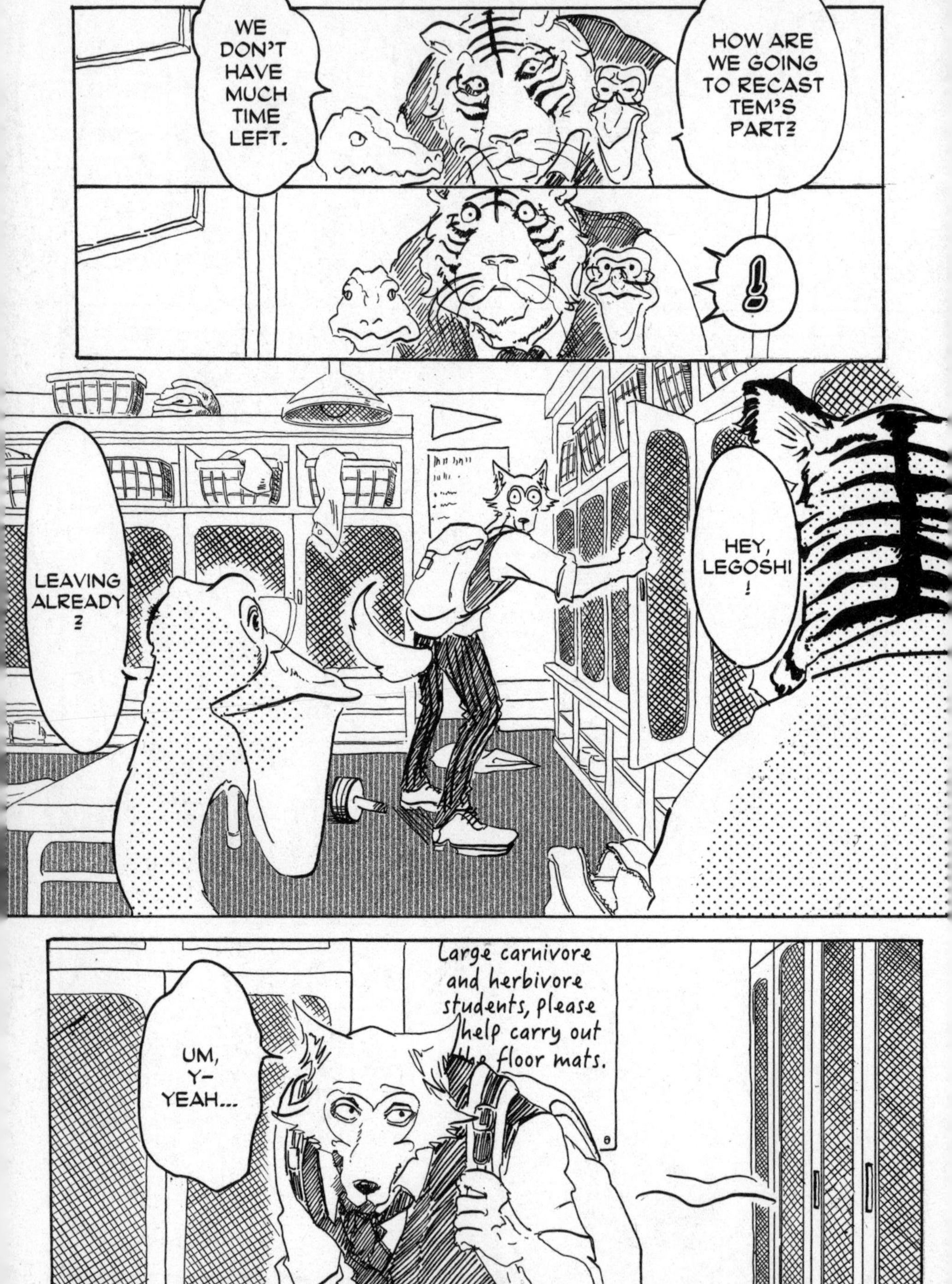
HOW ARE WE GOING TO RECAST TEM'S PART?
WE DON'T HAVE MUCH TIME LEFT.
!
HEY, LEGOSHI!
LEAVING ALREADY?
Large carnivore and herbivore students, please help carry out the floor mats.
UM, Y-YEAH...

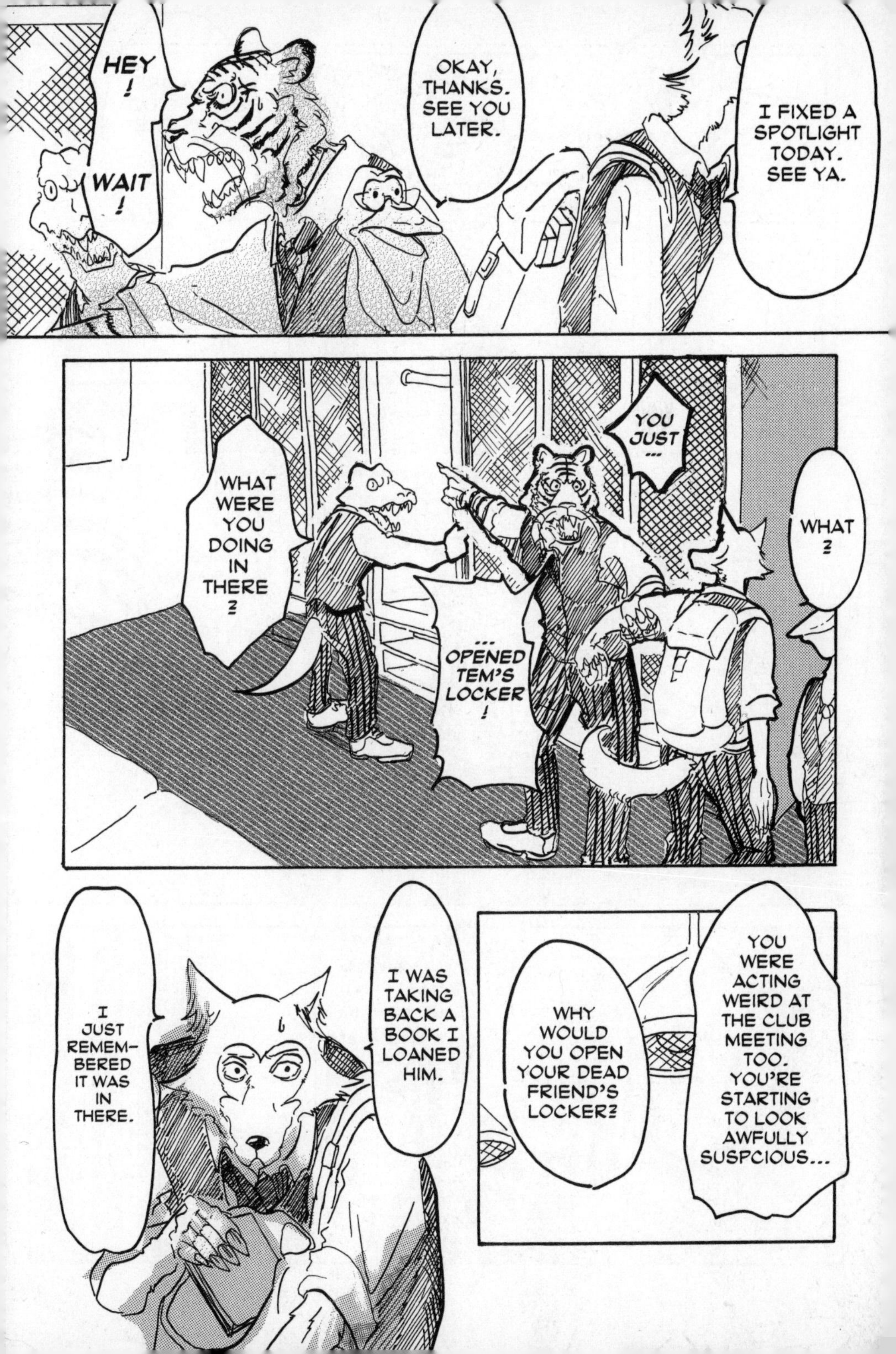
I FIXED A SPOTLIGHT TODAY. SEE YA.
OKAY, THANKS. SEE YOU LATER.
HEY! WAIT!
WHAT?
YOU JUST...
...OPENED TEM'S LOCKER!
WHAT WERE YOU DOING IN THERE?
YOU WERE ACTING WEIRD AT THE CLUB MEETING TOO. YOU'RE STARTING TO LOOK AWFULLY SUSPCIOUS...
WHY WOULD YOU OPEN YOUR DEAD FRIEND'S LOCKER?
I WAS TAKING BACK A BOOK I LOANED HIM.
I JUST REMEM-BERED IT WAS IN THERE.

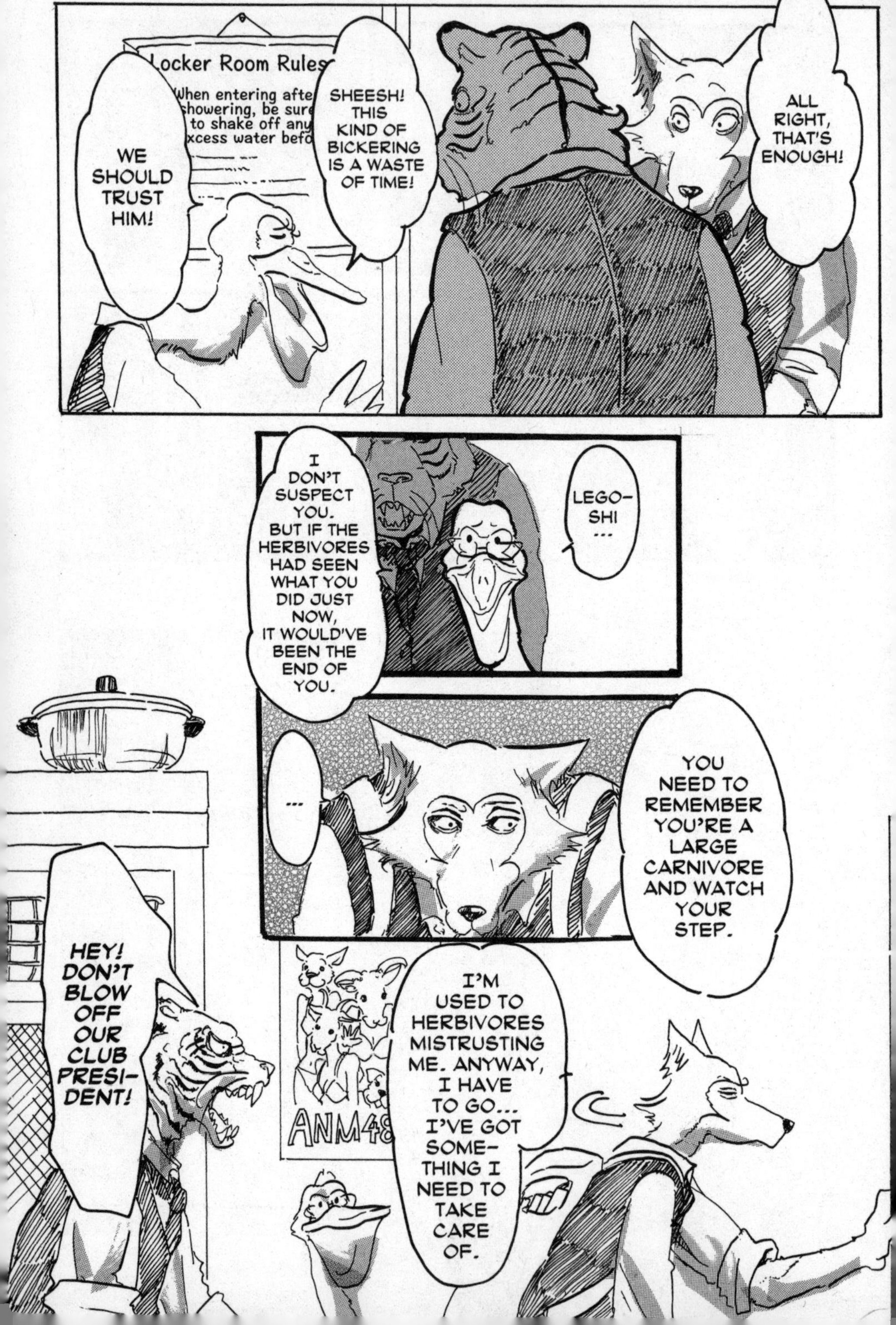
ALL RIGHT, THAT'S ENOUGH!
SHEESH! THIS KIND OF BICKERING IS A WASTE OF TIME!
Locker Room Rules
WE SHOULD TRUST HIM!
LEGO-SHI...
I DON'T SUSPECT YOU. BUT IF THE HERBIVORES HAD SEEN WHAT YOU DID JUST NOW, IT WOULD'VE BEEN THE END OF YOU.
YOU NEED TO REMEMBER YOU'RE A LARGE CARNIVORE AND WATCH YOUR STEP.
...
I'M USED TO HERBIVORES MISTRUSTING ME. ANYWAY, I HAVE TO GO... I'VE GOT SOMETHING I NEED TO TAKE CARE OF.
HEY! DON'T BLOW OFF OUR CLUB PRESIDENT!

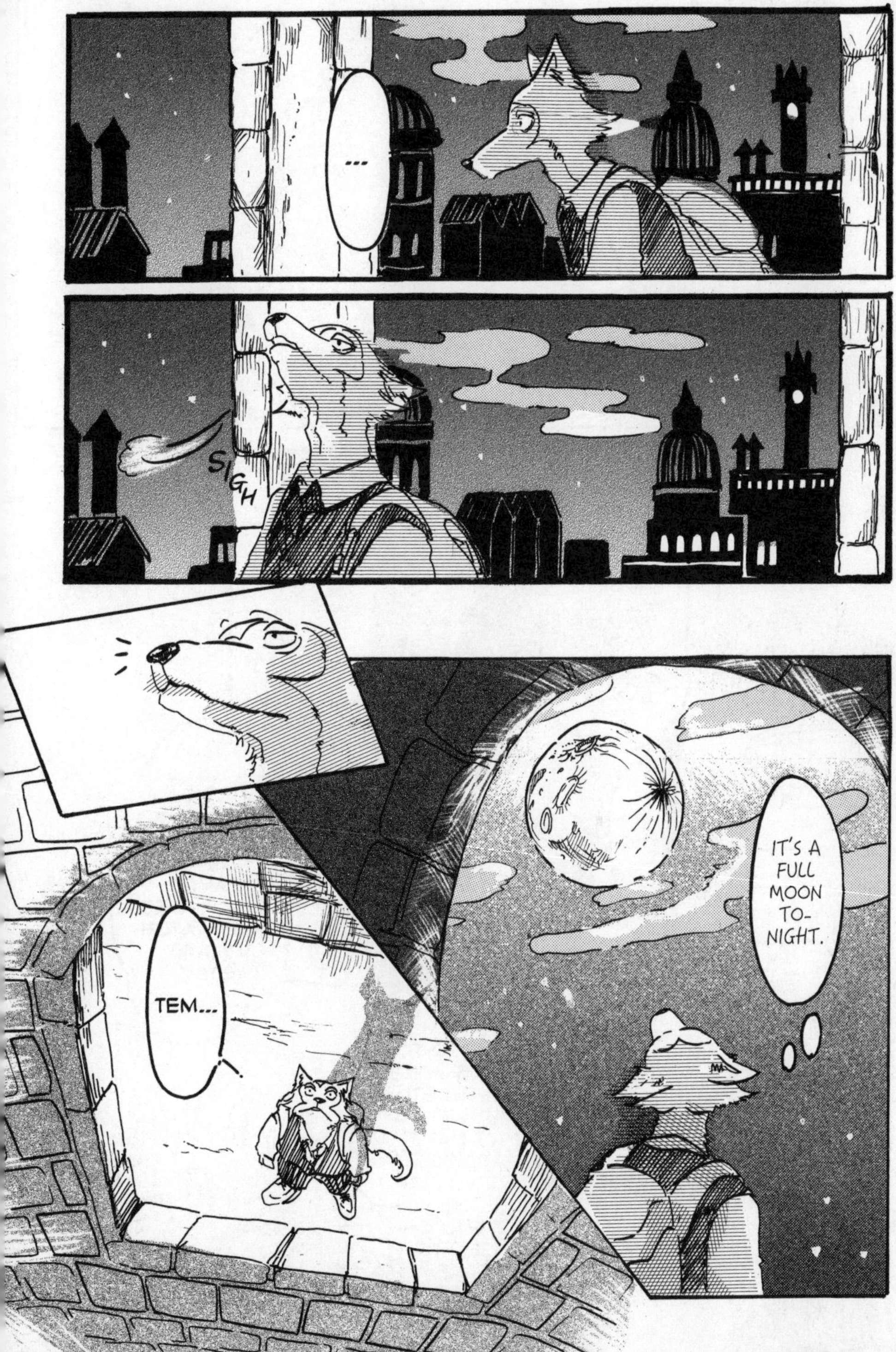
...
SIGH
IT'S A FULL MOON TO-NIGHT.
TEM...

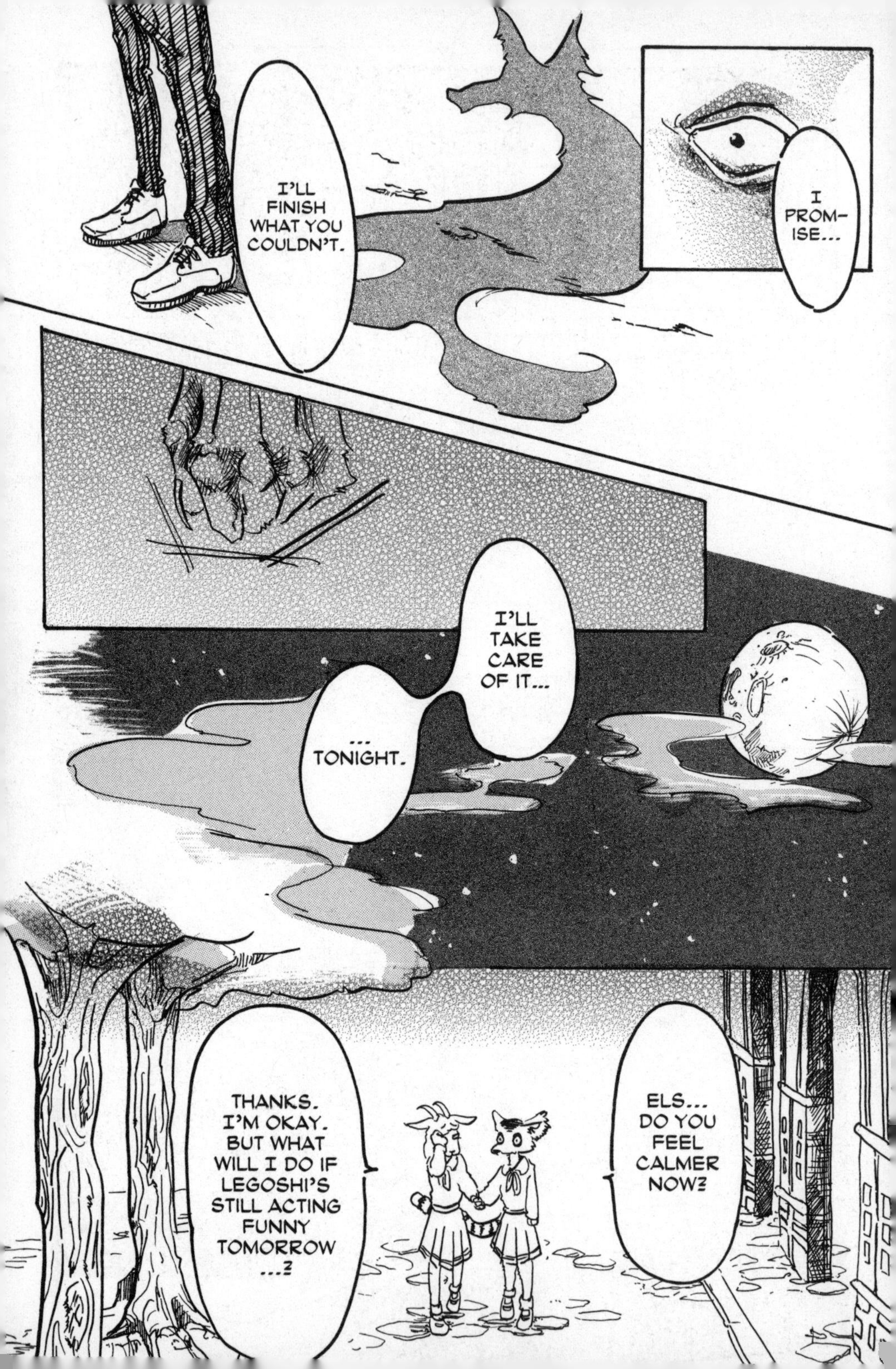

I PROMISE...
I'LL FINISH WHAT YOU COULDN'T.
I'LL TAKE CARE OF IT...
...TONIGHT.
ELS... DO YOU FEEL CALMER NOW?
THANKS. I'M OKAY. BUT WHAT WILL I DO IF LEGOSHI'S STILL ACTING FUNNY TOMORROW...?

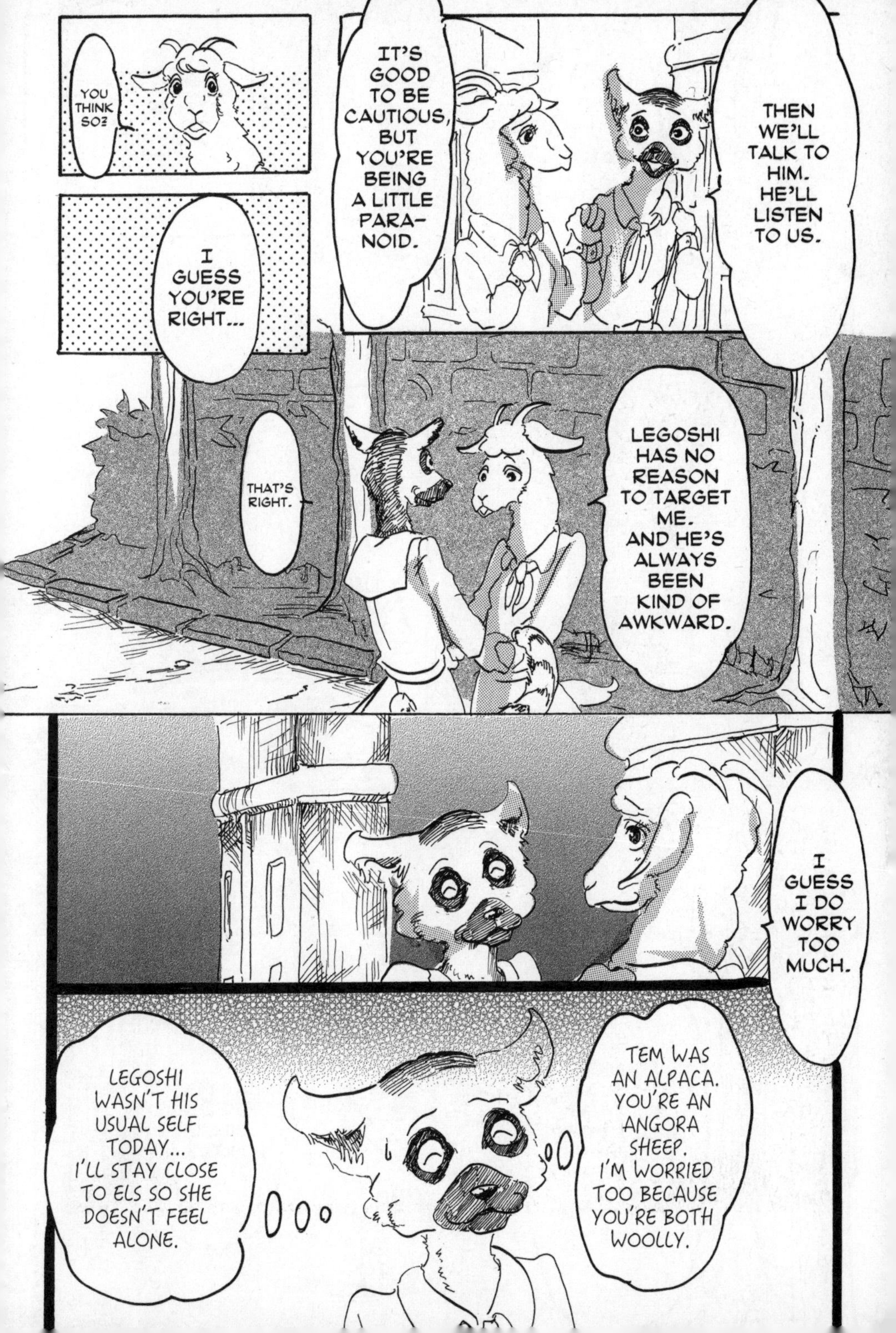
THEN WE'LL TALK TO HIM. HE'LL LISTEN TO US.
IT'S GOOD TO BE CAUTIOUS, BUT YOU'RE BEING A LITTLE PARA-NOID.
YOU THINK SO?
I GUESS YOU'RE RIGHT...
LEGOSHI HAS NO REASON TO TARGET ME. AND HE'S ALWAYS BEEN KIND OF AWKWARD.
THAT'S RIGHT.
I GUESS I DO WORRY TOO MUCH.
TEM WAS AN ALPACA. YOU'RE AN ANGORA SHEEP. I'M WORRIED TOO BECAUSE YOU'RE BOTH WOOLLY.
LEGOSHI WASN'T HIS USUAL SELF TODAY... I'LL STAY CLOSE TO ELS SO SHE DOESN'T FEEL ALONE.

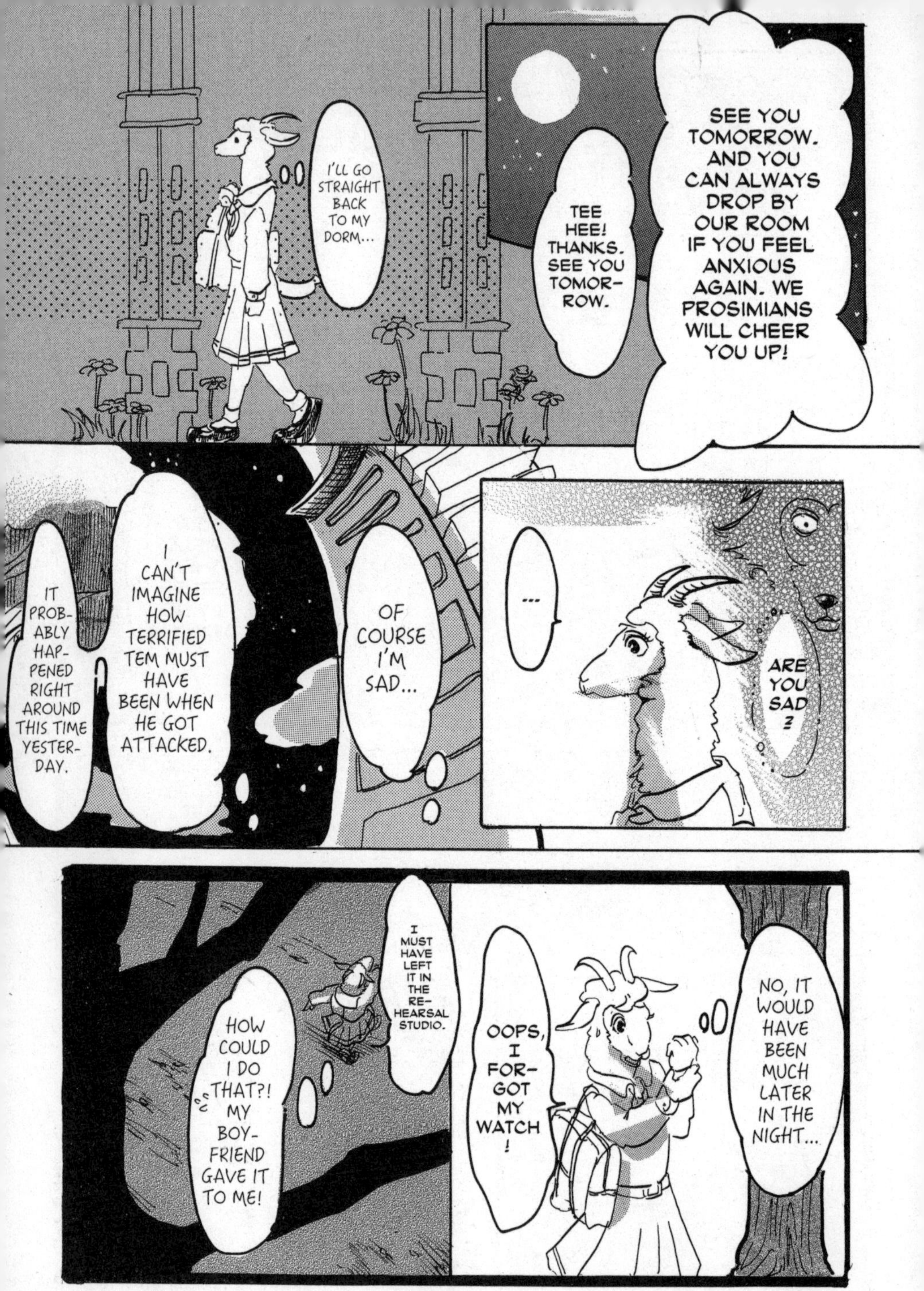
SEE YOU TOMORROW. AND YOU CAN ALWAYS DROP BY OUR ROOM IF YOU FEEL ANXIOUS AGAIN. WE PROSIMIANS WILL CHEER YOU UP!
TEE HEE! THANKS. SEE YOU TOMOR-ROW.
I'LL GO STRAIGHT BACK TO MY DORM...
ARE YOU SAD?
...
OF COURSE I'M SAD...
I CAN'T IMAGINE HOW TERRIFIED TEM MUST HAVE BEEN WHEN HE GOT ATTACKED.
IT PROB-ABLY HAP-PENED RIGHT AROUND THIS TIME YESTER-DAY.
NO, IT WOULD HAVE BEEN MUCH LATER IN THE NIGHT...
OOPS, I FOR-GOT MY WATCH!
I MUST HAVE LEFT IT IN THE RE-HEARSAL STUDIO.
HOW COULD I DO THAT?! MY BOY-FRIEND GAVE IT TO ME!

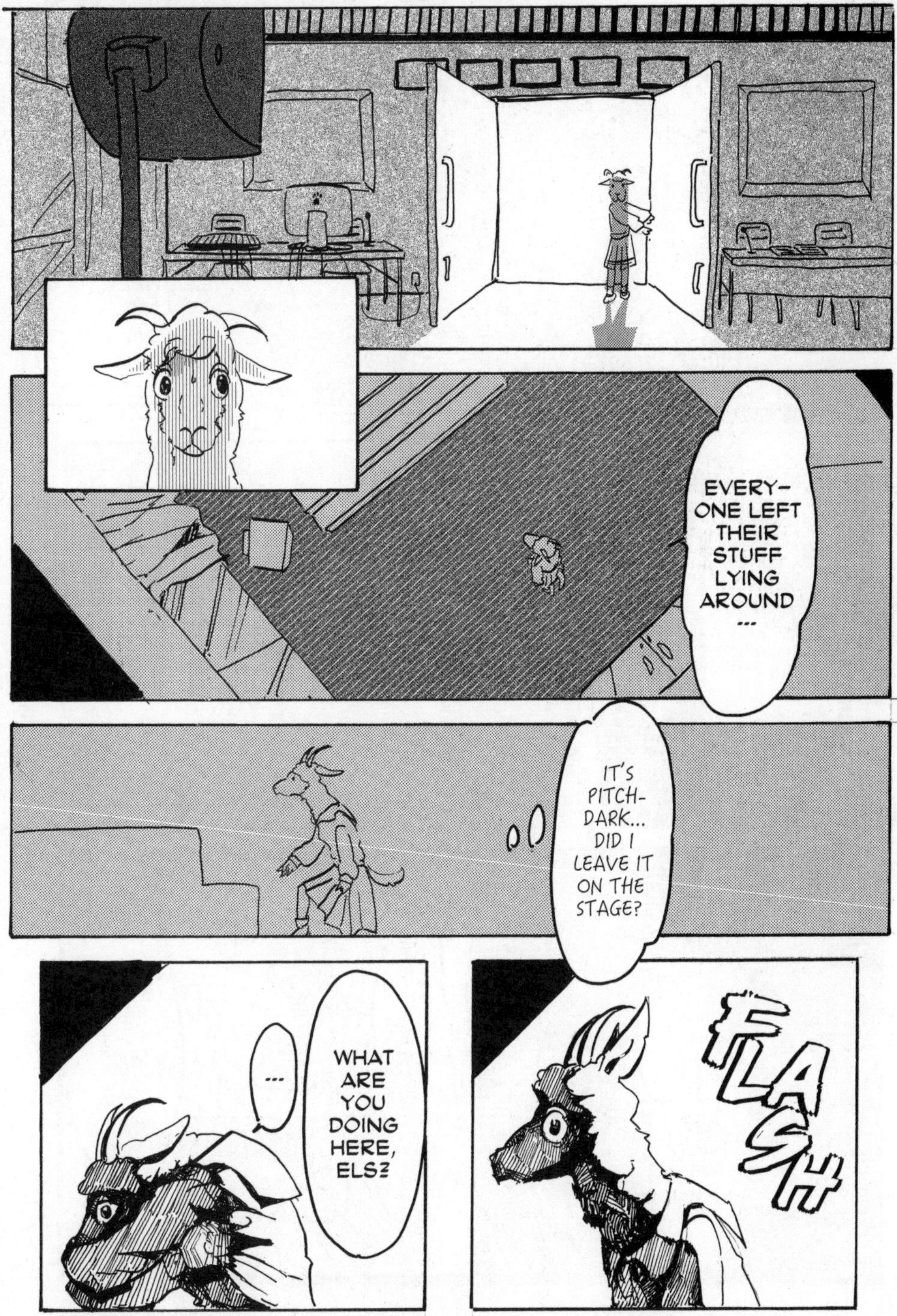
EVERY-ONE LEFT THEIR STUFF LYING AROUND...
IT'S PITCH-DARK... DID I LEAVE IT ON THE STAGE?
FLASH
WHAT ARE YOU DOING HERE, ELS?
...

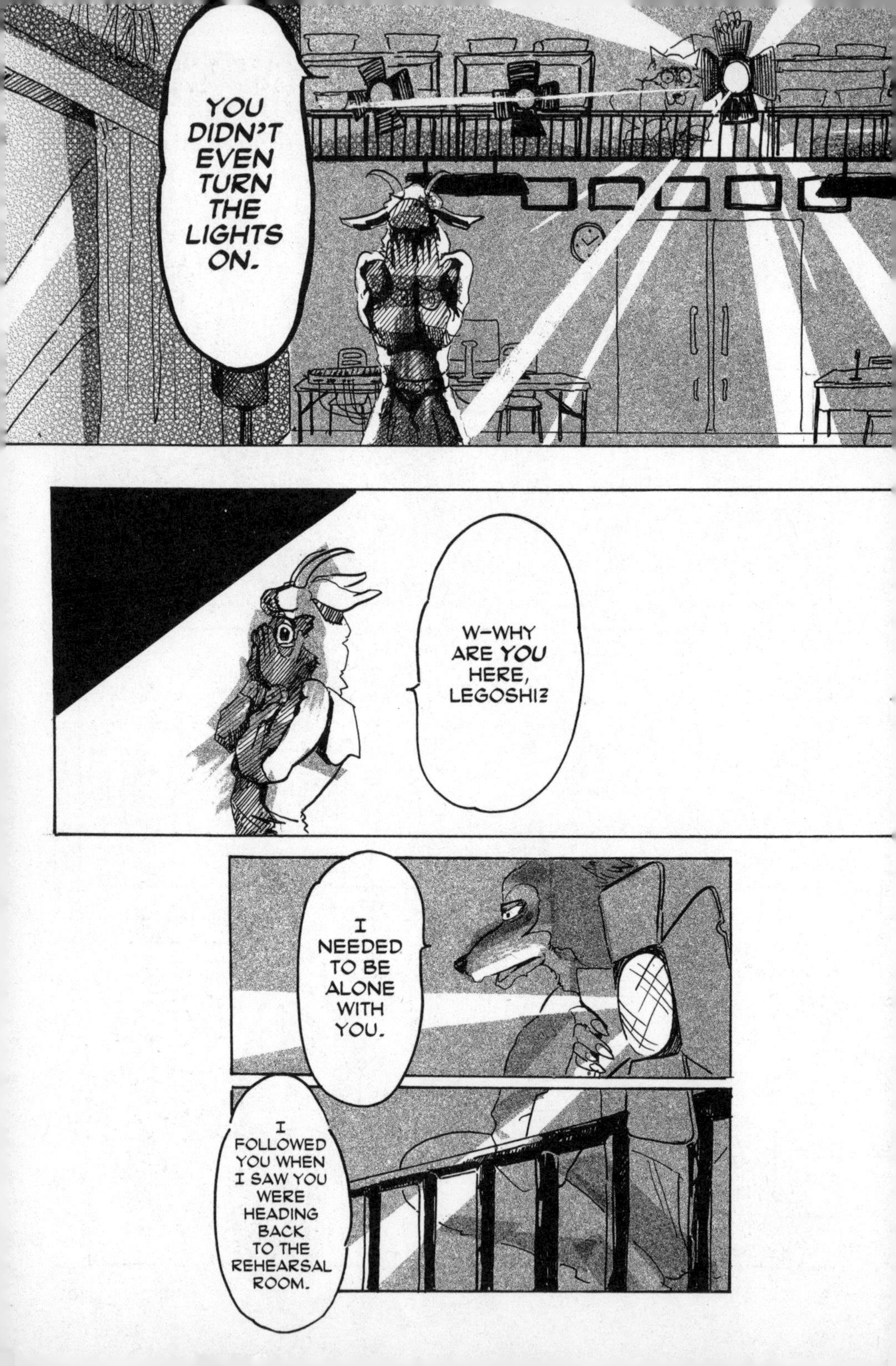
YOU DIDN'T EVEN TURN THE LIGHTS ON.
W-WHY ARE YOU HERE, LEGOSHI?
I NEEDED TO BE ALONE WITH YOU.
I FOLLOWED YOU WHEN I SAW YOU WERE HEADING BACK TO THE REHEARSAL ROOM.

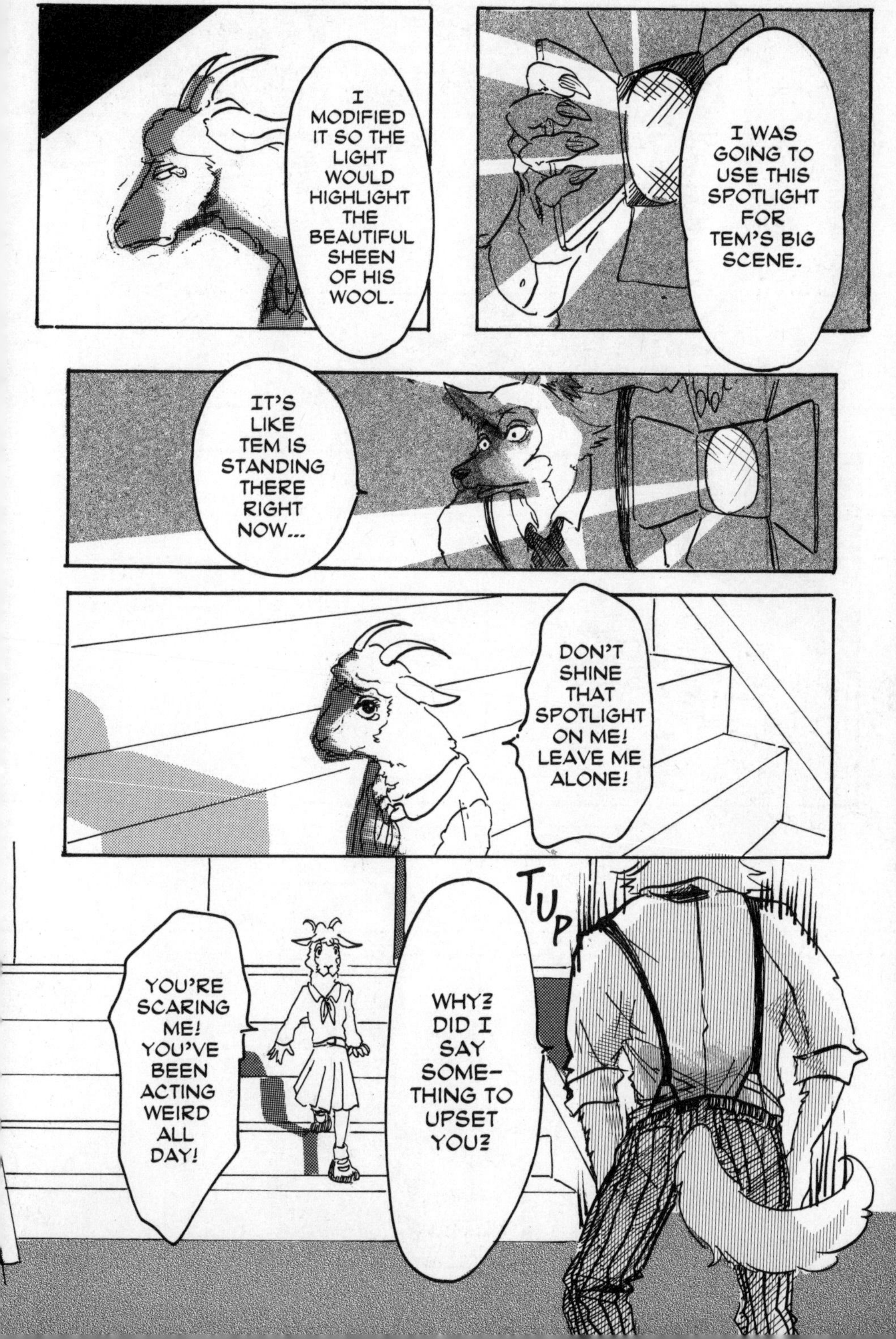
I WAS GOING TO USE THIS SPOTLIGHT FOR TEM'S BIG SCENE.
I MODIFIED IT SO THE LIGHT WOULD HIGHLIGHT THE BEAUTIFUL SHEEN OF HIS WOOL.
IT'S LIKE TEM IS STANDING THERE RIGHT NOW...
DON'T SHINE THAT SPOTLIGHT ON ME! LEAVE ME ALONE!
TUP
WHY? DID I SAY SOME-THING TO UPSET YOU?
YOU'RE SCARING ME! YOU'VE BEEN ACTING WEIRD ALL DAY!

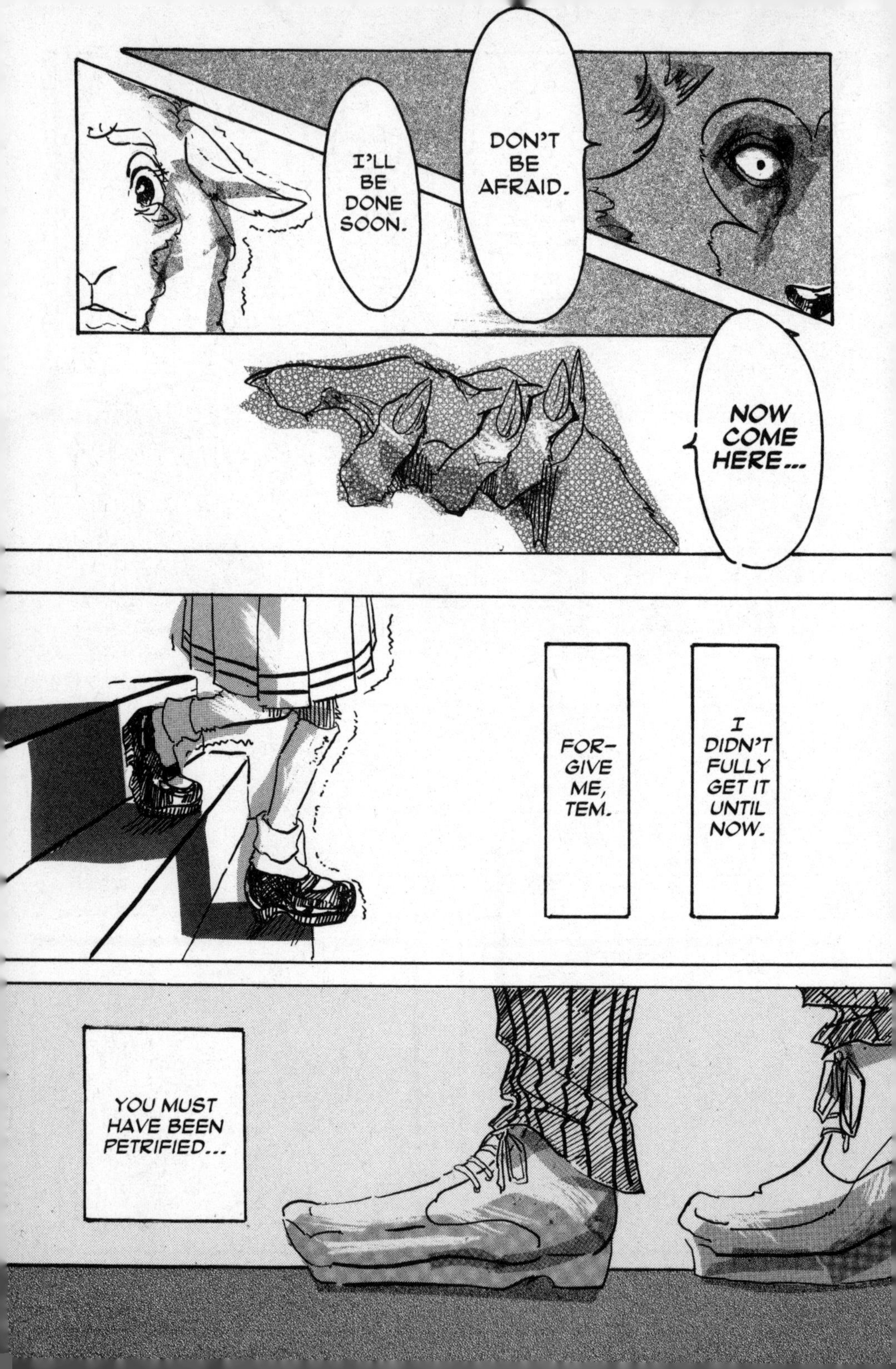
DON'T BE AFRAID.
I'LL BE DONE SOON.
NOW COME HERE...
I DIDN'T FULLY GET IT UNTIL NOW.
FOR-GIVE ME, TEM.
YOU MUST HAVE BEEN PETRIFIED...

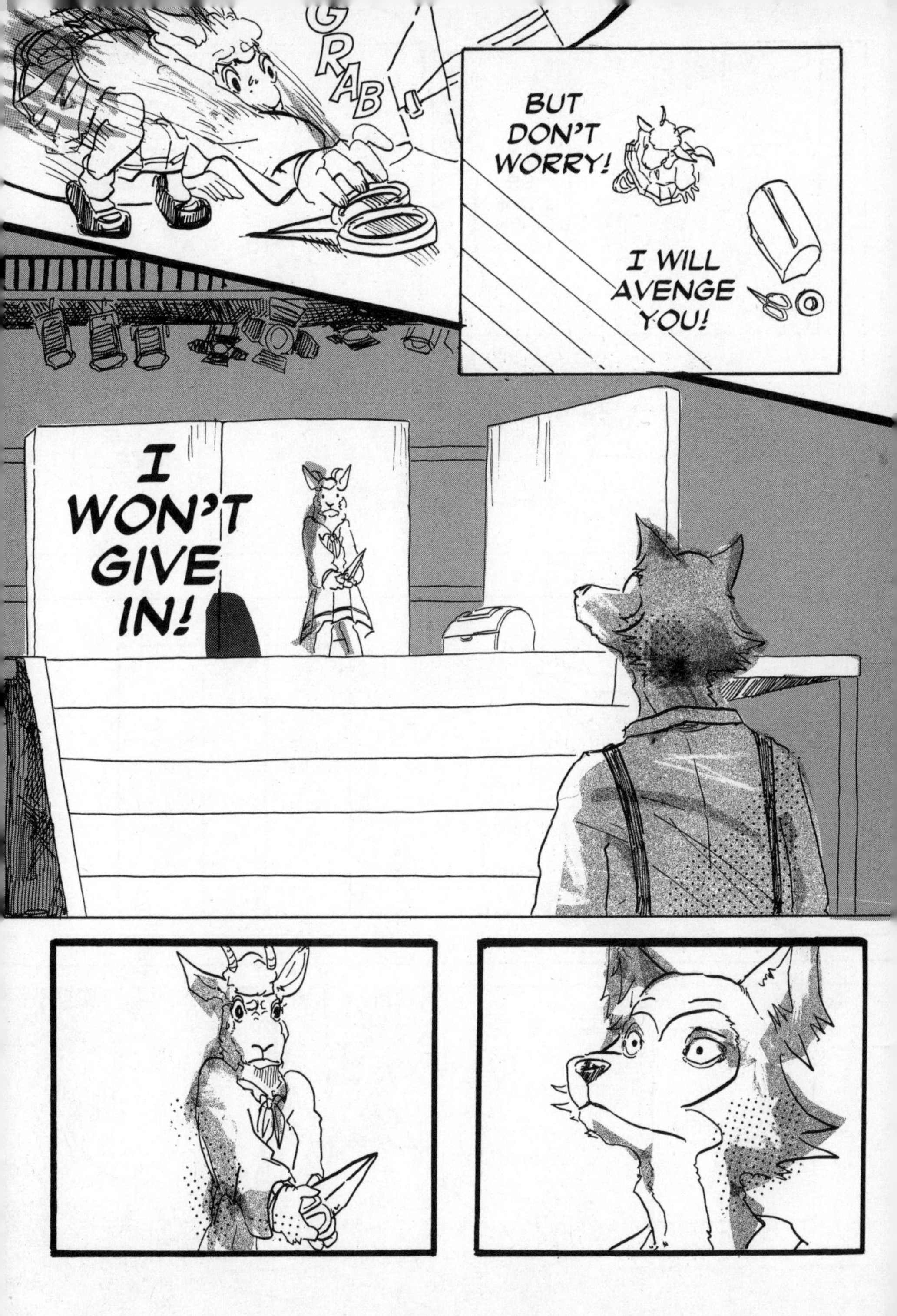
BUT DON'T WORRY!
I WILL AVENGE YOU!
GRAB
I WON'T GIVE IN!

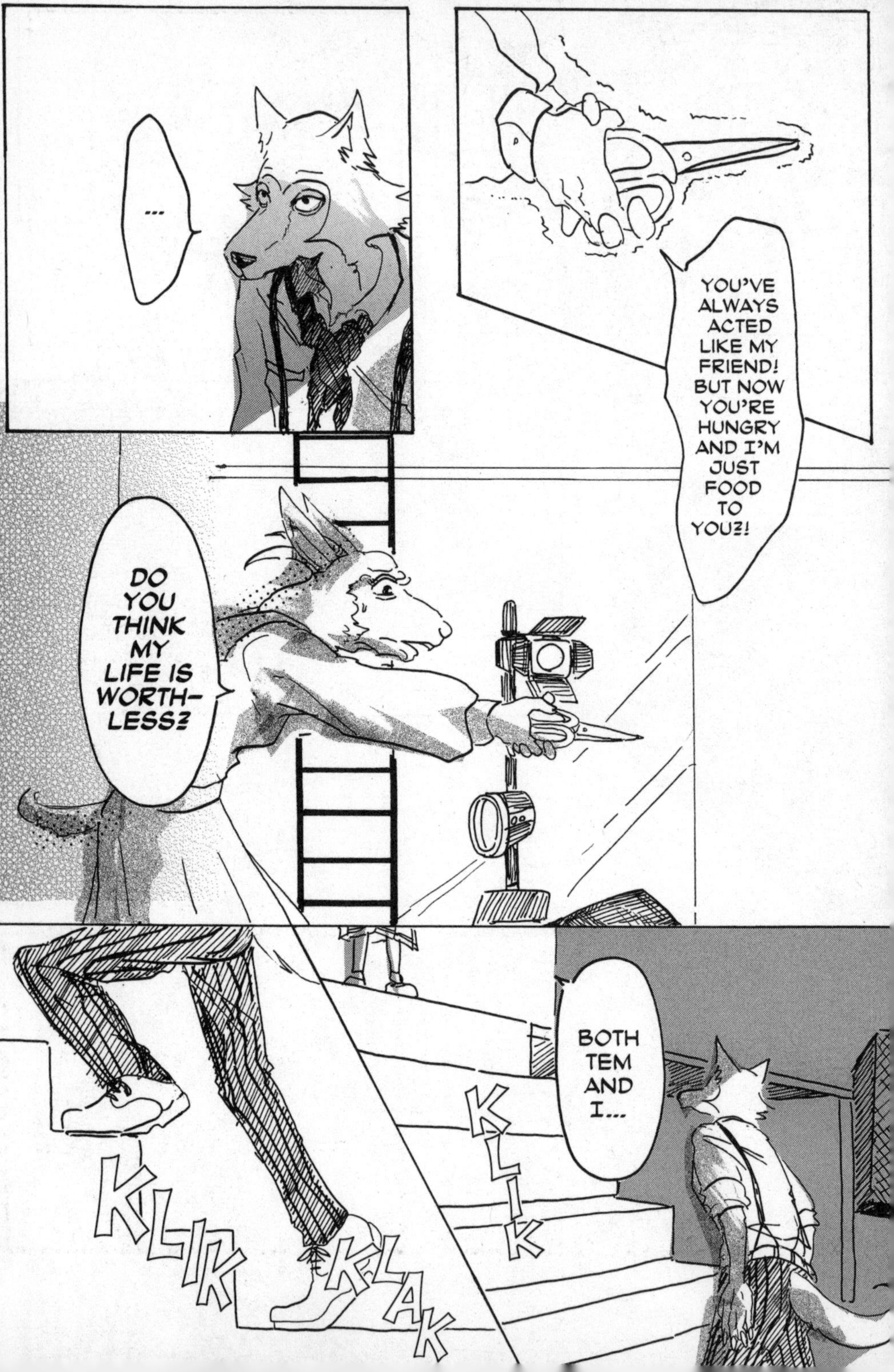
YOU'VE ALWAYS ACTED LIKE MY FRIEND! BUT NOW YOU'RE HUNGRY AND I'M JUST FOOD TO YOU?!
...
DO YOU THINK MY LIFE IS WORTH-LESS?
BOTH TEM AND I...
KLIK
KLIK
KLAK

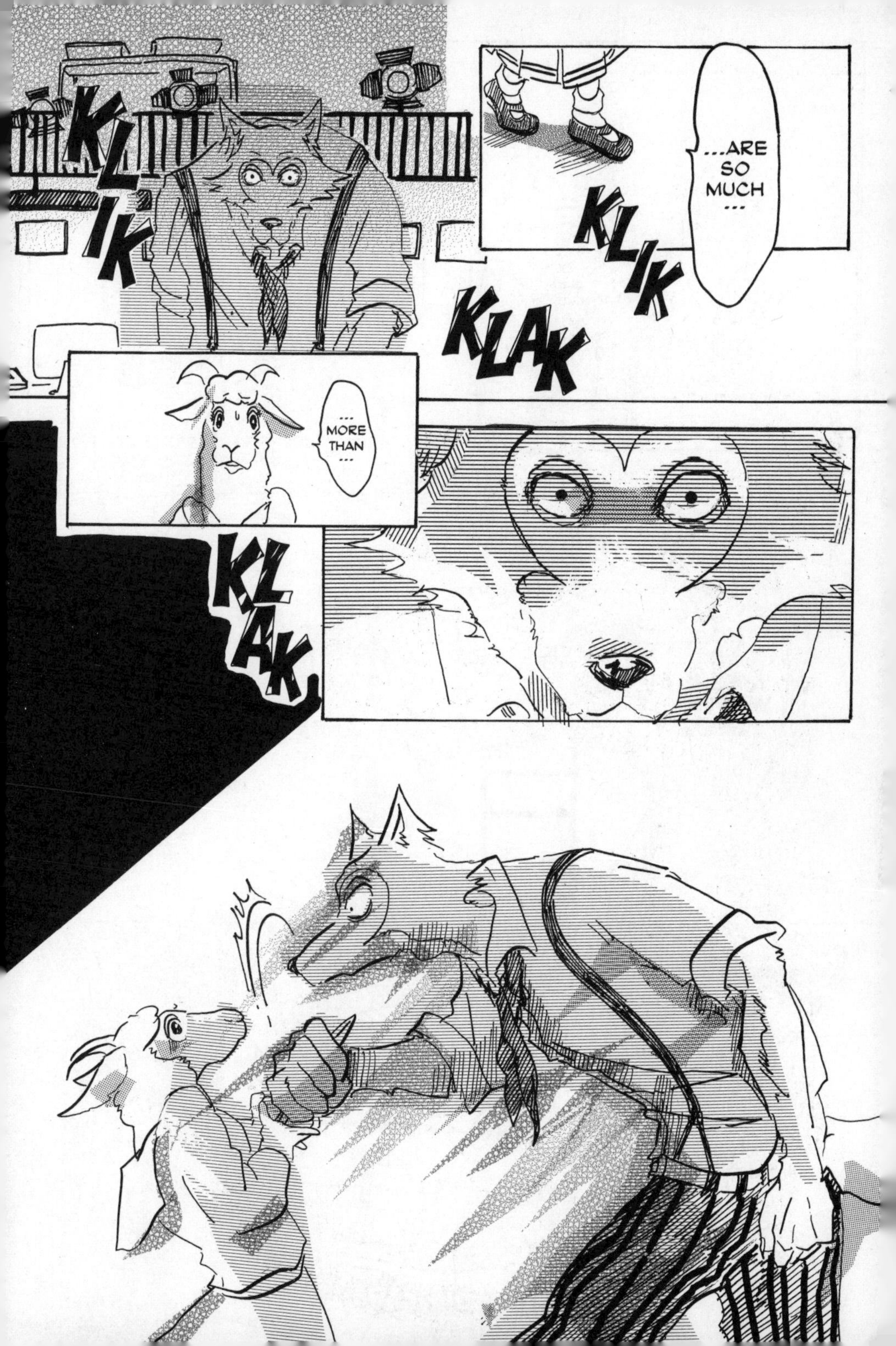
...ARE SO MUCH ...
KLIK
KLAK
KLIK
... MORE THAN ...
KLAK

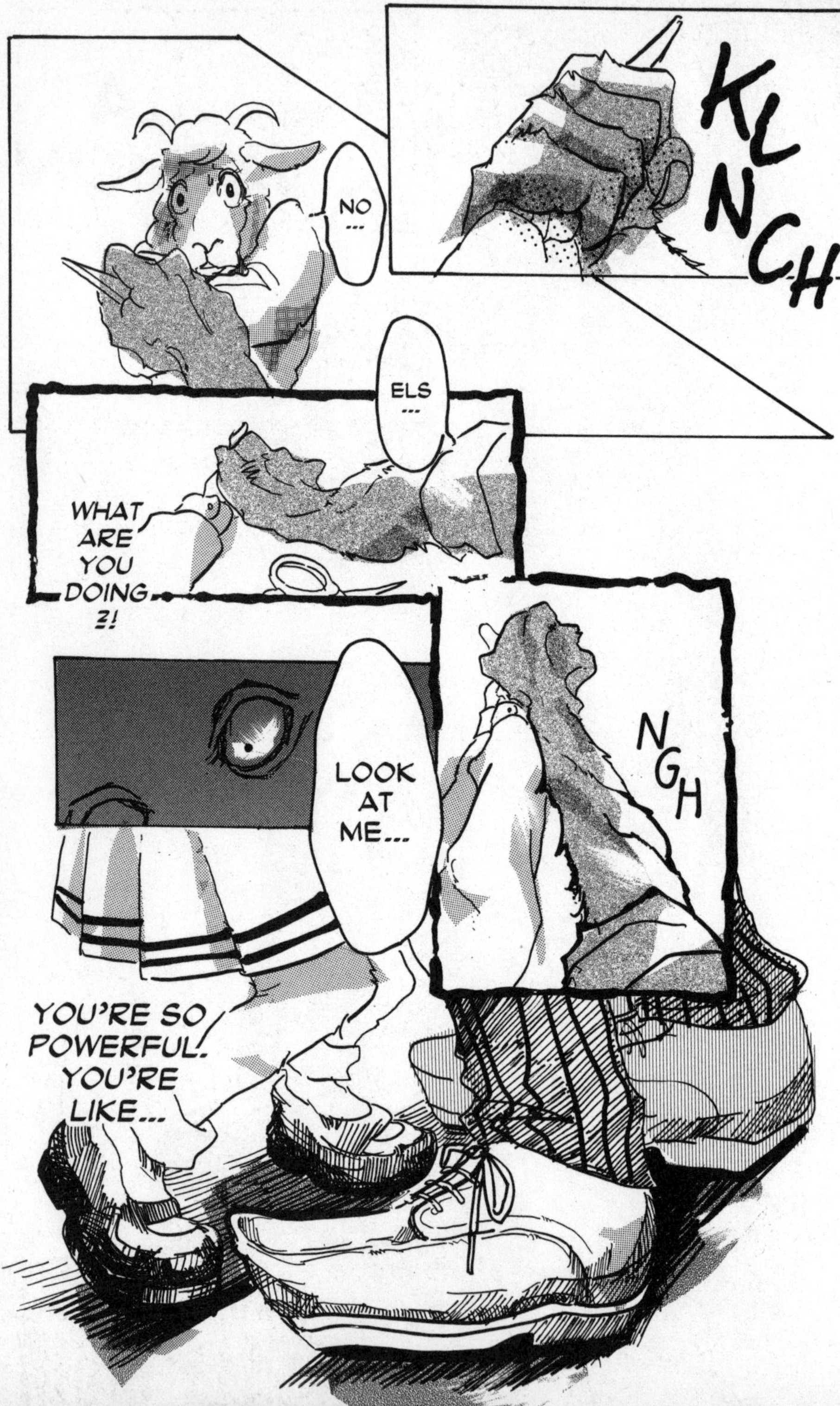
KLNCH
NO...
ELS...
WHAT ARE YOU DOING?!
NGH
LOOK AT ME...
YOU'RE SO POWERFUL. YOU'RE LIKE...

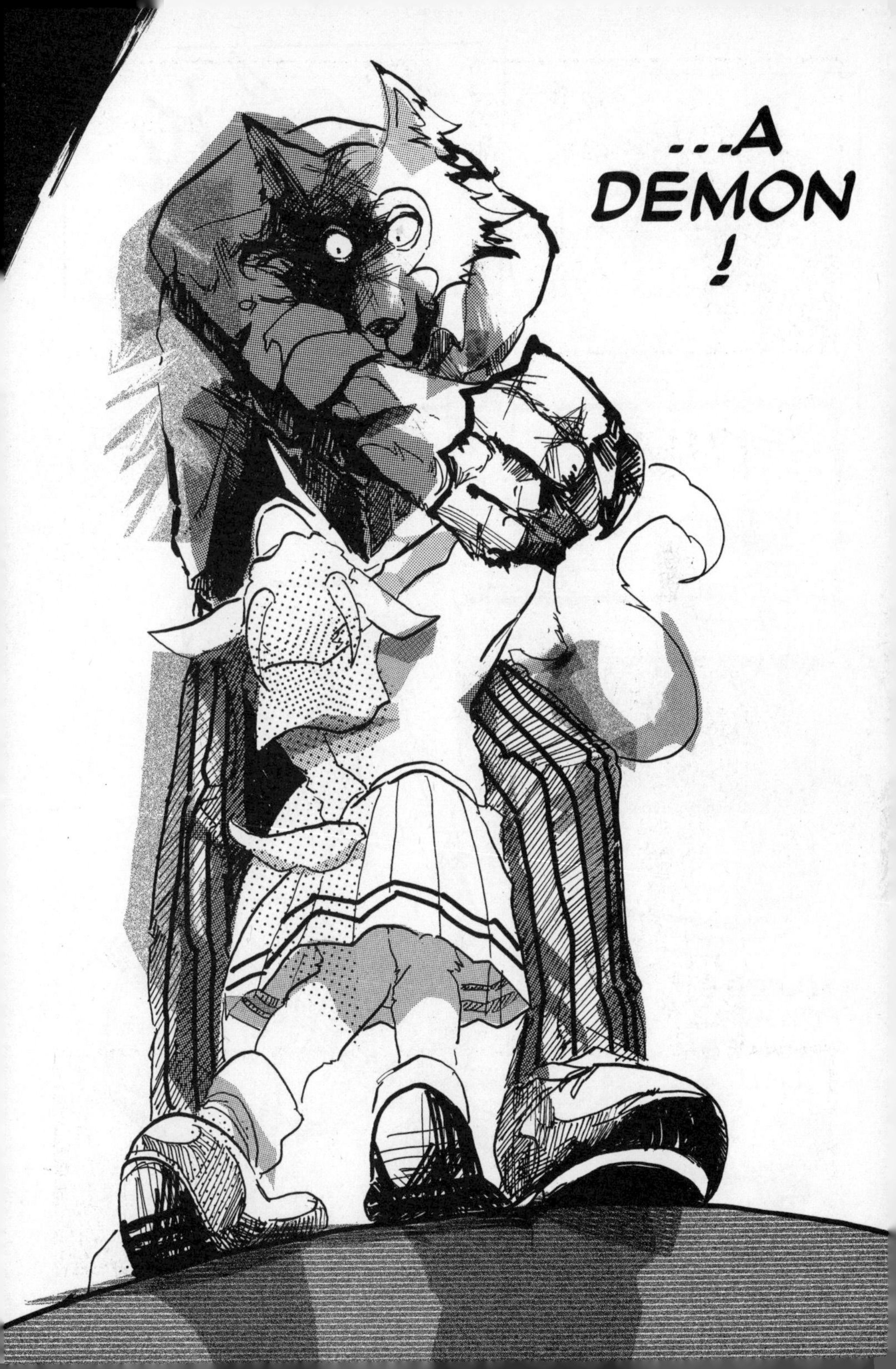
...A DEMON!

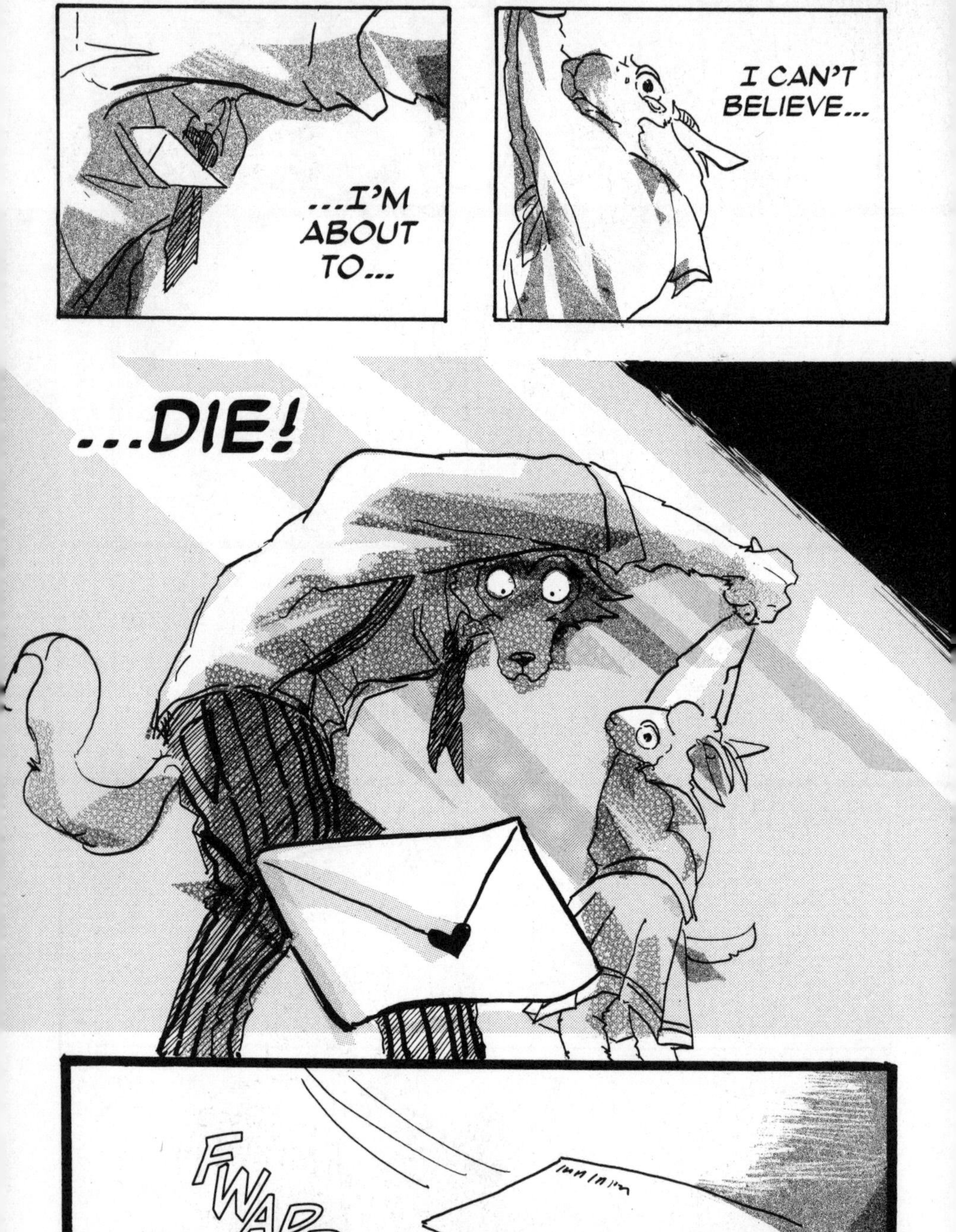
I CAN'T BELIEVE...
...I'M ABOUT TO...
...DIE!
FWAPPA

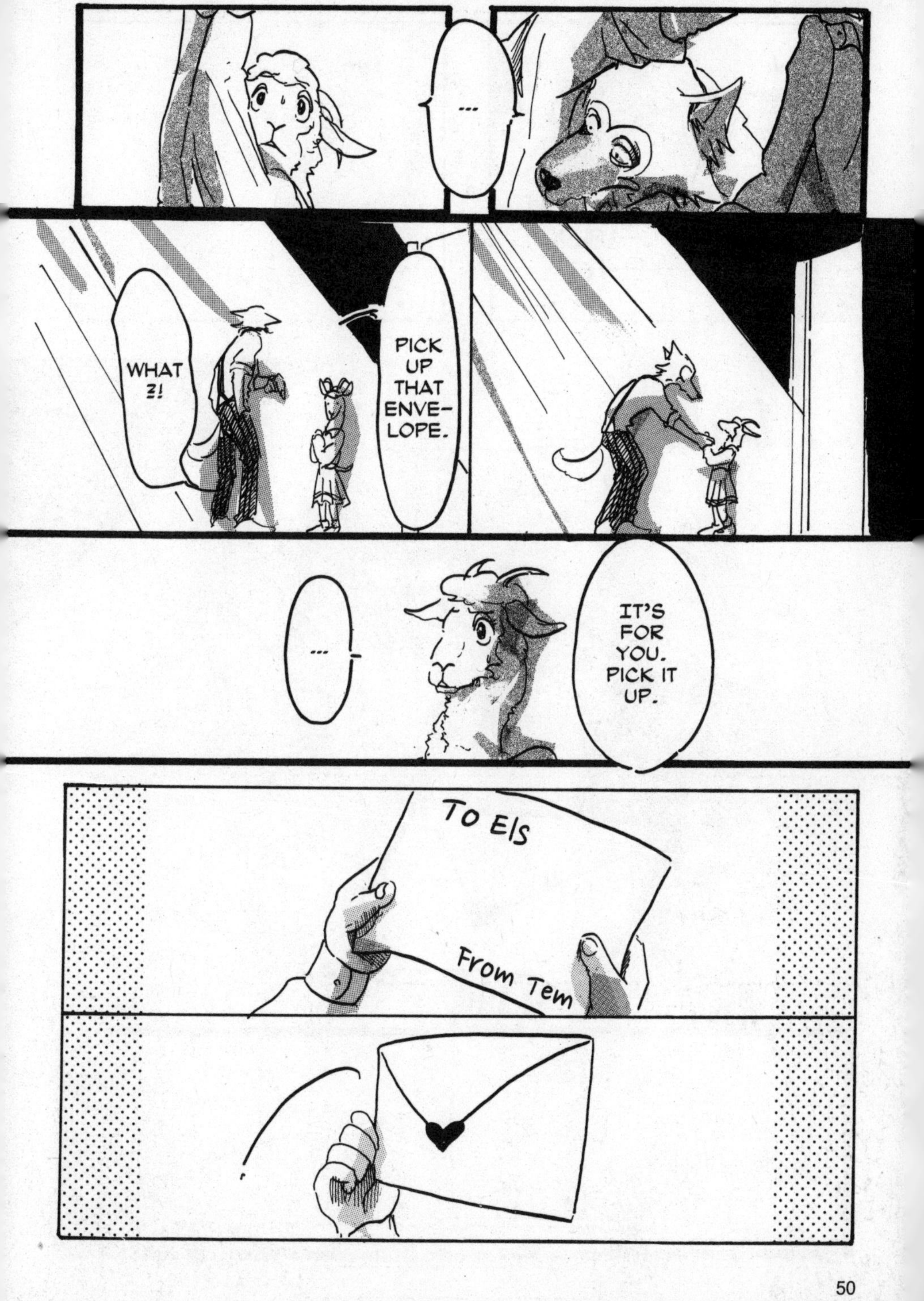
...
PICK UP THAT ENVELOPE.
WHAT?!
IT'S FOR YOU. PICK IT UP.
...
To Els
From Tem

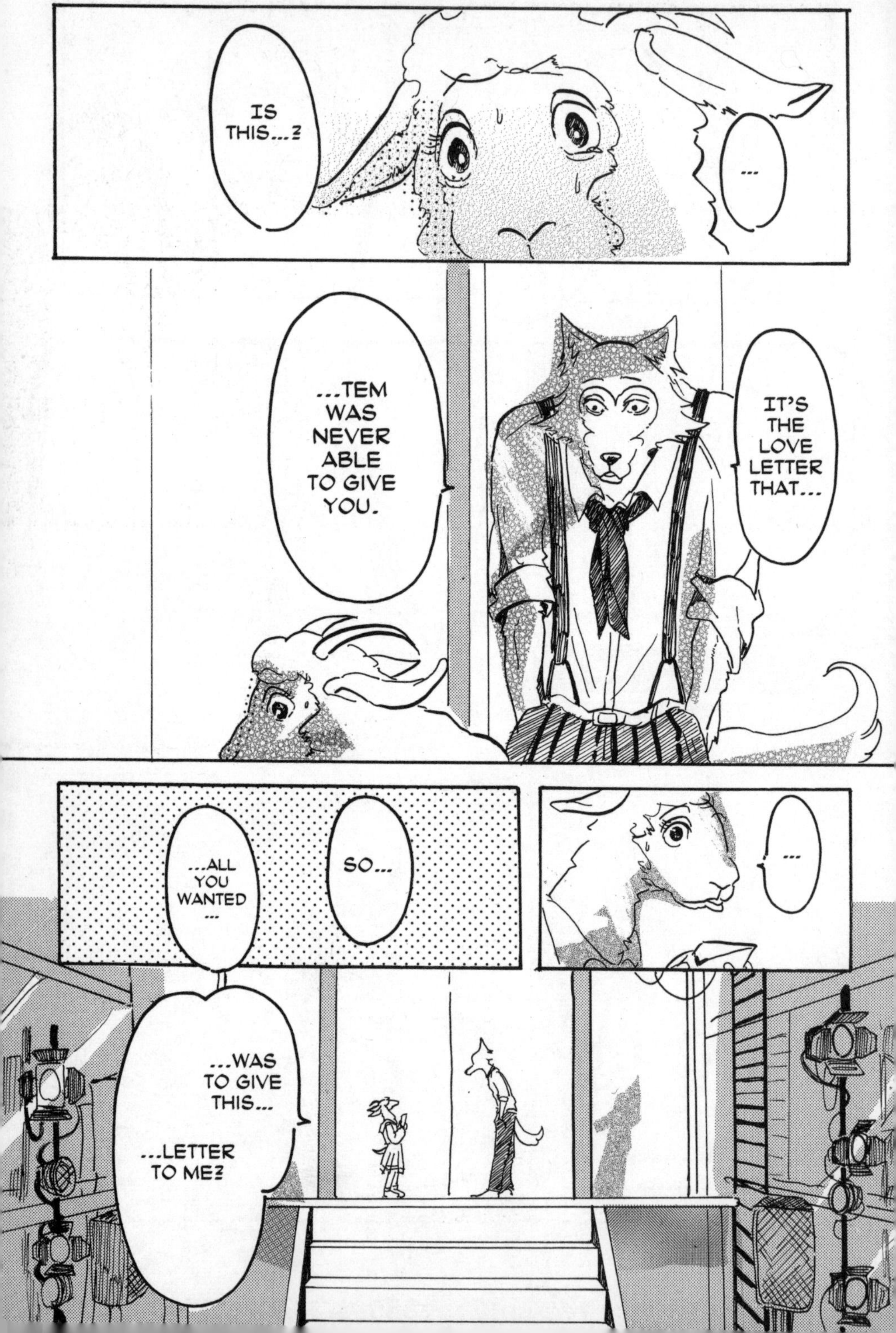
...
IS THIS...?
IT'S THE LOVE LETTER THAT...
...TEM WAS NEVER ABLE TO GIVE YOU.
...
SO...
...ALL YOU WANTED ...
...WAS TO GIVE THIS...
...LETTER TO ME?

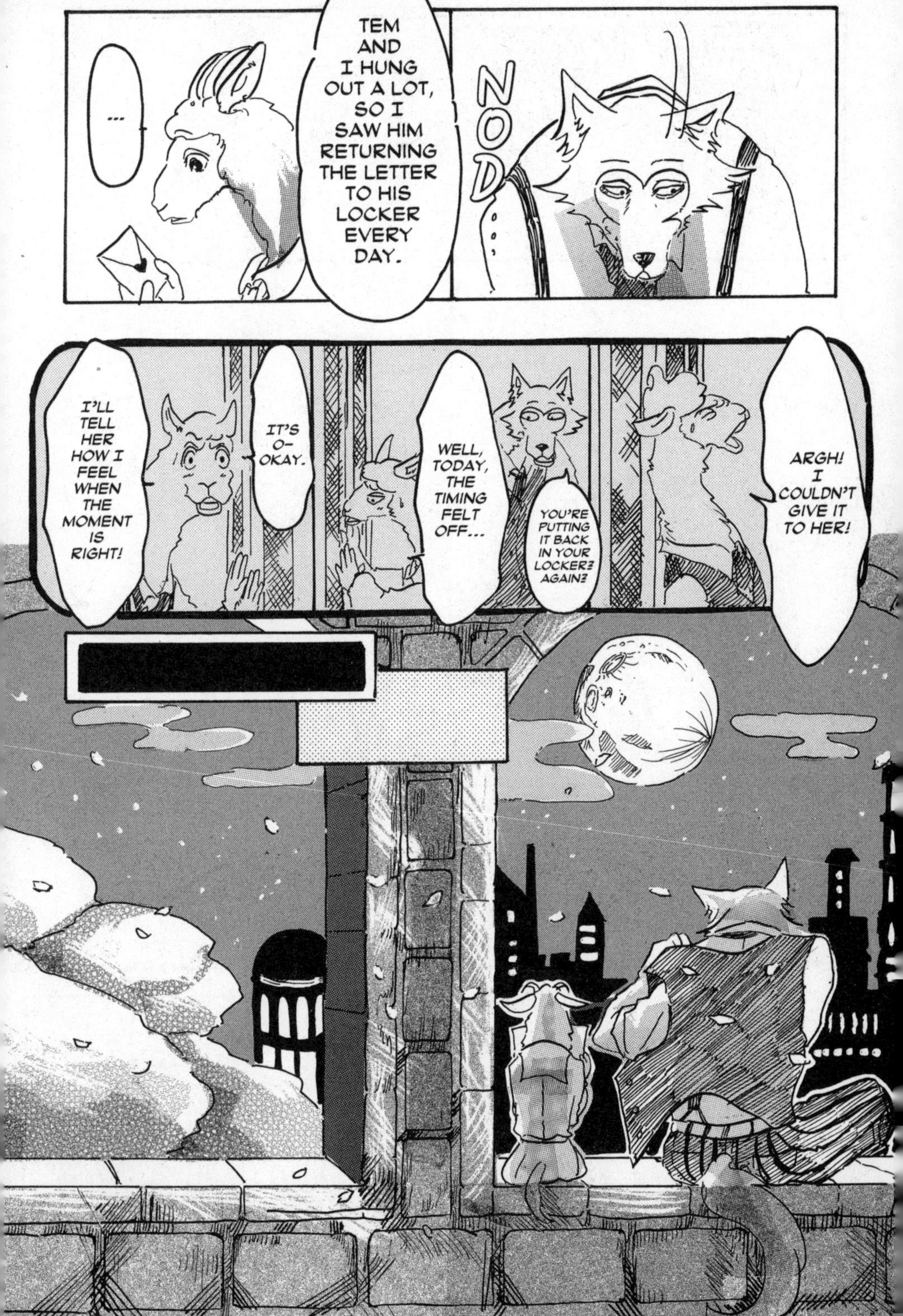
NOD...
TEM AND I HUNG OUT A LOT, SO I SAW HIM RETURNING THE LETTER TO HIS LOCKER EVERY DAY.
...
ARGH! I COULDN'T GIVE IT TO HER!
YOU'RE PUTTING IT BACK IN YOUR LOCKER? AGAIN?
WELL, TODAY, THE TIMING FELT OFF...
IT'S O-OKAY.
I'LL TELL HER HOW I FEEL WHEN THE MOMENT IS RIGHT!

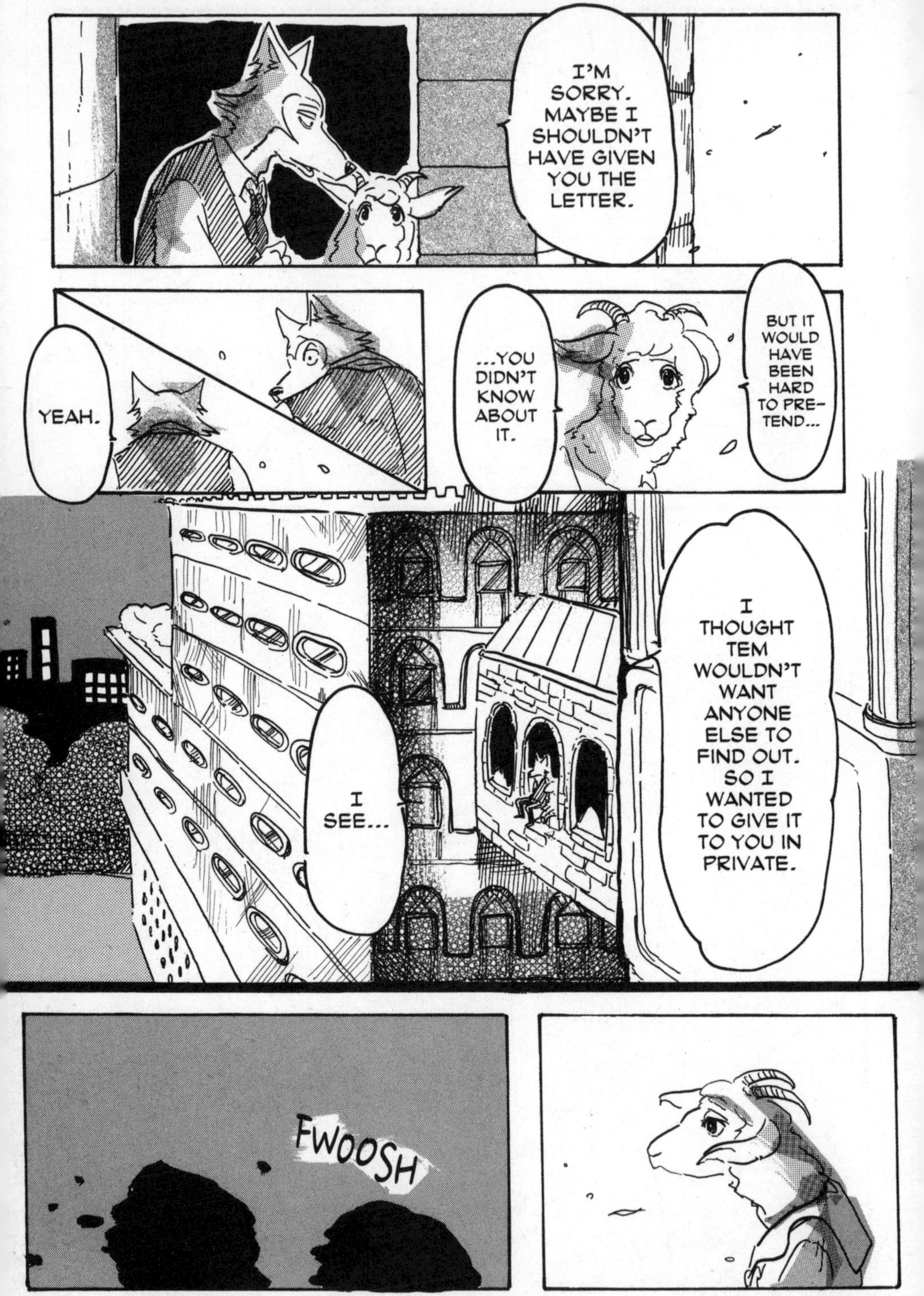
I'M SORRY. MAYBE I SHOULDN'T HAVE GIVEN YOU THE LETTER.
BUT IT WOULD HAVE BEEN HARD TO PRE-TEND...
...YOU DIDN'T KNOW ABOUT IT.
YEAH.
I THOUGHT TEM WOULDN'T WANT ANYONE ELSE TO FIND OUT. SO I WANTED TO GIVE IT TO YOU IN PRIVATE.
I SEE...
FWOOSH

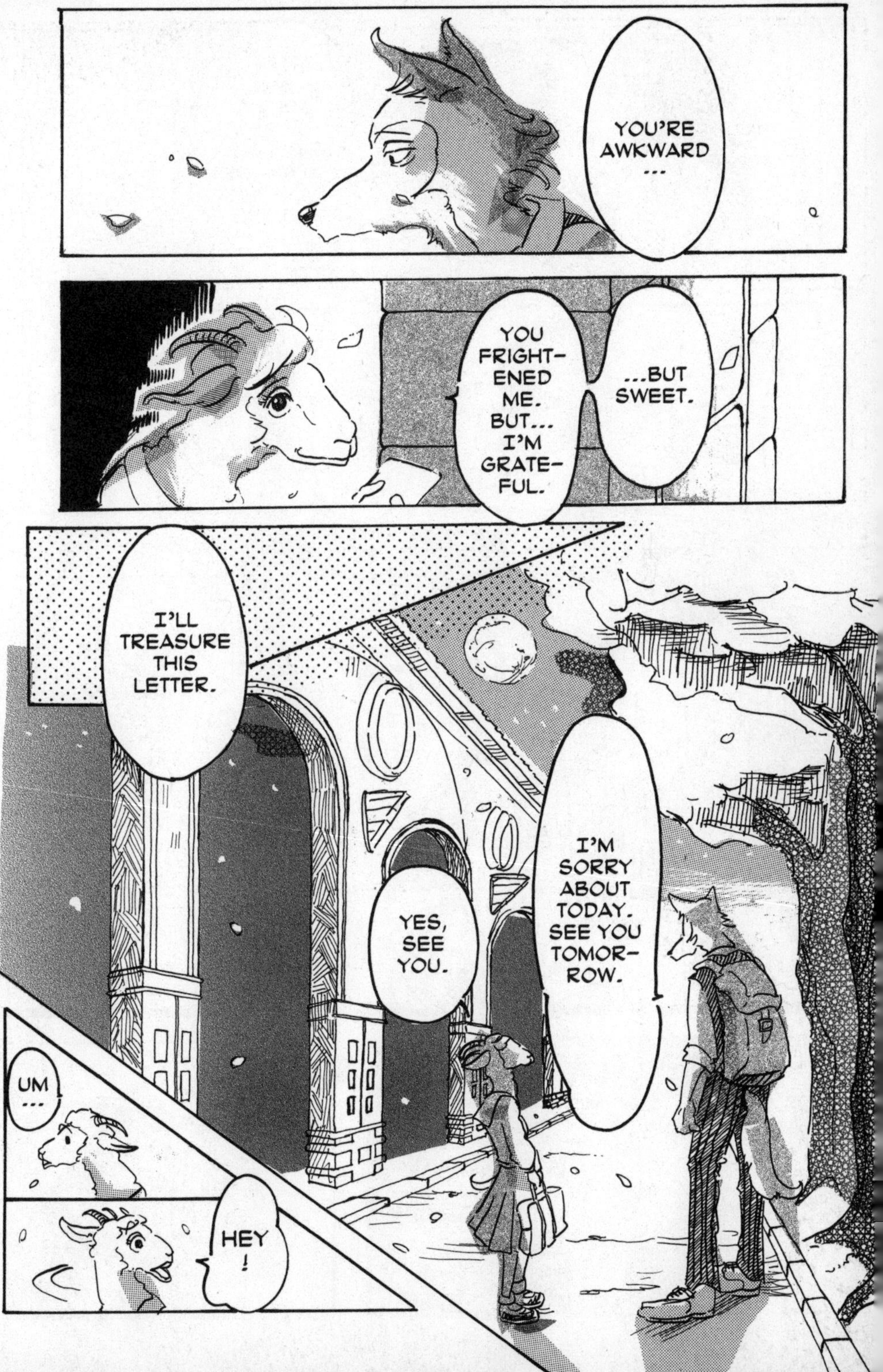
YOU'RE AWKWARD ...
...BUT SWEET.
YOU FRIGHT-ENED ME. BUT... I'M GRATE-FUL.
I'LL TREASURE THIS LETTER.
I'M SORRY ABOUT TODAY. SEE YOU TOMOR-ROW.
YES, SEE YOU.
UM ...
HEY !

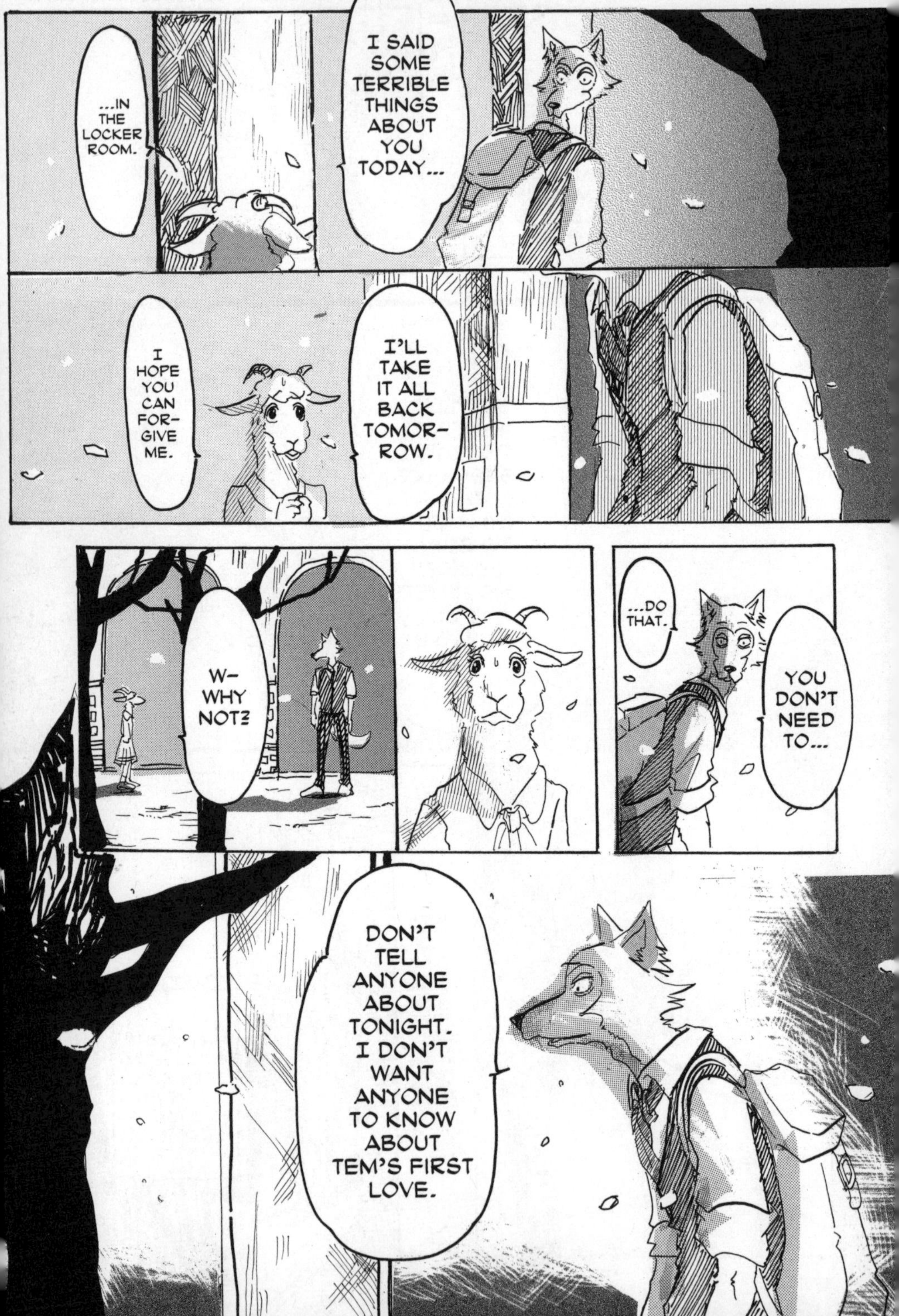
I SAID SOME TERRIBLE THINGS ABOUT YOU TODAY...
...IN THE LOCKER ROOM.
I'LL TAKE IT ALL BACK TOMORROW.
I HOPE YOU CAN FORGIVE ME.
YOU DON'T NEED TO...
...DO THAT.
W-WHY NOT?
DON'T TELL ANYONE ABOUT TONIGHT. I DON'T WANT ANYONE TO KNOW ABOUT TEM'S FIRST LOVE.

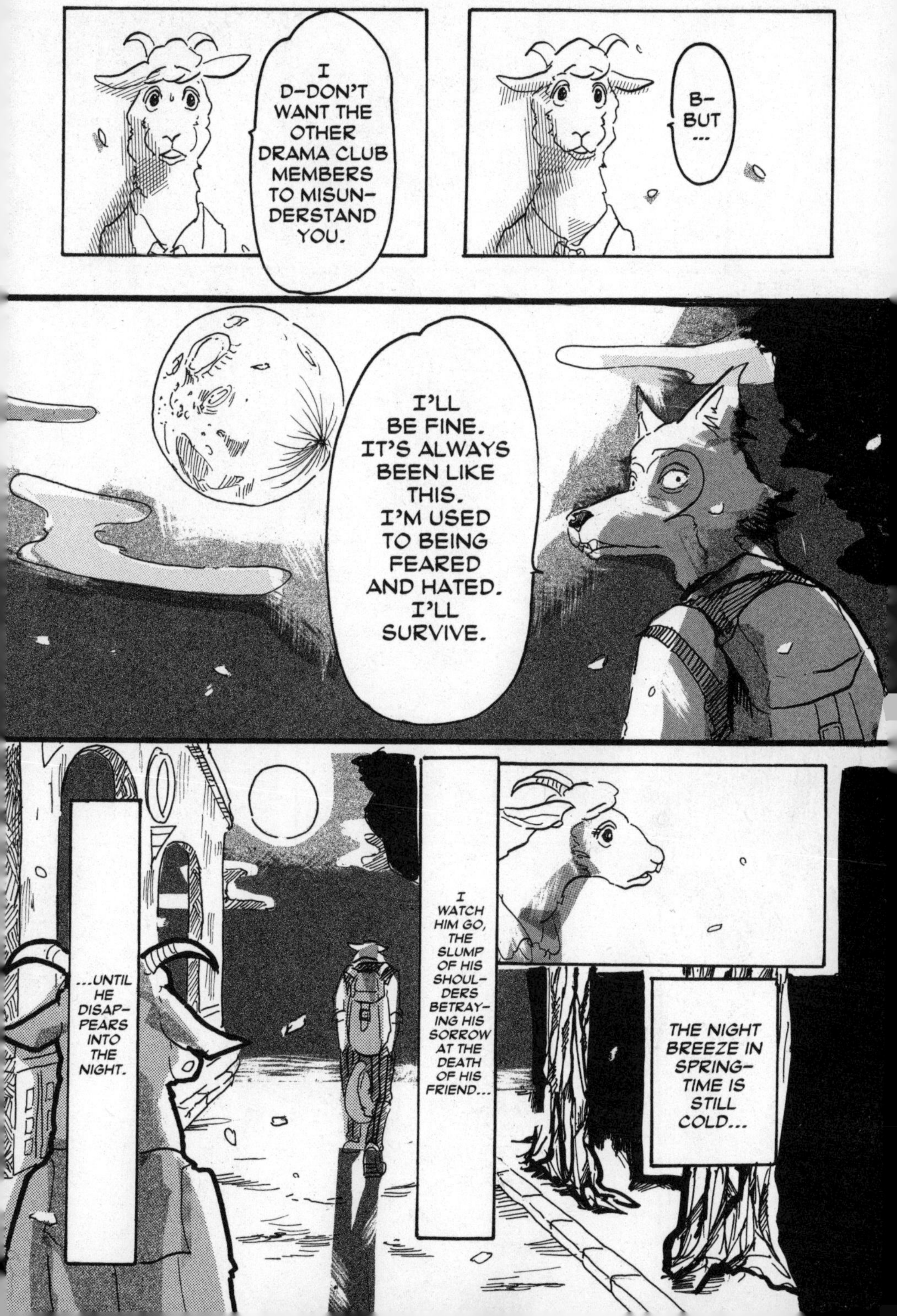

B-BUT...
I D-DON'T WANT THE OTHER DRAMA CLUB MEMBERS TO MISUNDERSTAND YOU.
I'LL BE FINE. IT'S ALWAYS BEEN LIKE THIS. I'M USED TO BEING FEARED AND HATED. I'LL SURVIVE.
THE NIGHT BREEZE IN SPRINGTIME IS STILL COLD...
I WATCH HIM GO, THE SLUMP OF HIS SHOULDERS BETRAYING HIS SORROW AT THE DEATH OF HIS FRIEND...
...UNTIL HE DISAPPEARS INTO THE NIGHT.

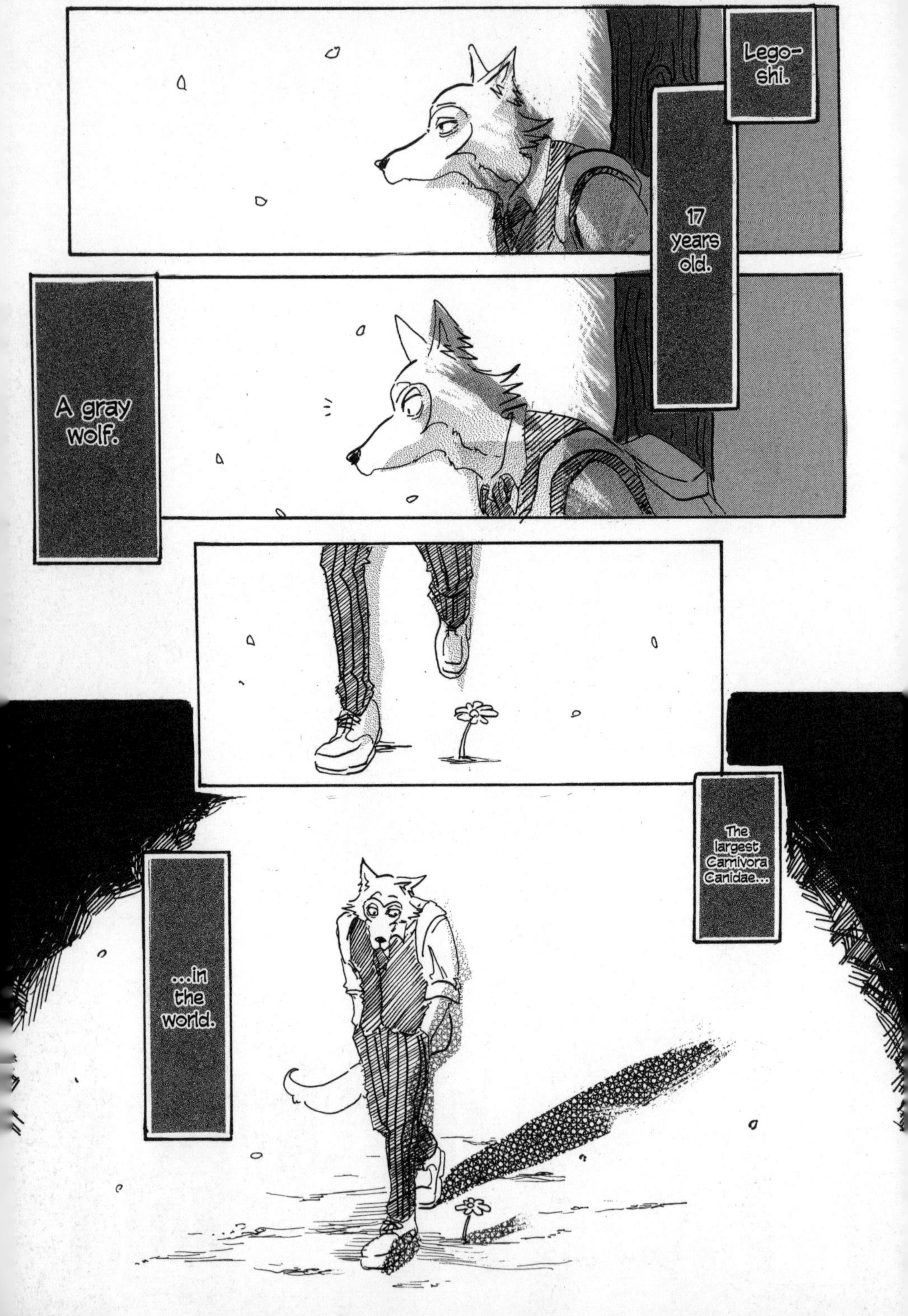
Lego-shi.
17 years old.
A gray wolf.
The largest Carnivora Canidae...
...in the world.

BEASTARS Vol.1

Chapter 2:
Rubbing Each Other the Wrong Way

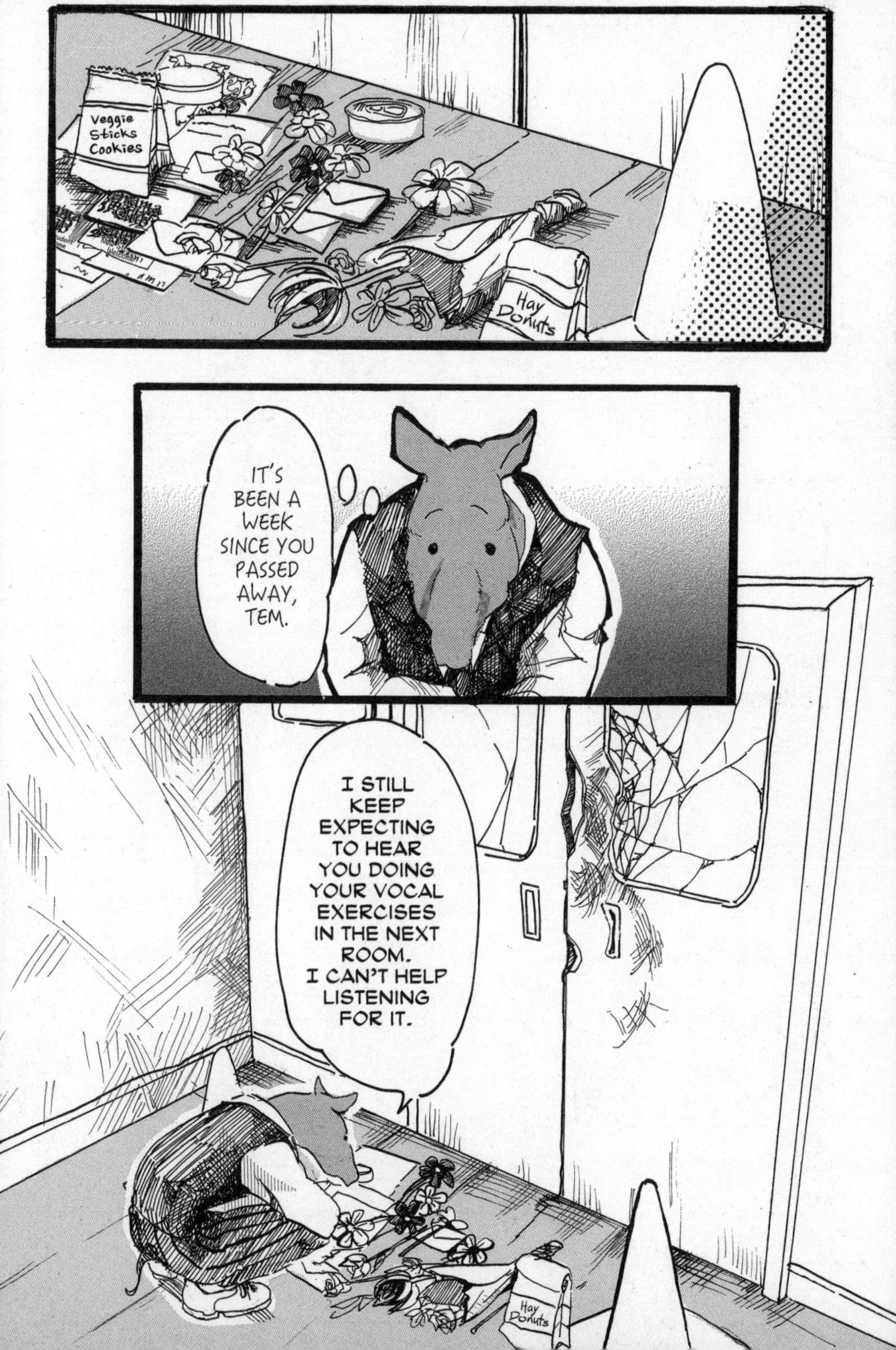
Veggie Sticks Cookies
Hay Donuts
IT'S BEEN A WEEK SINCE YOU PASSED AWAY, TEM.
I STILL KEEP EXPECTING TO HEAR YOU DOING YOUR VOCAL EXERCISES IN THE NEXT ROOM. I CAN'T HELP LISTENING FOR IT.
Hay Donuts

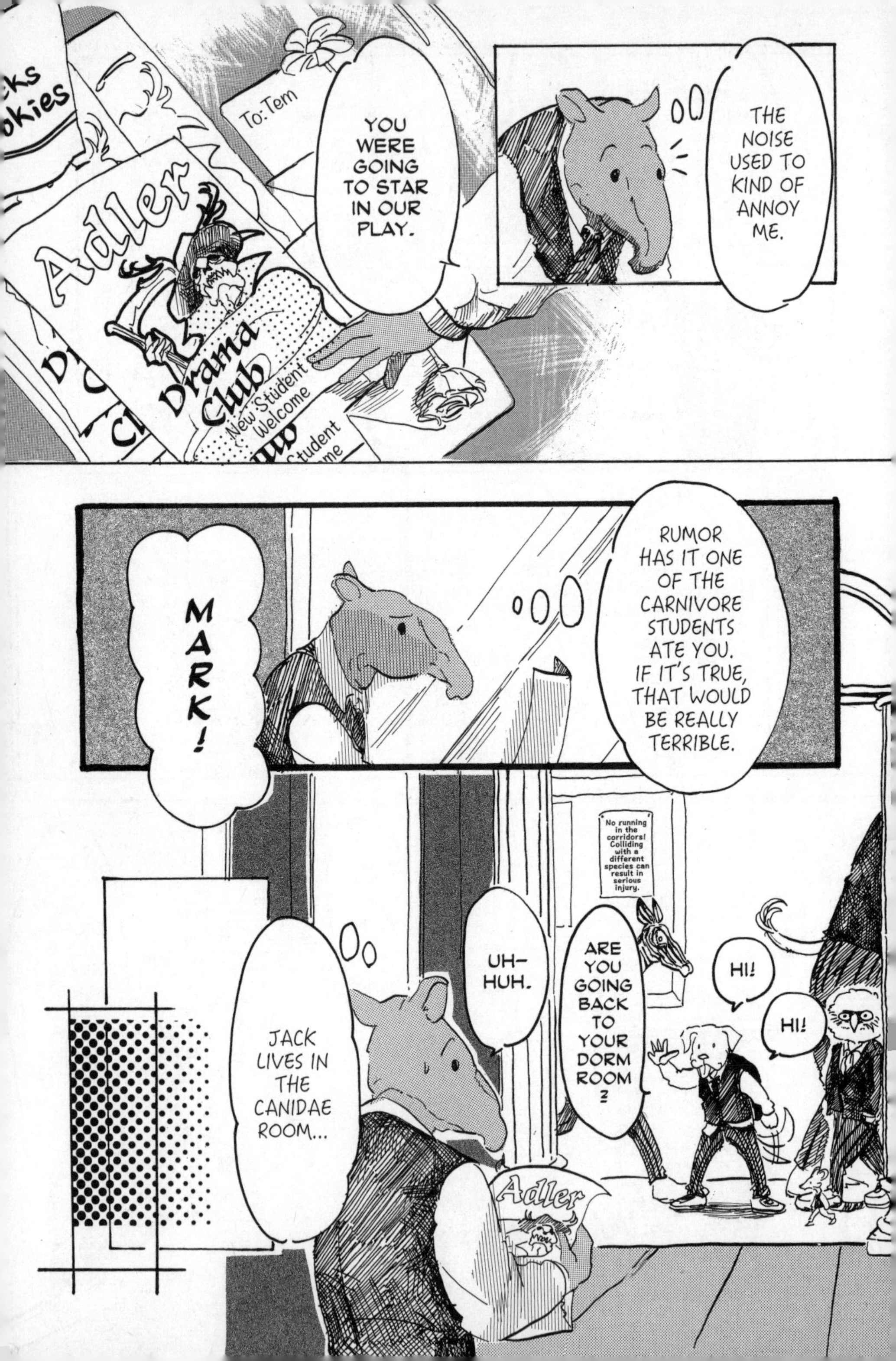
THE NOISE USED TO KIND OF ANNOY ME.
YOU WERE GOING TO STAR IN OUR PLAY.
To: Tem
Adler
Drama Club
New Student Welcome
RUMOR HAS IT ONE OF THE CARNIVORE STUDENTS ATE YOU. IF IT'S TRUE, THAT WOULD BE REALLY TERRIBLE.
MARK!
No running in the corridors! Colliding with a different species can result in serious injury.
HI!
HI!
ARE YOU GOING BACK TO YOUR DORM ROOM?
UH-HUH.
JACK LIVES IN THE CANIDAE ROOM...
Adler

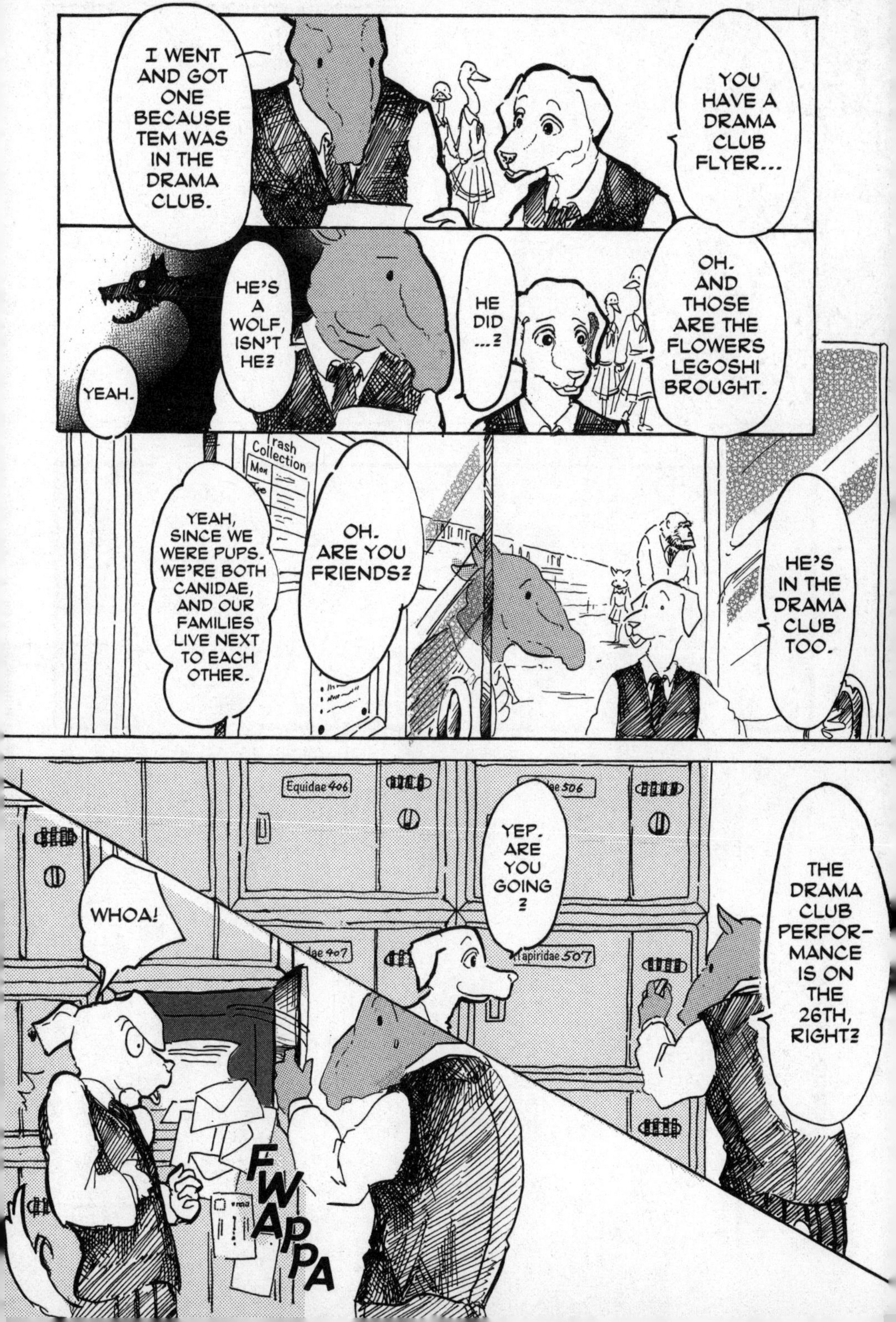

YOU HAVE A DRAMA CLUB FLYER...
I WENT AND GOT ONE BECAUSE TEM WAS IN THE DRAMA CLUB.
OH. AND THOSE ARE THE FLOWERS LEGOSHI BROUGHT.
HE DID...?
HE'S A WOLF, ISN'T HE?
YEAH.
HE'S IN THE DRAMA CLUB TOO.
OH. ARE YOU FRIENDS?
YEAH, SINCE WE WERE PUPS. WE'RE BOTH CANIDAE, AND OUR FAMILIES LIVE NEXT TO EACH OTHER.
rash Collection
Mon
THE DRAMA CLUB PERFORMANCE IS ON THE 26TH, RIGHT?
YEP. ARE YOU GOING?
Equidae 406
dae 506
dae 407
Tapiridae 507
WHOA!
FWAPPA

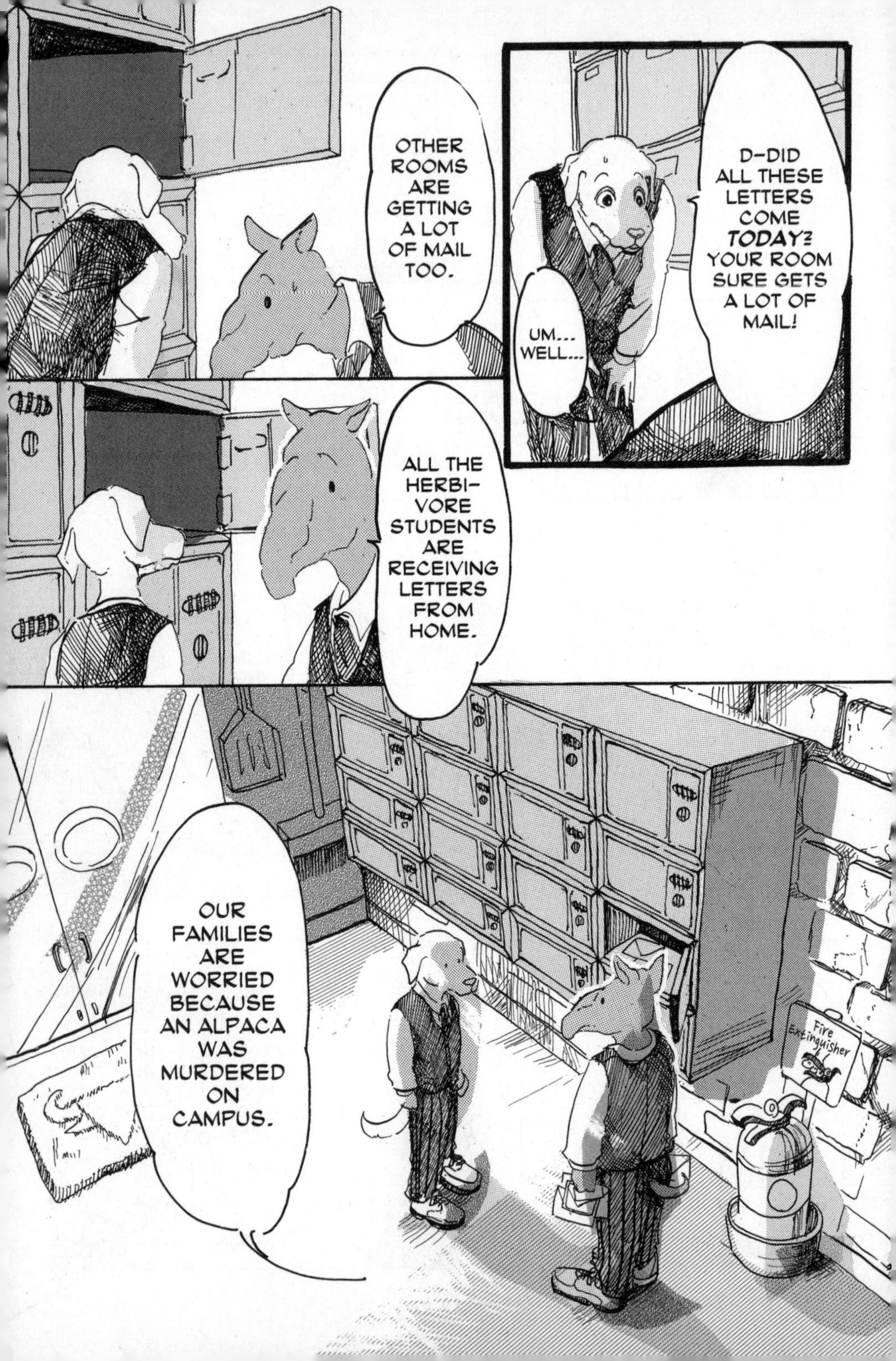
D-DID ALL THESE LETTERS COME *TODAY*?! YOUR ROOM SURE GETS A LOT OF MAIL!
UM... WELL...
OTHER ROOMS ARE GETTING A LOT OF MAIL TOO.
ALL THE HERBI-VORE STUDENTS ARE RECEIVING LETTERS FROM HOME.
OUR FAMILIES ARE WORRIED BECAUSE AN ALPACA WAS MURDERED ON CAMPUS.
Fire Extinguisher

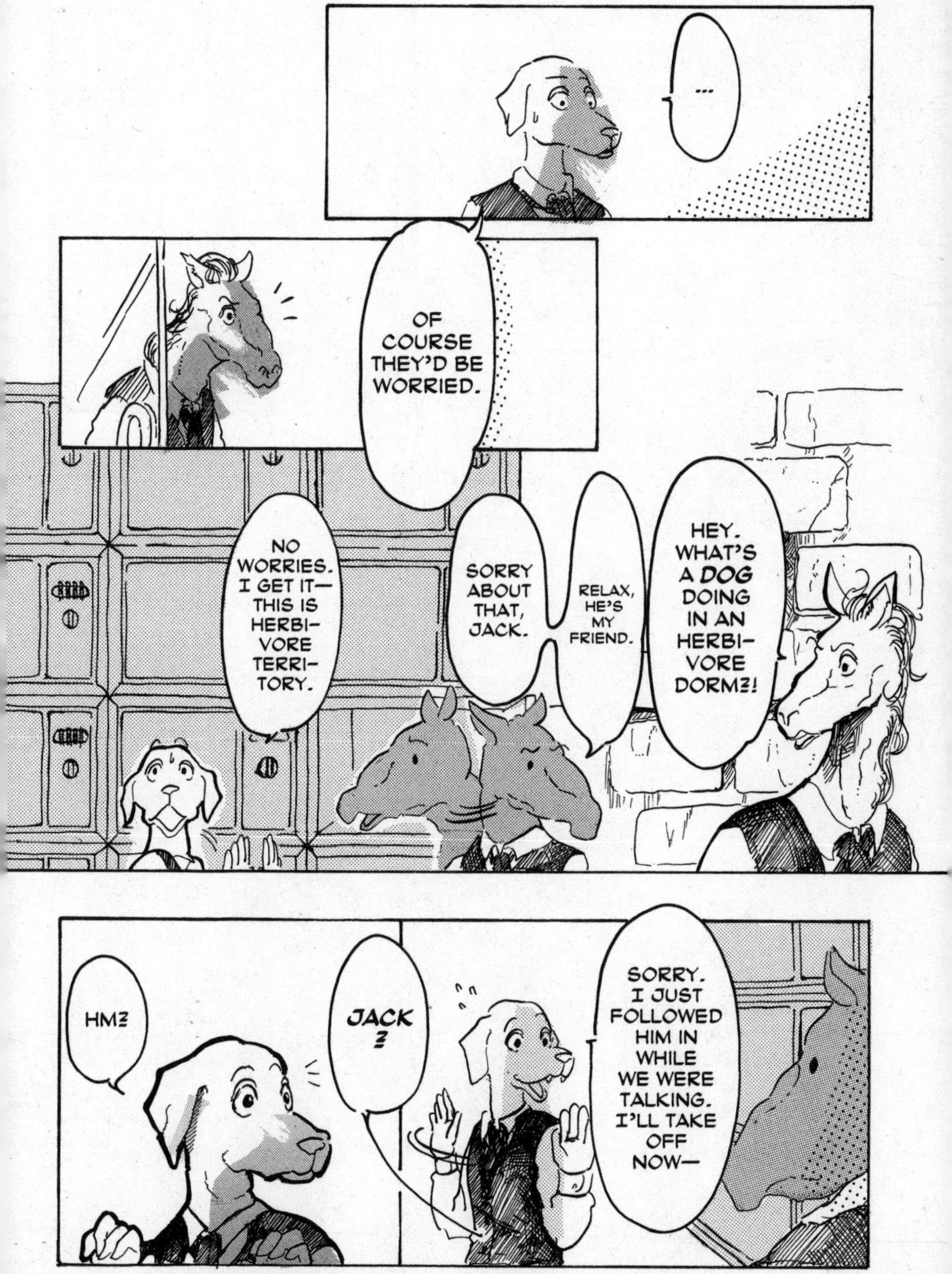
...
OF COURSE THEY'D BE WORRIED.
HEY. WHAT'S A DOG DOING IN AN HERBIVORE DORM?!
RELAX, HE'S MY FRIEND.
SORRY ABOUT THAT, JACK.
NO WORRIES. I GET IT— THIS IS HERBIVORE TERRITORY.
SORRY. I JUST FOLLOWED HIM IN WHILE WE WERE TALKING. I'LL TAKE OFF NOW—
JACK?
HM?

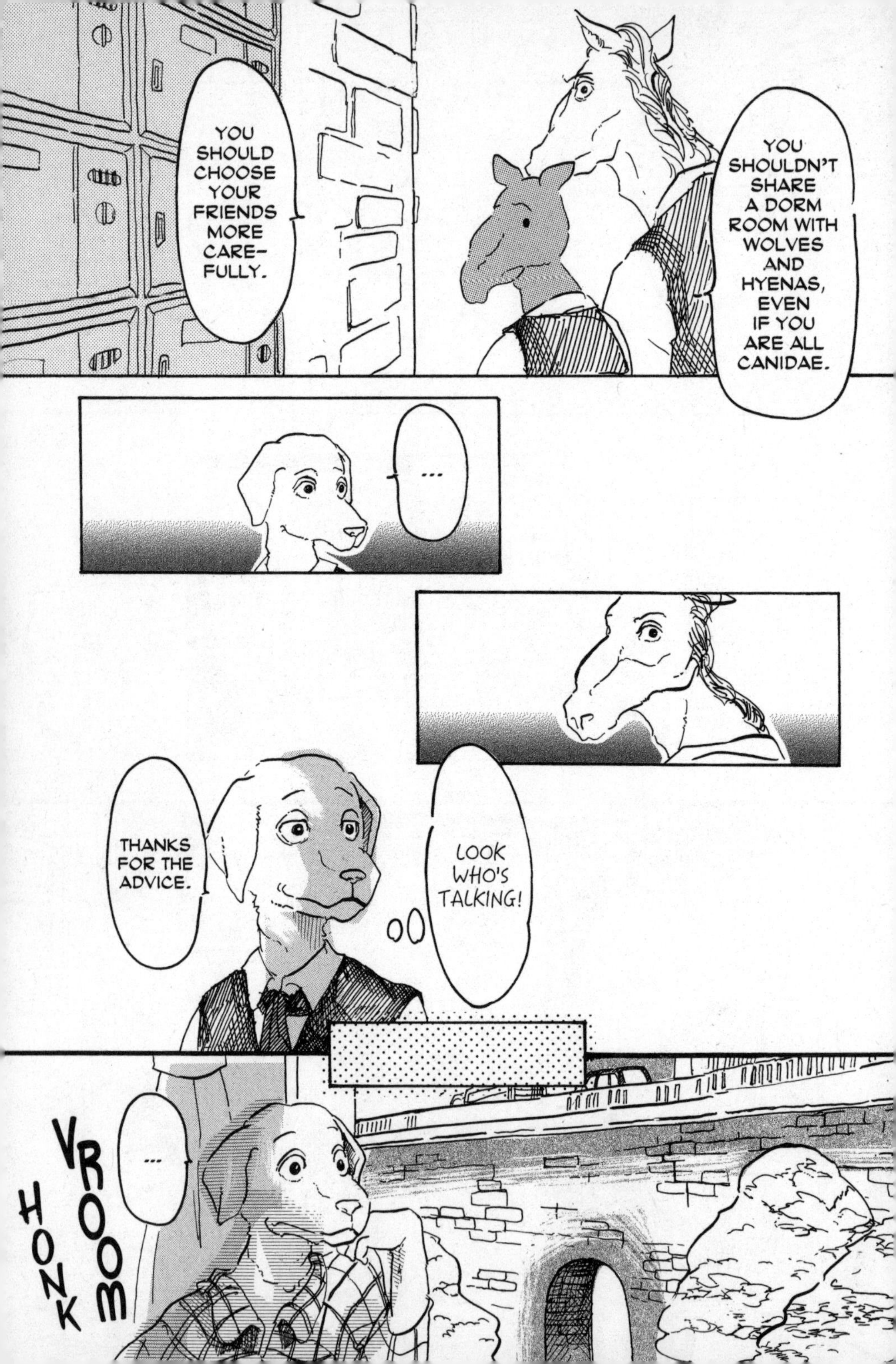
YOU SHOULDN'T SHARE A DORM ROOM WITH WOLVES AND HYENAS, EVEN IF YOU ARE ALL CANIDAE.
YOU SHOULD CHOOSE YOUR FRIENDS MORE CARE-FULLY.
...
LOOK WHO'S TALKING!
THANKS FOR THE ADVICE.
VROOM
HONK
...

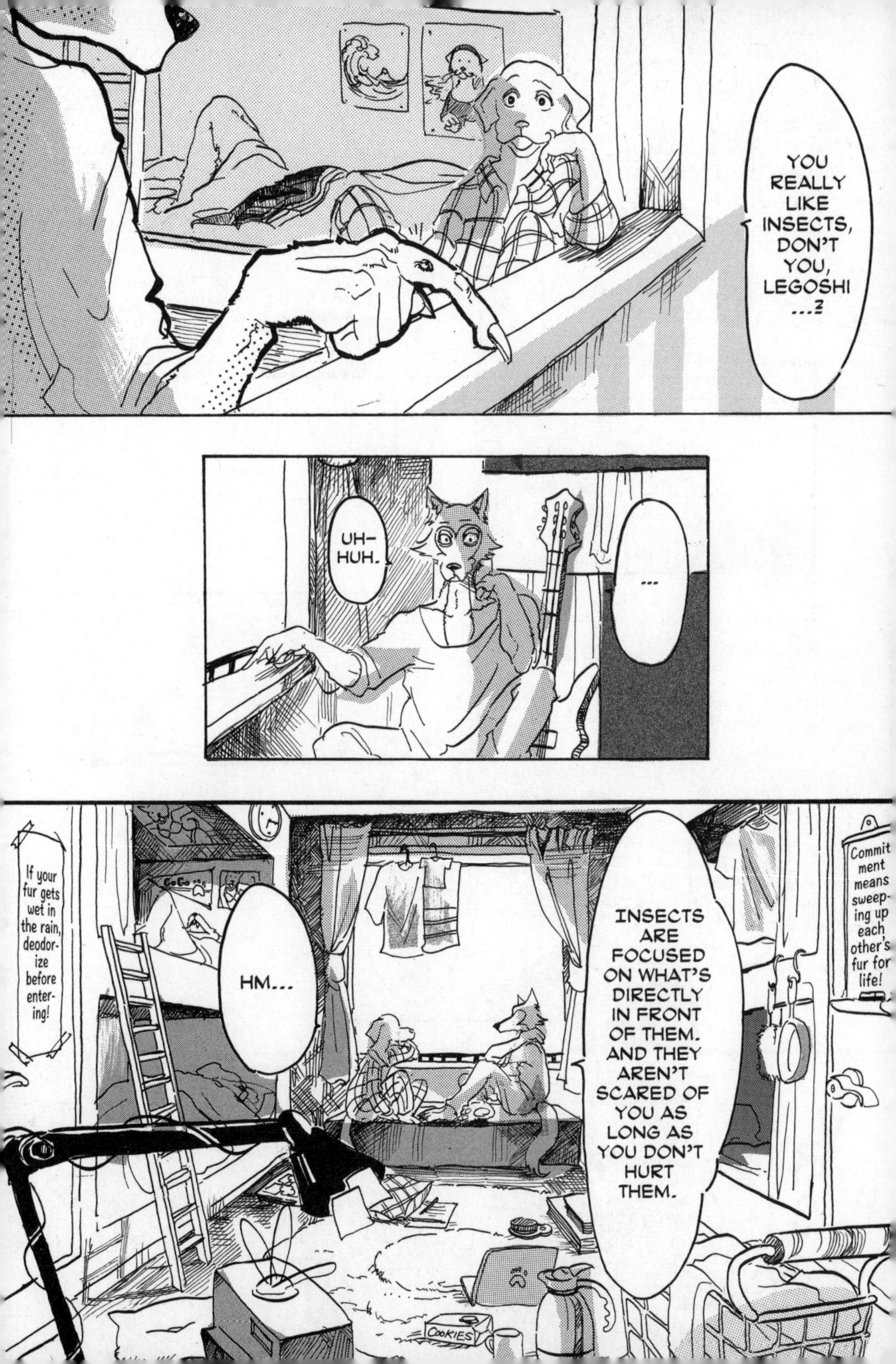
YOU REALLY LIKE INSECTS, DON'T YOU, LEGOSHI...?
...
UH-HUH.
Commitment means sweeping up each other's fur for life!
INSECTS ARE FOCUSED ON WHAT'S DIRECTLY IN FRONT OF THEM. AND THEY AREN'T SCARED OF YOU AS LONG AS YOU DON'T HURT THEM.
HM...
If your fur gets wet in the rain, deodorize before entering!
COOKIES

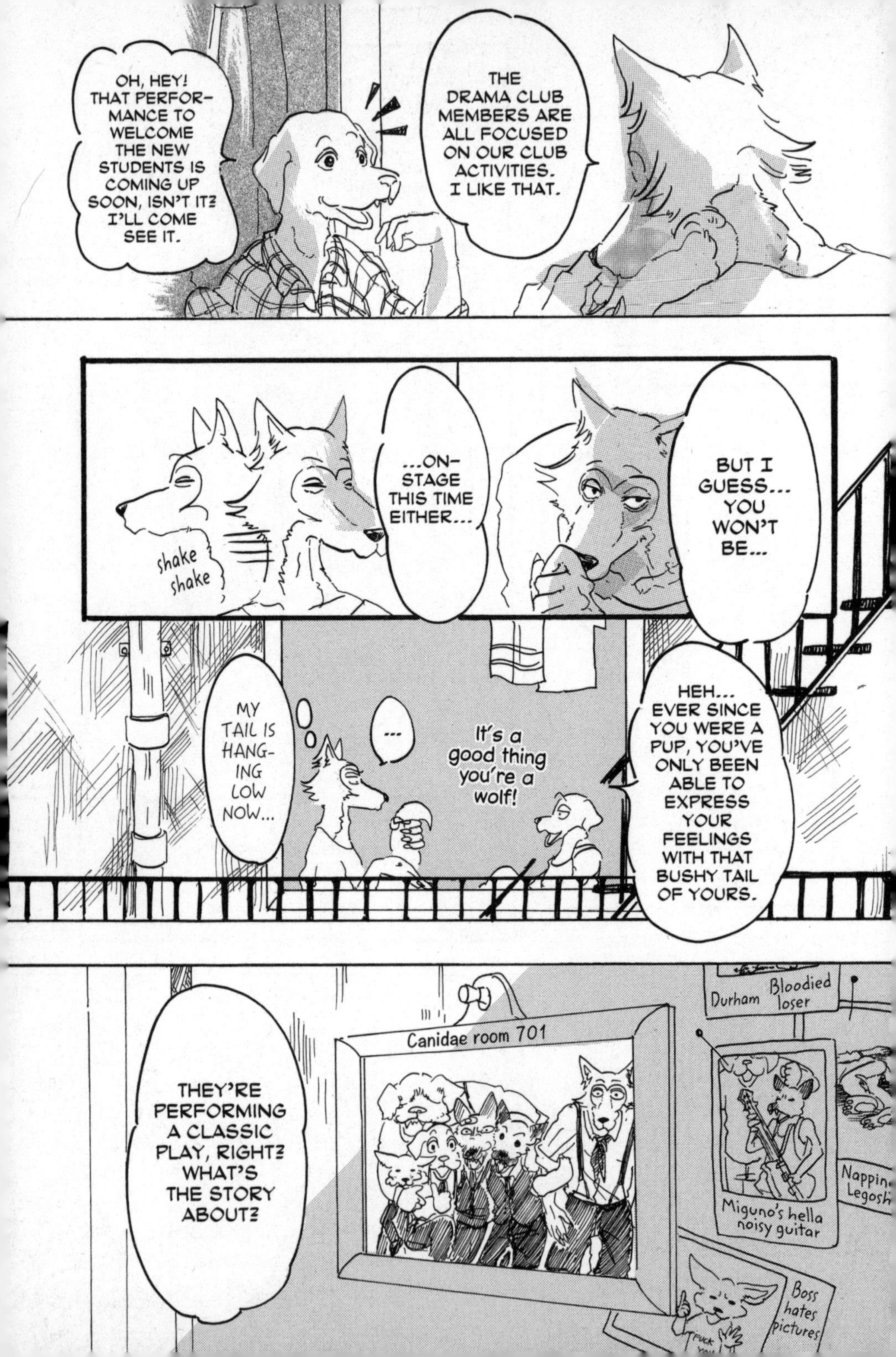
THE DRAMA CLUB MEMBERS ARE ALL FOCUSED ON OUR CLUB ACTIVITIES. I LIKE THAT.
OH, HEY! THAT PERFORMANCE TO WELCOME THE NEW STUDENTS IS COMING UP SOON, ISN'T IT? I'LL COME SEE IT.
BUT I GUESS... YOU WON'T BE...
...ON-STAGE THIS TIME EITHER...
shake shake
HEH... EVER SINCE YOU WERE A PUP, YOU'VE ONLY BEEN ABLE TO EXPRESS YOUR FEELINGS WITH THAT BUSHY TAIL OF YOURS.
It's a good thing you're a wolf!
...
MY TAIL IS HANGING LOW NOW...
Durham Bloodied loser
Nappin Legosh
Miguno's hella noisy guitar
Boss hates pictures
Canidae room 701
THEY'RE PERFORMING A CLASSIC PLAY, RIGHT? WHAT'S THE STORY ABOUT?

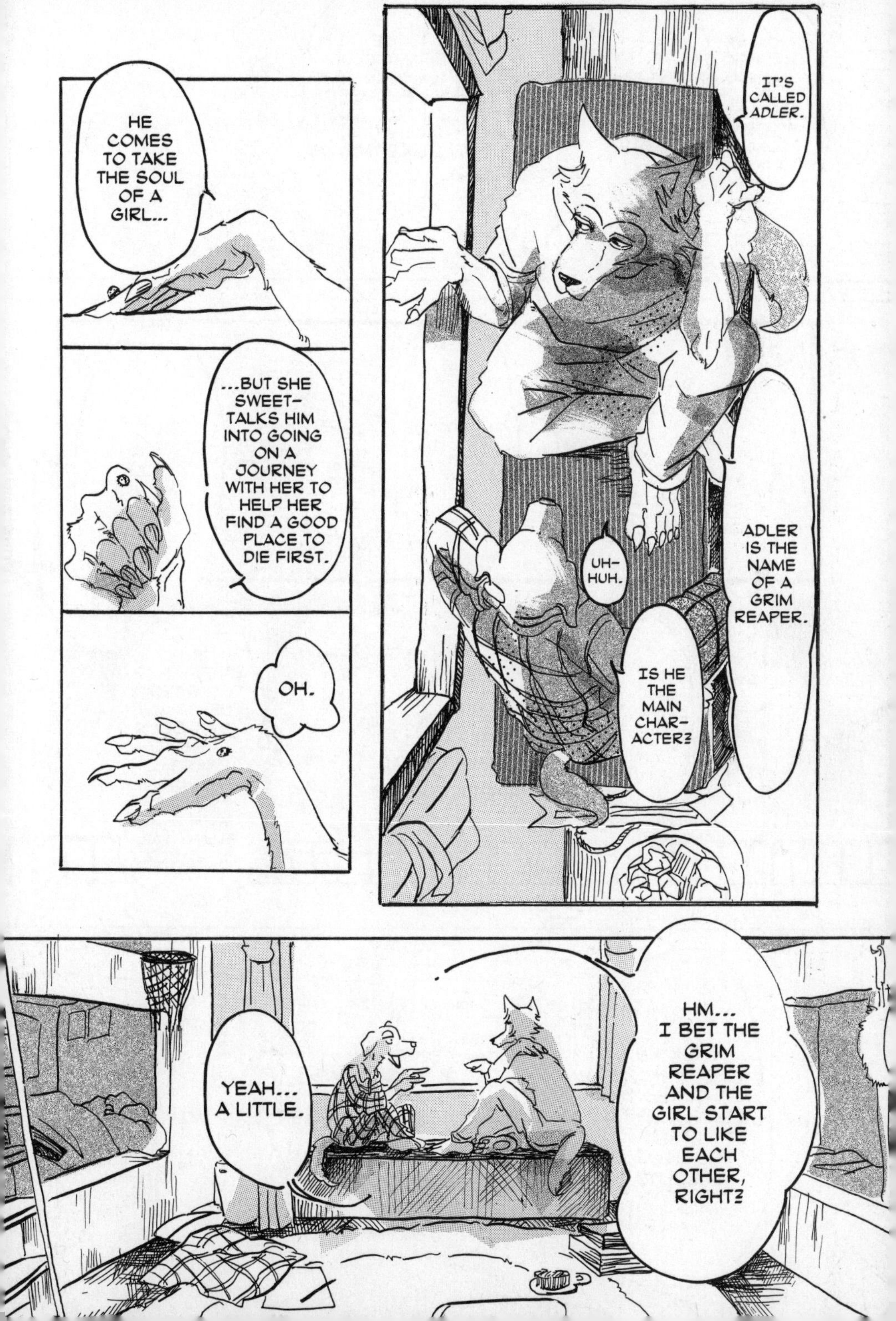
IT'S CALLED ADLER.
ADLER IS THE NAME OF A GRIM REAPER.
UH-HUH.
IS HE THE MAIN CHARACTER?
HE COMES TO TAKE THE SOUL OF A GIRL...
...BUT SHE SWEET-TALKS HIM INTO GOING ON A JOURNEY WITH HER TO HELP HER FIND A GOOD PLACE TO DIE FIRST.
OH.
HM... I BET THE GRIM REAPER AND THE GIRL START TO LIKE EACH OTHER, RIGHT?
YEAH... A LITTLE.

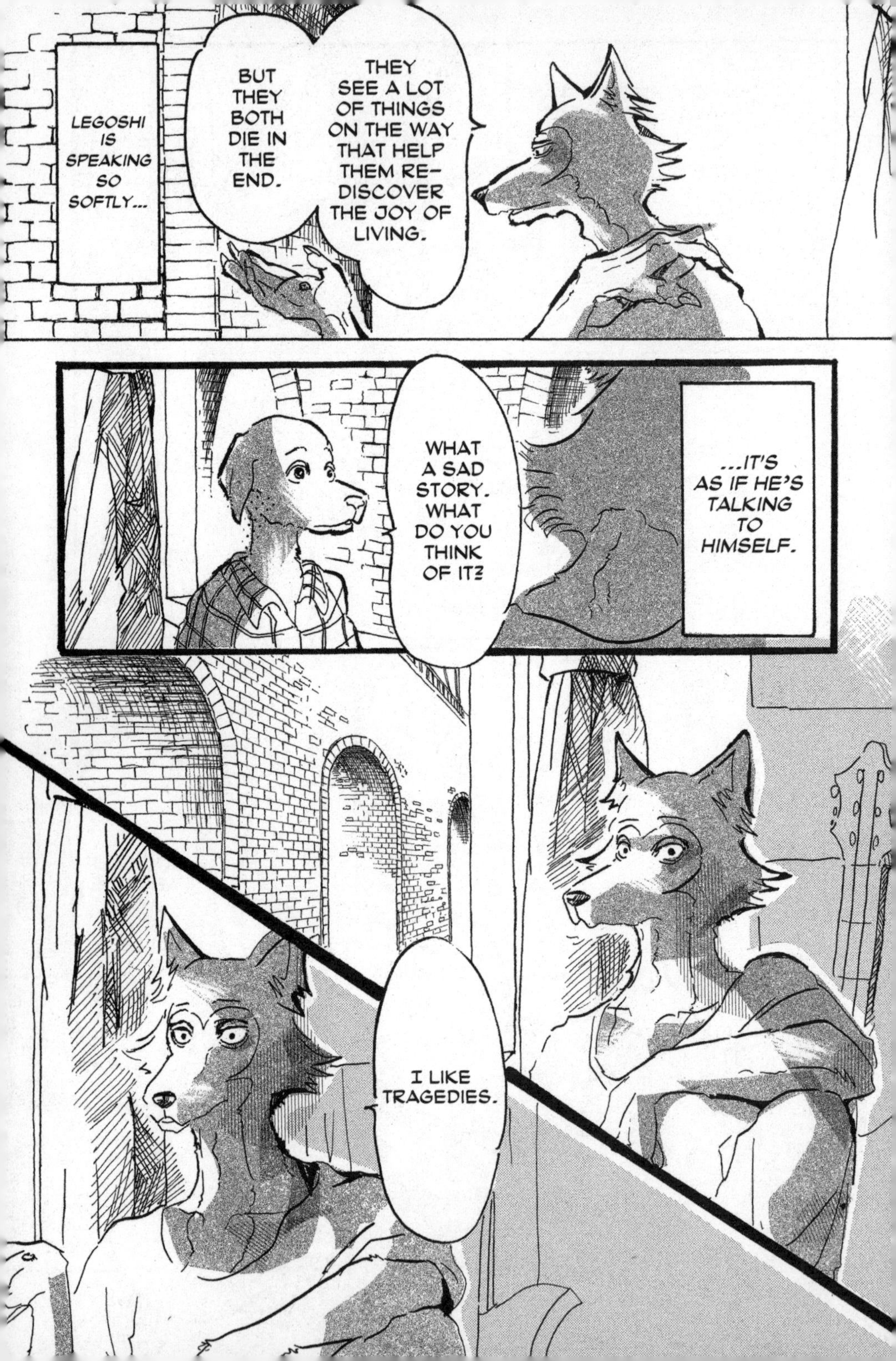
THEY SEE A LOT OF THINGS ON THE WAY THAT HELP THEM RE-DISCOVER THE JOY OF LIVING.
BUT THEY BOTH DIE IN THE END.
LEGOSHI IS SPEAKING SO SOFTLY...
...IT'S AS IF HE'S TALKING TO HIMSELF.
WHAT A SAD STORY. WHAT DO YOU THINK OF IT?
I LIKE TRAGEDIES.

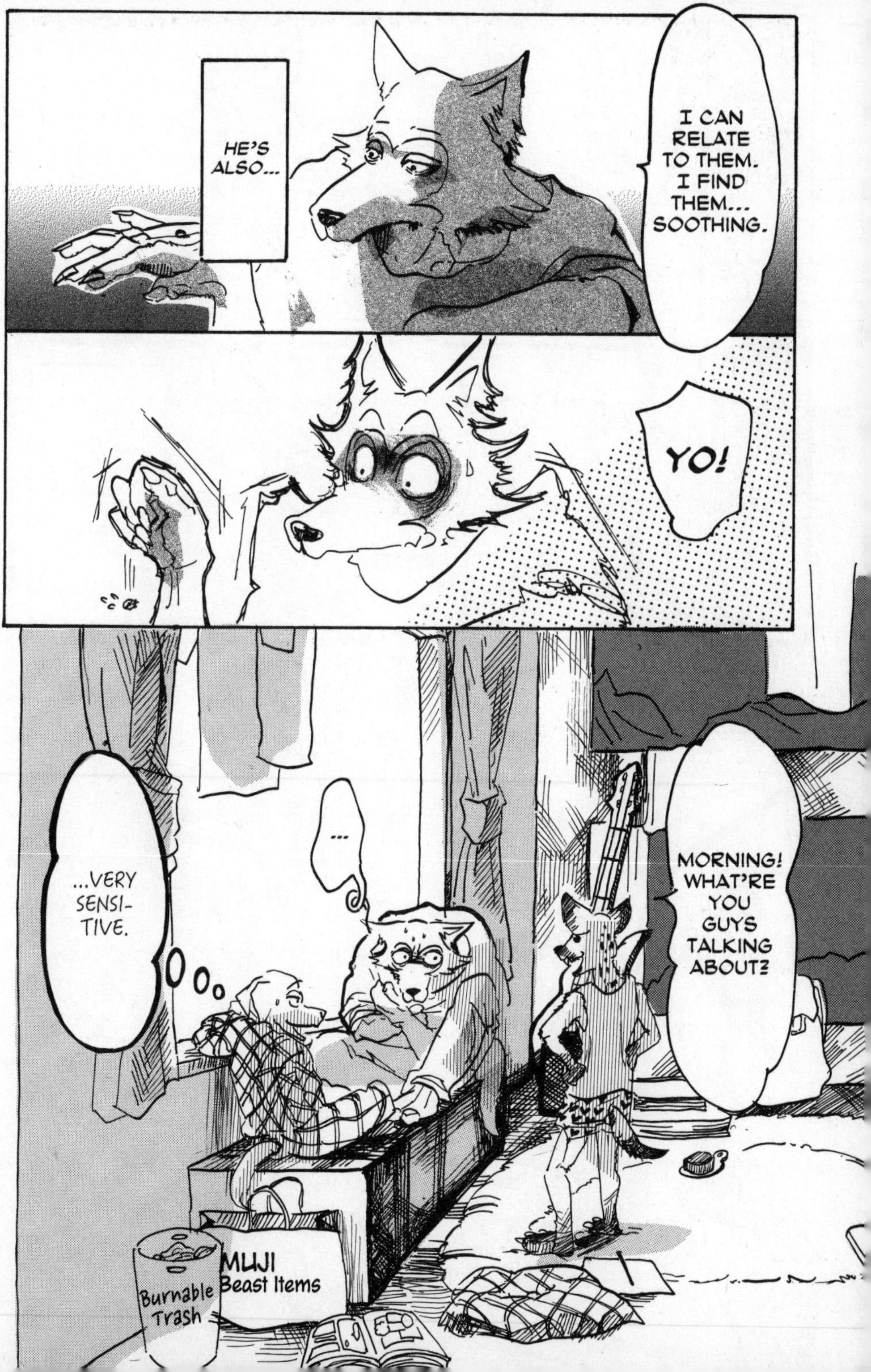
I CAN RELATE TO THEM. I FIND THEM... SOOTHING.
HE'S ALSO...
YO!
MORNING! WHAT'RE YOU GUYS TALKING ABOUT?
...
...VERY SENSI-TIVE.
MUJI Beast Items
Burnable Trash

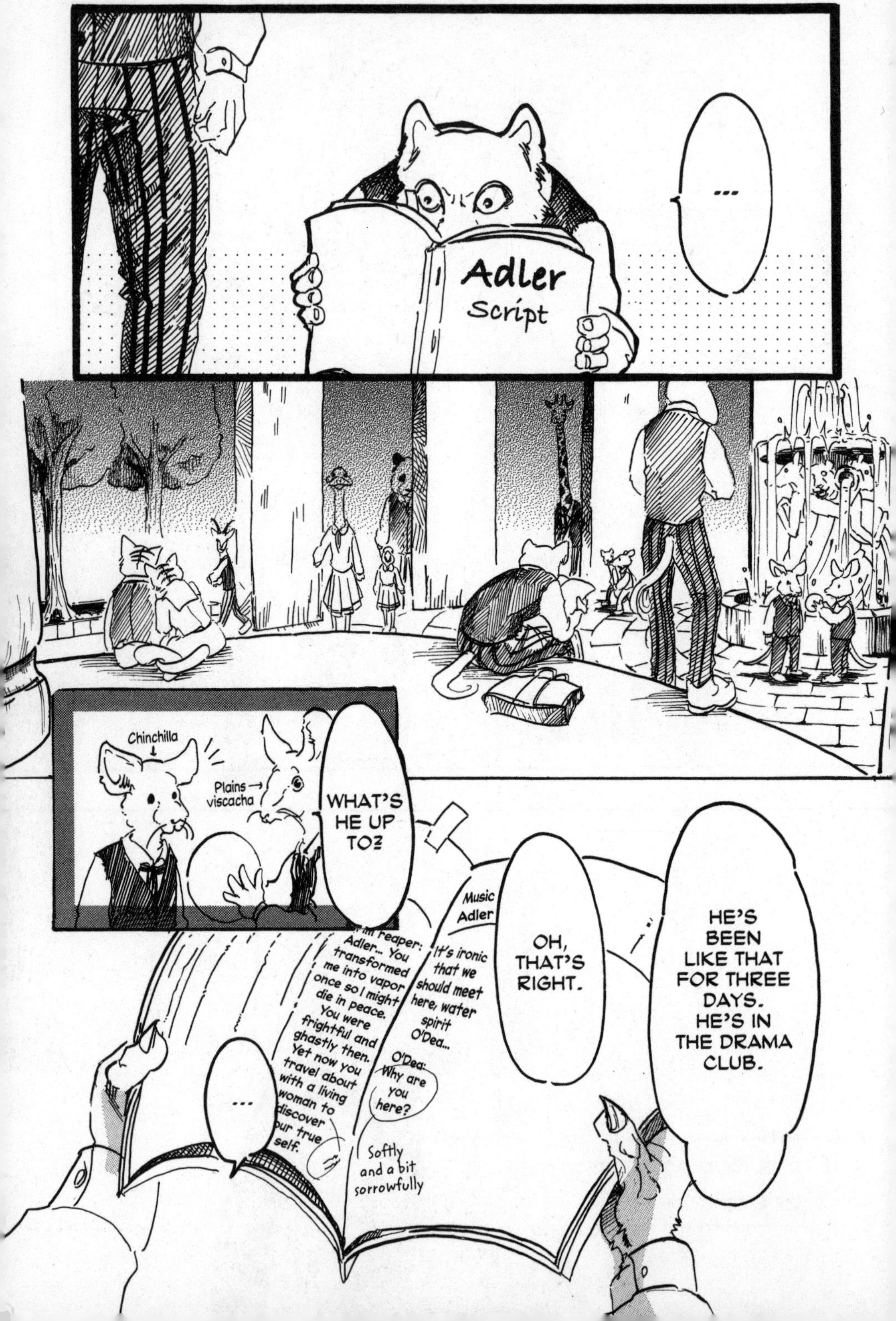
...
Adler
Script
Chinchilla
Plains viscacha
WHAT'S HE UP TO?
HE'S BEEN LIKE THAT FOR THREE DAYS. HE'S IN THE DRAMA CLUB.
OH, THAT'S RIGHT.
Music
Adler
It's ironic that we should meet here, water spirit O'Dea...
O'Dea: Why are you here?
Softly and a bit sorrowfully
rim reaper: Adler... You transformed me into vapor once so I might die in peace. You were frightful and ghastly then. Yet now you travel about with a living woman to discover our true self.
...

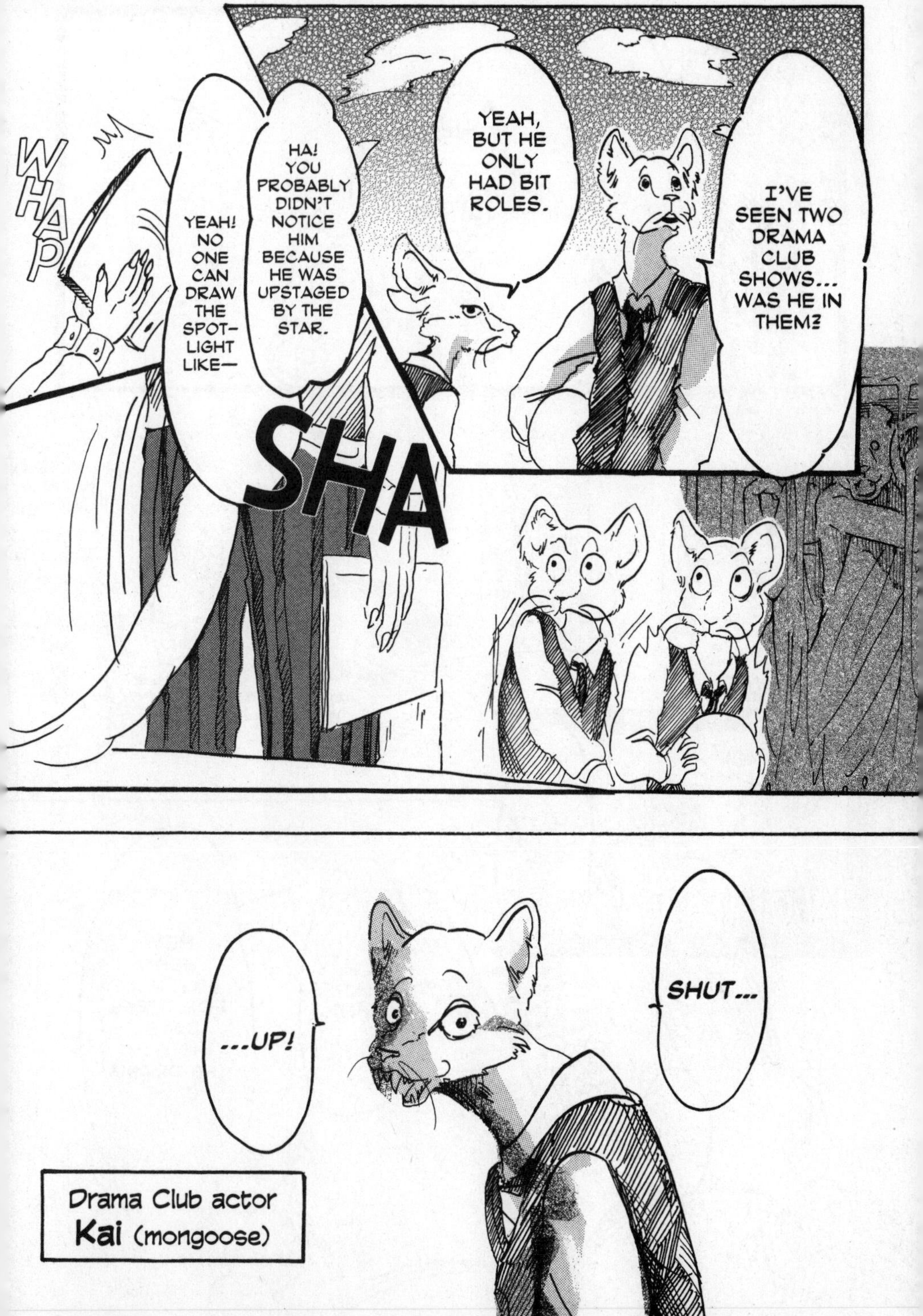
I'VE SEEN TWO DRAMA CLUB SHOWS... WAS HE IN THEM?
YEAH, BUT HE ONLY HAD BIT ROLES.
HA! YOU PROBABLY DIDN'T NOTICE HIM BECAUSE HE WAS UPSTAGED BY THE STAR.
YEAH! NO ONE CAN DRAW THE SPOT-LIGHT LIKE—
WHAP
SHA
SHUT...
...UP!
Drama Club actor
Kai (mongoose)

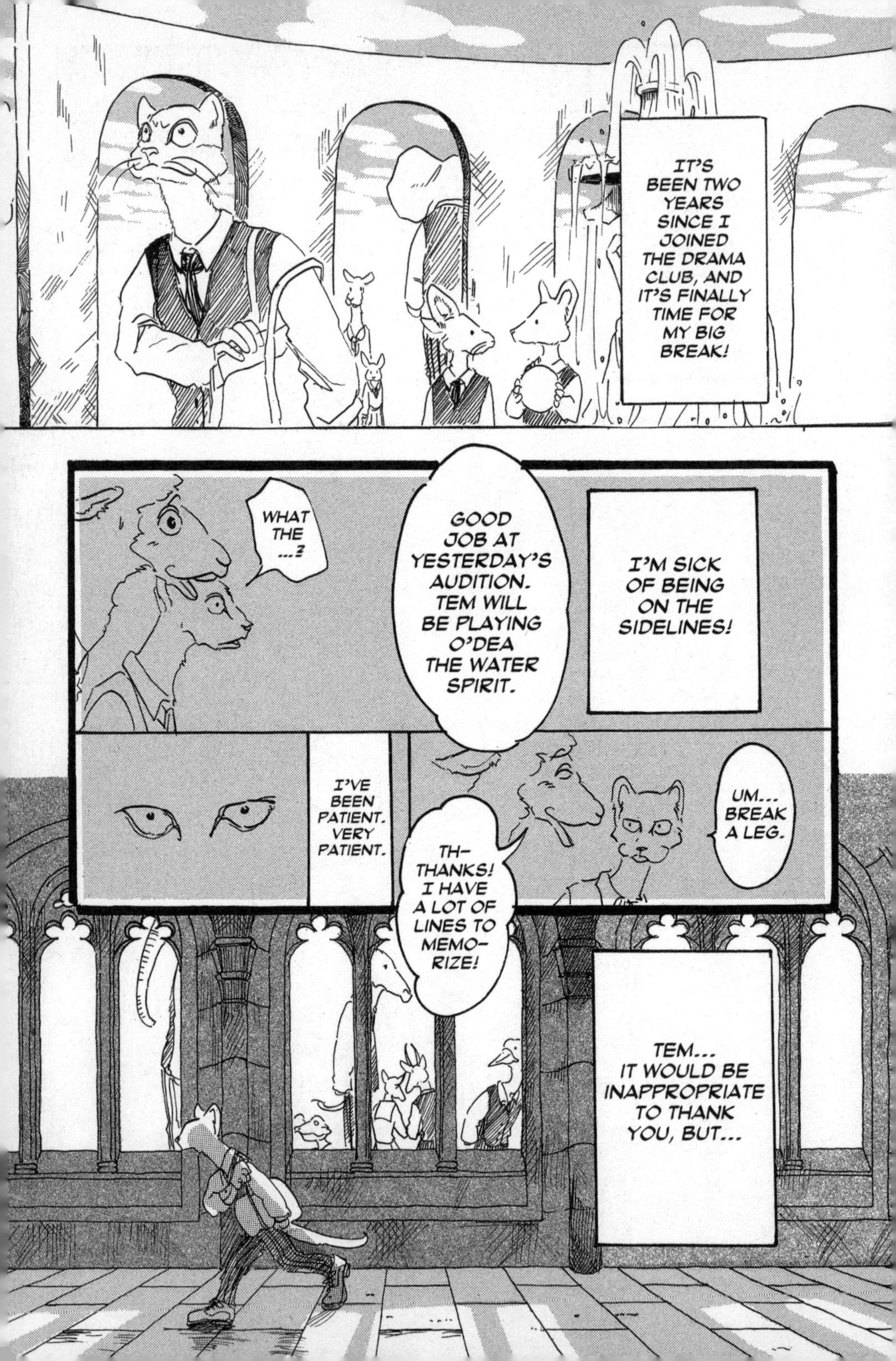
IT'S BEEN TWO YEARS SINCE I JOINED THE DRAMA CLUB, AND IT'S FINALLY TIME FOR MY BIG BREAK!
I'M SICK OF BEING ON THE SIDELINES!
GOOD JOB AT YESTERDAY'S AUDITION. TEM WILL BE PLAYING O'DEA THE WATER SPIRIT.
WHAT THE ...?
UM... BREAK A LEG.
TH-THANKS! I HAVE A LOT OF LINES TO MEMO-RIZE!
I'VE BEEN PATIENT. VERY PATIENT.
TEM... IT WOULD BE INAPPROPRIATE TO THANK YOU, BUT...

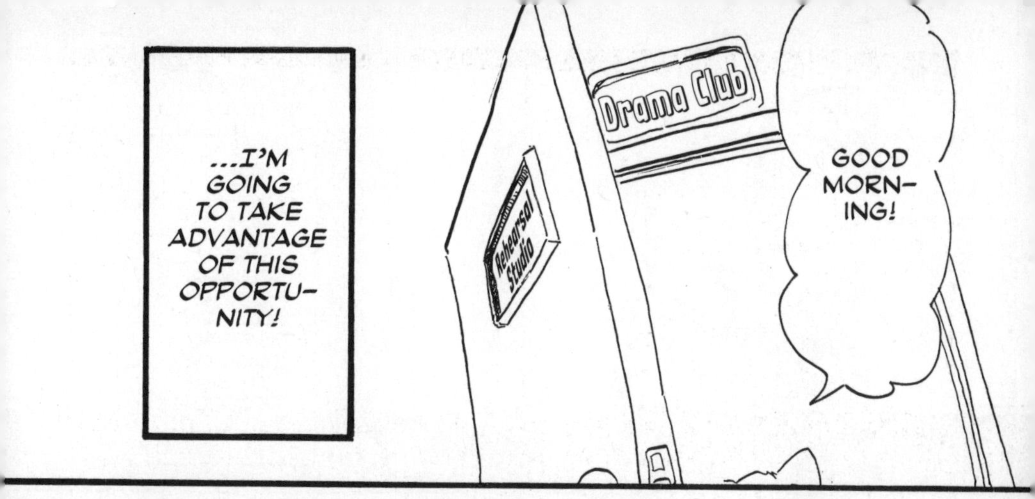
GOOD MORNING!
Drama Club
Rehearsal Studio
...I'M GOING TO TAKE ADVANTAGE OF THIS OPPORTUNITY!

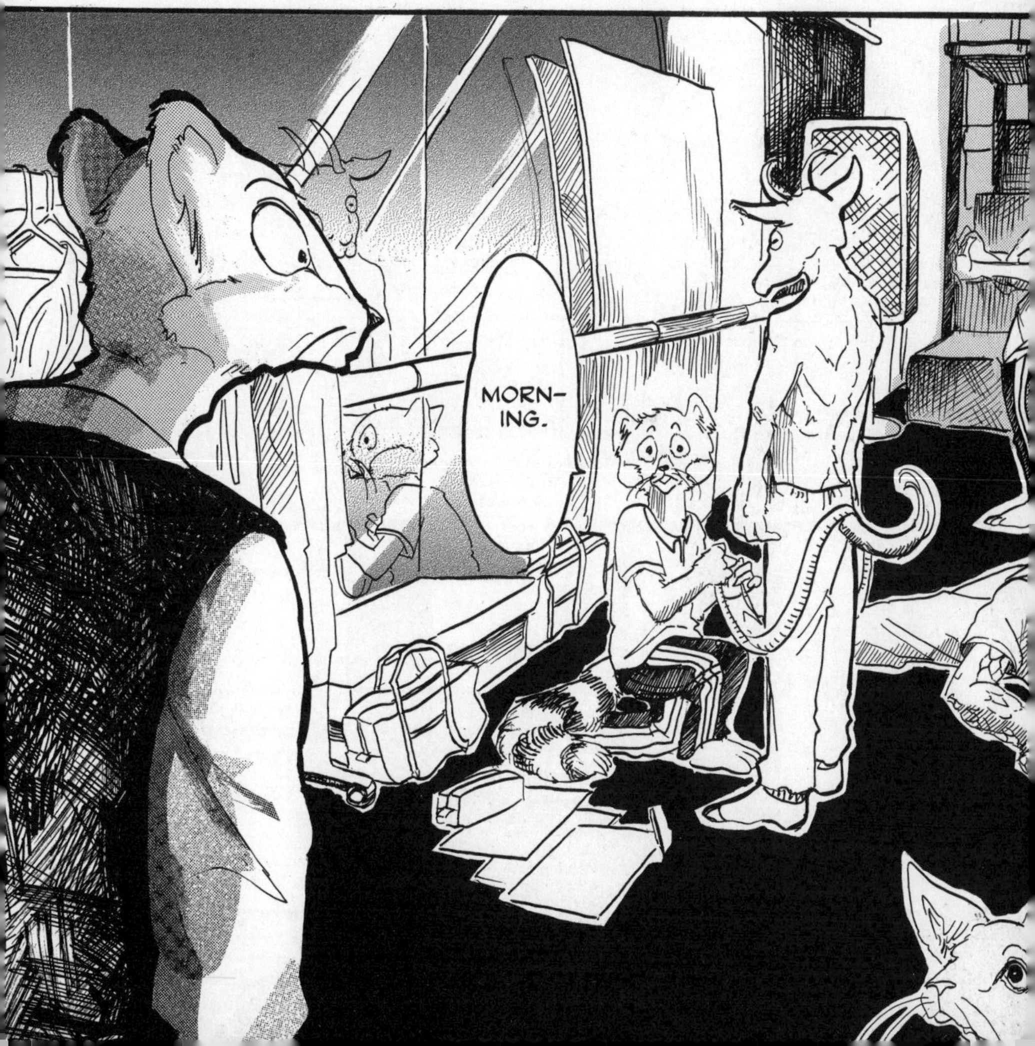
MORNING.

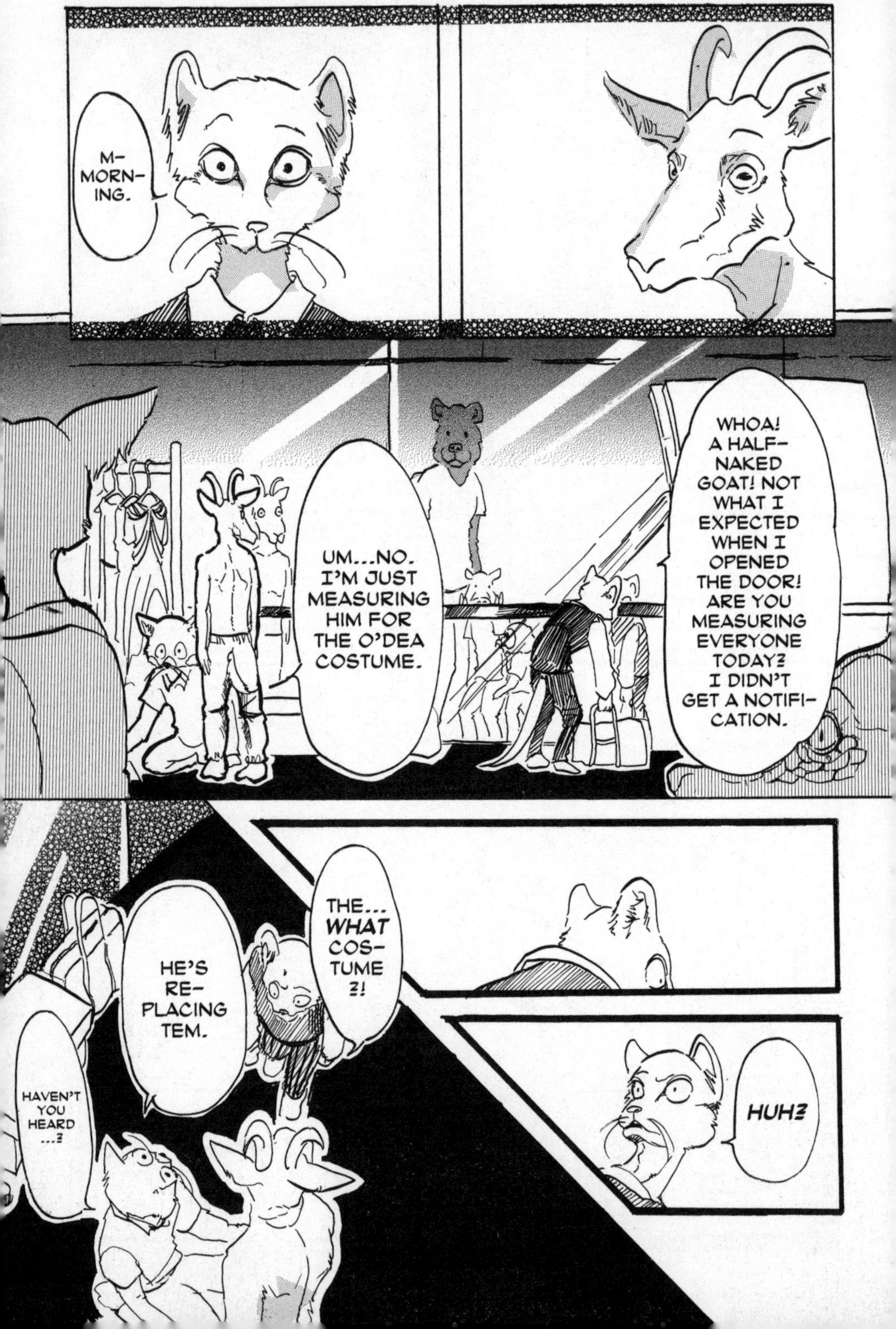
M-MORNING.
WHOA! A HALF-NAKED GOAT! NOT WHAT I EXPECTED WHEN I OPENED THE DOOR! ARE YOU MEASURING EVERYONE TODAY? I DIDN'T GET A NOTIFICATION.
UM...NO. I'M JUST MEASURING HIM FOR THE O'DEA COSTUME.
HUH?
THE... *WHAT* COSTUME?!
HE'S REPLACING TEM.
HAVEN'T YOU HEARD...?

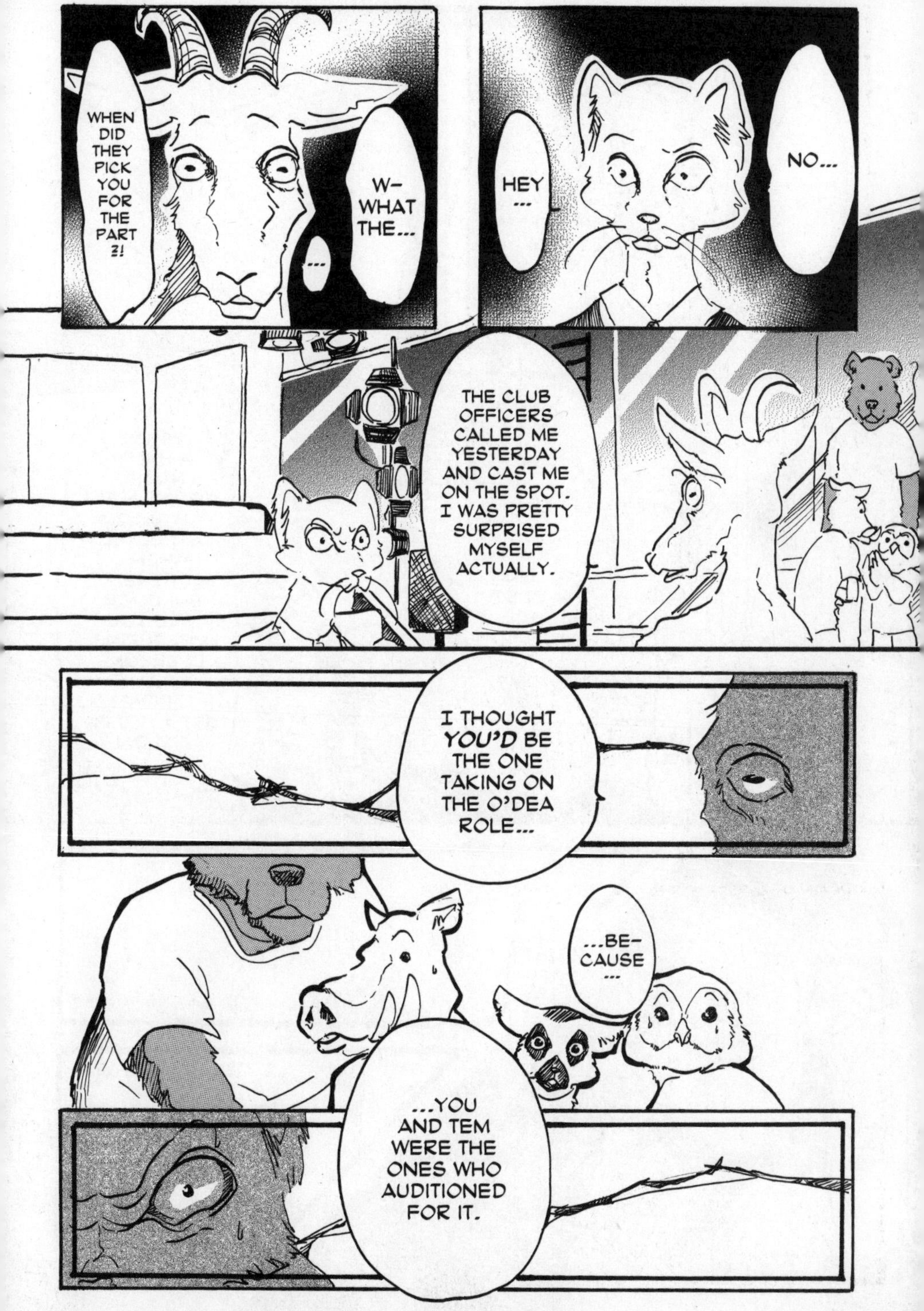
NO...
HEY ...
W-WHAT THE...
...
WHEN DID THEY PICK YOU FOR THE PART?!
THE CLUB OFFICERS CALLED ME YESTERDAY AND CAST ME ON THE SPOT. I WAS PRETTY SURPRISED MYSELF ACTUALLY.
I THOUGHT *YOU'D* BE THE ONE TAKING ON THE O'DEA ROLE...
...BE-CAUSE ...
...YOU AND TEM WERE THE ONES WHO AUDITIONED FOR IT.

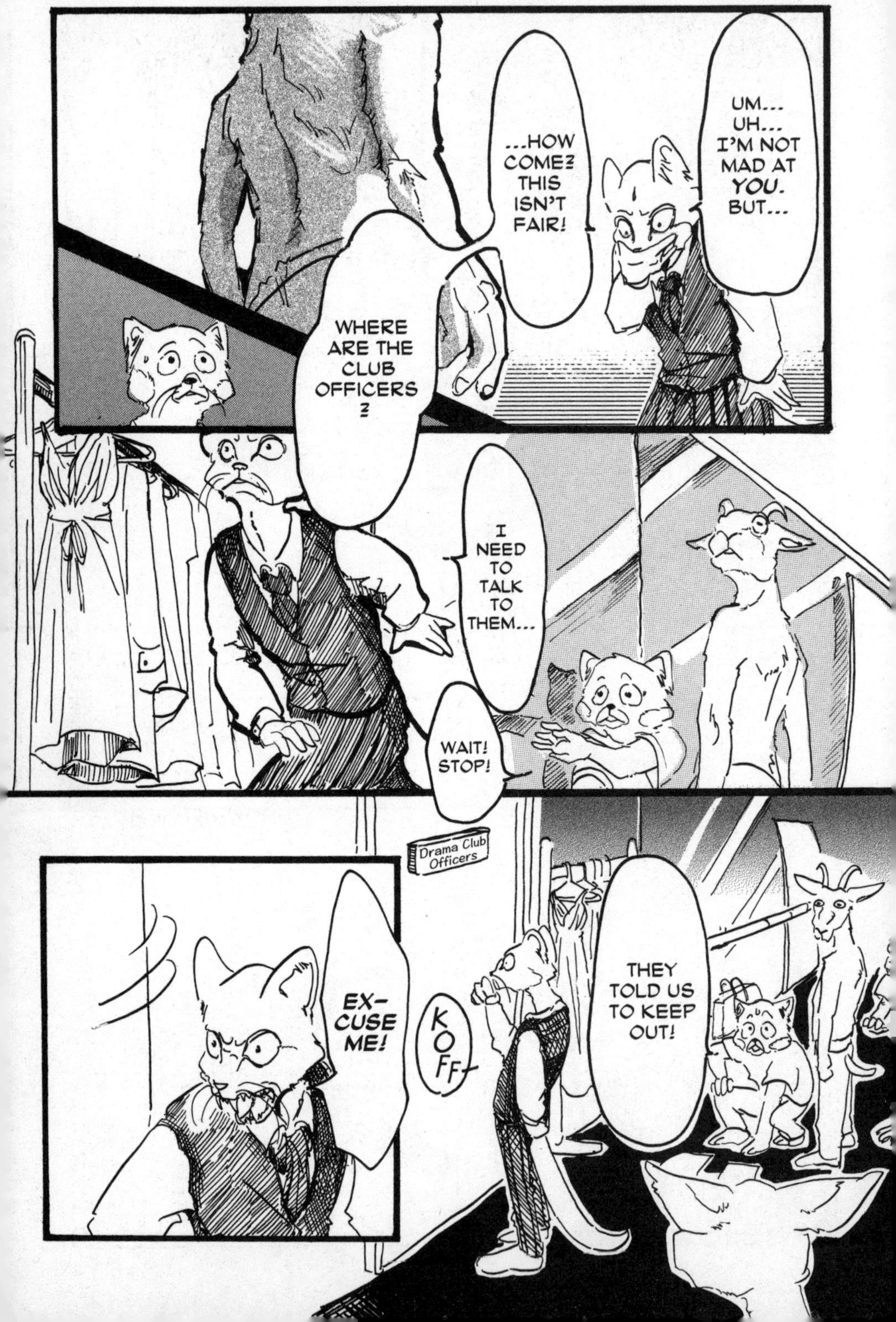
UM... UH... I'M NOT MAD AT *YOU*. BUT...
...HOW COME? THIS ISN'T FAIR!
WHERE ARE THE CLUB OFFICERS?
I NEED TO TALK TO THEM...
WAIT! STOP!
Drama Club Officers
THEY TOLD US TO KEEP OUT!
KOFF
EX-CUSE ME!

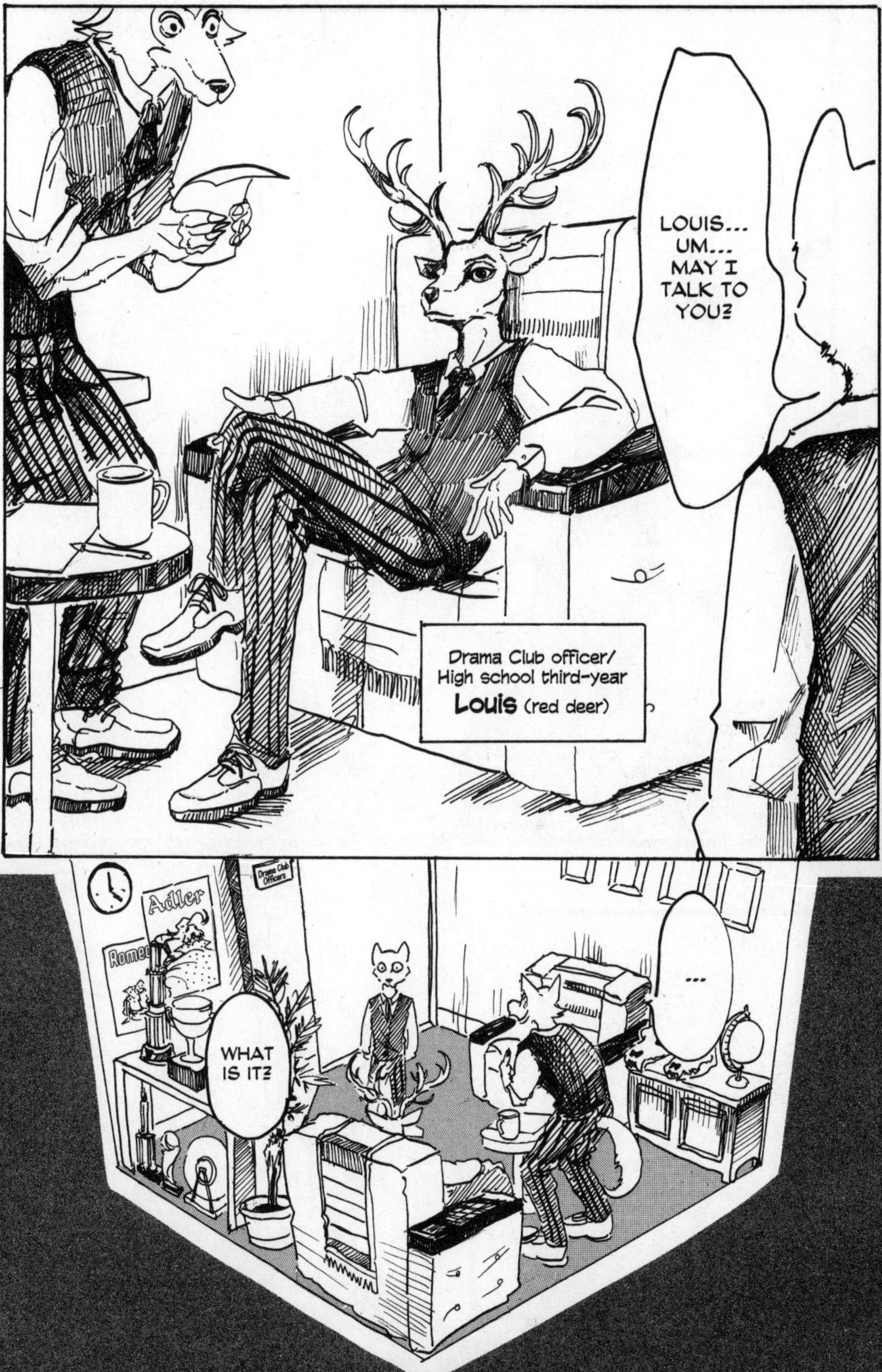
LOUIS... UM... MAY I TALK TO YOU?
Drama Club officer/ High school third-year Louis (red deer)
...
WHAT IS IT?
Drama Club Officers
Adler
Romeo

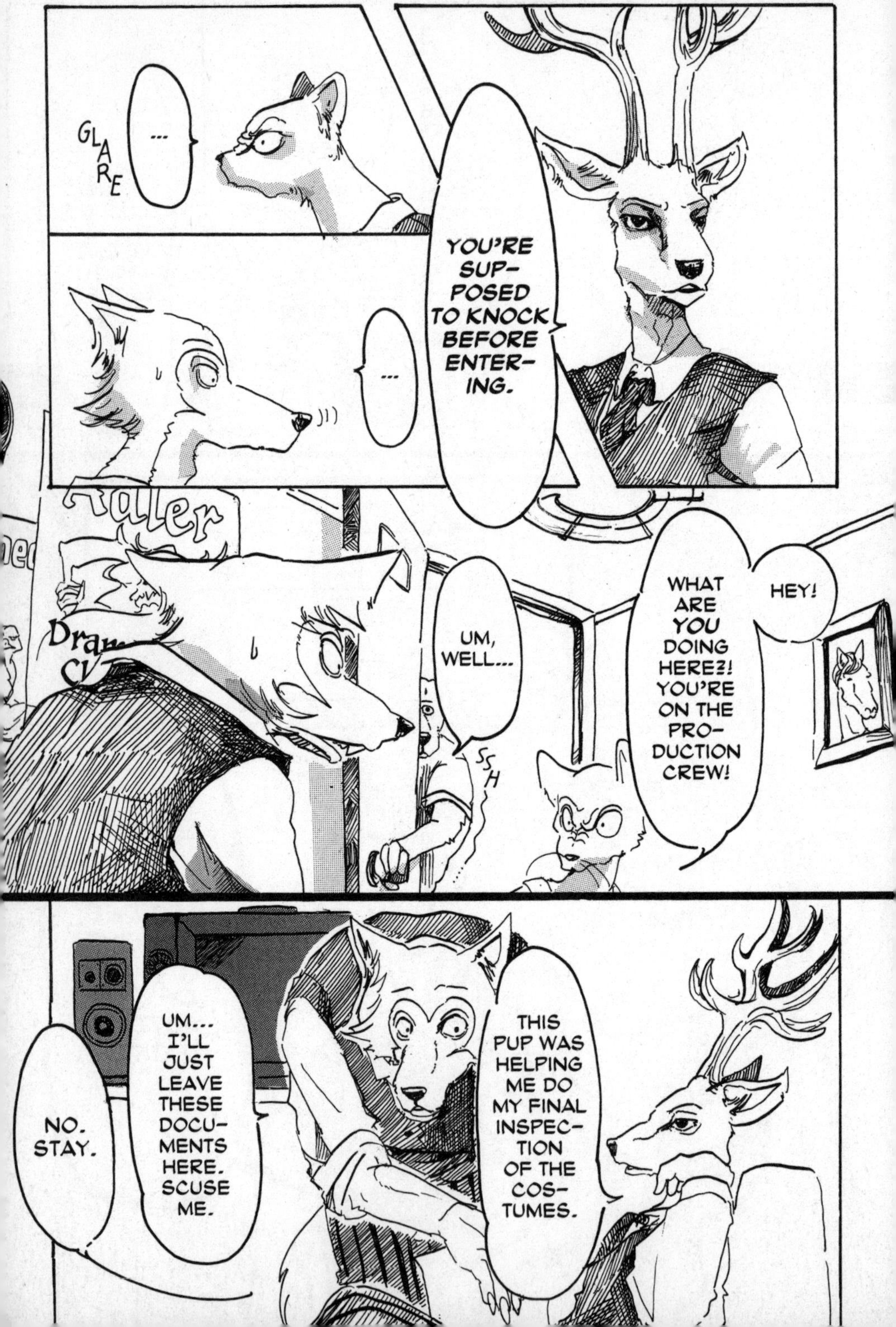

YOU'RE SUP-POSED TO KNOCK BEFORE ENTER-ING.
GLARE
...
...
HEY!
WHAT ARE YOU DOING HERE?! YOU'RE ON THE PRO-DUCTION CREW!
UM, WELL...
SSH
THIS PUP WAS HELPING ME DO MY FINAL INSPEC-TION OF THE COS-TUMES.
UM... I'LL JUST LEAVE THESE DOCU-MENTS HERE. SCUSE ME.
NO. STAY.

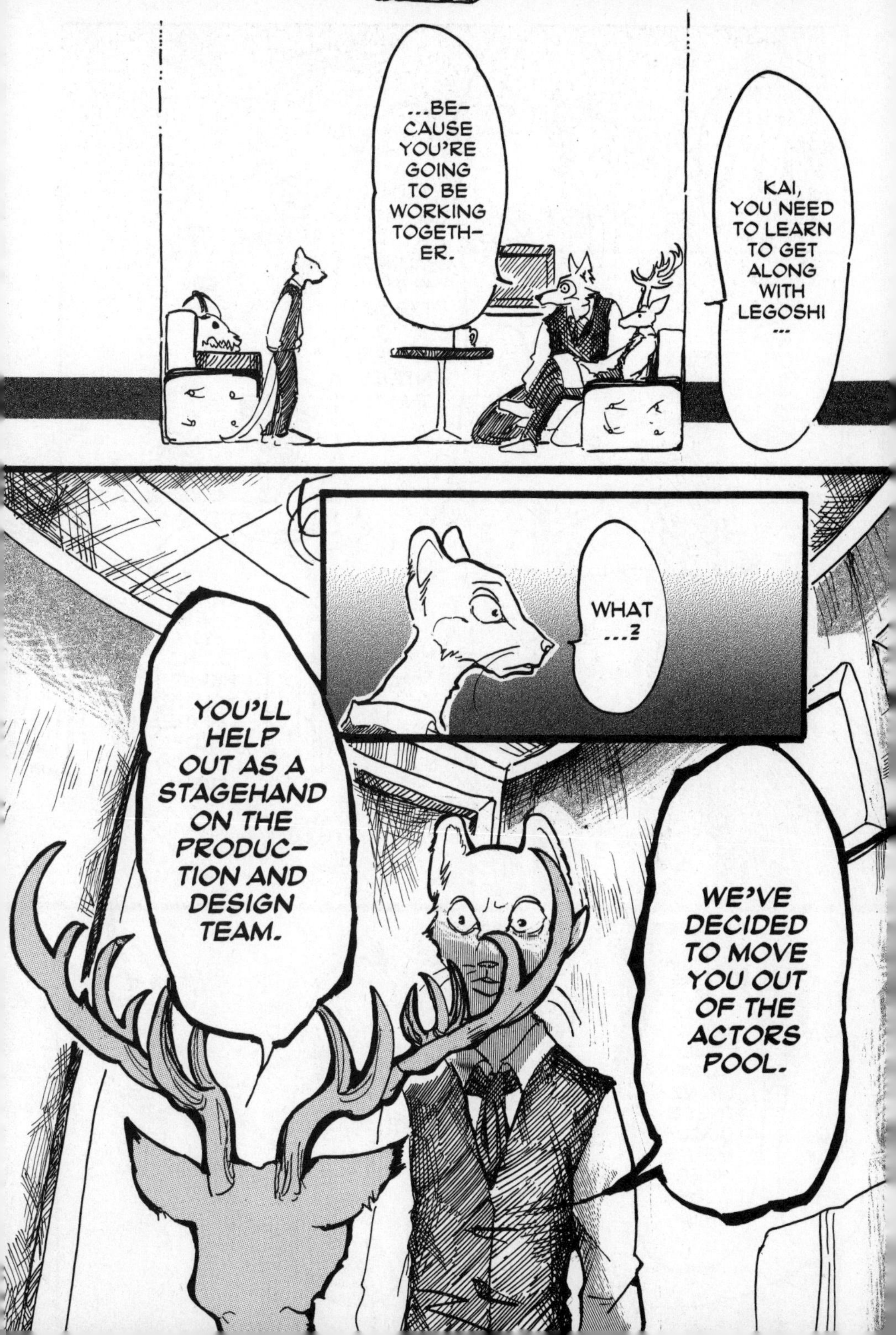
KAI, YOU NEED TO LEARN TO GET ALONG WITH LEGOSHI ...
...BE-CAUSE YOU'RE GOING TO BE WORKING TOGETH-ER.
WHAT ...?
WE'VE DECIDED TO MOVE YOU OUT OF THE ACTORS POOL.
YOU'LL HELP OUT AS A STAGEHAND ON THE PRODUCTION AND DESIGN TEAM.

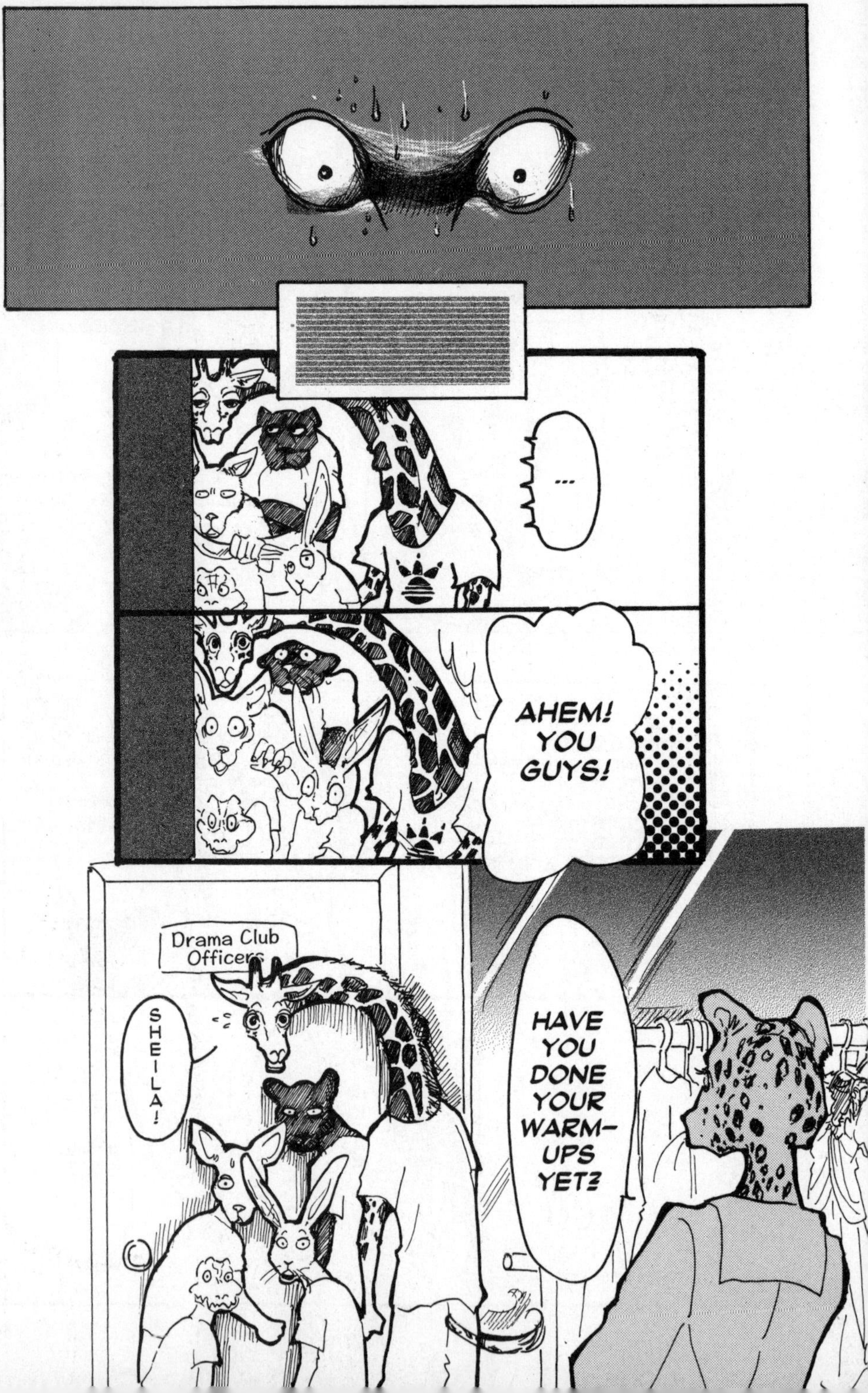
...
AHEM! YOU GUYS!
HAVE YOU DONE YOUR WARM-UPS YET?
Drama Club Officers
SHEILA!

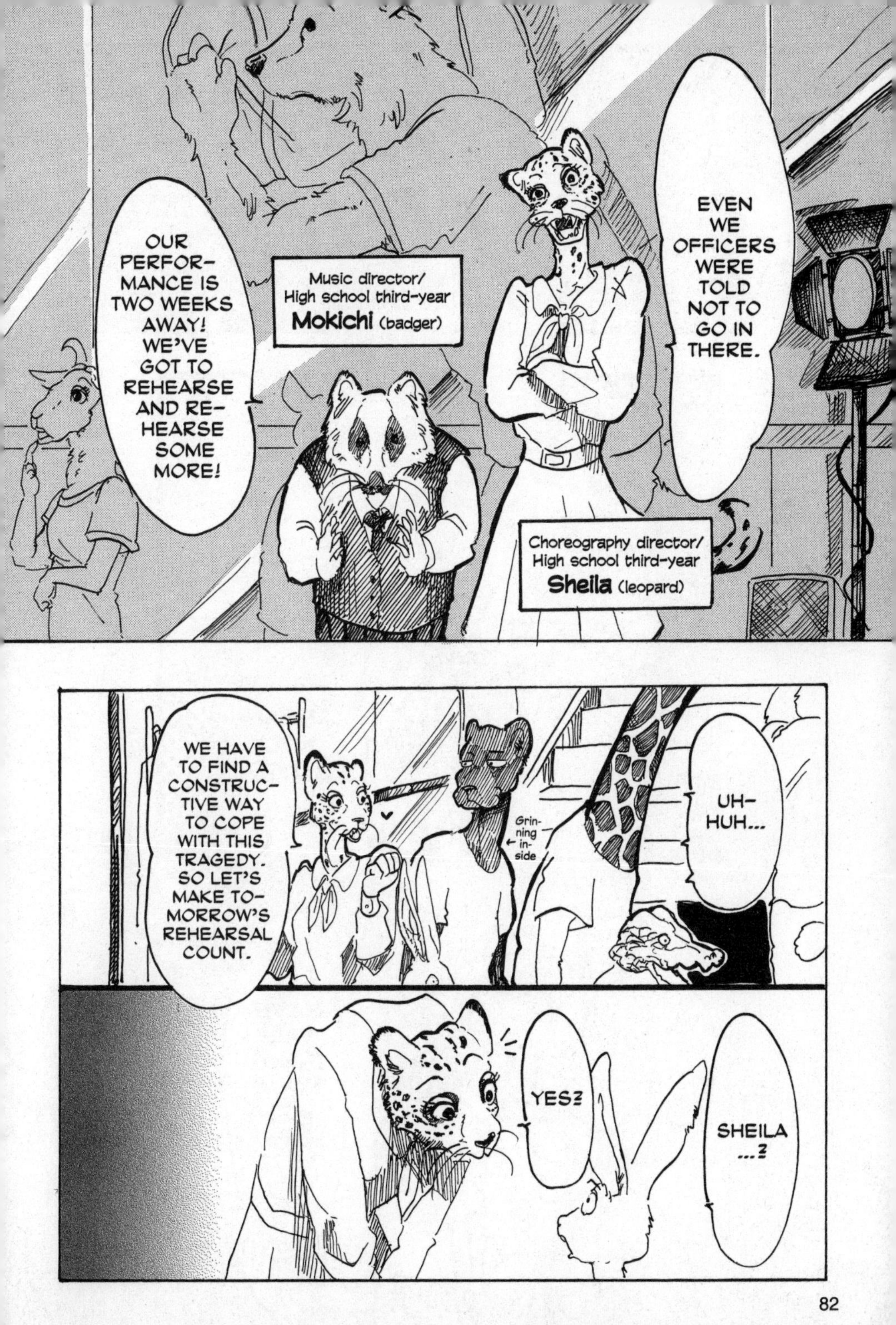
EVEN WE OFFICERS WERE TOLD NOT TO GO IN THERE.
Music director/ High school third-year **Mokichi** (badger)
OUR PERFORMANCE IS TWO WEEKS AWAY! WE'VE GOT TO REHEARSE AND REHEARSE SOME MORE!
Choreography director/ High school third-year **Sheila** (leopard)
UH-HUH...
Grinning inside
WE HAVE TO FIND A CONSTRUCTIVE WAY TO COPE WITH THIS TRAGEDY. SO LET'S MAKE TOMORROW'S REHEARSAL COUNT.
SHEILA ...?
YES?

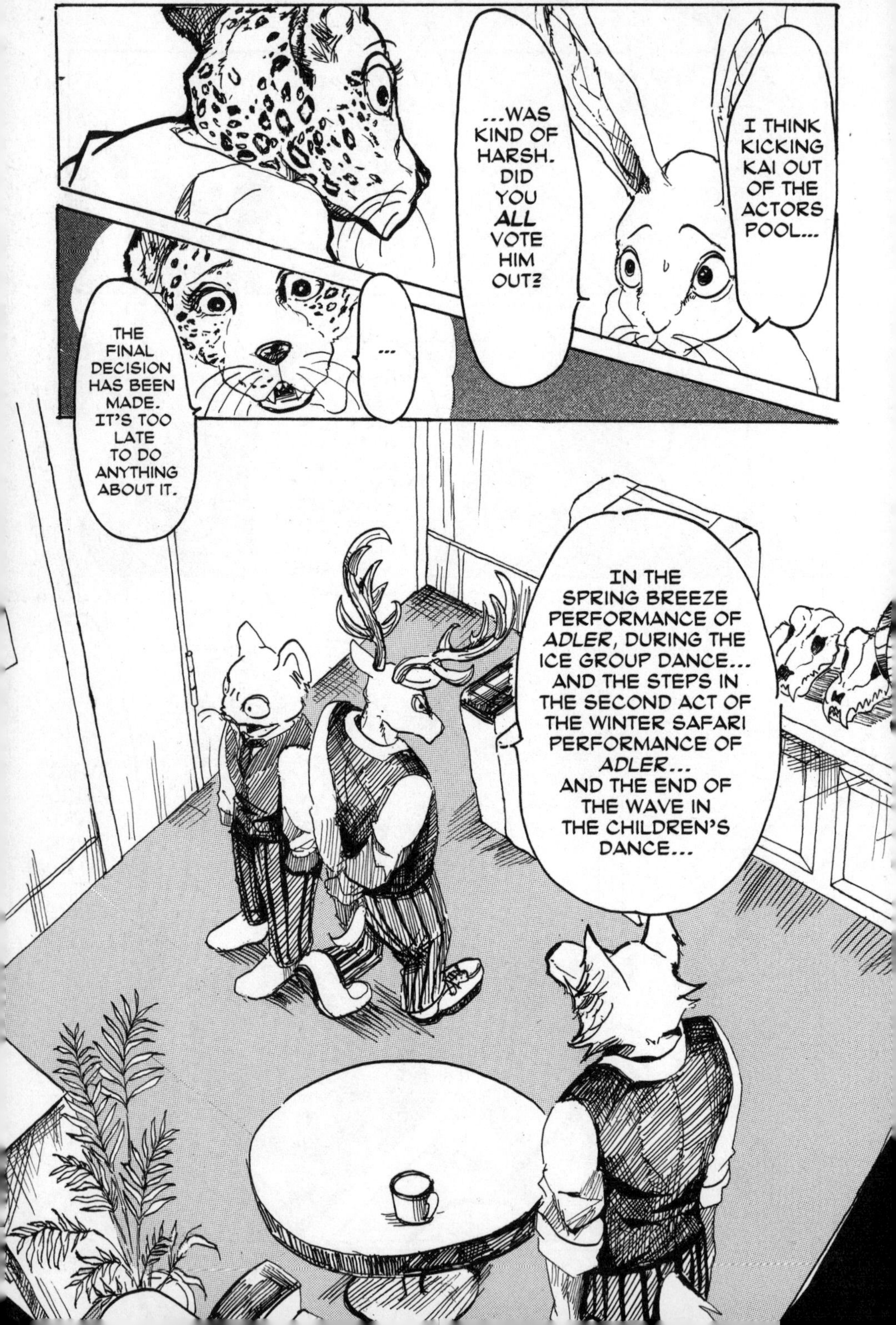
I THINK KICKING KAI OUT OF THE ACTORS POOL...
...WAS KIND OF HARSH. DID YOU ALL VOTE HIM OUT?
...
THE FINAL DECISION HAS BEEN MADE. IT'S TOO LATE TO DO ANYTHING ABOUT IT.
IN THE SPRING BREEZE PERFORMANCE OF ADLER, DURING THE ICE GROUP DANCE... AND THE STEPS IN THE SECOND ACT OF THE WINTER SAFARI PERFORMANCE OF ADLER... AND THE END OF THE WAVE IN THE CHILDREN'S DANCE...

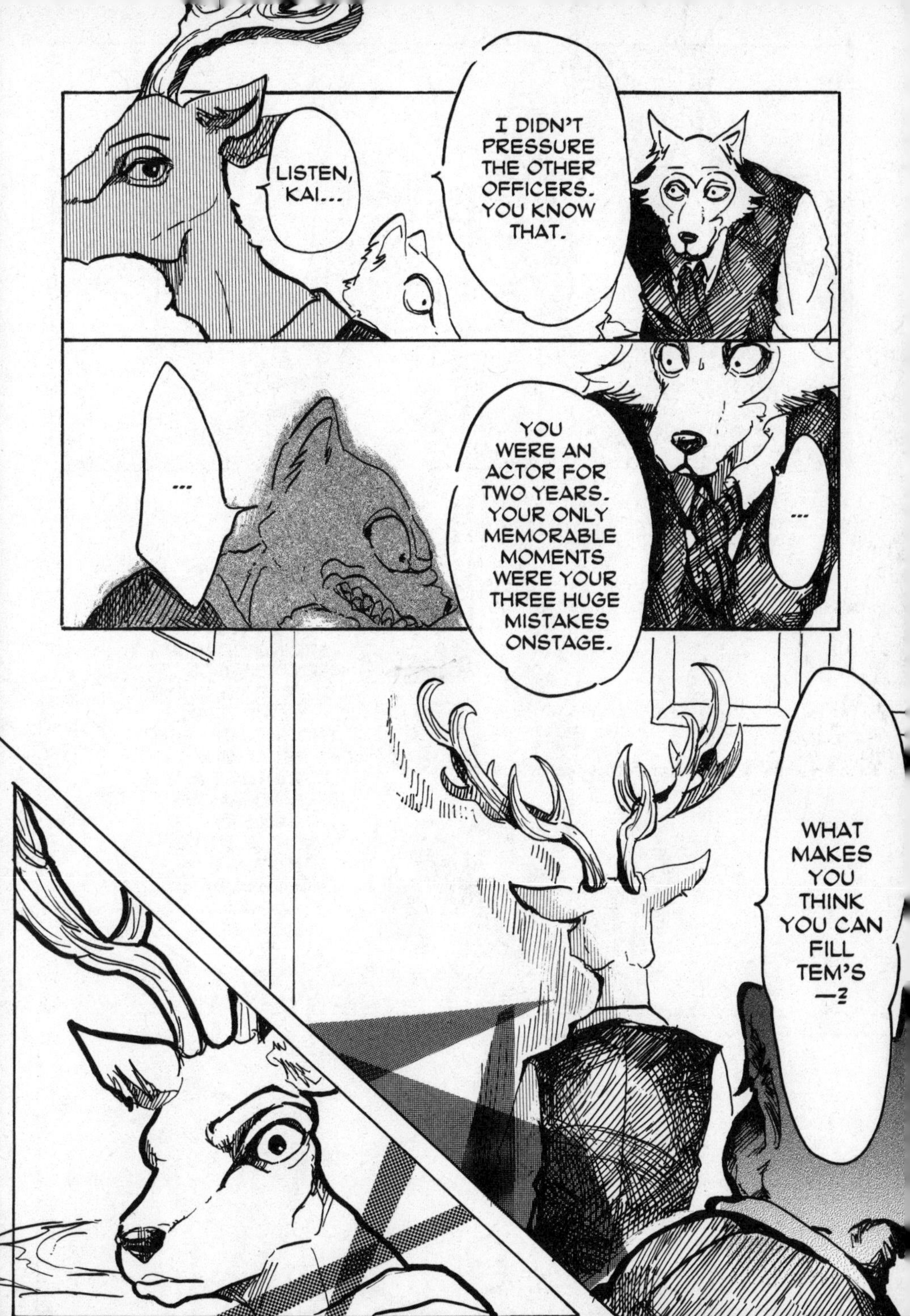
I DIDN'T PRESSURE THE OTHER OFFICERS. YOU KNOW THAT.
LISTEN, KAI...
...
YOU WERE AN ACTOR FOR TWO YEARS. YOUR ONLY MEMORABLE MOMENTS WERE YOUR THREE HUGE MISTAKES ONSTAGE.
...
WHAT MAKES YOU THINK YOU CAN FILL TEM'S —?

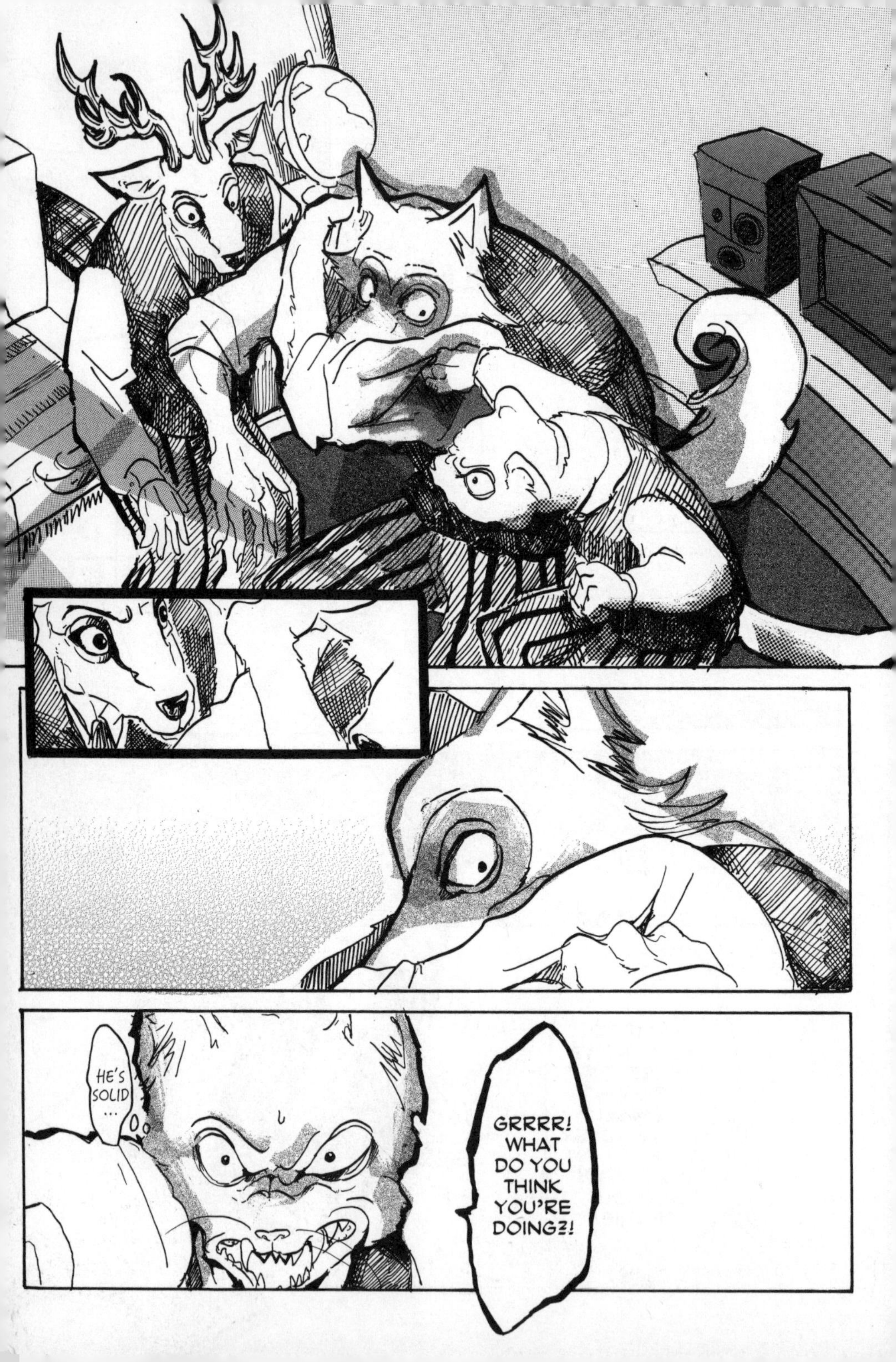
GRRRR! WHAT DO YOU THINK YOU'RE DOING?!
HE'S SOLID...

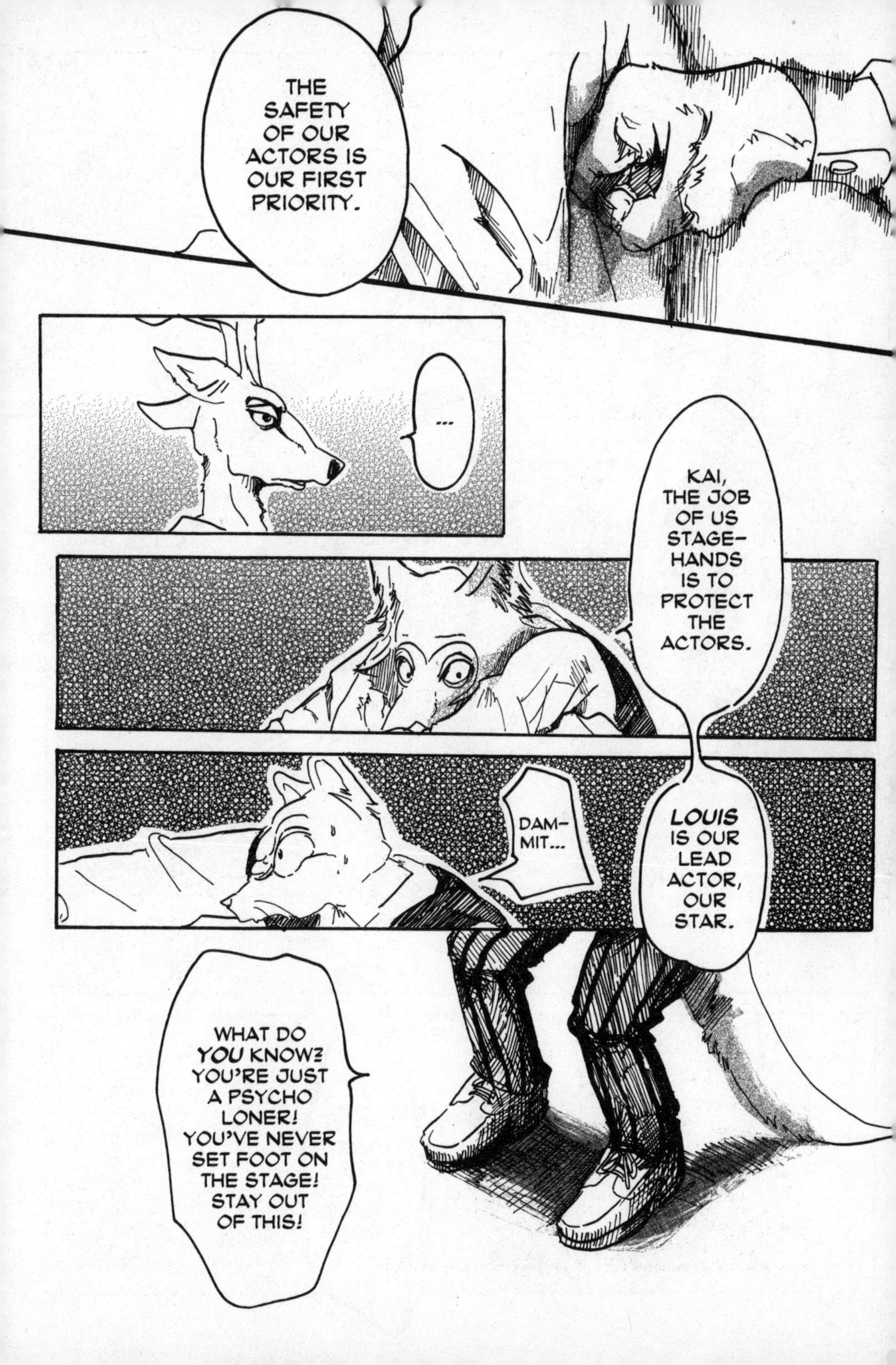
THE SAFETY OF OUR ACTORS IS OUR FIRST PRIORITY.
...
KAI, THE JOB OF US STAGE-HANDS IS TO PROTECT THE ACTORS.
LOUIS IS OUR LEAD ACTOR, OUR STAR.
DAM-MIT...
WHAT DO *YOU* KNOW? YOU'RE JUST A PSYCHO LONER! YOU'VE NEVER SET FOOT ON THE STAGE! STAY OUT OF THIS!

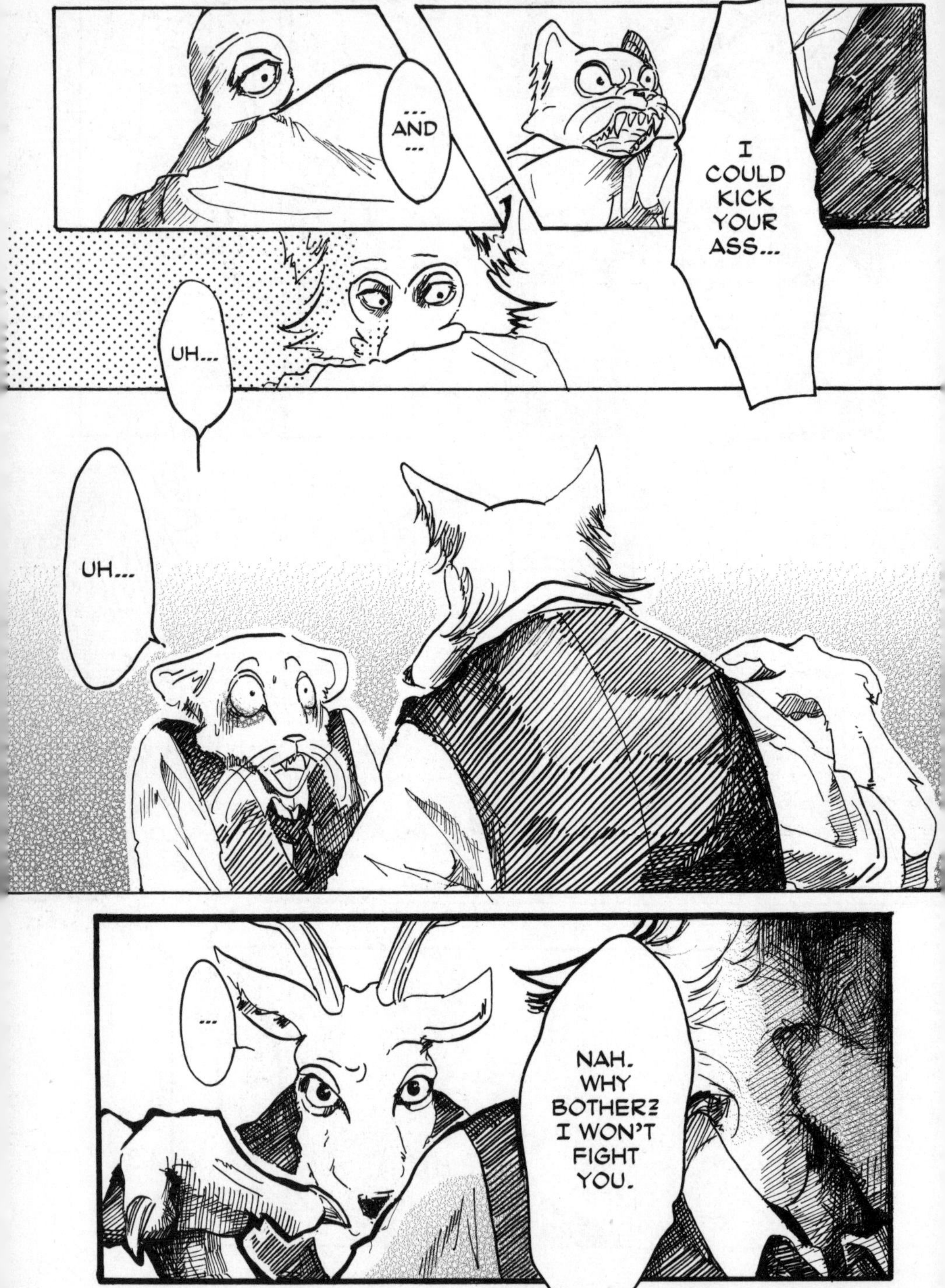
I COULD KICK YOUR ASS...
...AND...
UH...
UH...
...
NAH. WHY BOTHER? I WON'T FIGHT YOU.

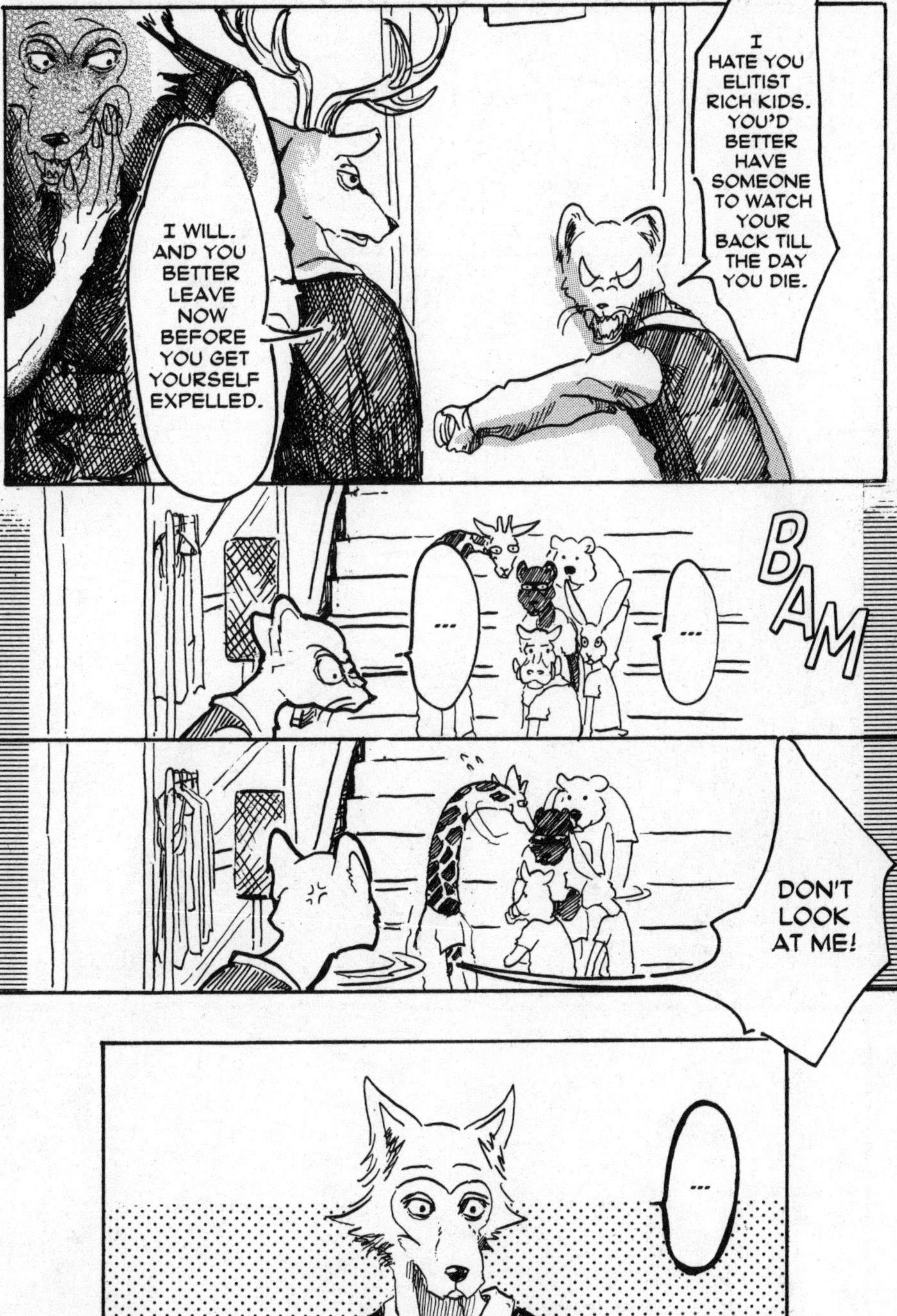
I HATE YOU ELITIST RICH KIDS. YOU'D BETTER HAVE SOMEONE TO WATCH YOUR BACK TILL THE DAY YOU DIE.
I WILL. AND YOU BETTER LEAVE NOW BEFORE YOU GET YOURSELF EXPELLED.
BAM
...
...
DON'T LOOK AT ME!
...

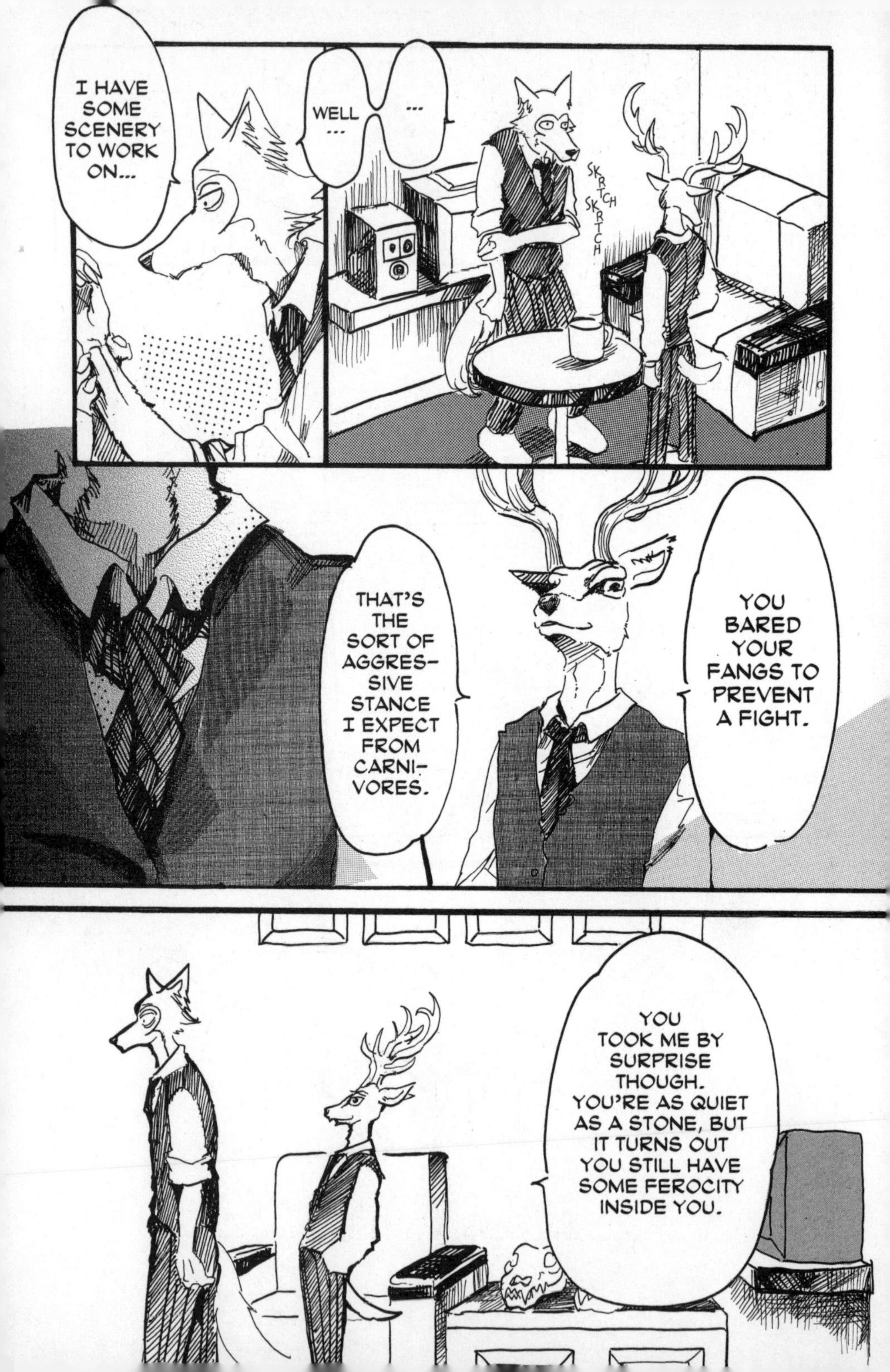
WELL ... ...
SKRTCH SKRTCH
I HAVE SOME SCENERY TO WORK ON...
YOU BARED YOUR FANGS TO PREVENT A FIGHT.
THAT'S THE SORT OF AGGRES-SIVE STANCE I EXPECT FROM CARNI-VORES.
YOU TOOK ME BY SURPRISE THOUGH. YOU'RE AS QUIET AS A STONE, BUT IT TURNS OUT YOU STILL HAVE SOME FEROCITY INSIDE YOU.

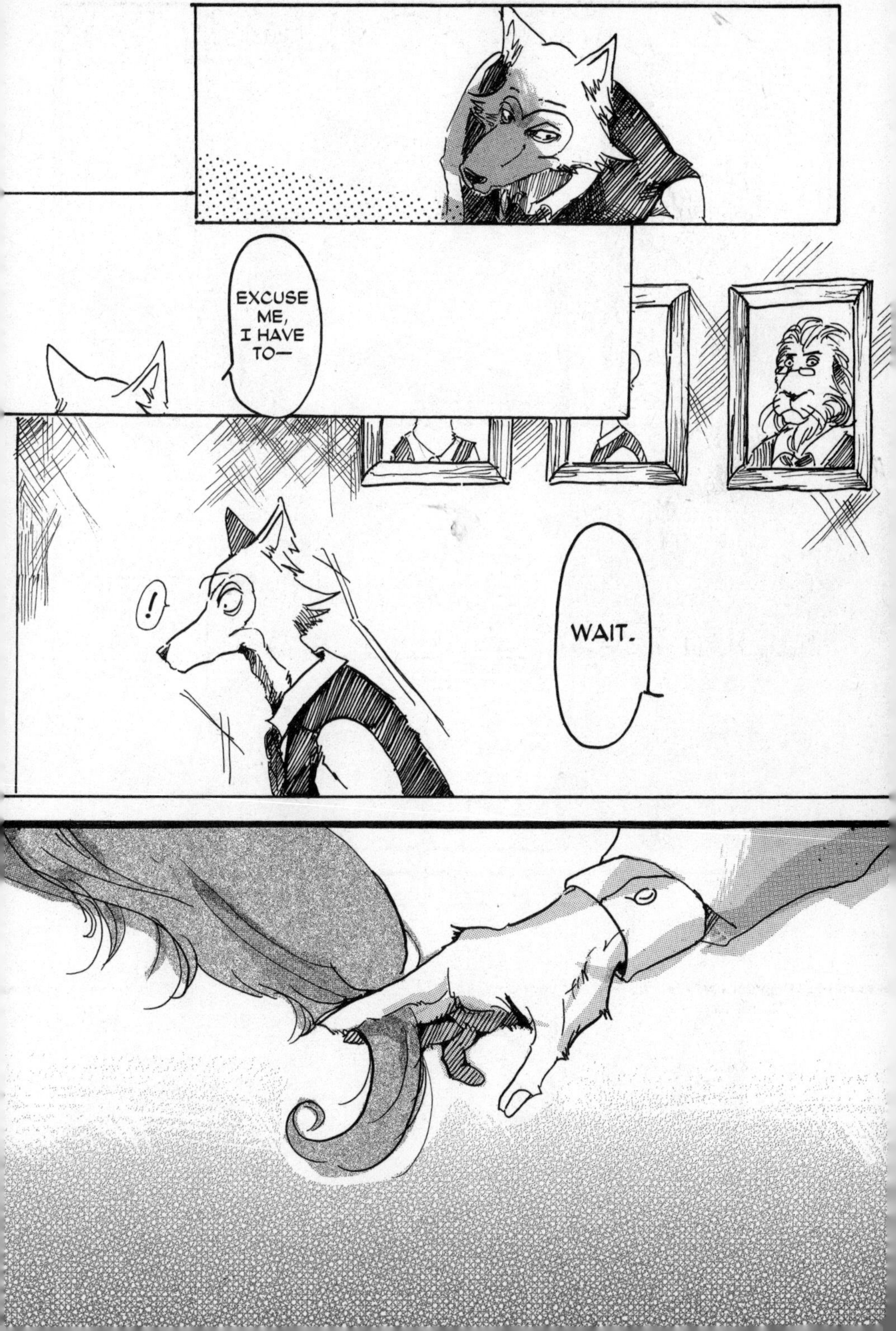
EXCUSE ME, I HAVE TO—
WAIT.
!

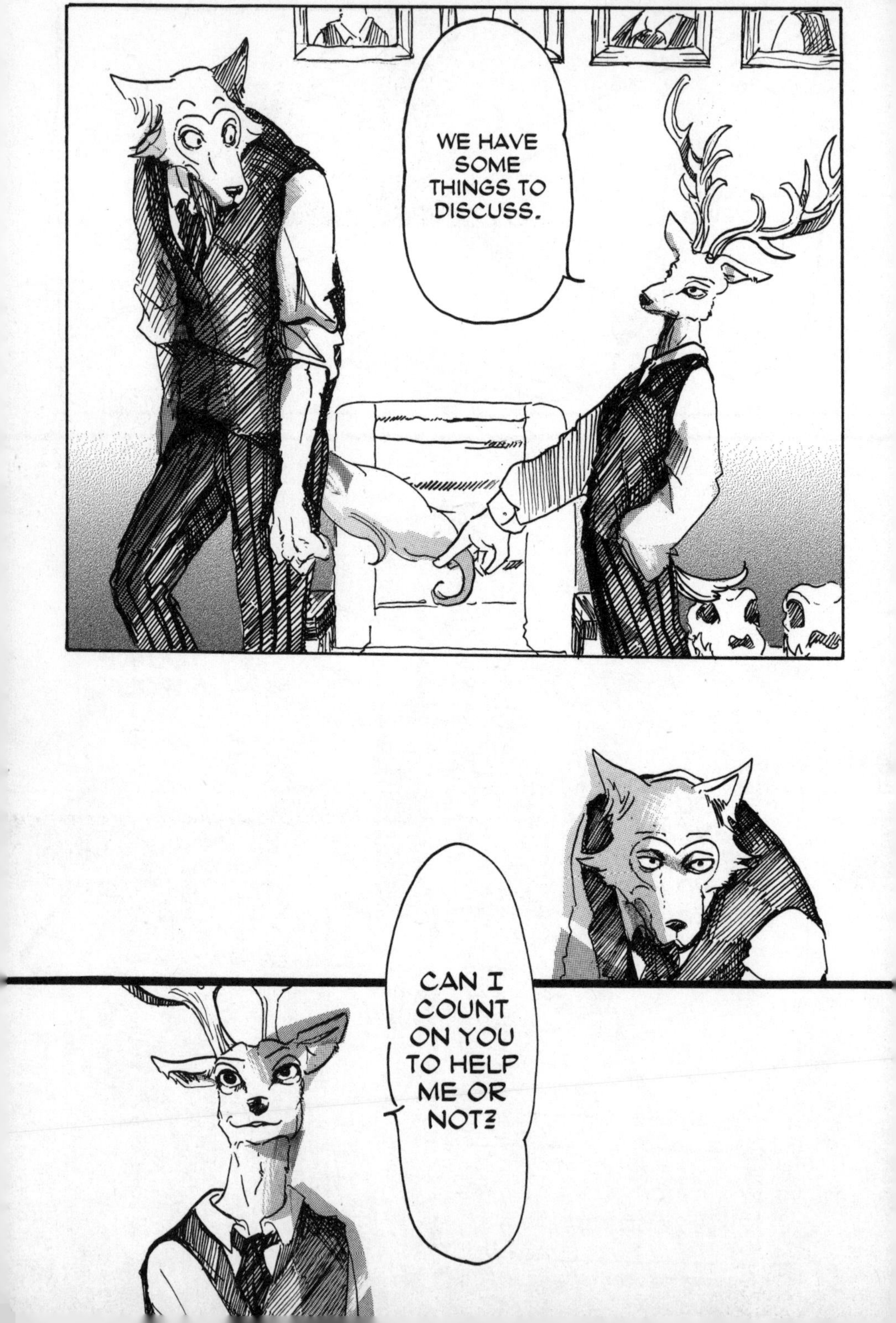
WE HAVE SOME THINGS TO DISCUSS.
CAN I COUNT ON YOU TO HELP ME OR NOT?

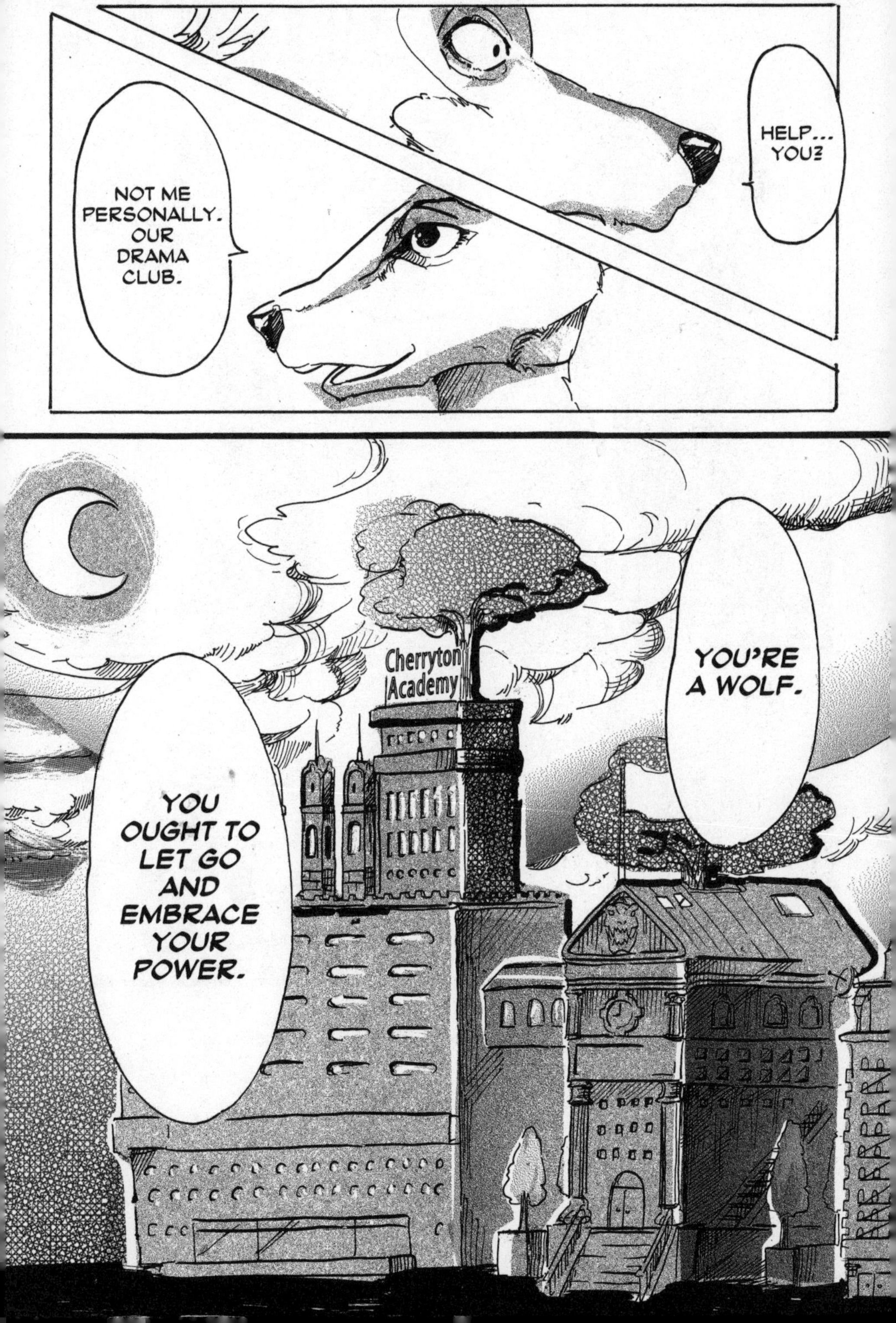
HELP... YOU?
NOT ME PERSONALLY. OUR DRAMA CLUB.
YOU'RE A WOLF.
Cherryton Academy
YOU OUGHT TO LET GO AND EMBRACE YOUR POWER.

Chapter 3:
A Warning in the Mist

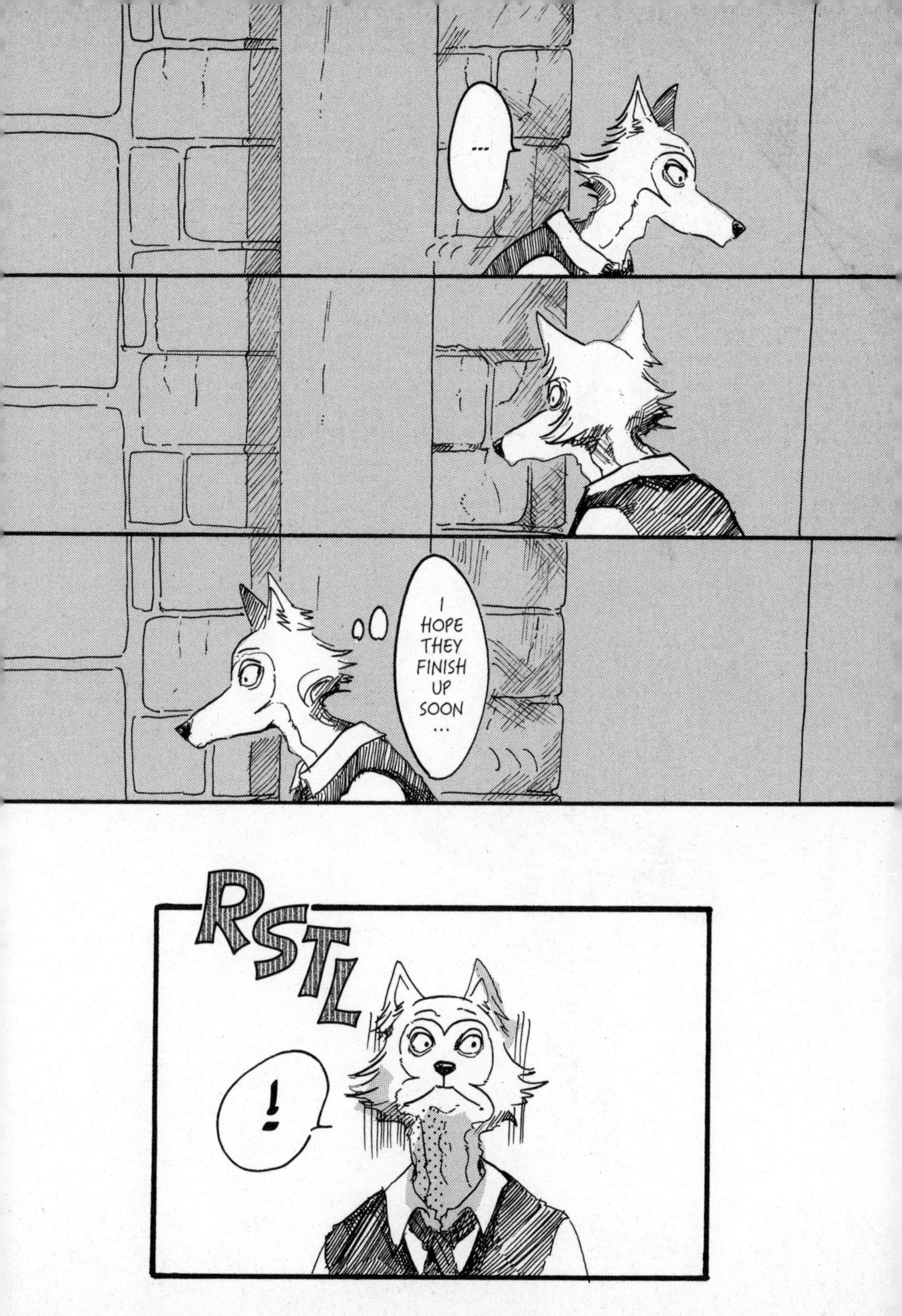
...
I HOPE THEY FINISH UP SOON...
RSTL
!

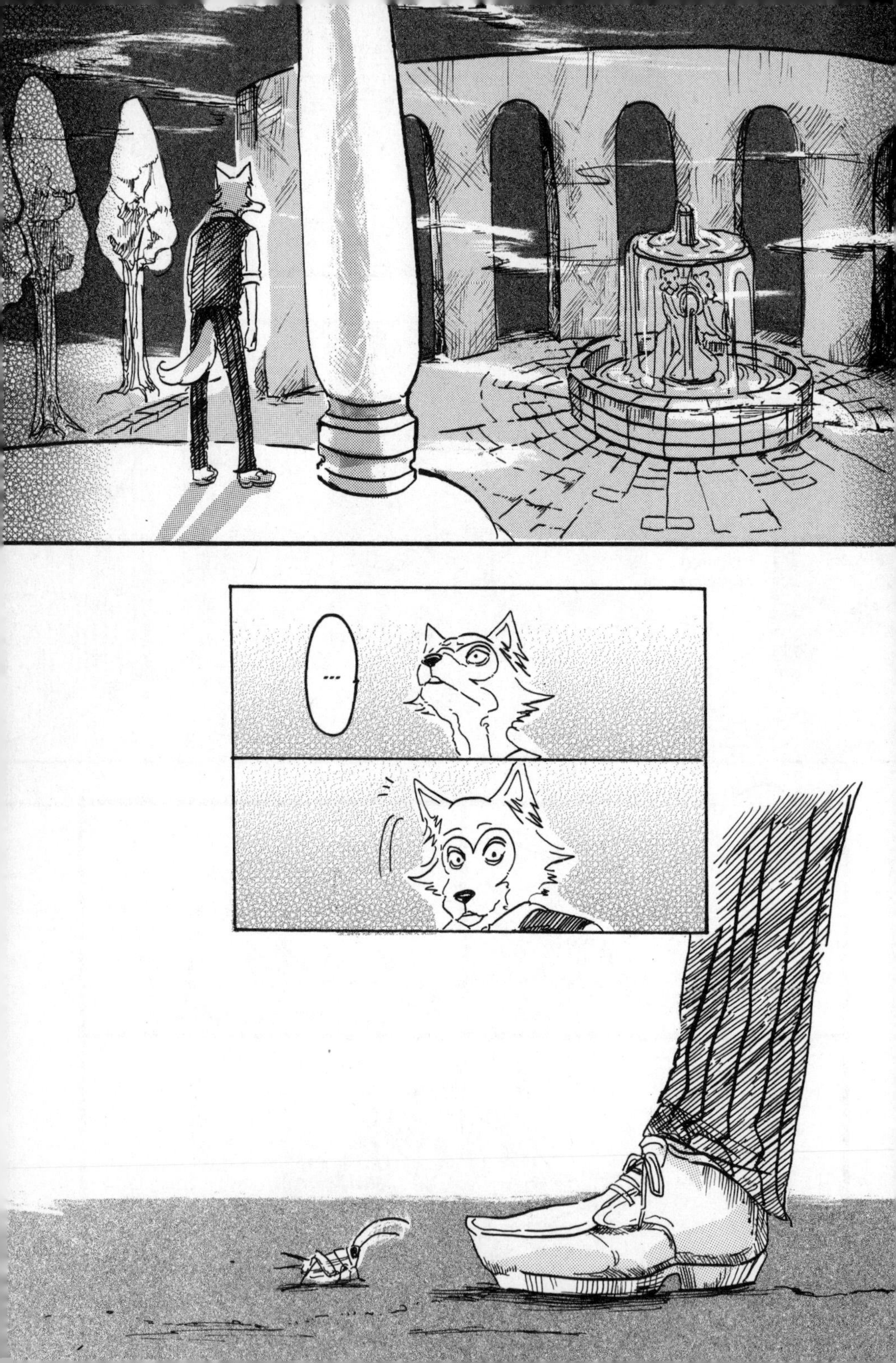
...

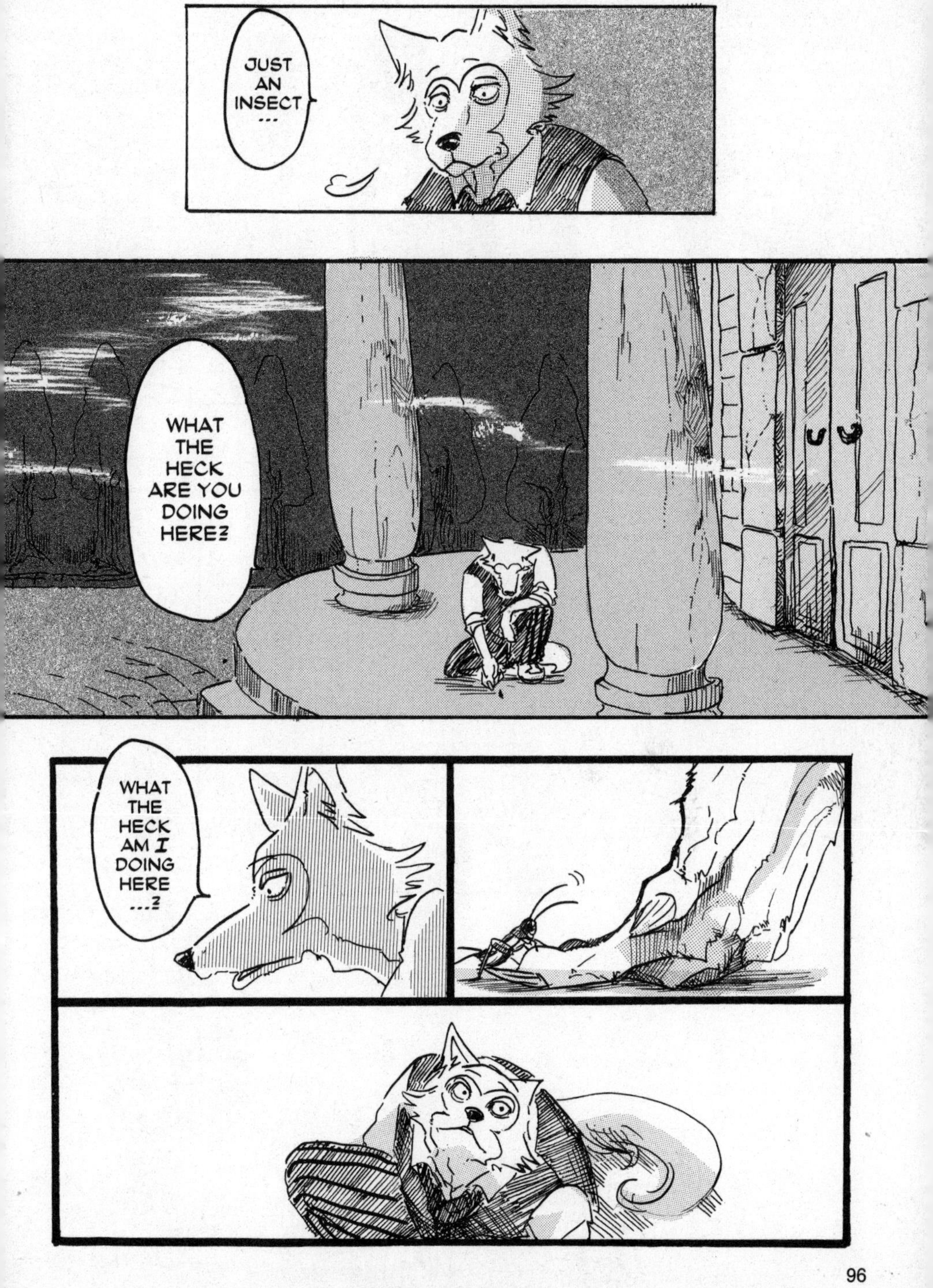
JUST AN INSECT...
WHAT THE HECK ARE YOU DOING HERE?
WHAT THE HECK AM *I* DOING HERE...?

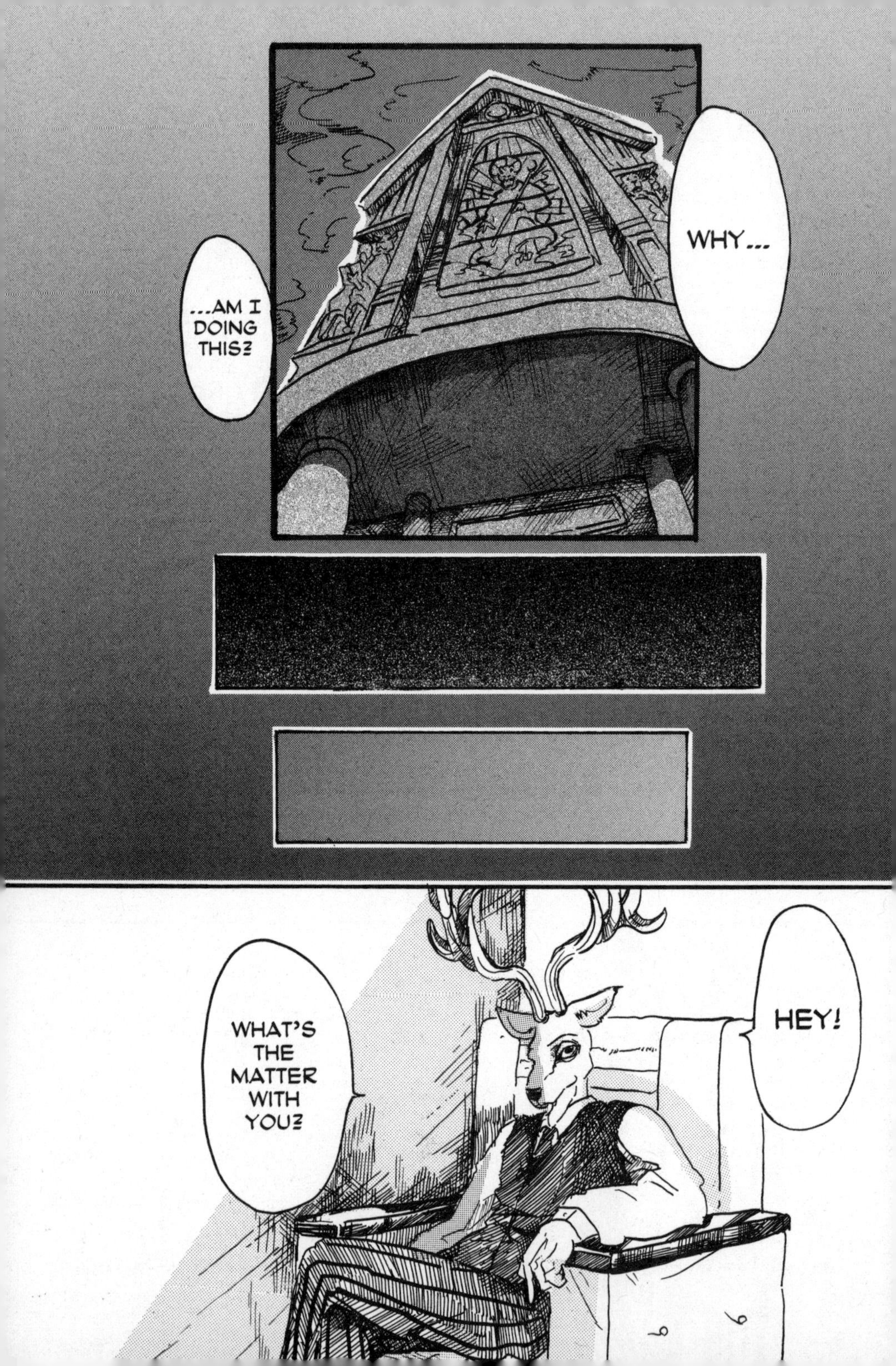
WHY...
...AM I DOING THIS?
HEY!
WHAT'S THE MATTER WITH YOU?

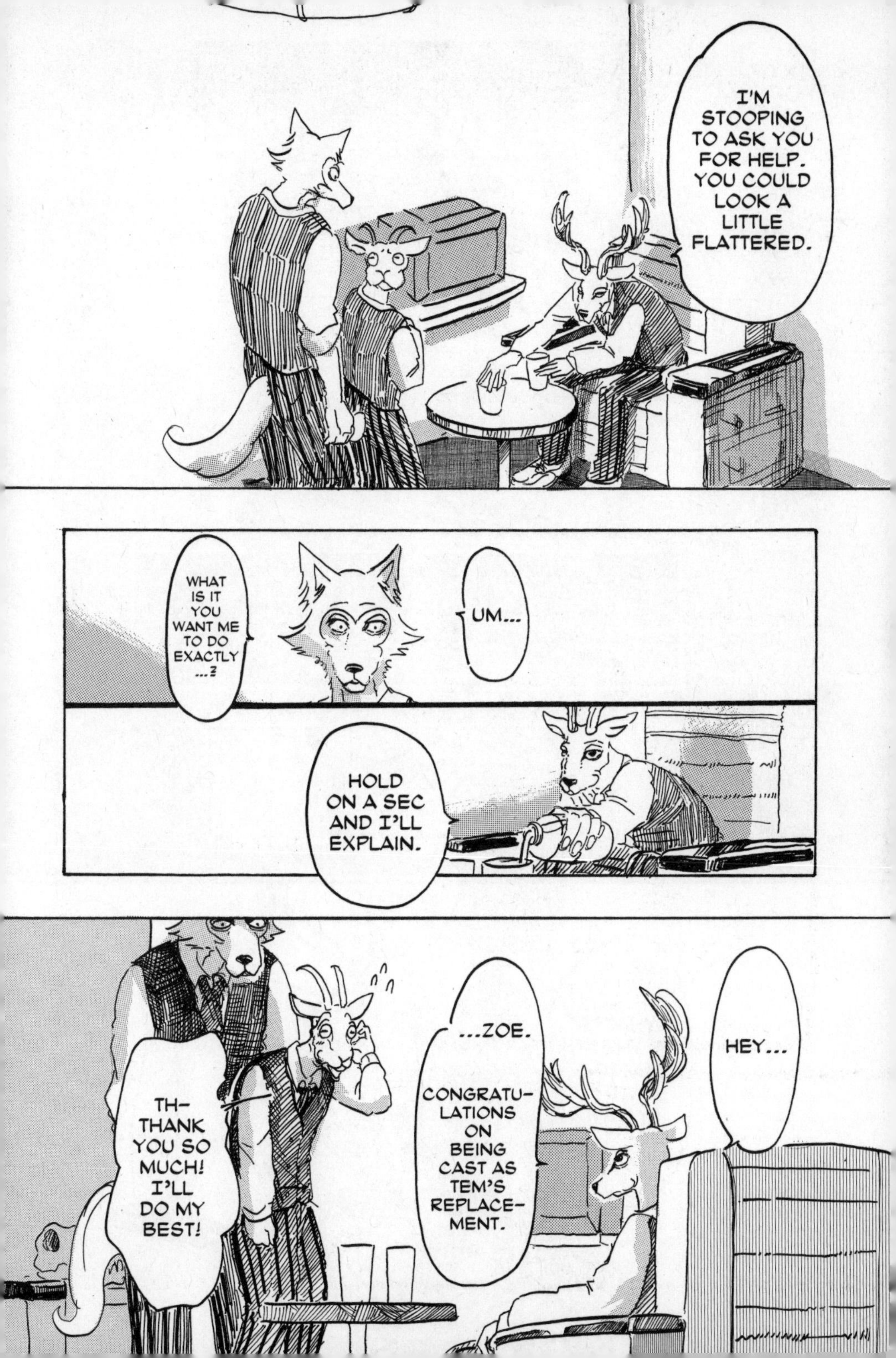
I'M STOOPING TO ASK YOU FOR HELP. YOU COULD LOOK A LITTLE FLATTERED.
UM...
WHAT IS IT YOU WANT ME TO DO EXACTLY...?
HOLD ON A SEC AND I'LL EXPLAIN.
HEY...
...ZOE.
CONGRATULATIONS ON BEING CAST AS TEM'S REPLACEMENT.
TH-THANK YOU SO MUCH! I'LL DO MY BEST!

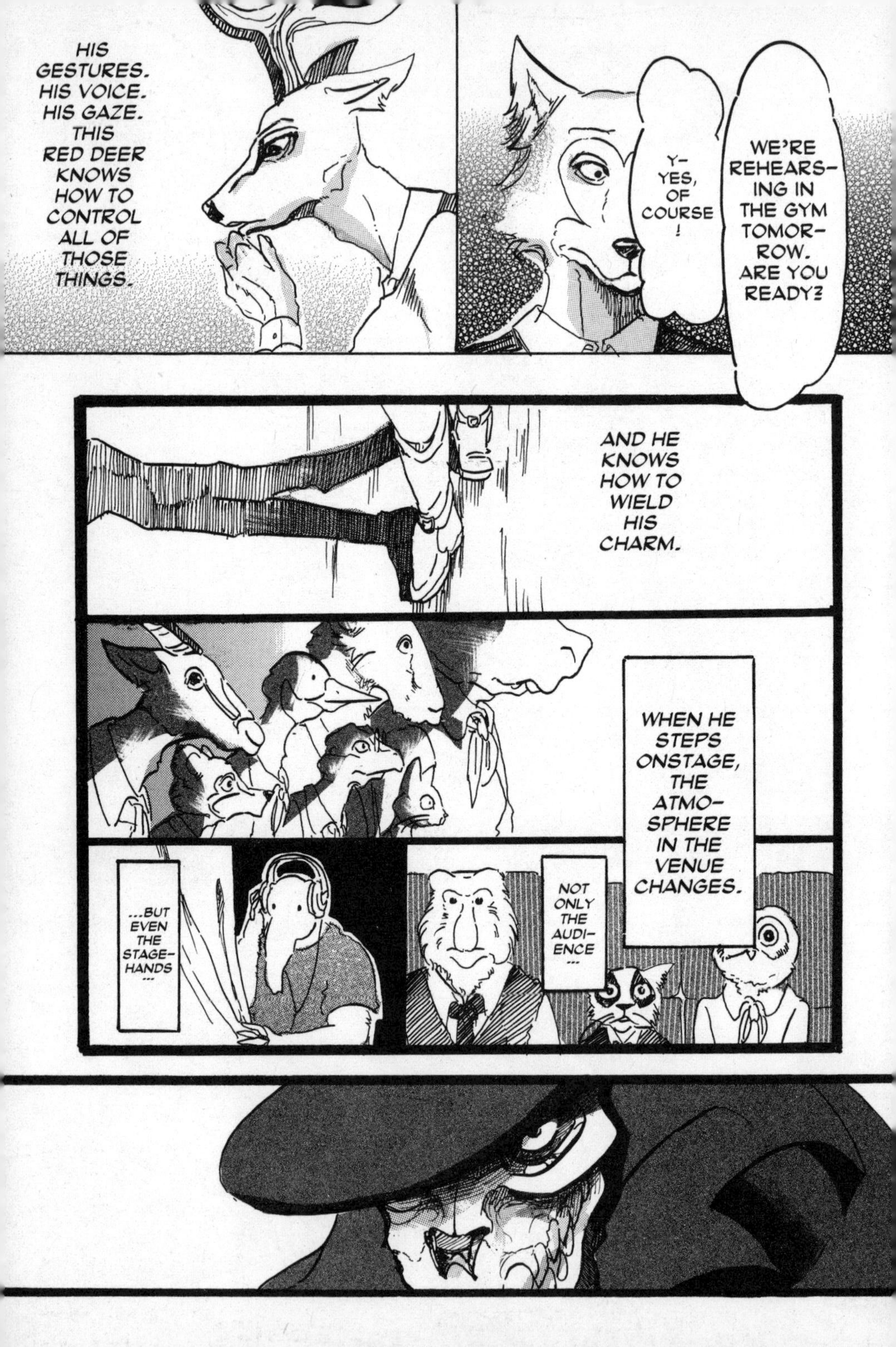

WE'RE REHEARSING IN THE GYM TOMORROW. ARE YOU READY?
Y-YES, OF COURSE!
HIS GESTURES. HIS VOICE. HIS GAZE. THIS RED DEER KNOWS HOW TO CONTROL ALL OF THOSE THINGS.
AND HE KNOWS HOW TO WIELD HIS CHARM.
WHEN HE STEPS ONSTAGE, THE ATMOSPHERE IN THE VENUE CHANGES.
NOT ONLY THE AUDIENCE...
...BUT EVEN THE STAGEHANDS...

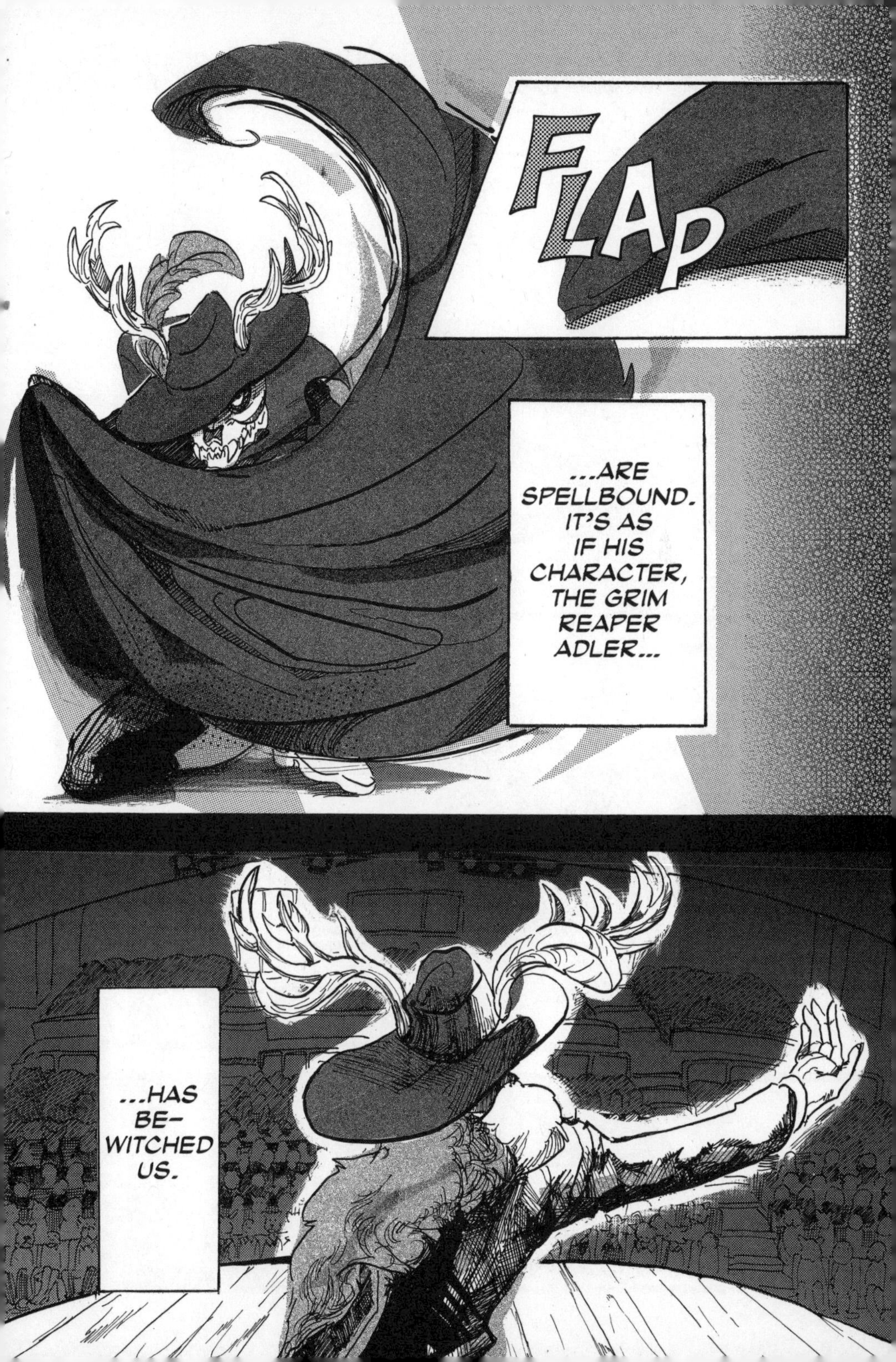
FLAP
...ARE SPELLBOUND. IT'S AS IF HIS CHARACTER, THE GRIM REAPER ADLER...
...HAS BE-WITCHED US.

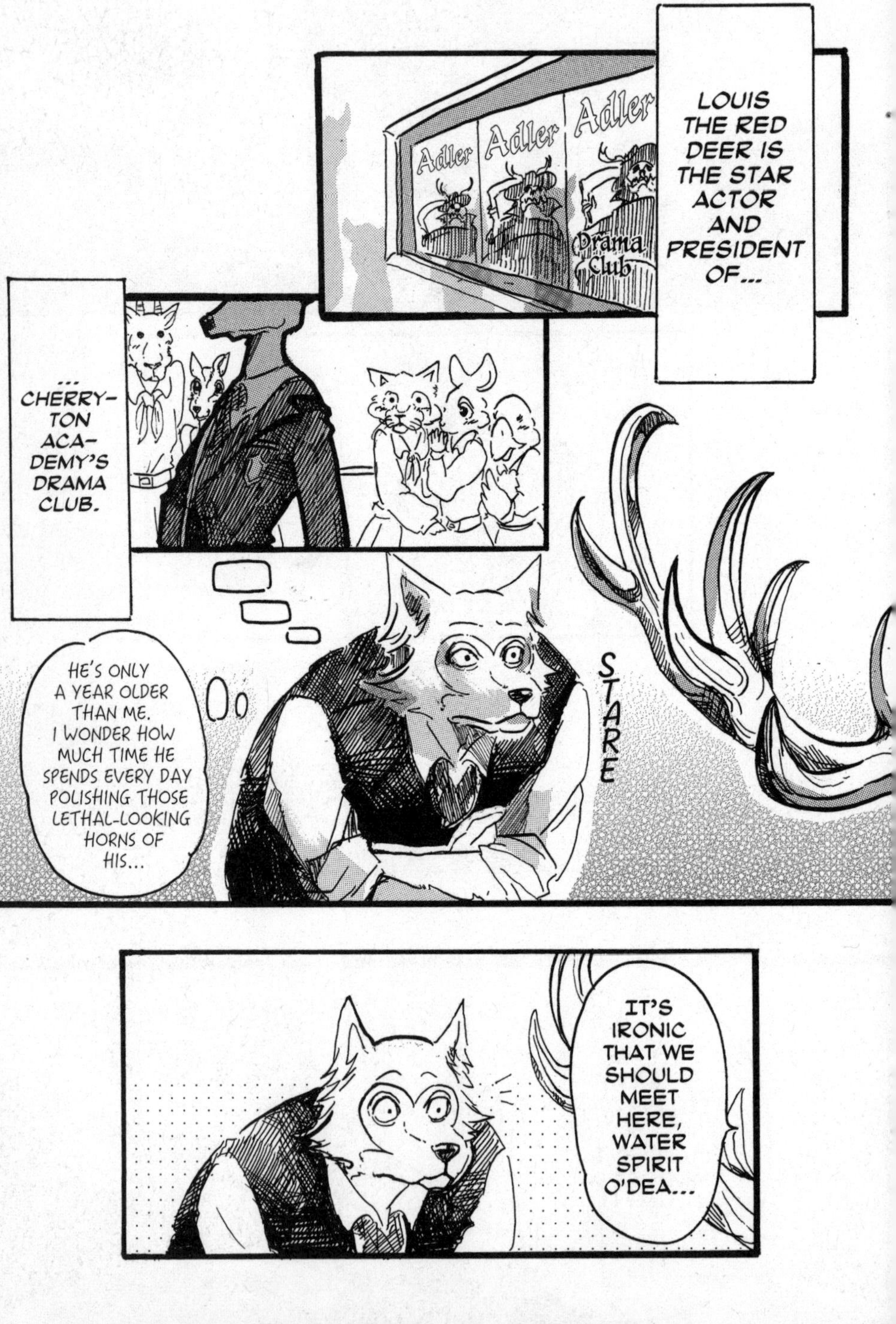
LOUIS THE RED DEER IS THE STAR ACTOR AND PRESIDENT OF...
Adler
Adler
Adler
Drama Club
...CHERRYTON ACADEMY'S DRAMA CLUB.
STARE
HE'S ONLY A YEAR OLDER THAN ME. I WONDER HOW MUCH TIME HE SPENDS EVERY DAY POLISHING THOSE LETHAL-LOOKING HORNS OF HIS...
IT'S IRONIC THAT WE SHOULD MEET HERE, WATER SPIRIT O'DEA...

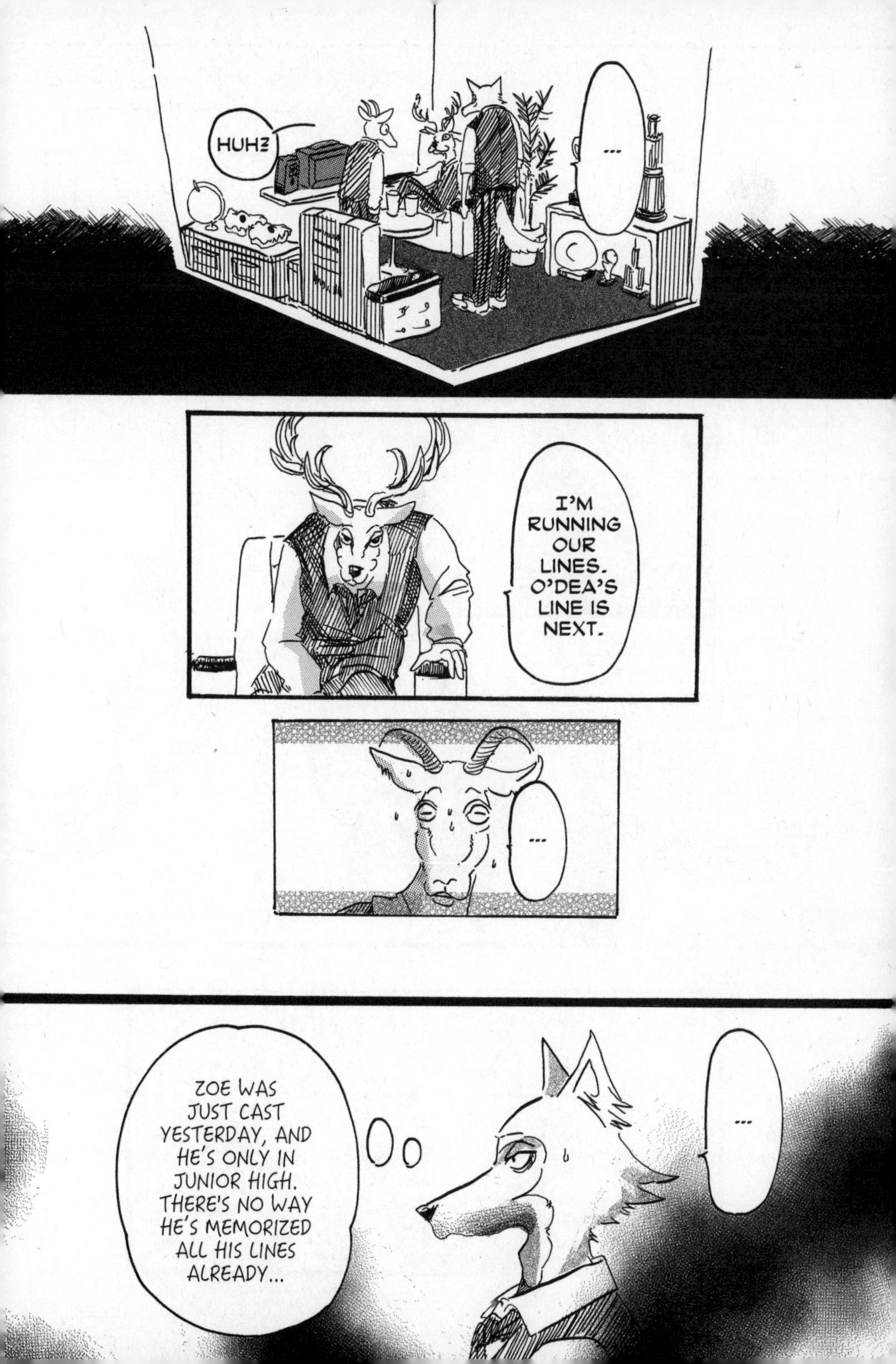
...
HUH?
I'M RUNNING OUR LINES. O'DEA'S LINE IS NEXT.
...
...
ZOE WAS JUST CAST YESTERDAY, AND HE'S ONLY IN JUNIOR HIGH. THERE'S NO WAY HE'S MEMORIZED ALL HIS LINES ALREADY...

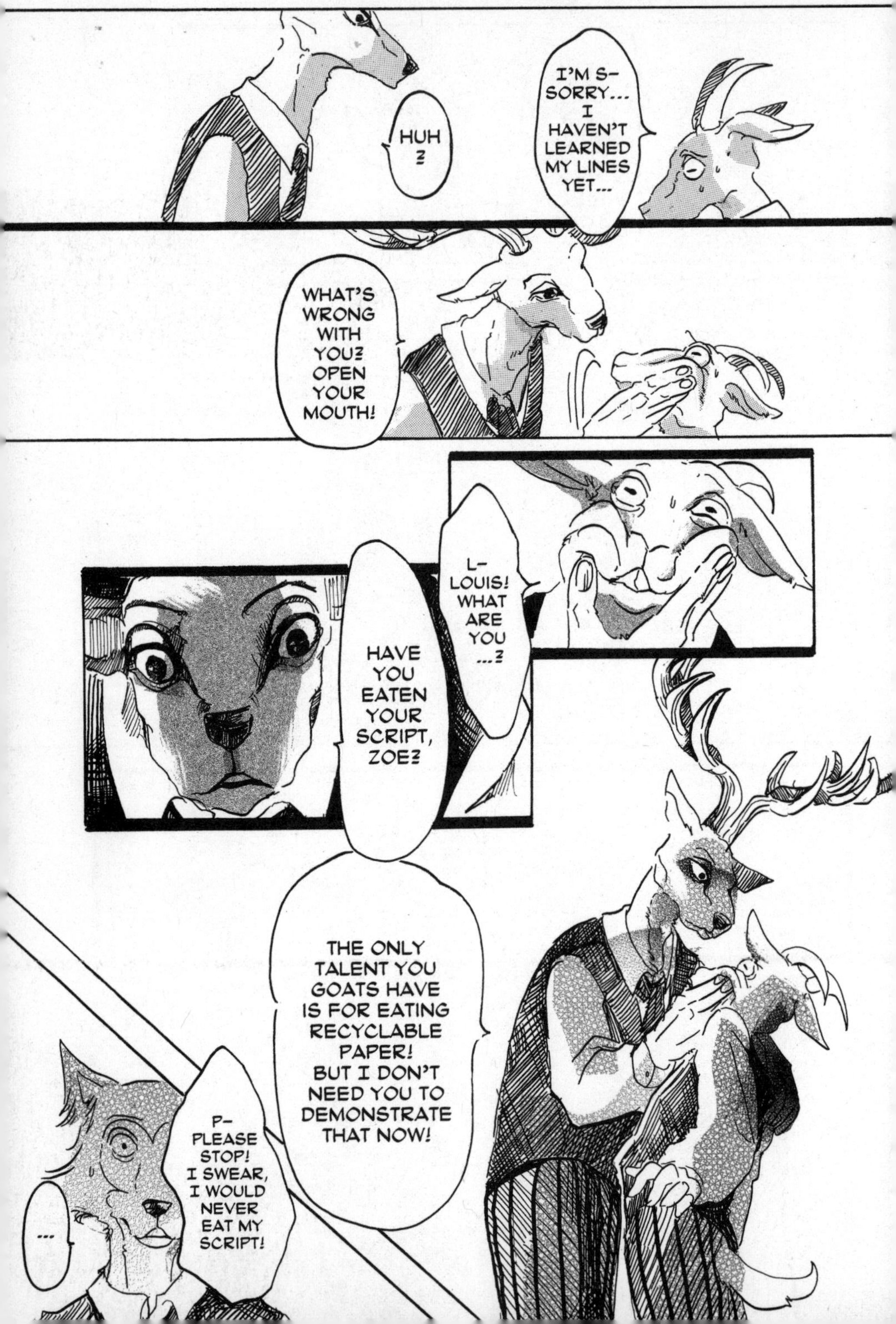

I'M S-SORRY... I HAVEN'T LEARNED MY LINES YET...
HUH?
WHAT'S WRONG WITH YOU? OPEN YOUR MOUTH!
L-LOUIS! WHAT ARE YOU ...?
HAVE YOU EATEN YOUR SCRIPT, ZOE?
THE ONLY TALENT YOU GOATS HAVE IS FOR EATING RECYCLABLE PAPER! BUT I DON'T NEED YOU TO DEMONSTRATE THAT NOW!
P-PLEASE STOP! I SWEAR, I WOULD NEVER EAT MY SCRIPT!
...

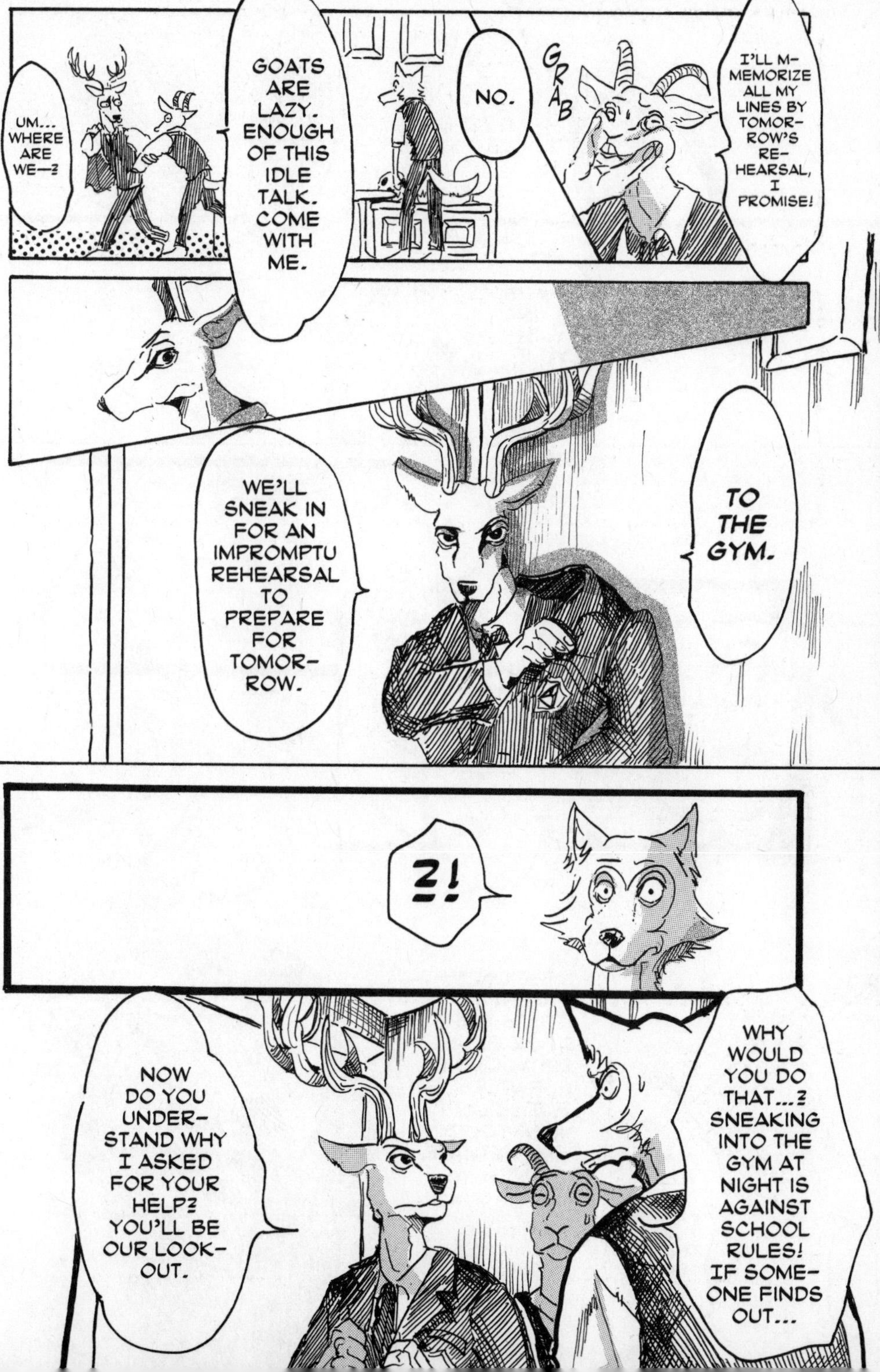
I'LL M-MEMORIZE ALL MY LINES BY TOMORROW'S REHEARSAL, I PROMISE!
GRAB
NO.
GOATS ARE LAZY. ENOUGH OF THIS IDLE TALK. COME WITH ME.
UM... WHERE ARE WE--?
TO THE GYM.
WE'LL SNEAK IN FOR AN IMPROMPTU REHEARSAL TO PREPARE FOR TOMORROW.
!?
WHY WOULD YOU DO THAT...? SNEAKING INTO THE GYM AT NIGHT IS AGAINST SCHOOL RULES! IF SOMEONE FINDS OUT...
NOW DO YOU UNDERSTAND WHY I ASKED FOR YOUR HELP? YOU'LL BE OUR LOOKOUT.

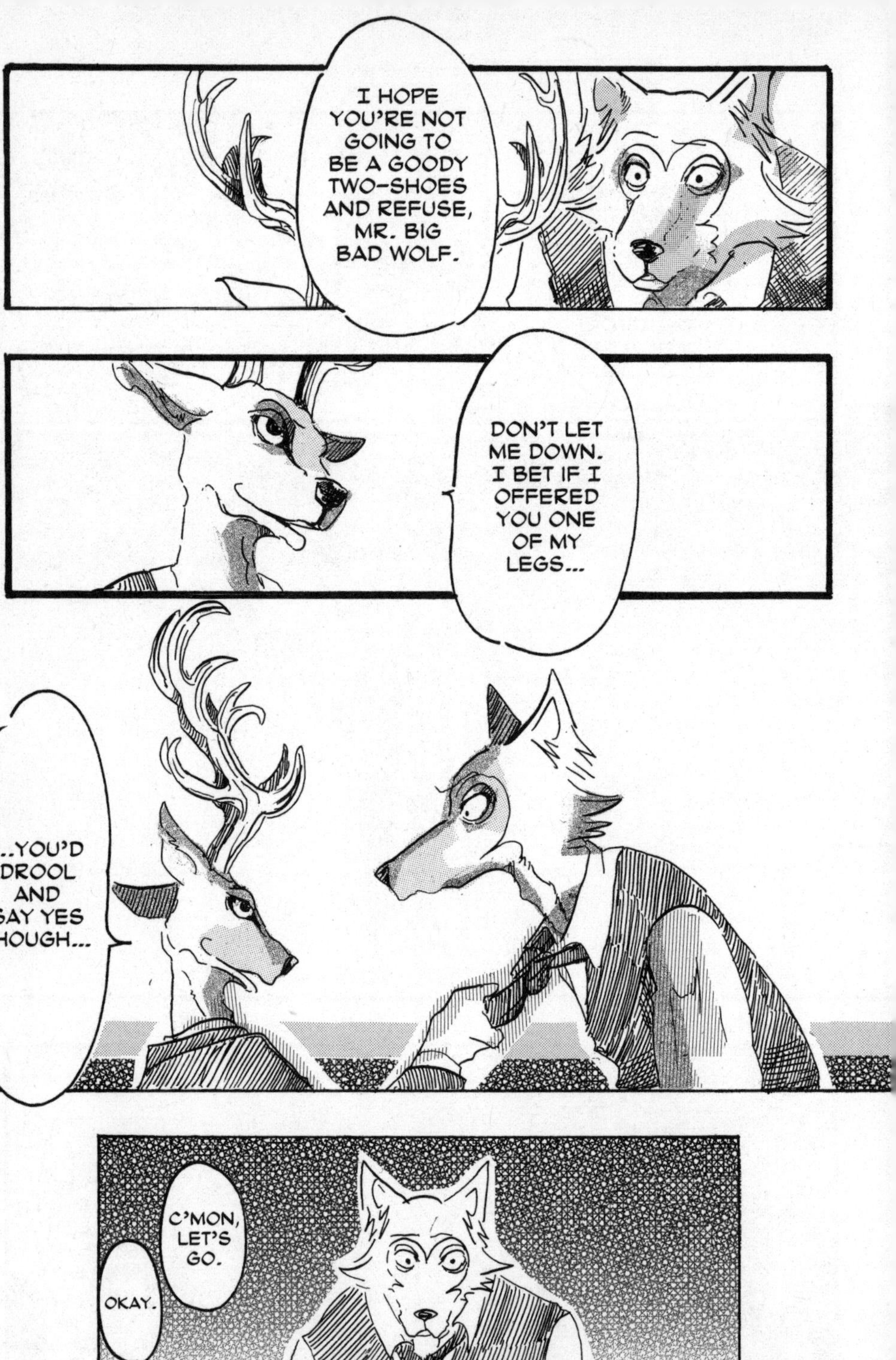
I HOPE YOU'RE NOT GOING TO BE A GOODY TWO-SHOES AND REFUSE, MR. BIG BAD WOLF.
DON'T LET ME DOWN. I BET IF I OFFERED YOU ONE OF MY LEGS...
...YOU'D DROOL AND SAY YES THOUGH...
C'MON, LET'S GO.
OKAY.

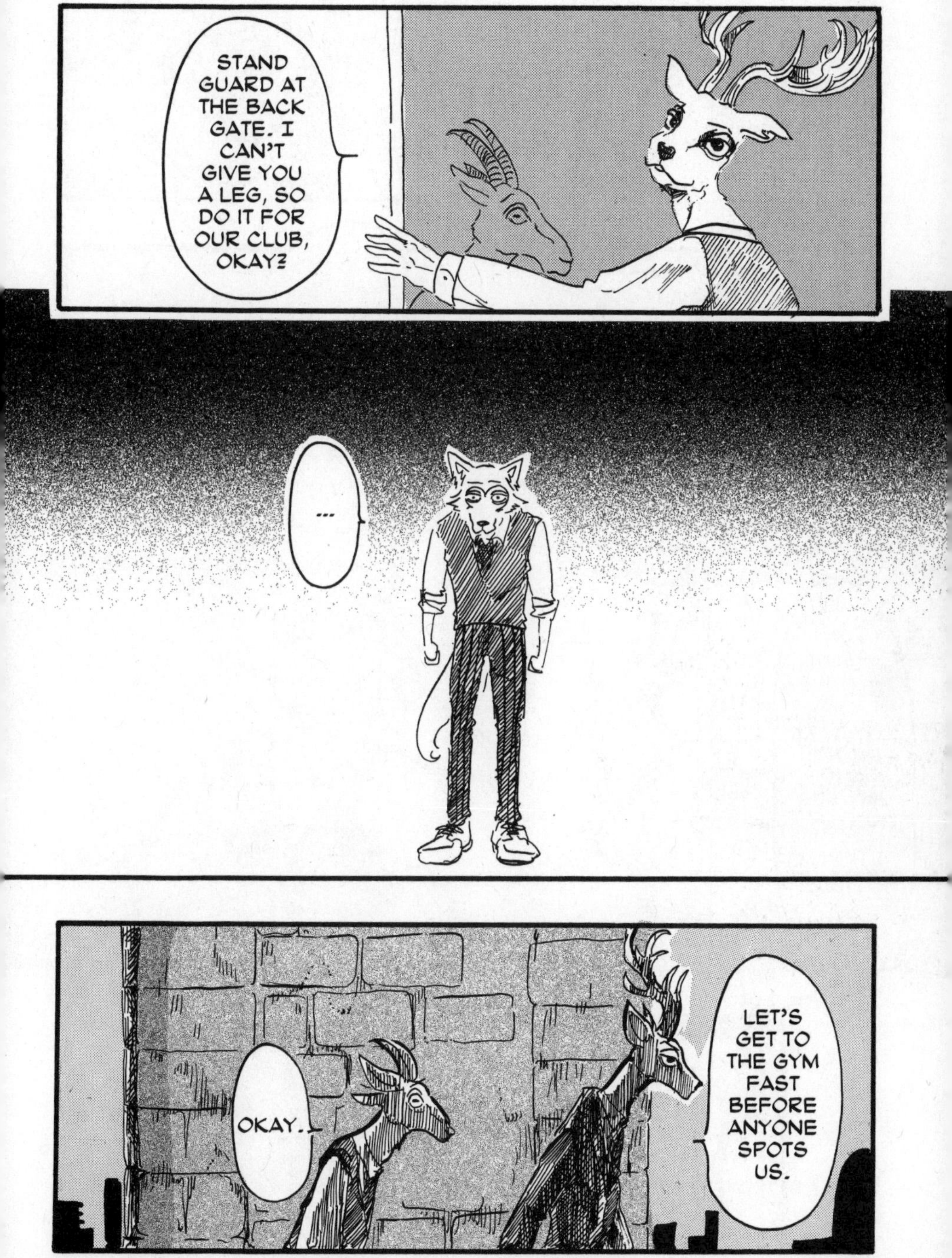
STAND GUARD AT THE BACK GATE. I CAN'T GIVE YOU A LEG, SO DO IT FOR OUR CLUB, OKAY?
...
LET'S GET TO THE GYM FAST BEFORE ANYONE SPOTS US.
OKAY..

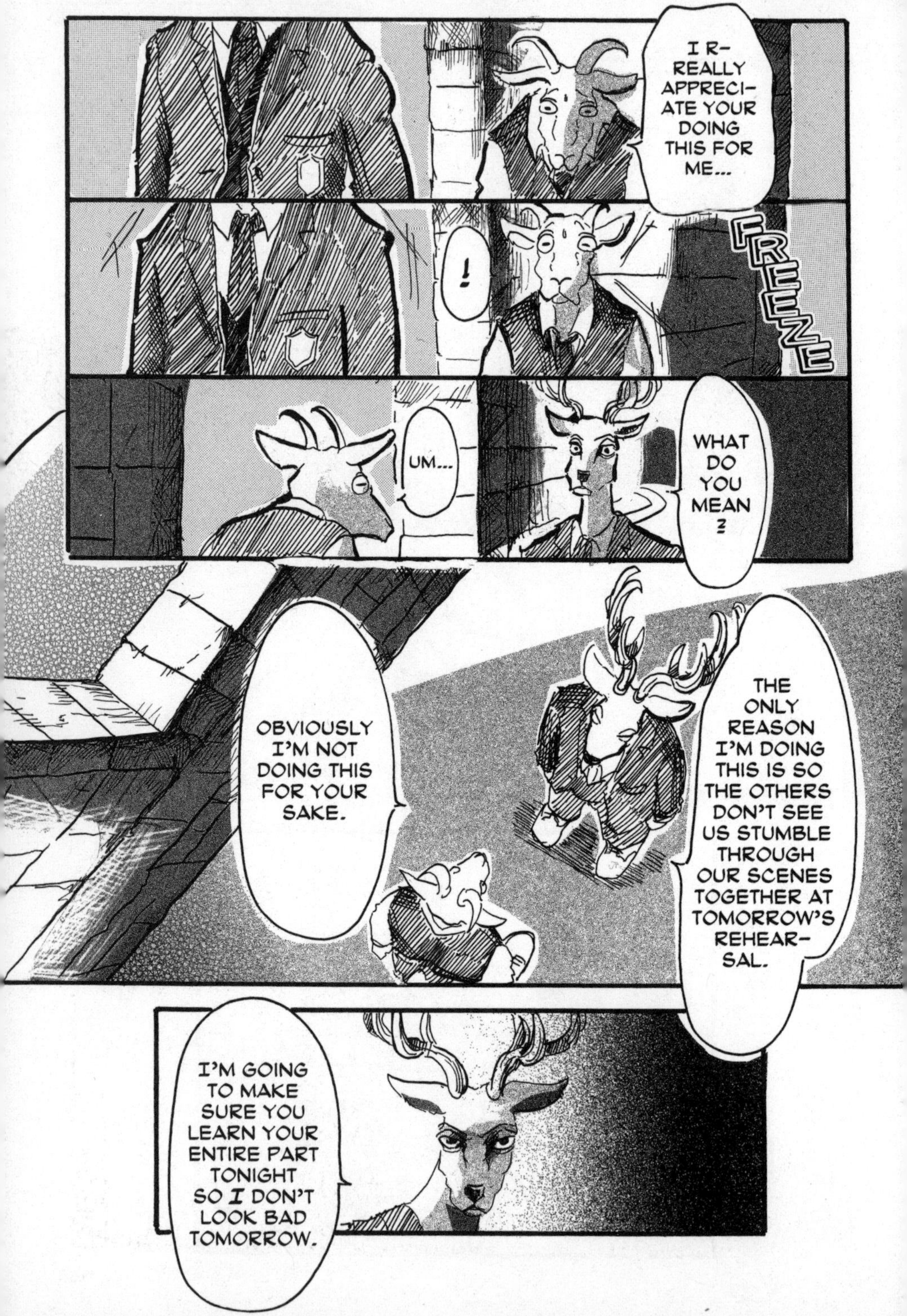
I R-REALLY APPRECIATE YOUR DOING THIS FOR ME...
FREEZE
!
WHAT DO YOU MEAN?
UM...
THE ONLY REASON I'M DOING THIS IS SO THE OTHERS DON'T SEE US STUMBLE THROUGH OUR SCENES TOGETHER AT TOMORROW'S REHEAR-SAL.
OBVIOUSLY I'M NOT DOING THIS FOR YOUR SAKE.
I'M GOING TO MAKE SURE YOU LEARN YOUR ENTIRE PART TONIGHT SO *I* DON'T LOOK BAD TOMORROW.

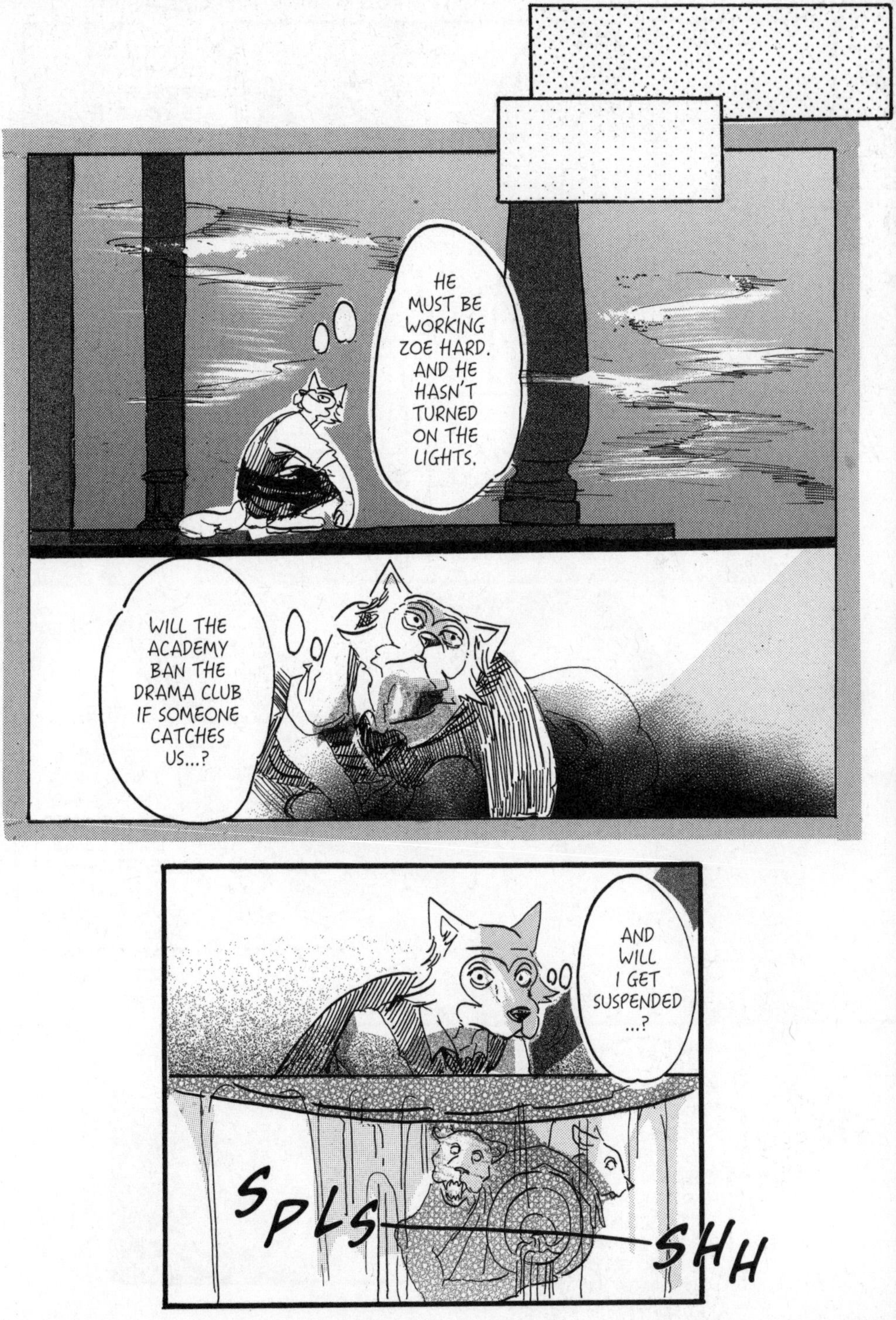
HE MUST BE WORKING ZOE HARD. AND HE HASN'T TURNED ON THE LIGHTS.
WILL THE ACADEMY BAN THE DRAMA CLUB IF SOMEONE CATCHES US...?
AND WILL I GET SUSPENDED ...?
SPLSSHH

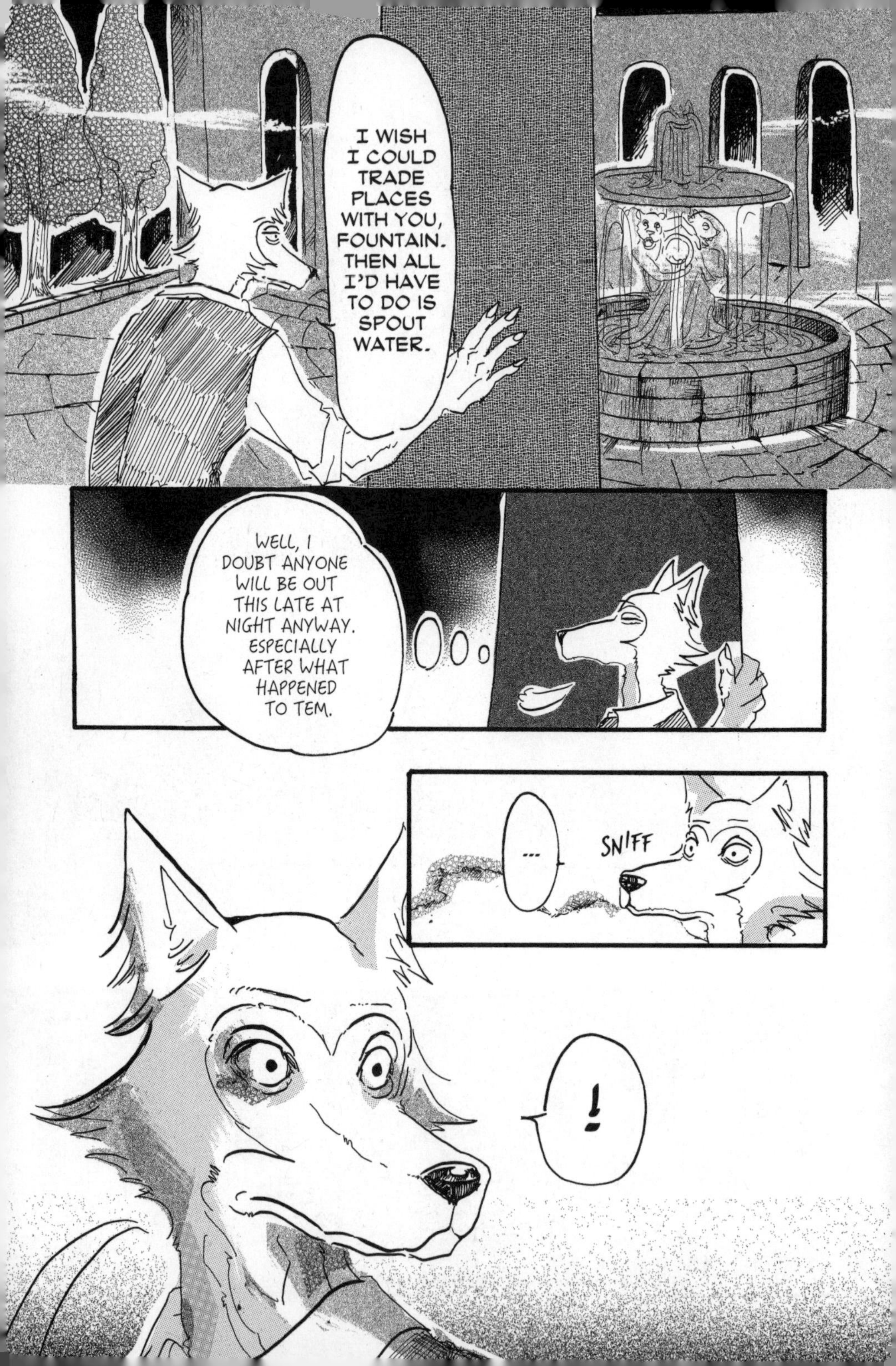

I WISH I COULD TRADE PLACES WITH YOU, FOUNTAIN. THEN ALL I'D HAVE TO DO IS SPOUT WATER.
WELL, I DOUBT ANYONE WILL BE OUT THIS LATE AT NIGHT ANYWAY. ESPECIALLY AFTER WHAT HAPPENED TO TEM.
SNIFF
...
!

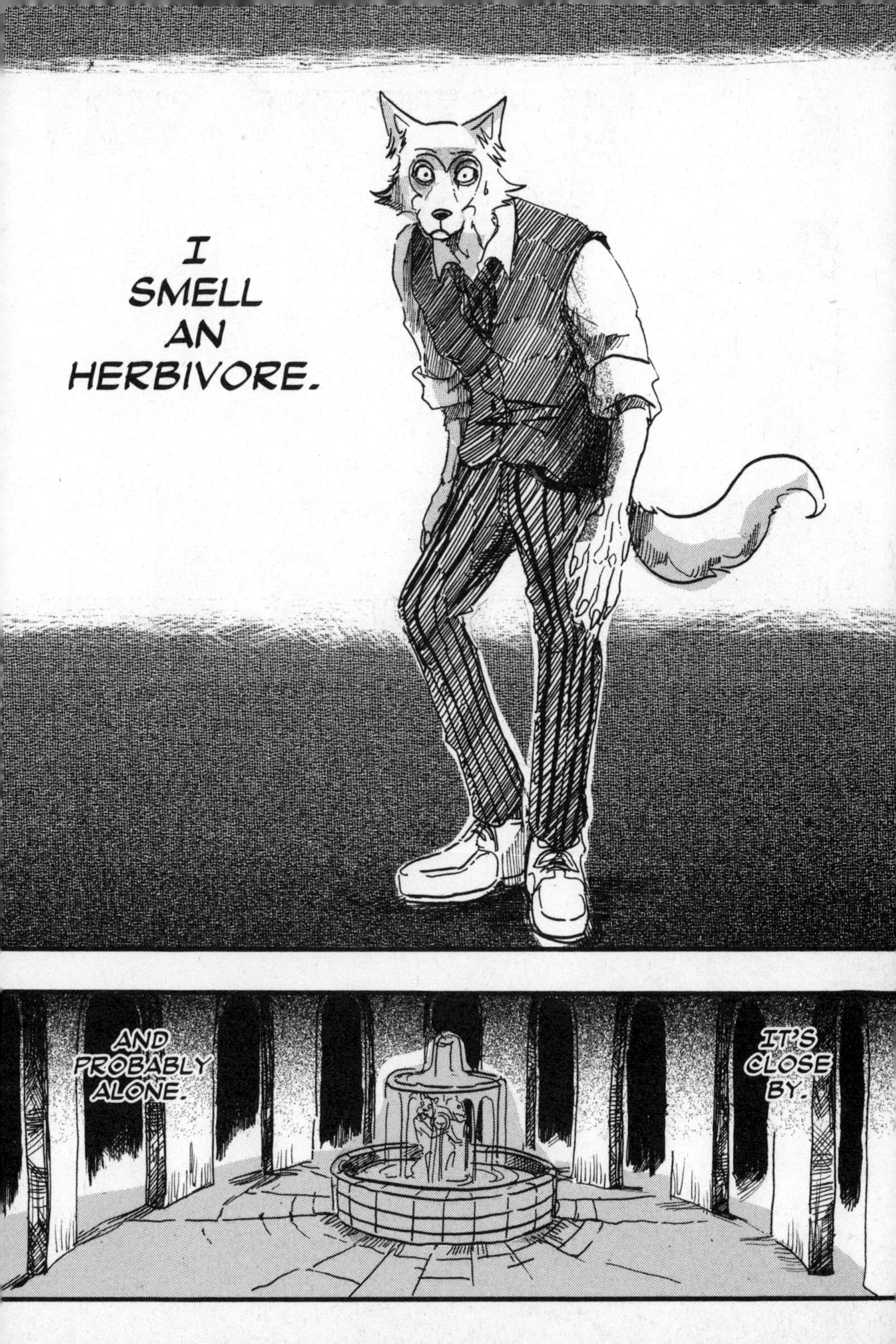
I SMELL AN HERBIVORE.
IT'S CLOSE BY.
AND PROBABLY ALONE.

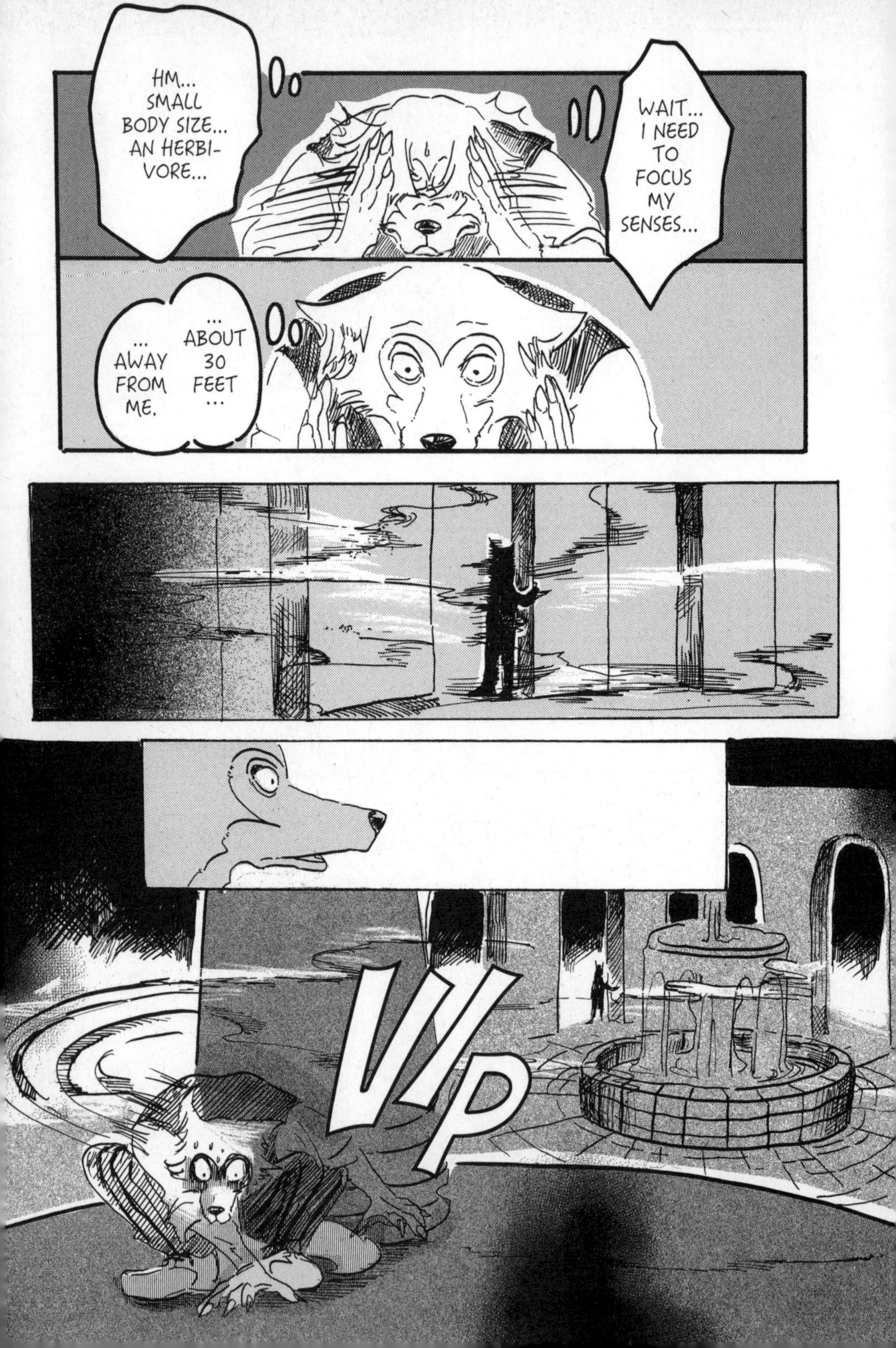
WAIT... I NEED TO FOCUS MY SENSES...
HM... SMALL BODY SIZE... AN HERBI-VORE...
... ABOUT 30 FEET ...
... AWAY FROM ME.
VIP

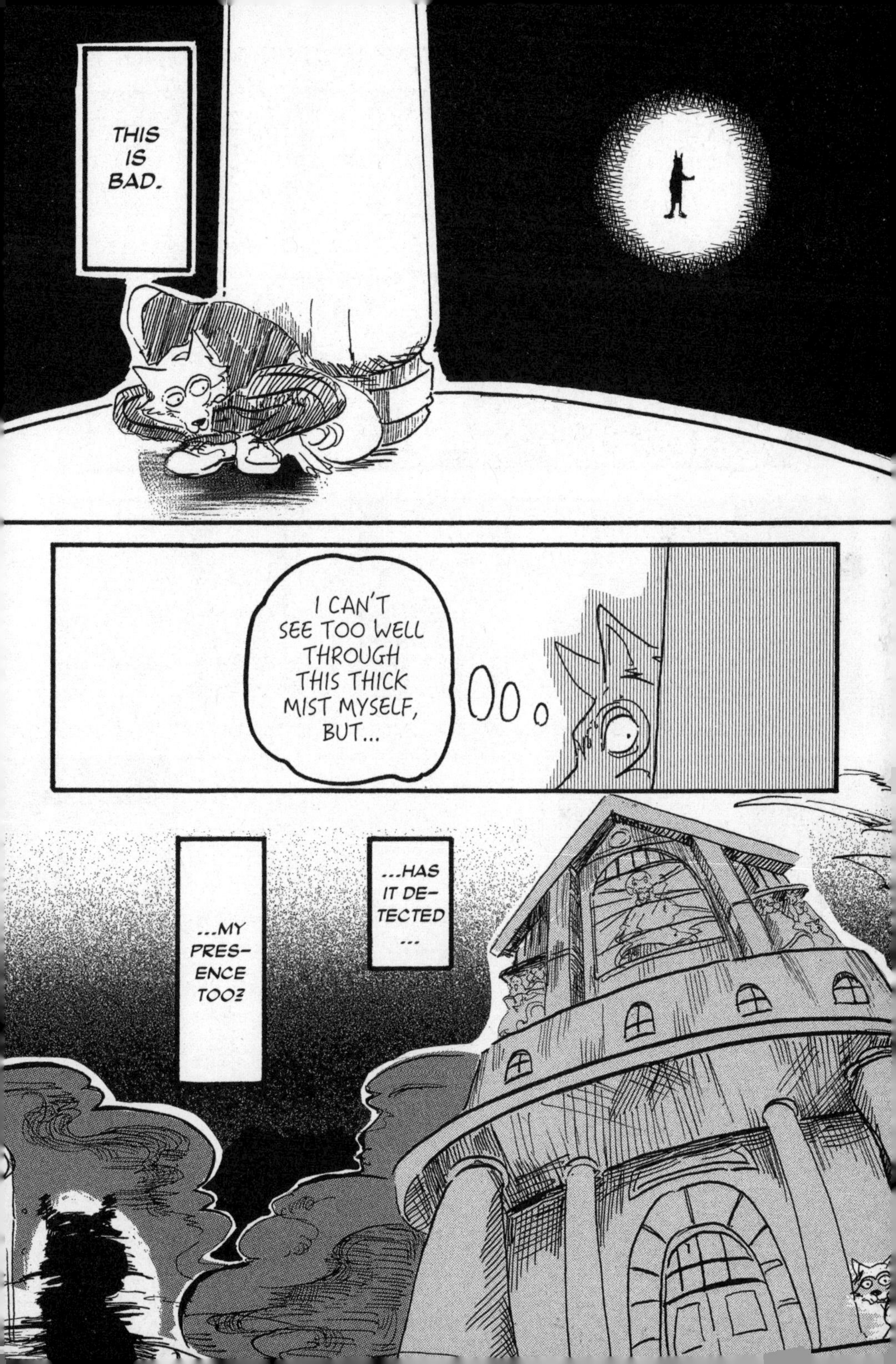
THIS IS BAD.
I CAN'T SEE TOO WELL THROUGH THIS THICK MIST MYSELF, BUT...
...HAS IT DE-TECTED ...
...MY PRES-ENCE TOO?

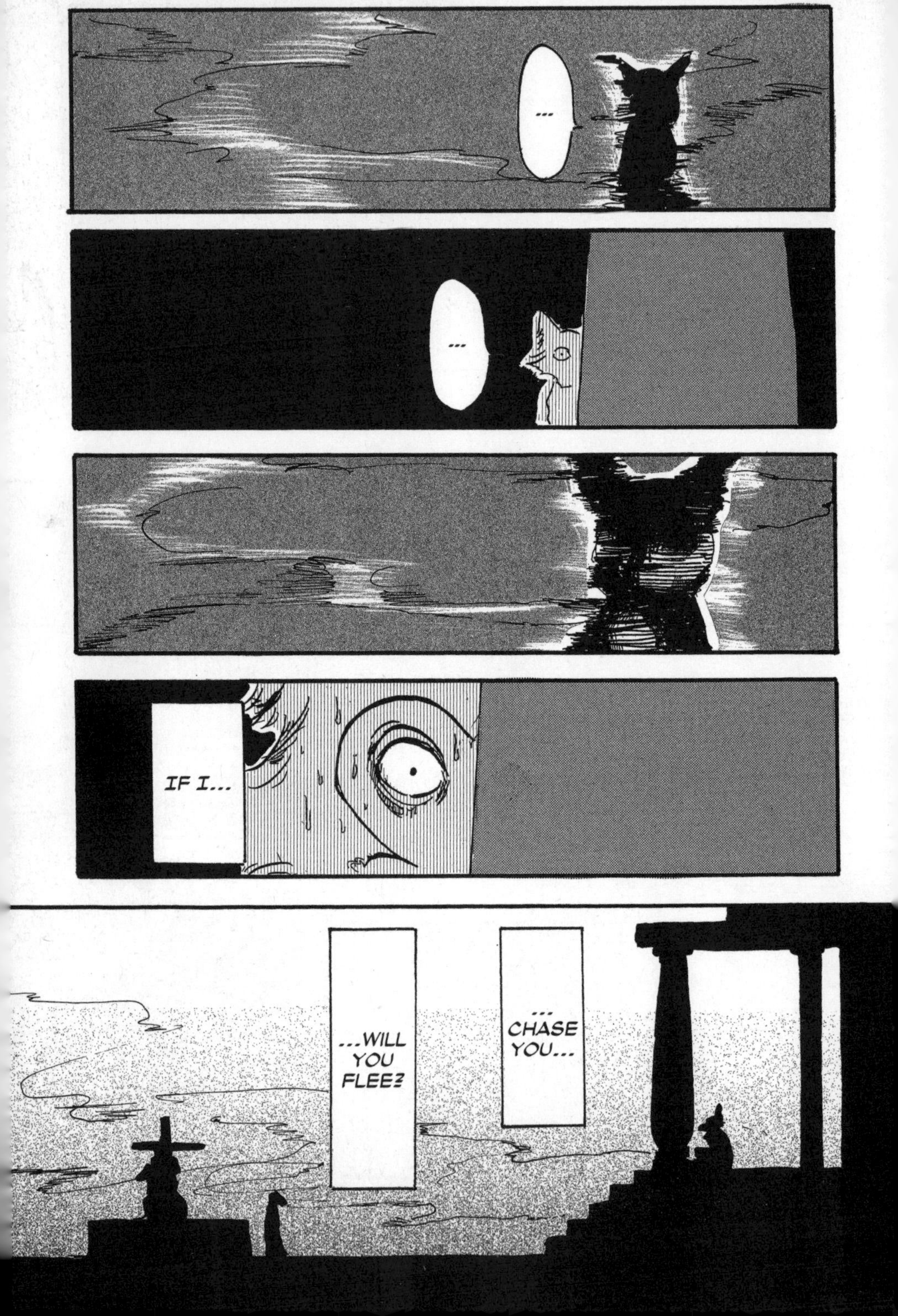
...
...
IF I...
...CHASE YOU...
...WILL YOU FLEE?

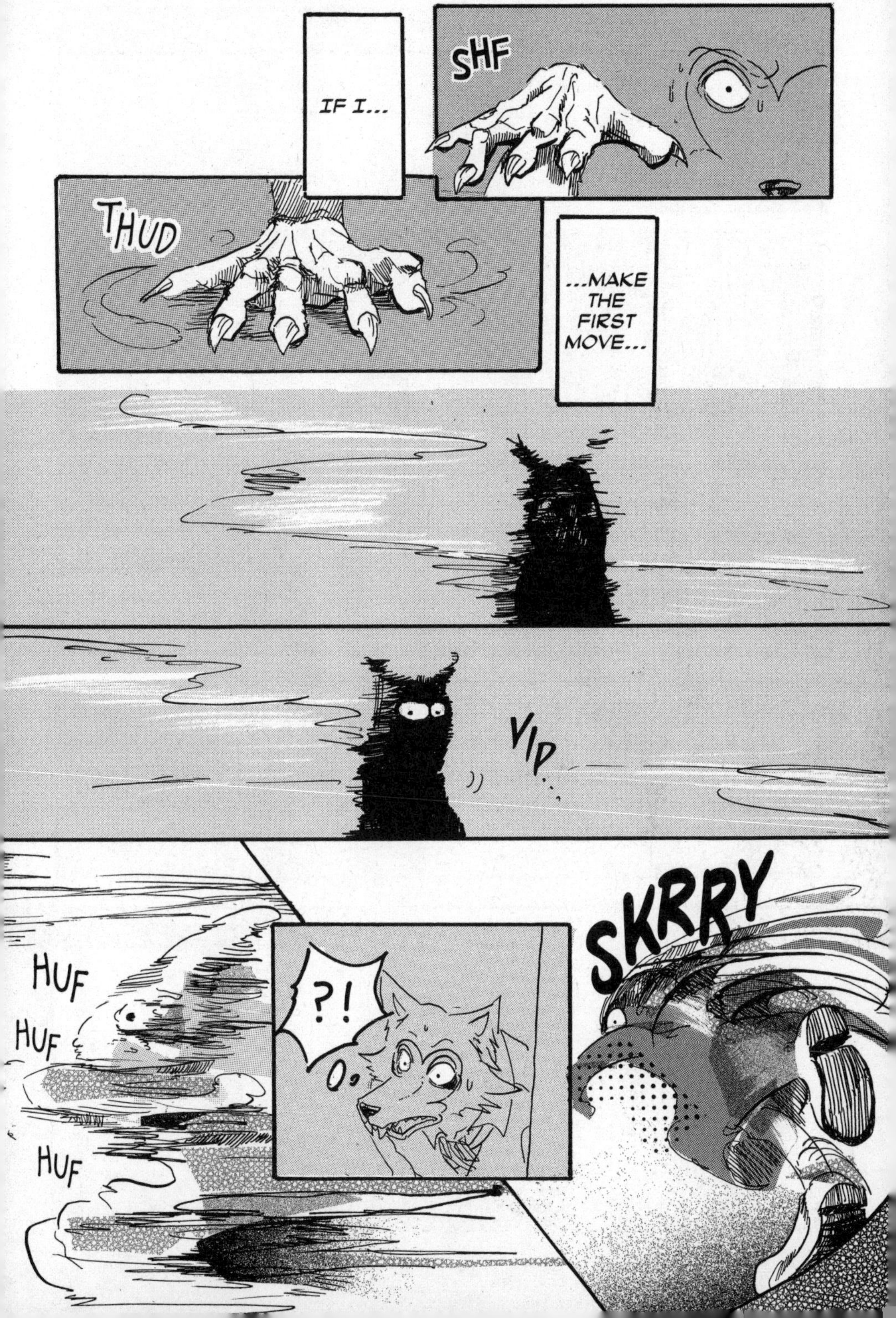
SHF
IF I...
...MAKE THE FIRST MOVE...
THUD
VIP...
SKRRY
?!
HUF
HUF
HUF

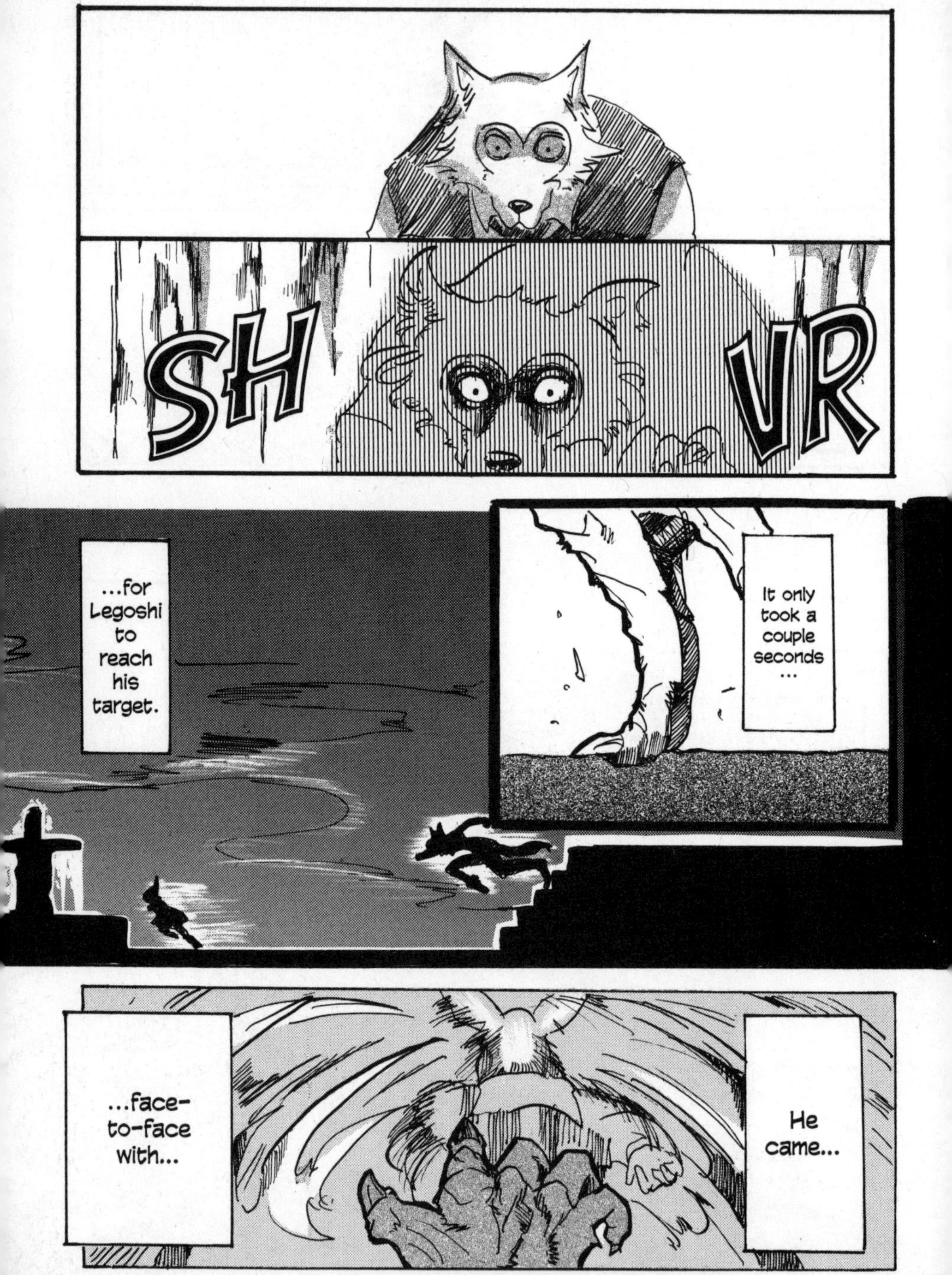
SH
VR
It only took a couple seconds...
...for Legoshi to reach his target.
He came...
...face-to-face with...

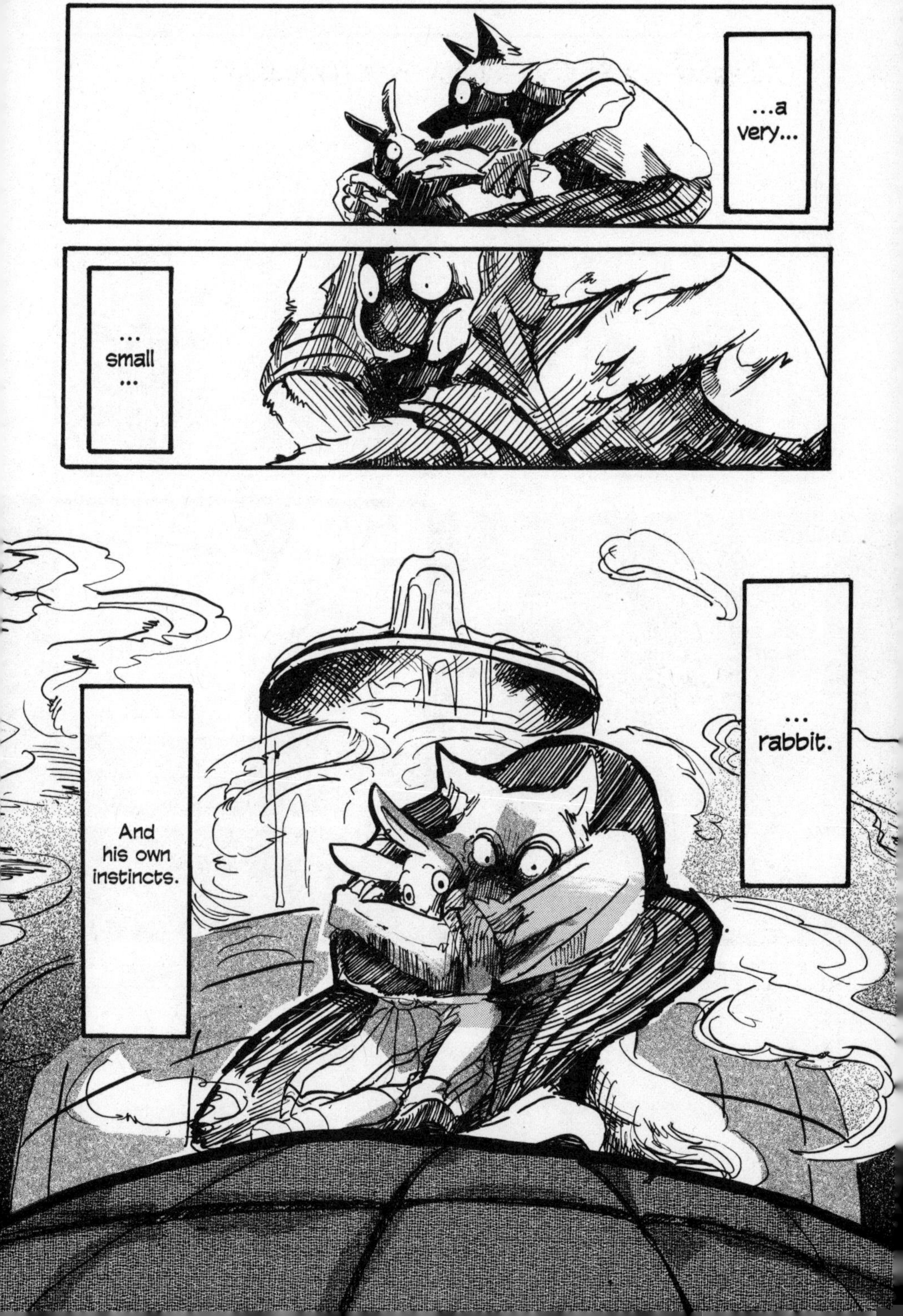
...a very...
... small ...
... rabbit.
And his own instincts.

Chapter 4: A Pretty Bad Day Even for Rabbits

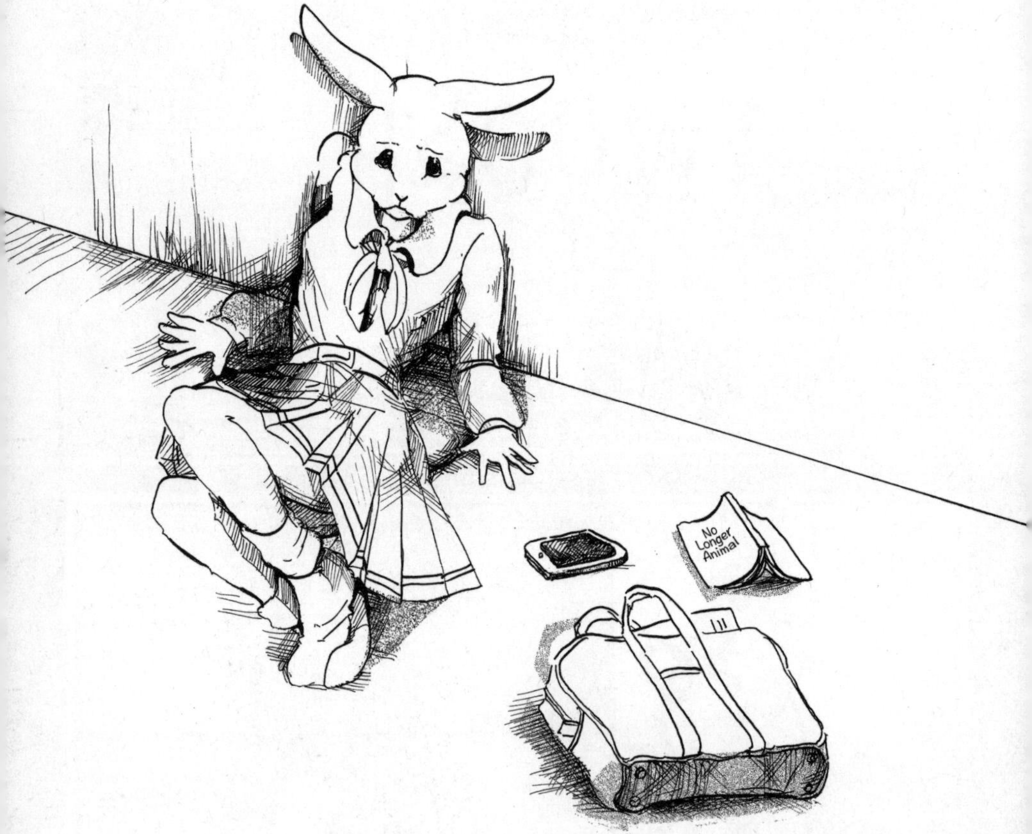
No Longer Animal

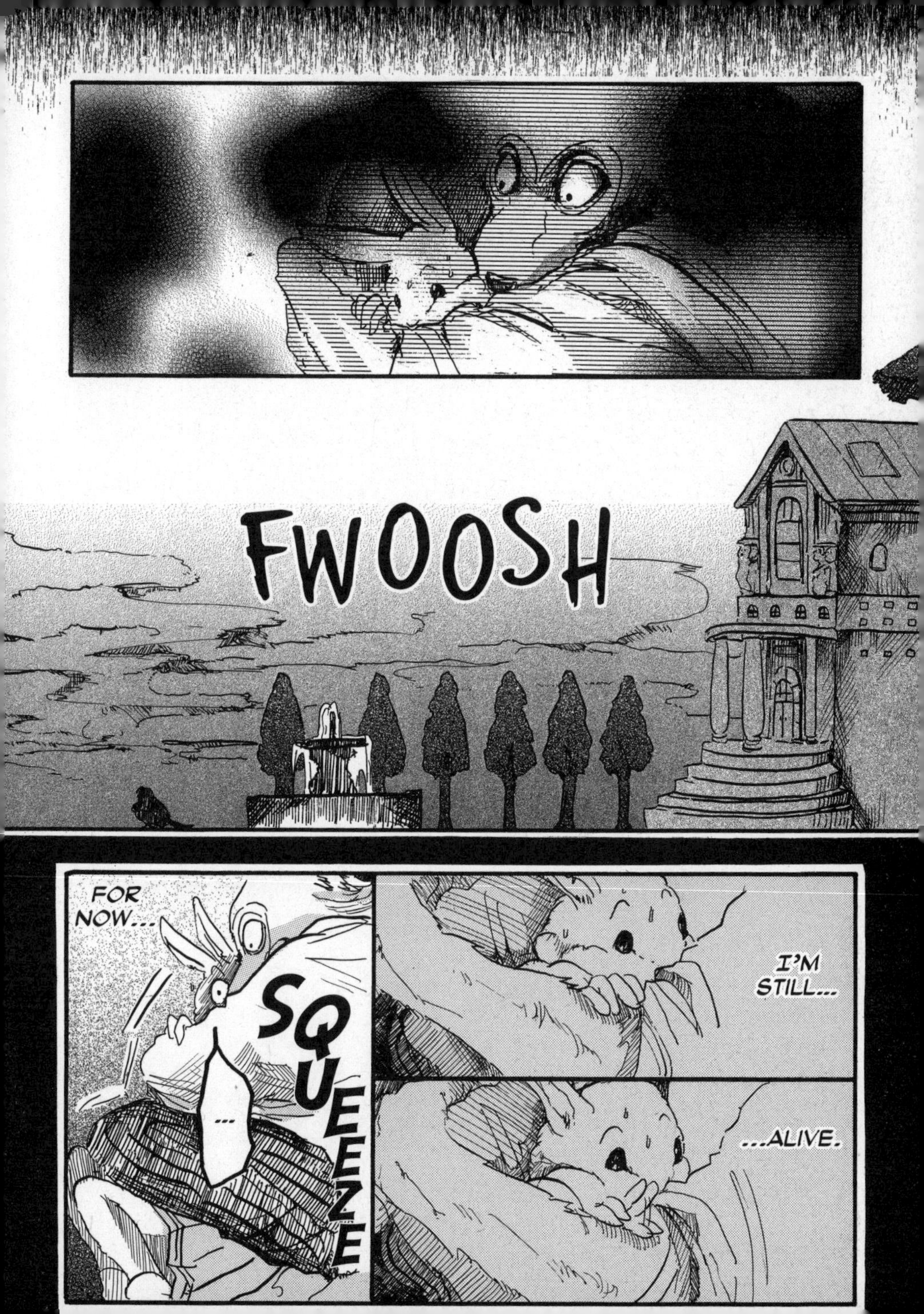
FWOOSH
FOR NOW...
SQUEEZE
...
I'M STILL...
...ALIVE.

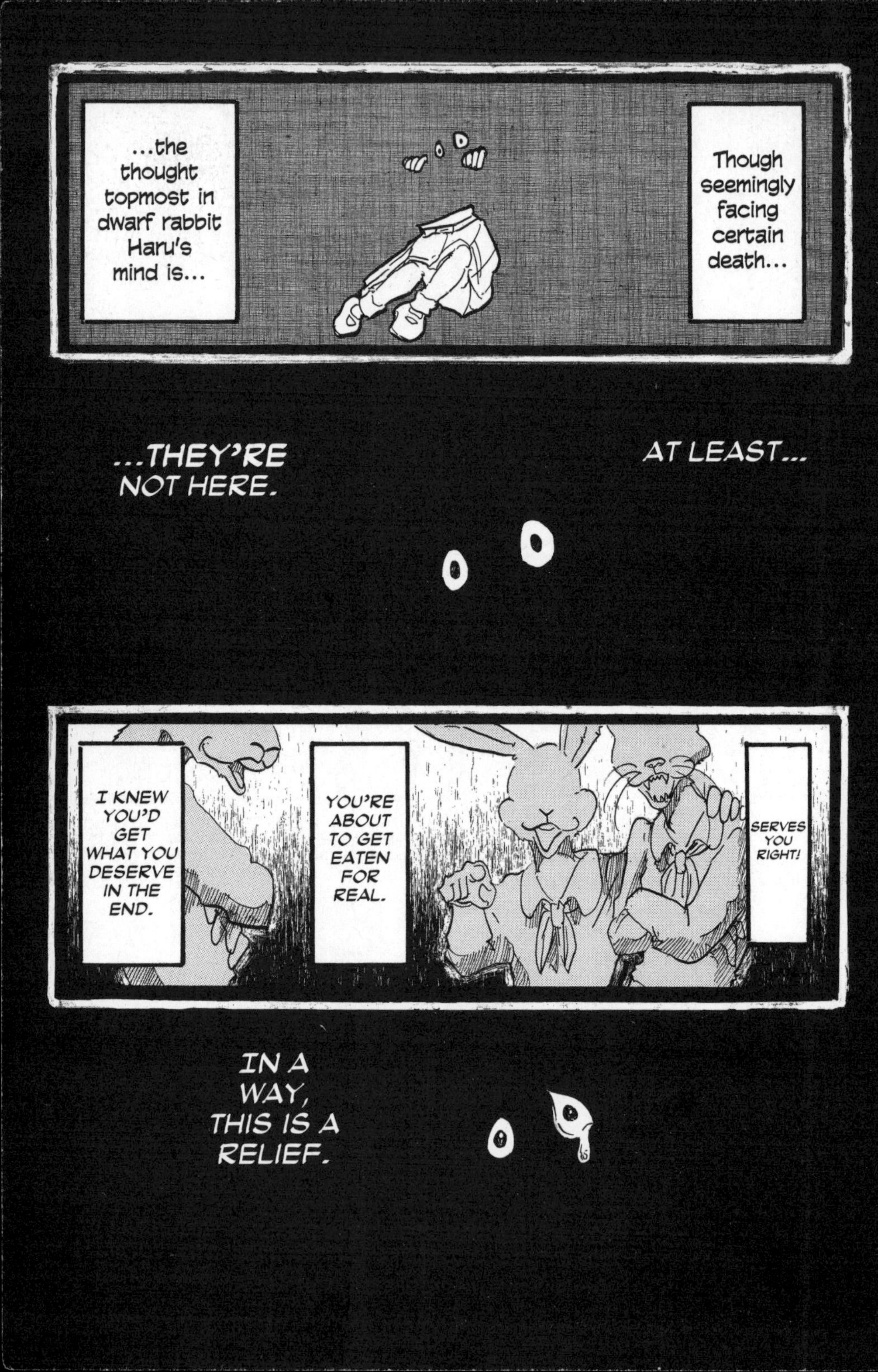
Though seemingly facing certain death...
...the thought topmost in dwarf rabbit Haru's mind is...
AT LEAST...
...THEY'RE NOT HERE.
SERVES YOU RIGHT!
YOU'RE ABOUT TO GET EATEN FOR REAL.
I KNEW YOU'D GET WHAT YOU DESERVE IN THE END.
IN A WAY, THIS IS A RELIEF.

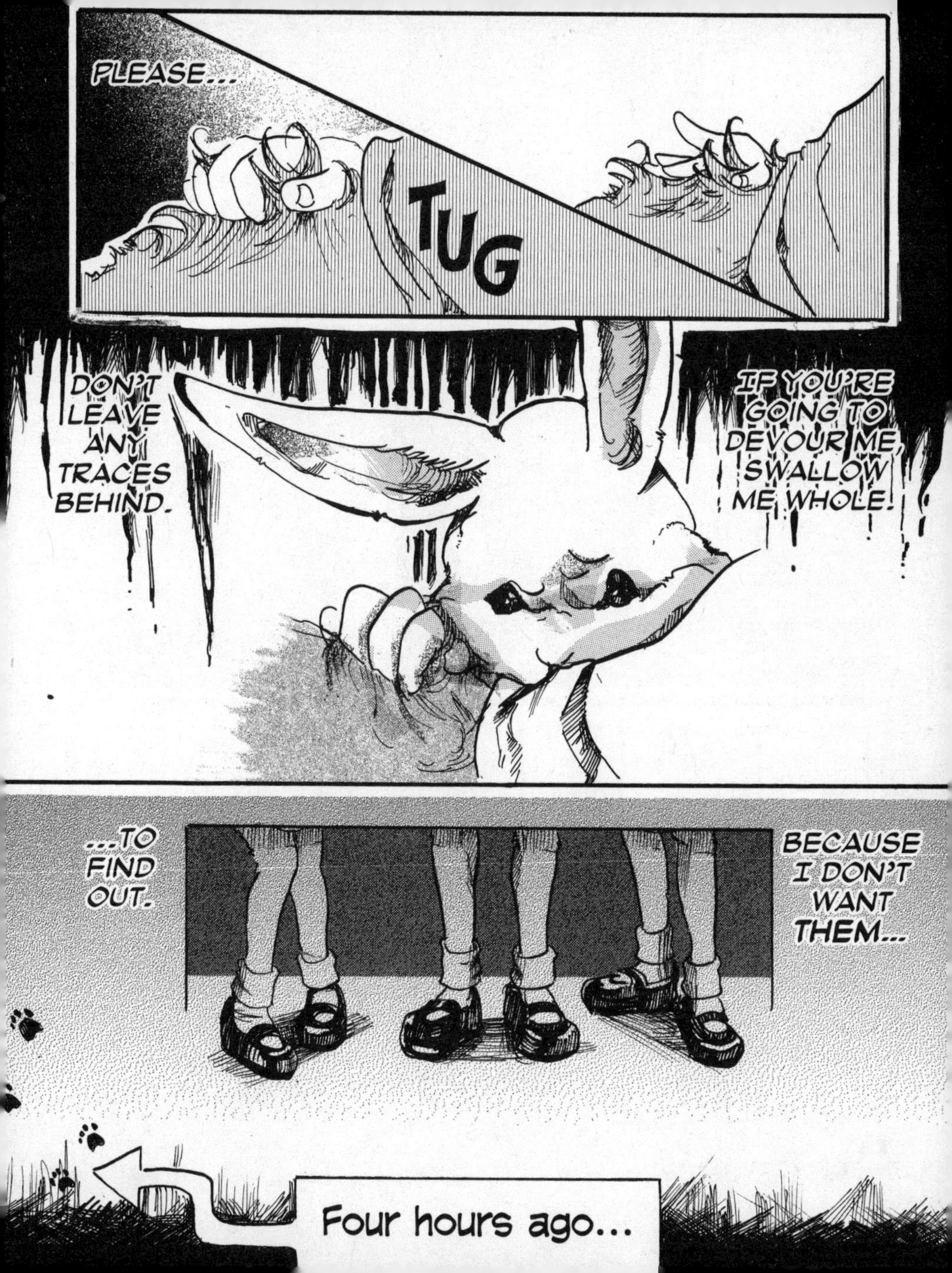
PLEASE...
TUG
IF YOU'RE GOING TO DEVOUR ME, SWALLOW ME WHOLE!
DON'T LEAVE ANY TRACES BEHIND.
BECAUSE I DON'T WANT THEM...
...TO FIND OUT.
Four hours ago...

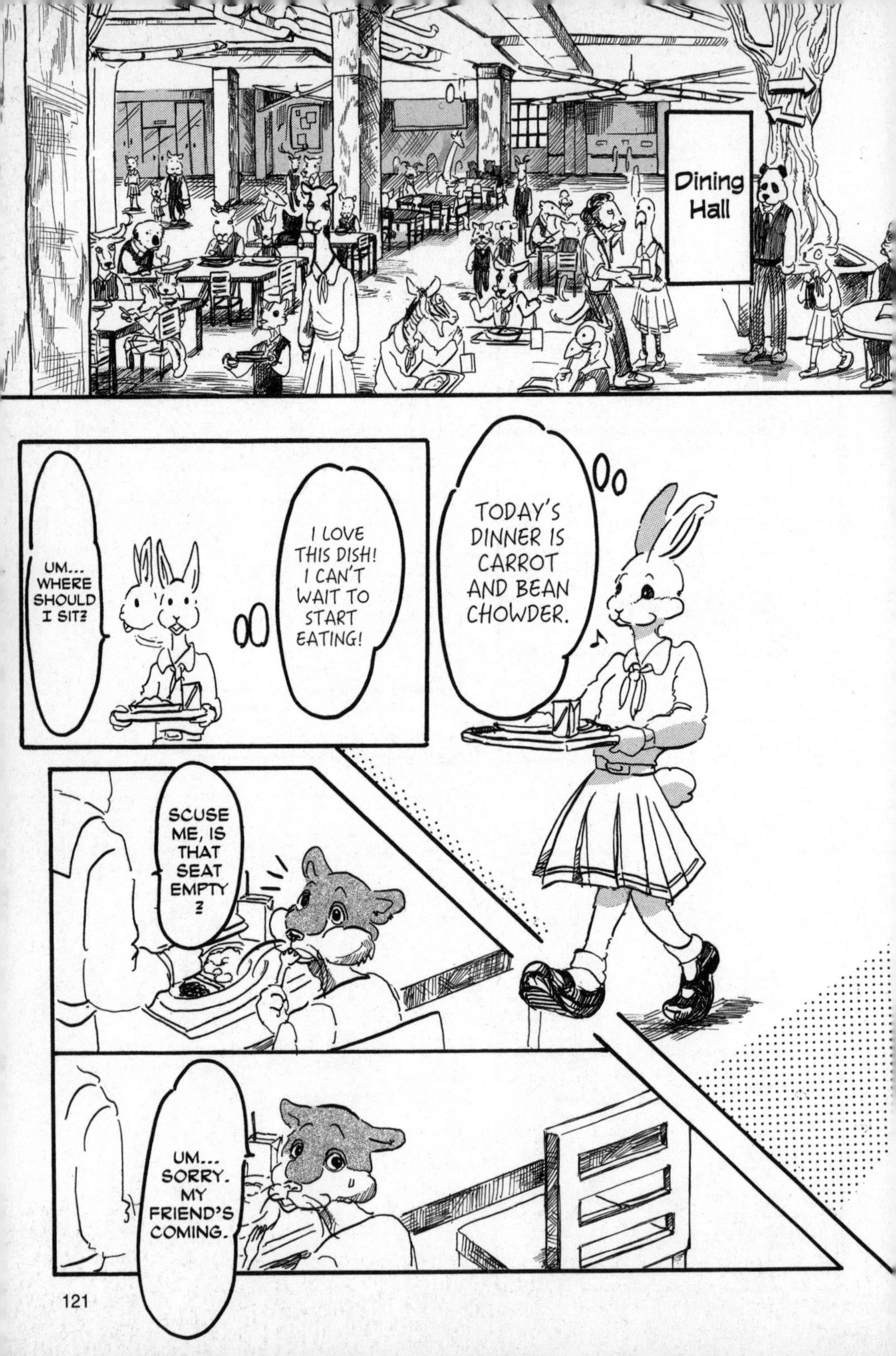
Dining Hall
TODAY'S DINNER IS CARROT AND BEAN CHOWDER.
I LOVE THIS DISH! I CAN'T WAIT TO START EATING!
UM... WHERE SHOULD I SIT?
SCUSE ME, IS THAT SEAT EMPTY?
UM... SORRY. MY FRIEND'S COMING.

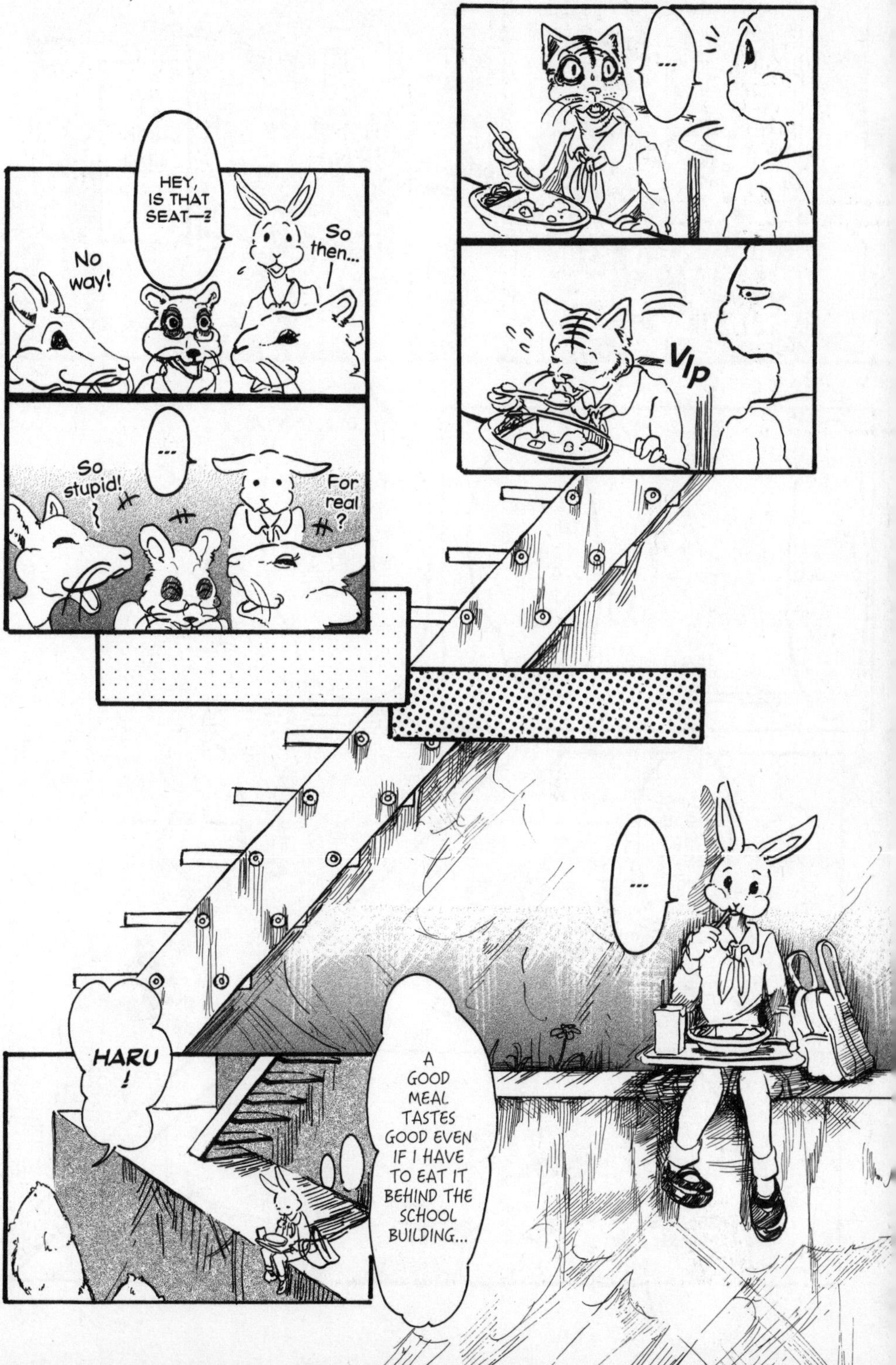
...
Vlp
HEY, IS THAT SEAT—?
So then...
No way!
...
For real?
So stupid!
...
A GOOD MEAL TASTES GOOD EVEN IF I HAVE TO EAT IT BEHIND THE SCHOOL BUILDING...
HARU!

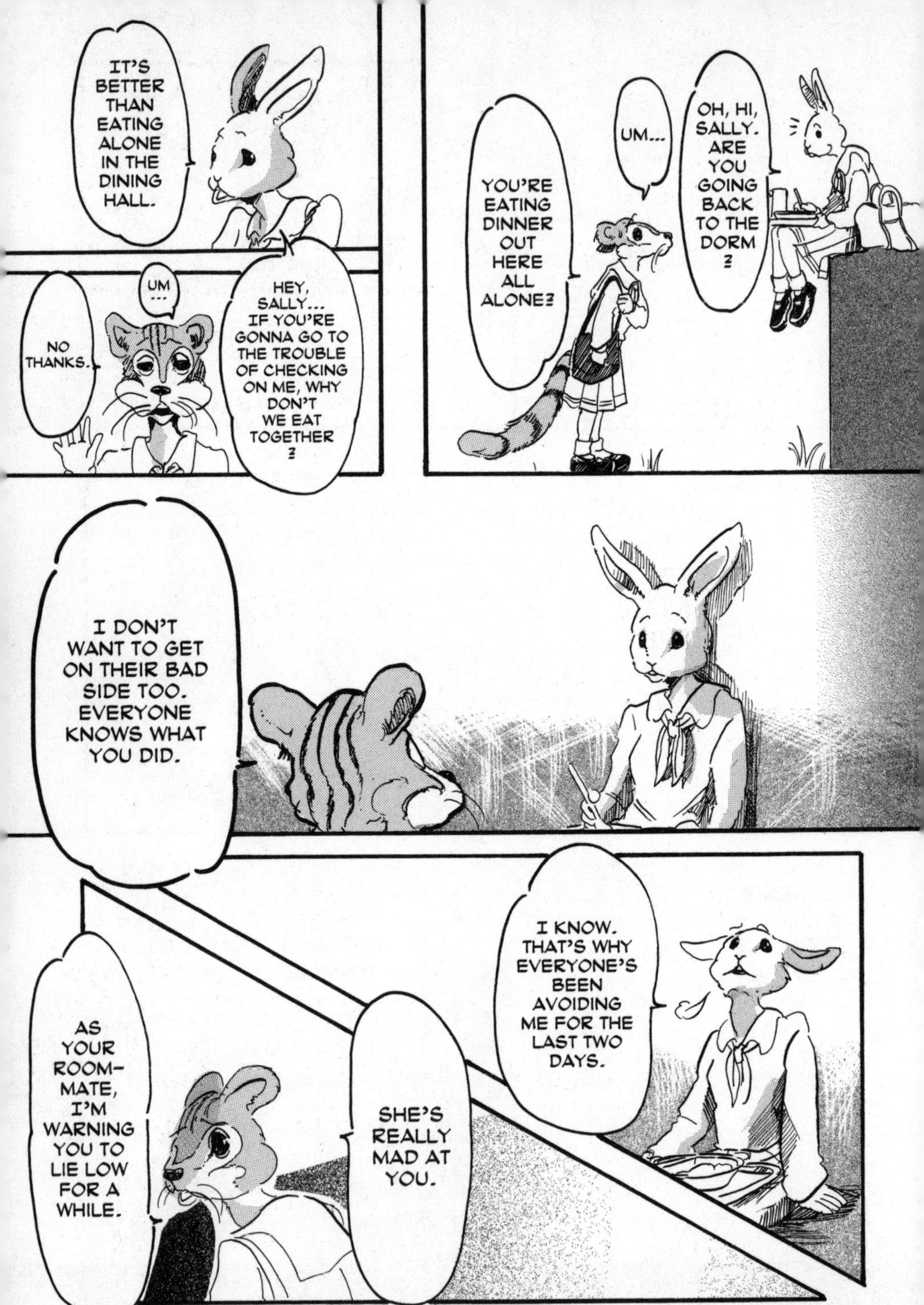
OH, HI, SALLY. ARE YOU GOING BACK TO THE DORM?
UM...
YOU'RE EATING DINNER OUT HERE ALL ALONE?
IT'S BETTER THAN EATING ALONE IN THE DINING HALL.
HEY, SALLY... IF YOU'RE GONNA GO TO THE TROUBLE OF CHECKING ON ME, WHY DON'T WE EAT TOGETHER?
UM ...
NO THANKS.
I DON'T WANT TO GET ON THEIR BAD SIDE TOO. EVERYONE KNOWS WHAT YOU DID.
I KNOW. THAT'S WHY EVERYONE'S BEEN AVOIDING ME FOR THE LAST TWO DAYS.
SHE'S REALLY MAD AT YOU.
AS YOUR ROOM-MATE, I'M WARNING YOU TO LIE LOW FOR A WHILE.

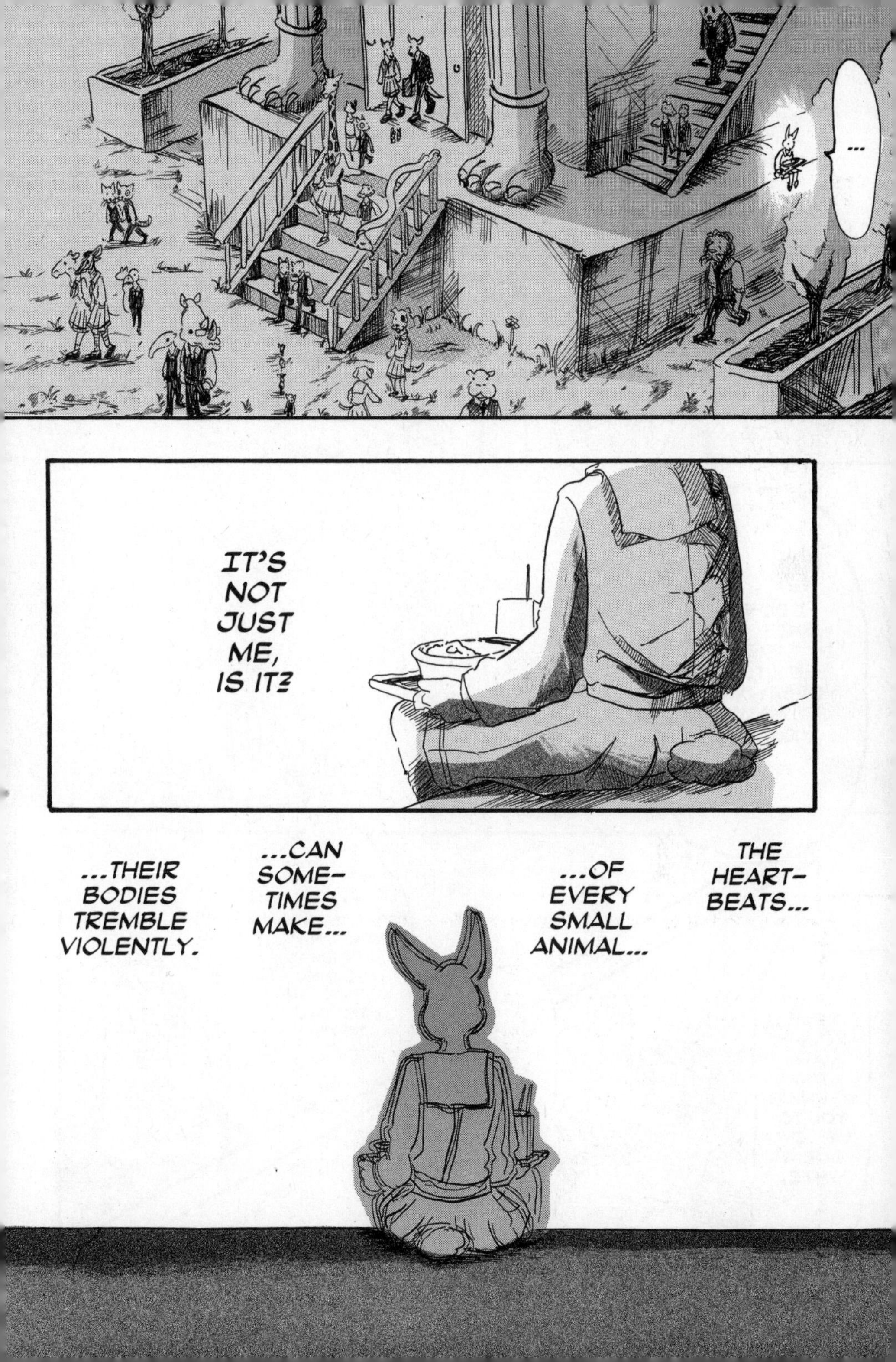
...
IT'S NOT JUST ME, IS IT?
THE HEART-BEATS...
...OF EVERY SMALL ANIMAL...
...CAN SOME-TIMES MAKE...
...THEIR BODIES TREMBLE VIOLENTLY.

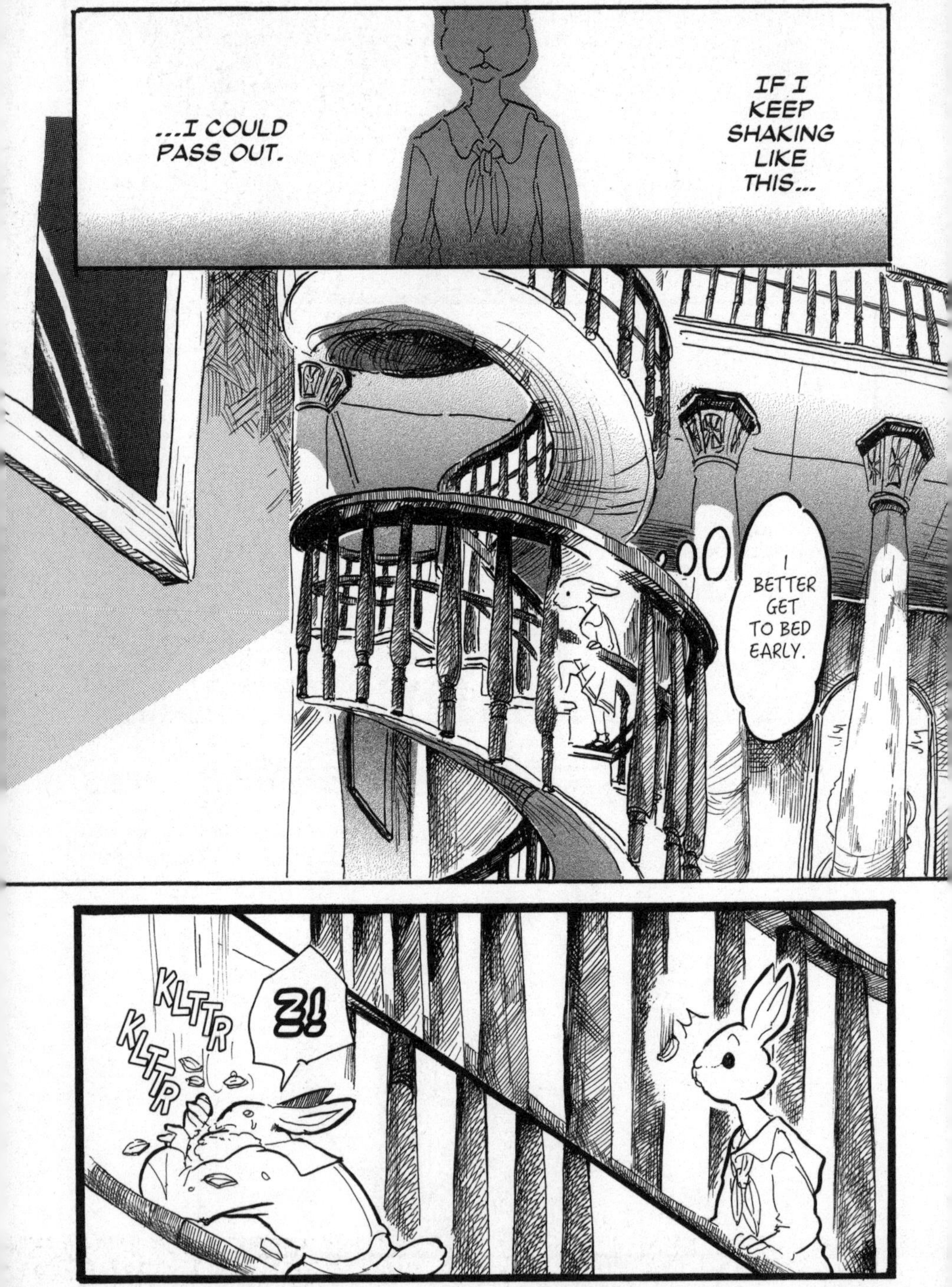
IF I KEEP SHAKING LIKE THIS...
...I COULD PASS OUT.
I BETTER GET TO BED EARLY.
Z!
KLTTR KLTTR

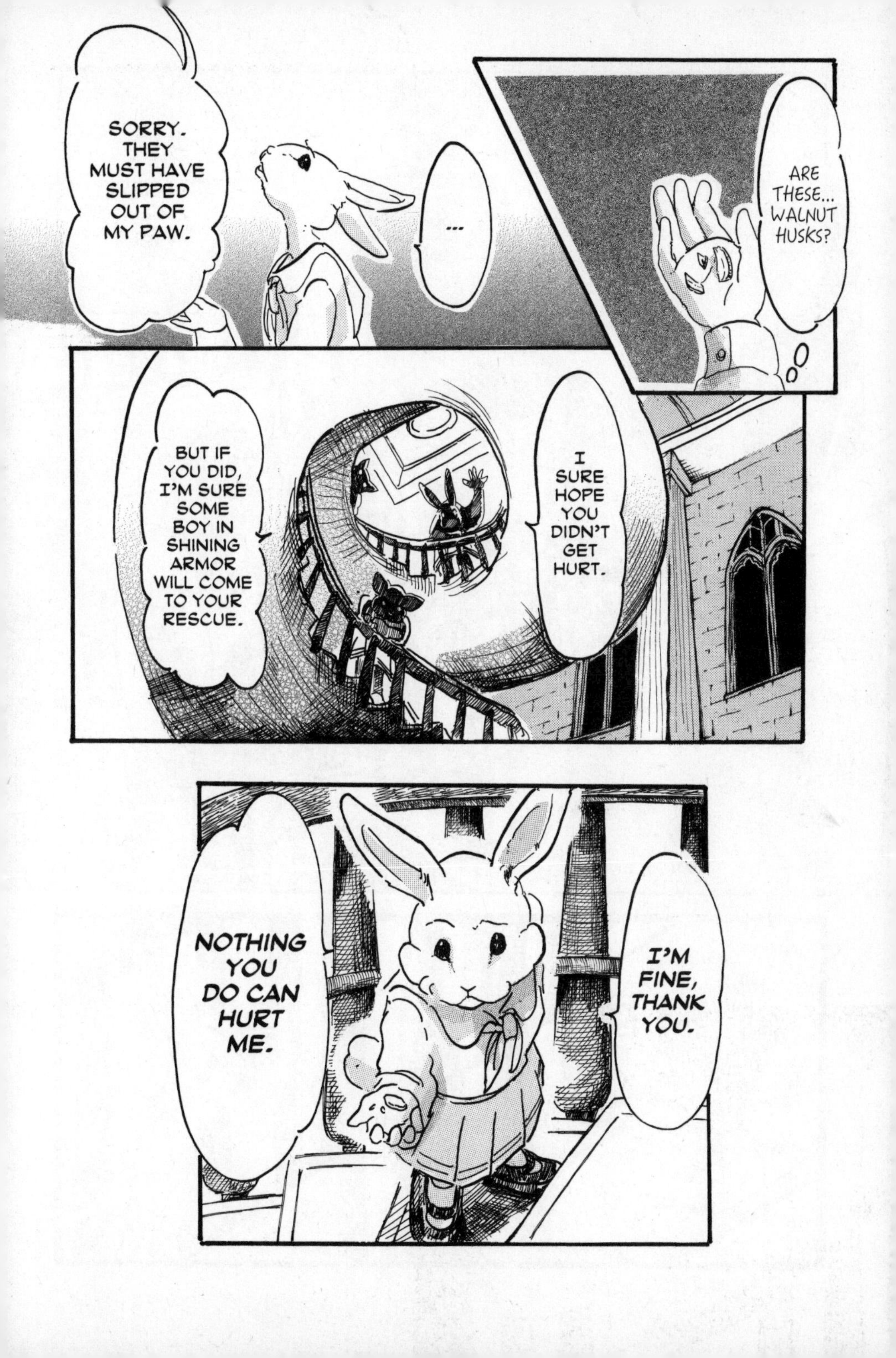
ARE THESE... WALNUT HUSKS?
...
SORRY. THEY MUST HAVE SLIPPED OUT OF MY PAW.
I SURE HOPE YOU DIDN'T GET HURT.
BUT IF YOU DID, I'M SURE SOME BOY IN SHINING ARMOR WILL COME TO YOUR RESCUE.
I'M FINE, THANK YOU.
NOTHING YOU DO CAN HURT ME.

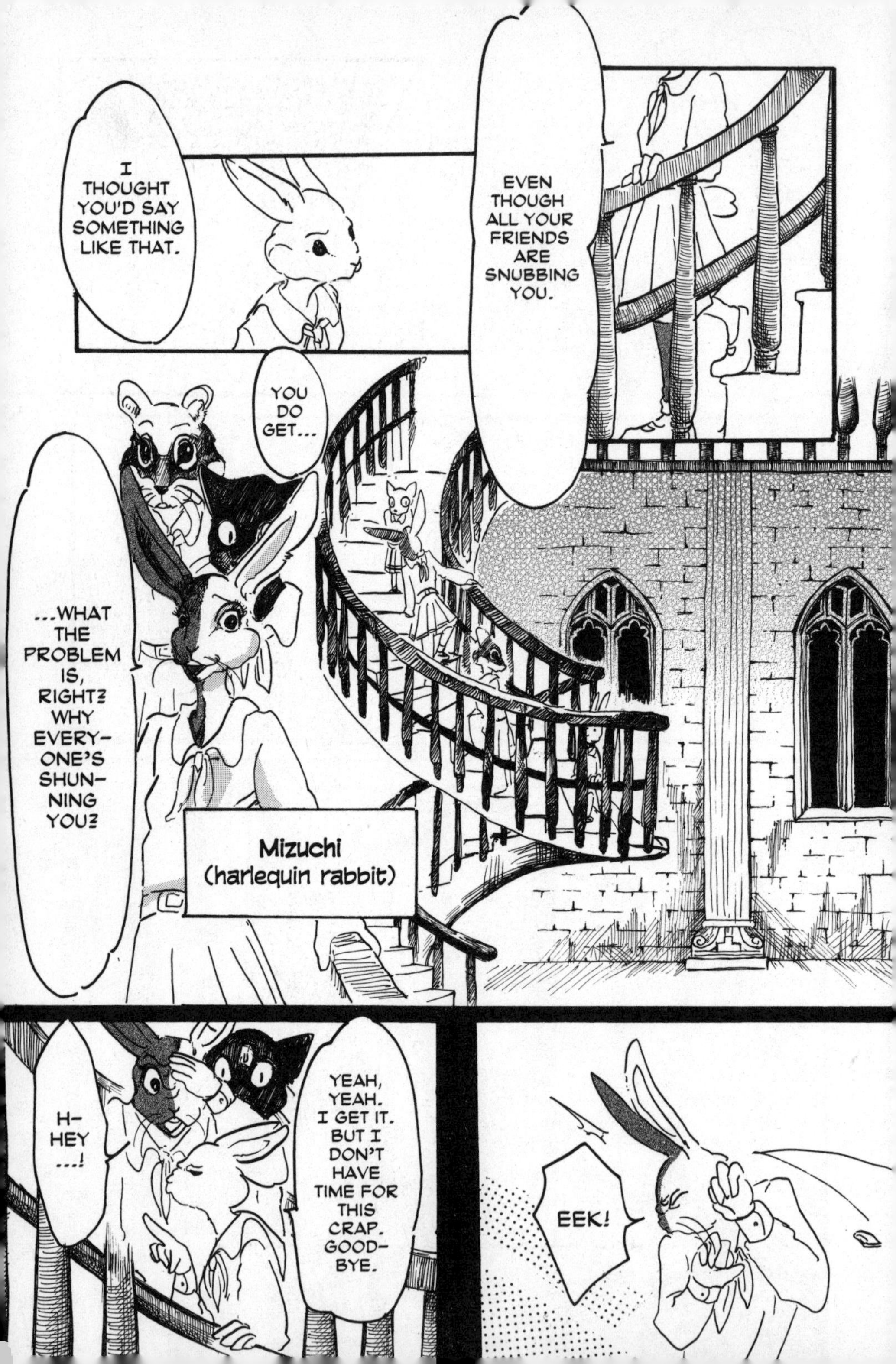
EVEN THOUGH ALL YOUR FRIENDS ARE SNUBBING YOU.
I THOUGHT YOU'D SAY SOMETHING LIKE THAT.
YOU DO GET...
...WHAT THE PROBLEM IS, RIGHT? WHY EVERYONE'S SHUNNING YOU?
Mizuchi (harlequin rabbit)
EEK!
YEAH, YEAH. I GET IT. BUT I DON'T HAVE TIME FOR THIS CRAP. GOODBYE.
H-HEY...!

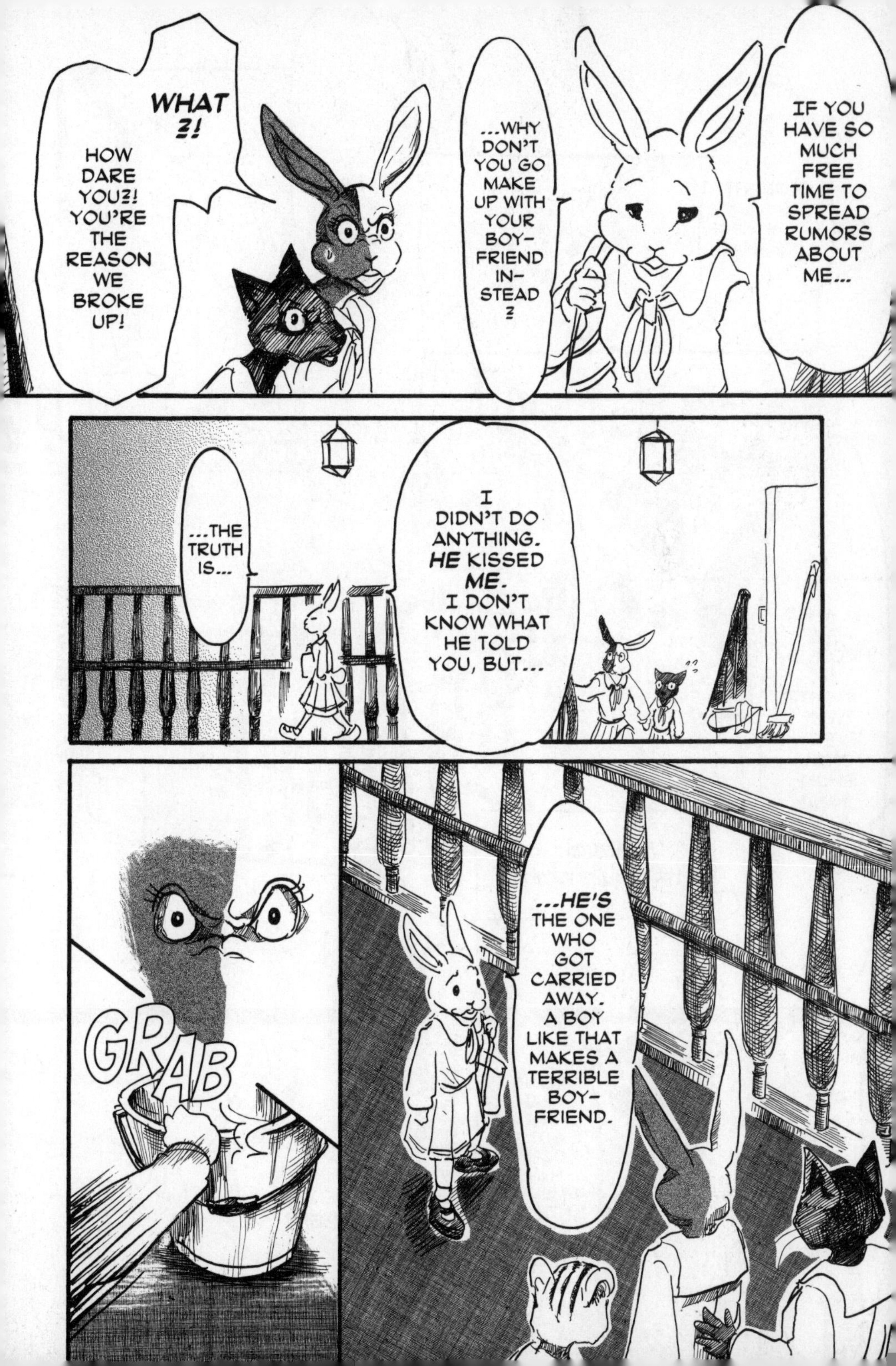
IF YOU HAVE SO MUCH FREE TIME TO SPREAD RUMORS ABOUT ME...
...WHY DON'T YOU GO MAKE UP WITH YOUR BOY-FRIEND IN-STEAD?
WHAT?!
HOW DARE YOU?! YOU'RE THE REASON WE BROKE UP!
...THE TRUTH IS...
I DIDN'T DO ANYTHING. HE KISSED ME. I DON'T KNOW WHAT HE TOLD YOU, BUT...
...HE'S THE ONE WHO GOT CARRIED AWAY. A BOY LIKE THAT MAKES A TERRIBLE BOY-FRIEND.
GRAB

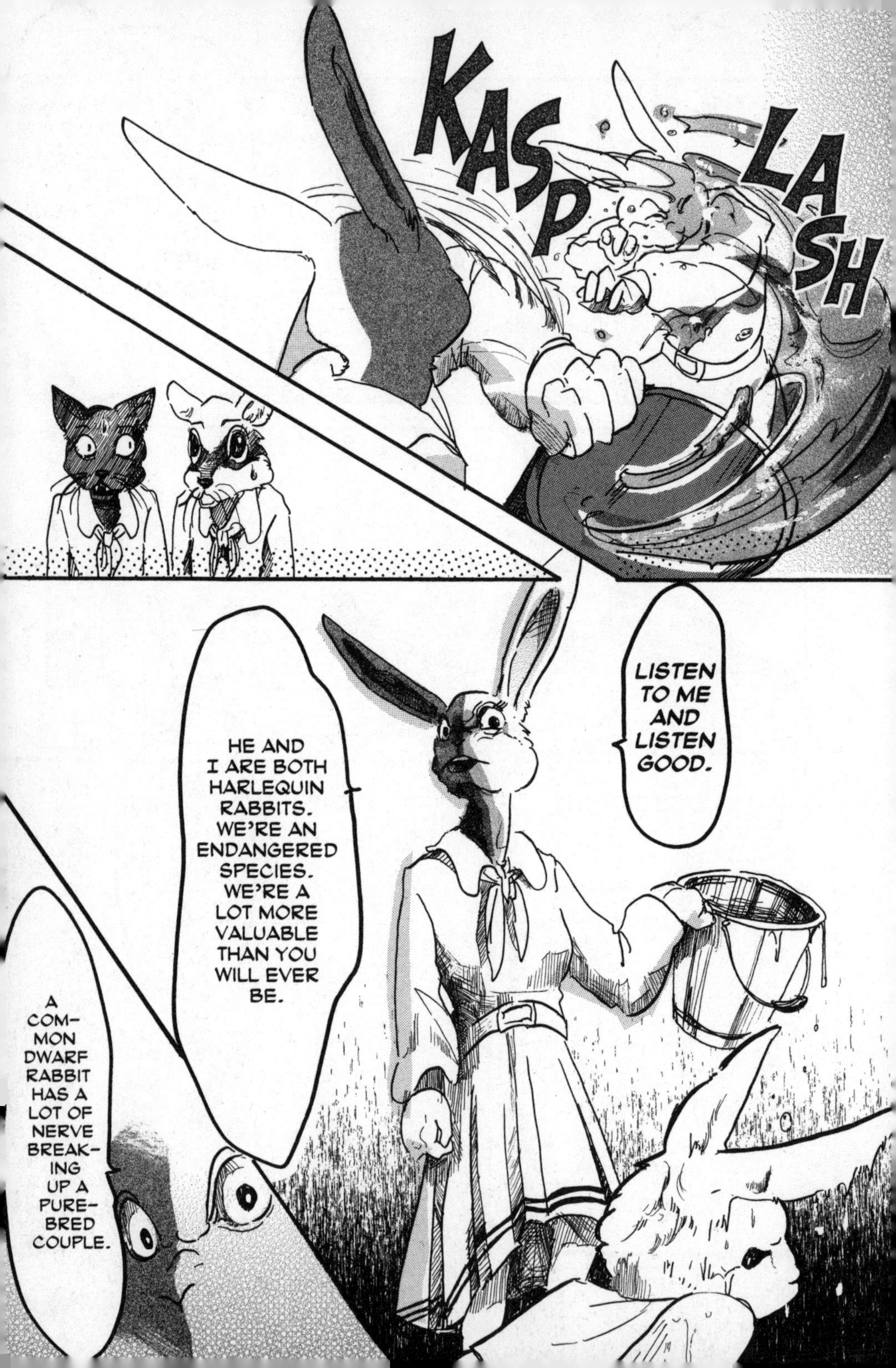
KASPLASH
LISTEN TO ME AND LISTEN GOOD.
HE AND I ARE BOTH HARLEQUIN RABBITS. WE'RE AN ENDANGERED SPECIES. WE'RE A LOT MORE VALUABLE THAN YOU WILL EVER BE.
A COMMON DWARF RABBIT HAS A LOT OF NERVE BREAKING UP A PUREBRED COUPLE.

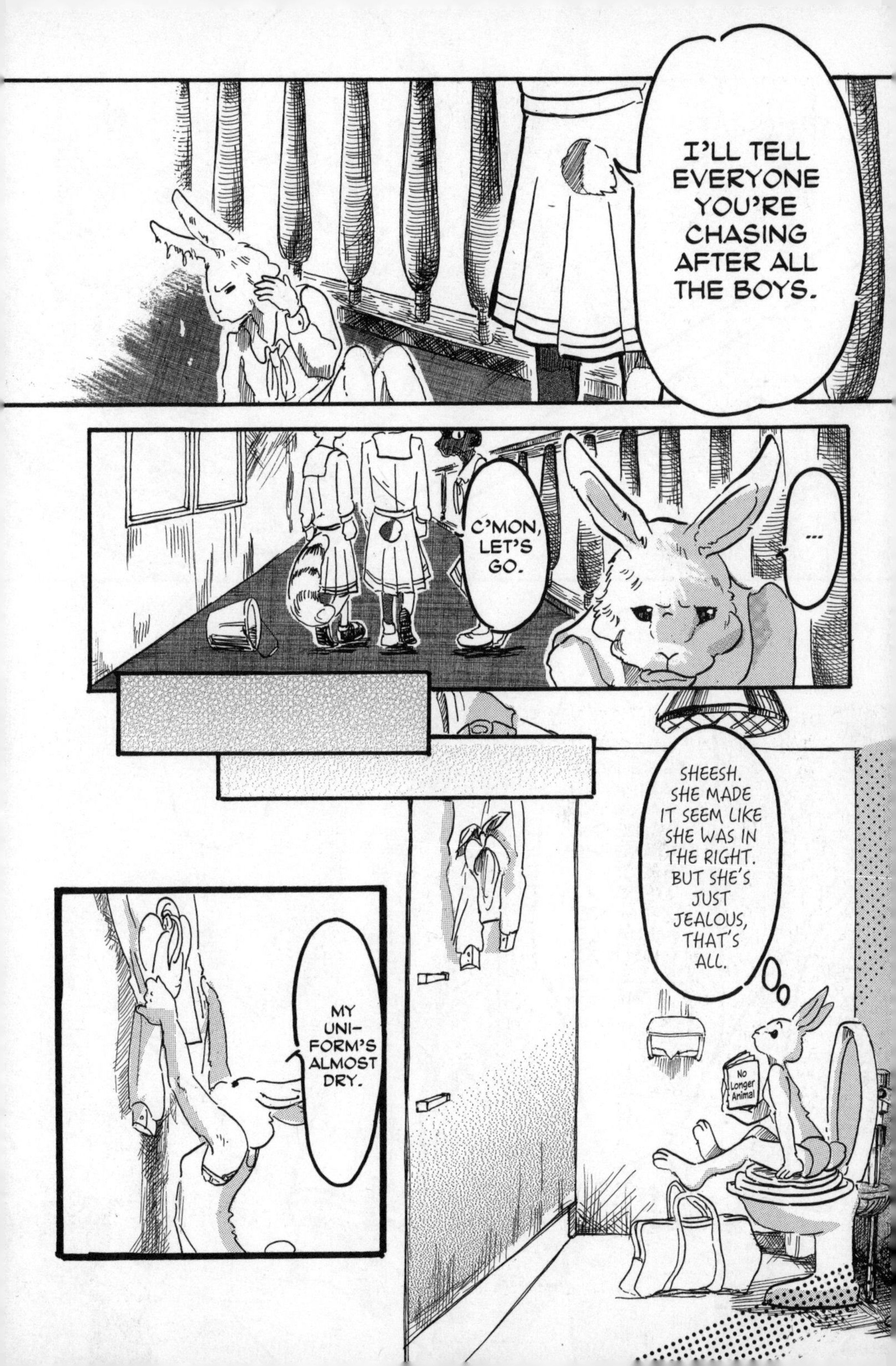
I'LL TELL EVERYONE YOU'RE CHASING AFTER ALL THE BOYS.
...
C'MON, LET'S GO.
SHEESH. SHE MADE IT SEEM LIKE SHE WAS IN THE RIGHT. BUT SHE'S JUST JEALOUS, THAT'S ALL.
No Longer Animal
MY UNI-FORM'S ALMOST DRY.

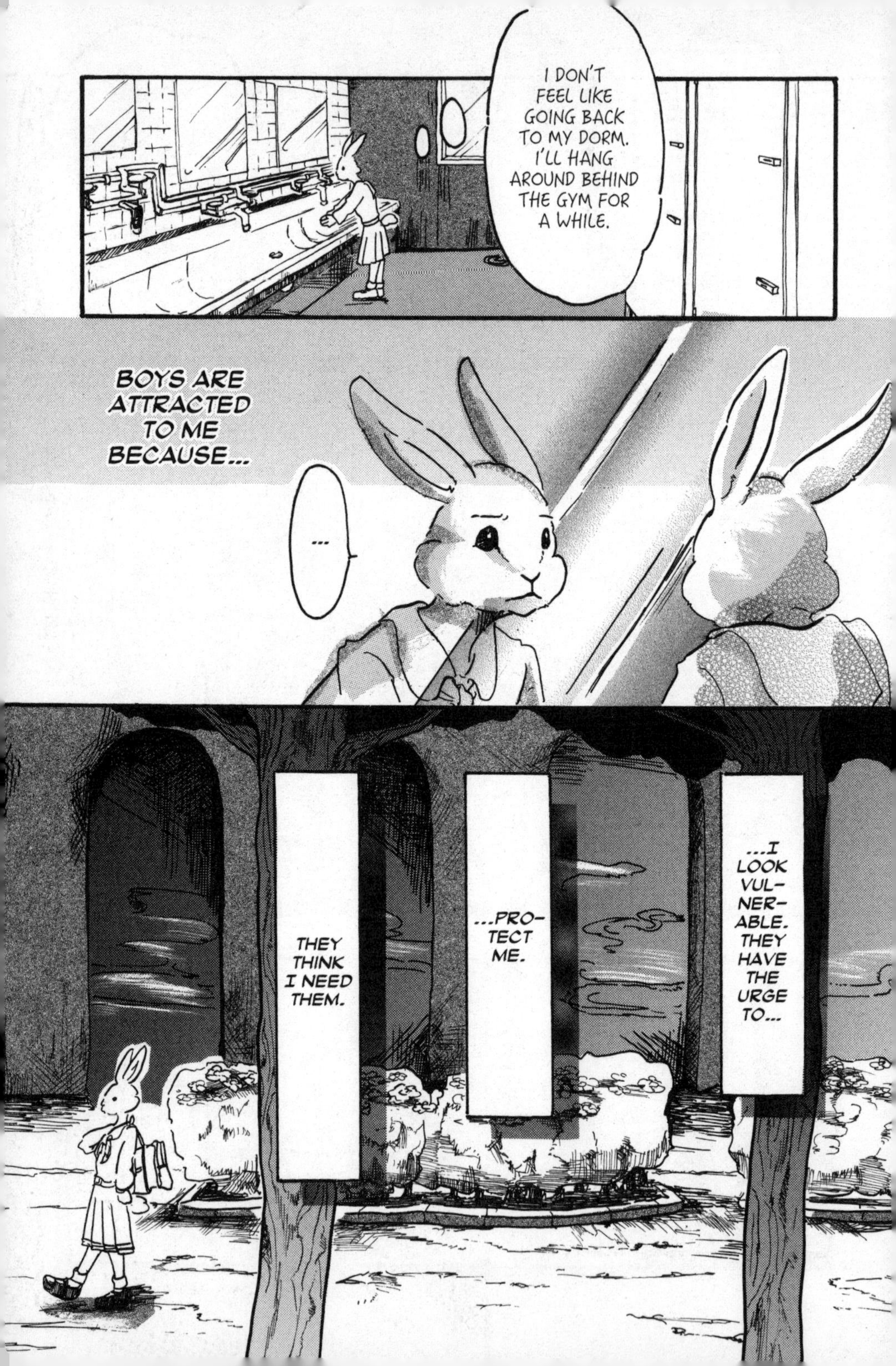
I DON'T FEEL LIKE GOING BACK TO MY DORM. I'LL HANG AROUND BEHIND THE GYM FOR A WHILE.
BOYS ARE ATTRACTED TO ME BECAUSE...
...
...I LOOK VUL-NER-ABLE. THEY HAVE THE URGE TO...
...PRO-TECT ME.
THEY THINK I NEED THEM.

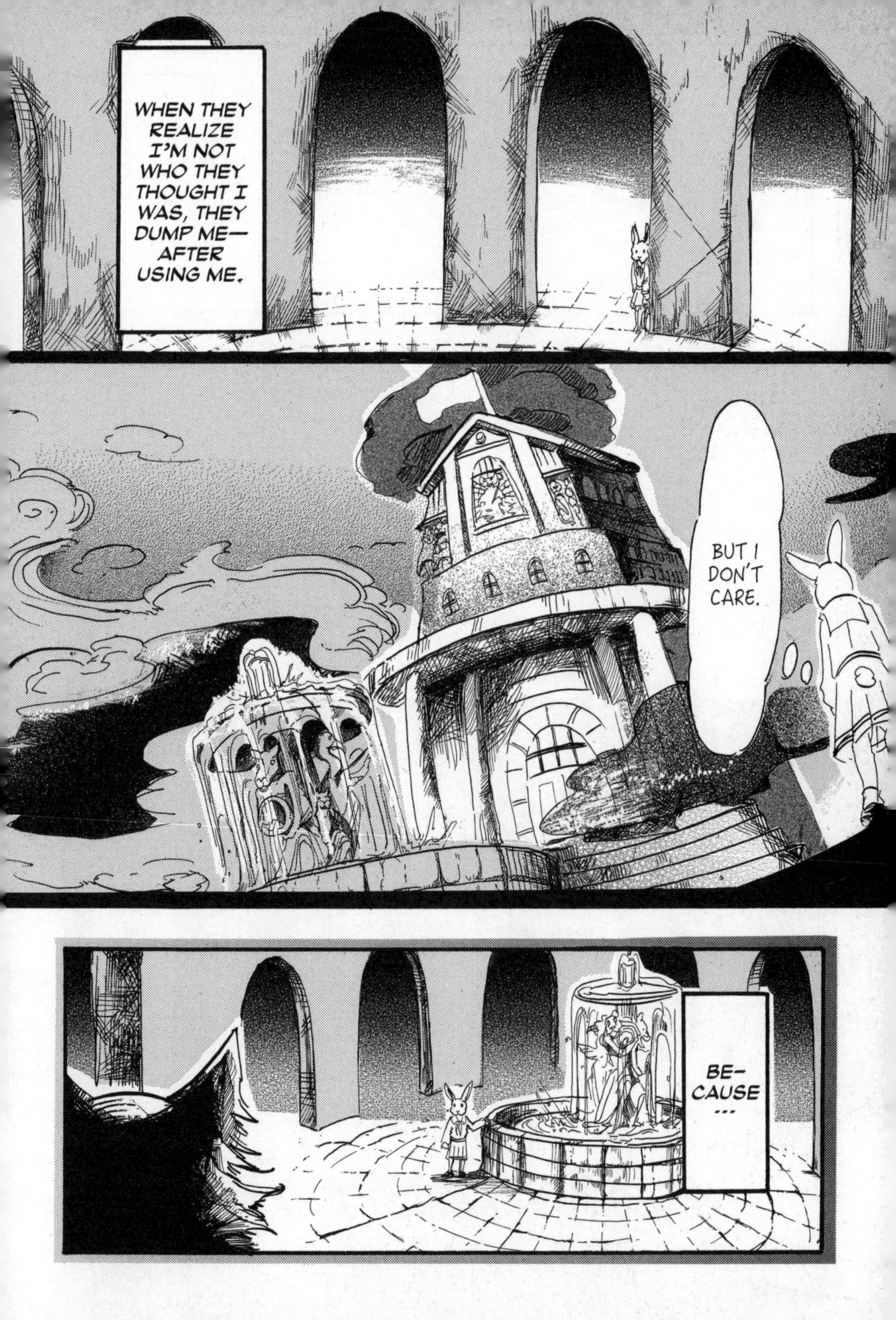
WHEN THEY REALIZE I'M NOT WHO THEY THOUGHT I WAS, THEY DUMP ME—AFTER USING ME.
BUT I DON'T CARE.
BE-CAUSE...

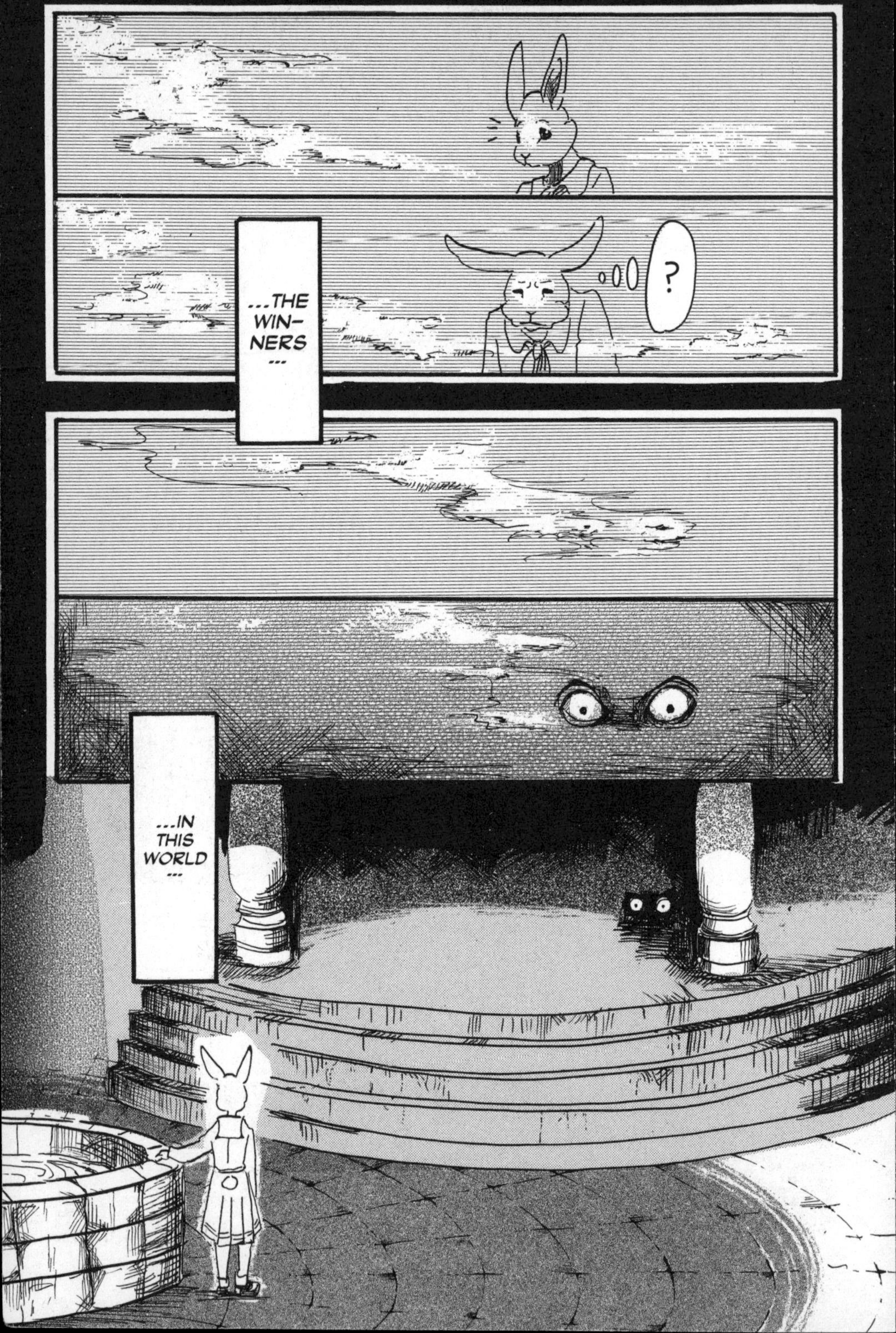
?
...THE WIN-NERS...
...IN THIS WORLD...

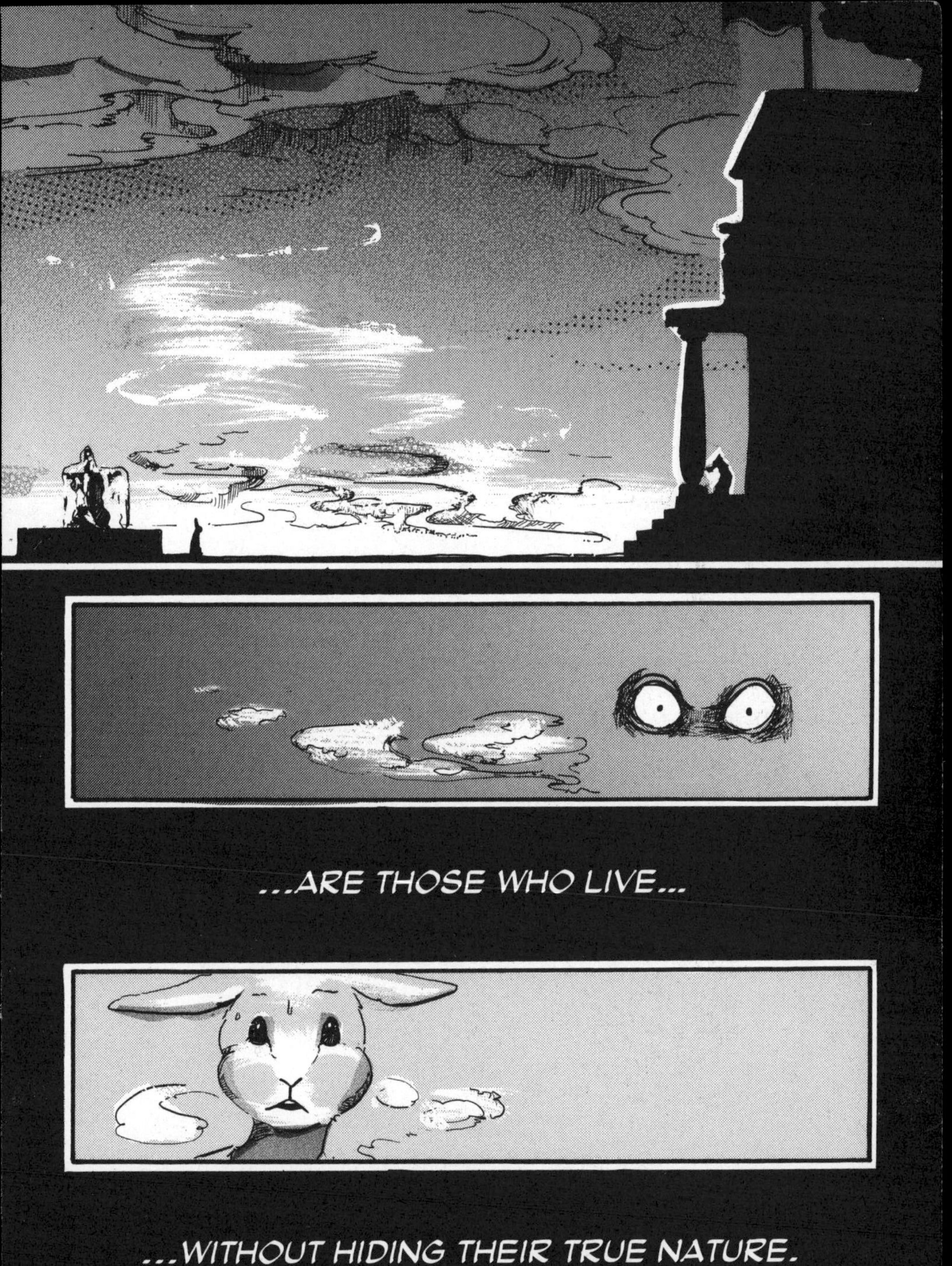
...ARE THOSE WHO LIVE...
...WITHOUT HIDING THEIR TRUE NATURE.

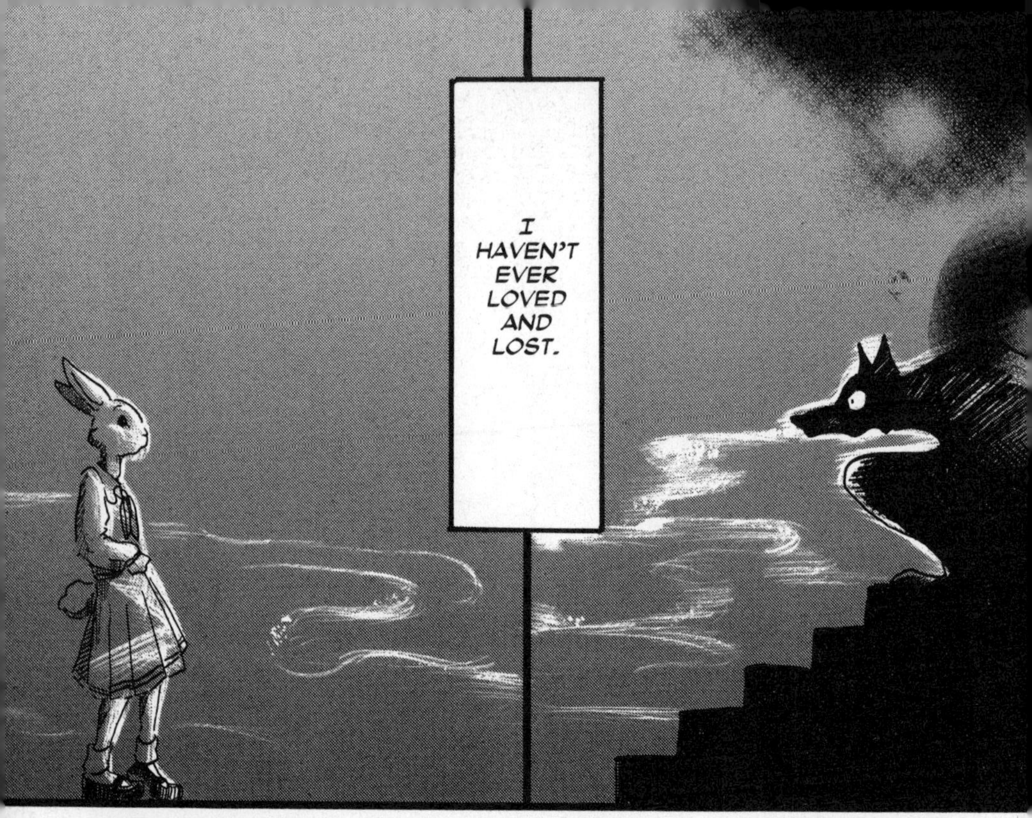
I HAVEN'T EVER LOVED AND LOST.

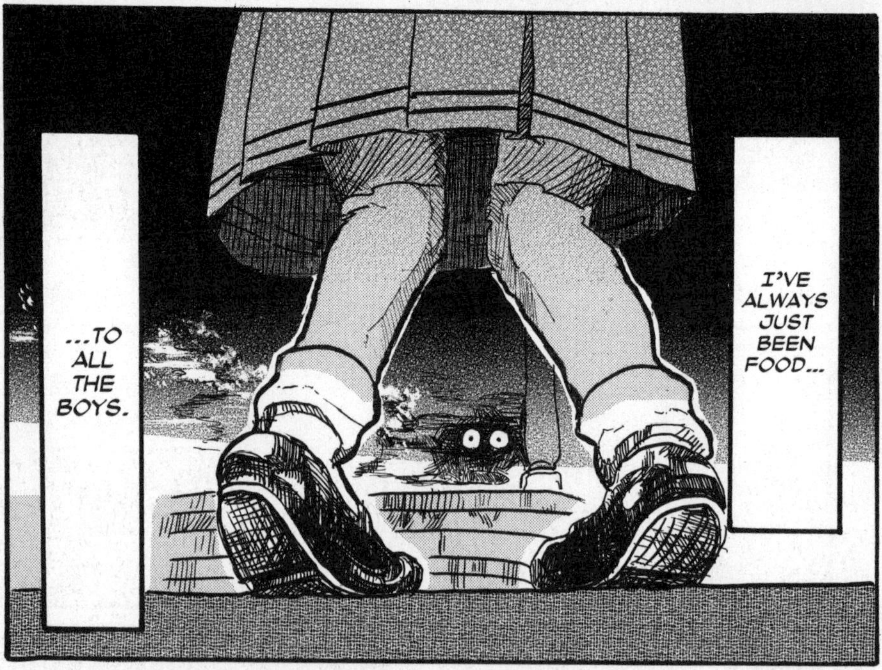
I'VE ALWAYS JUST BEEN FOOD...
...TO ALL THE BOYS.

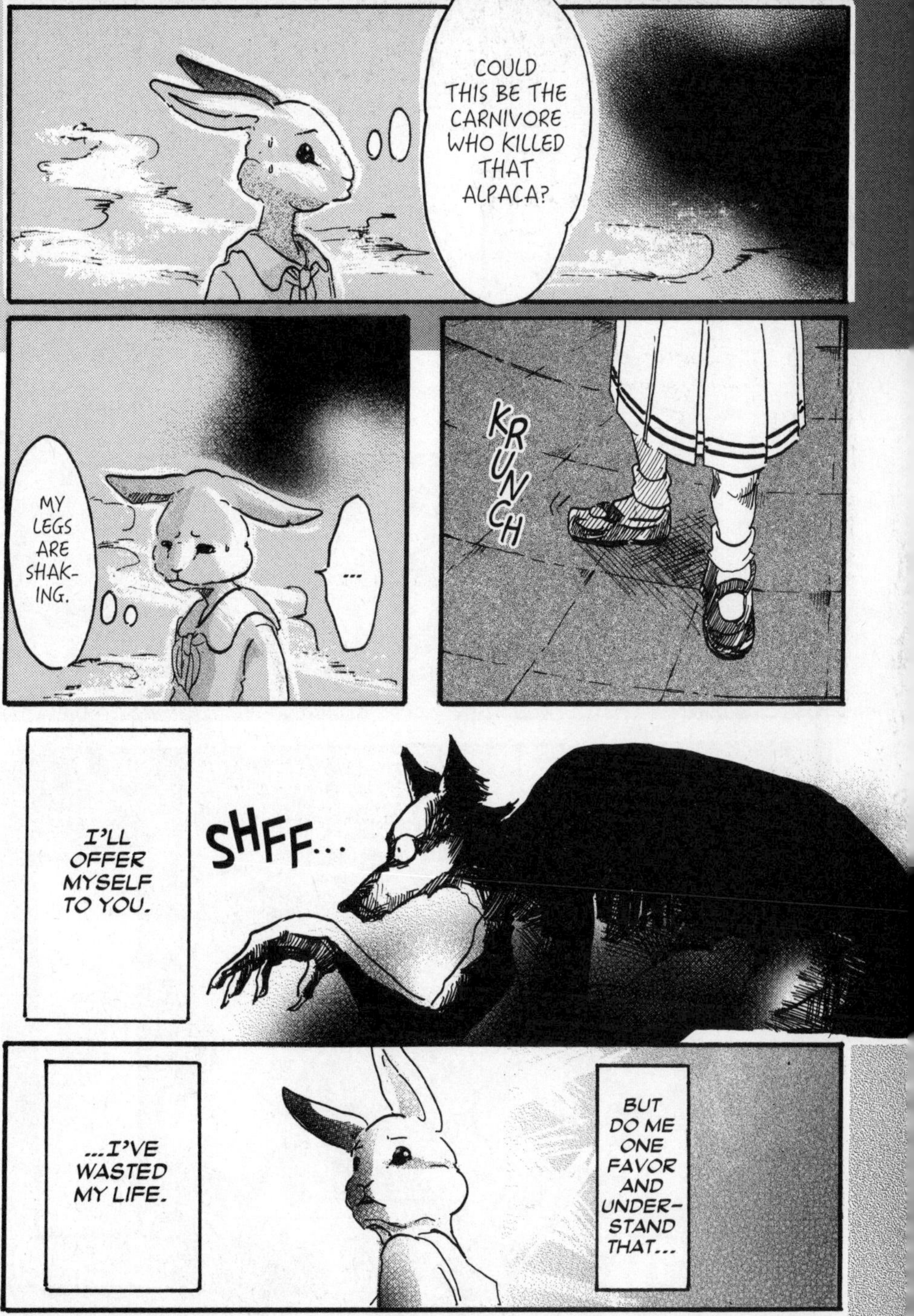
COULD THIS BE THE CARNIVORE WHO KILLED THAT ALPACA?
KRUNCH
...
MY LEGS ARE SHAK-ING.
SHFF...
I'LL OFFER MYSELF TO YOU.
BUT DO ME ONE FAVOR AND UNDER-STAND THAT...
...I'VE WASTED MY LIFE.

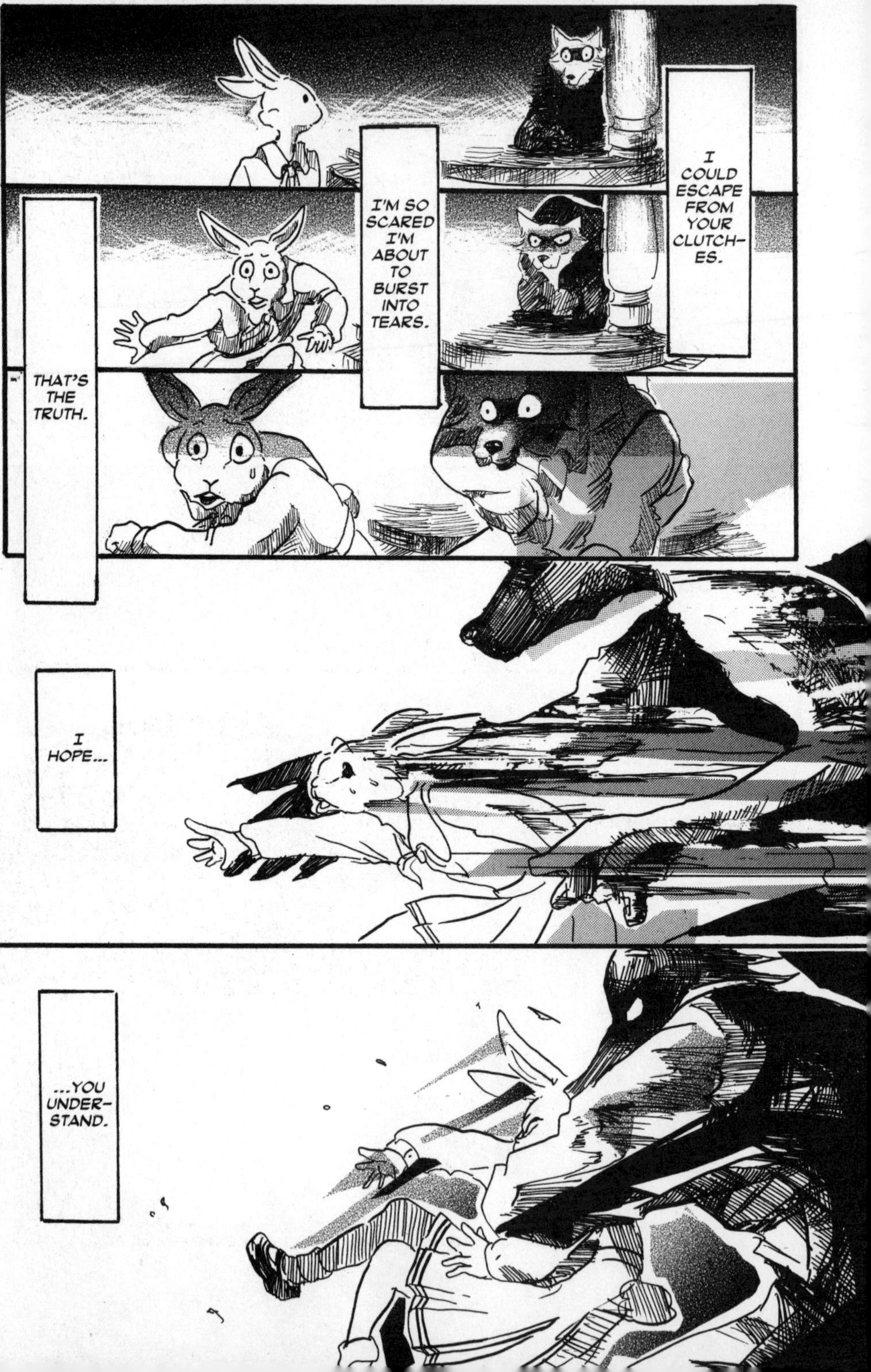
I COULD ESCAPE FROM YOUR CLUTCHES.
I'M SO SCARED I'M ABOUT TO BURST INTO TEARS.
THAT'S THE TRUTH.
I HOPE...
...YOU UNDERSTAND.

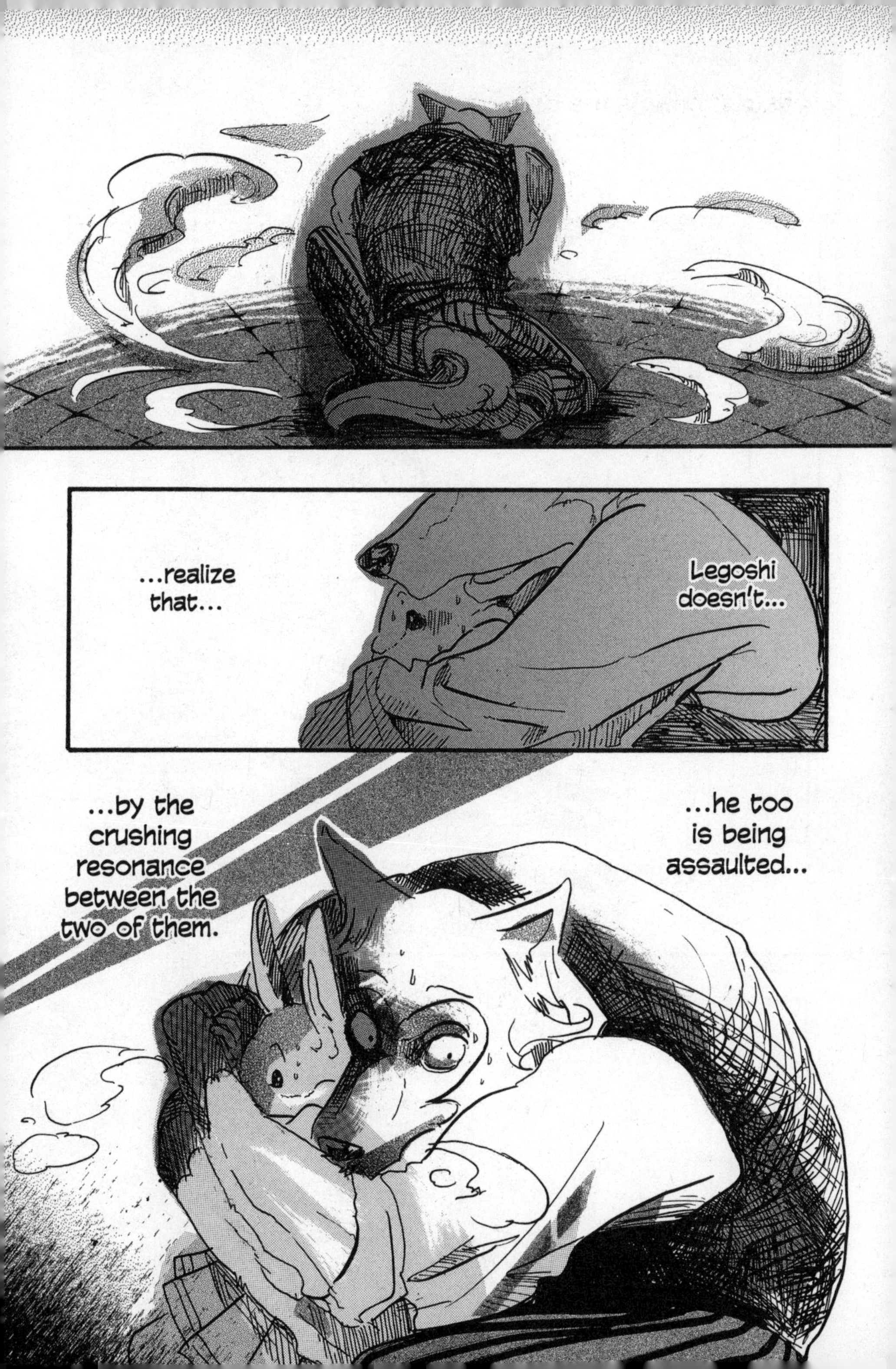
Legoshi doesn't...
...realize that...
...he too is being assaulted...
...by the crushing resonance between the two of them.

Chapter 5: Hey, It's Us!

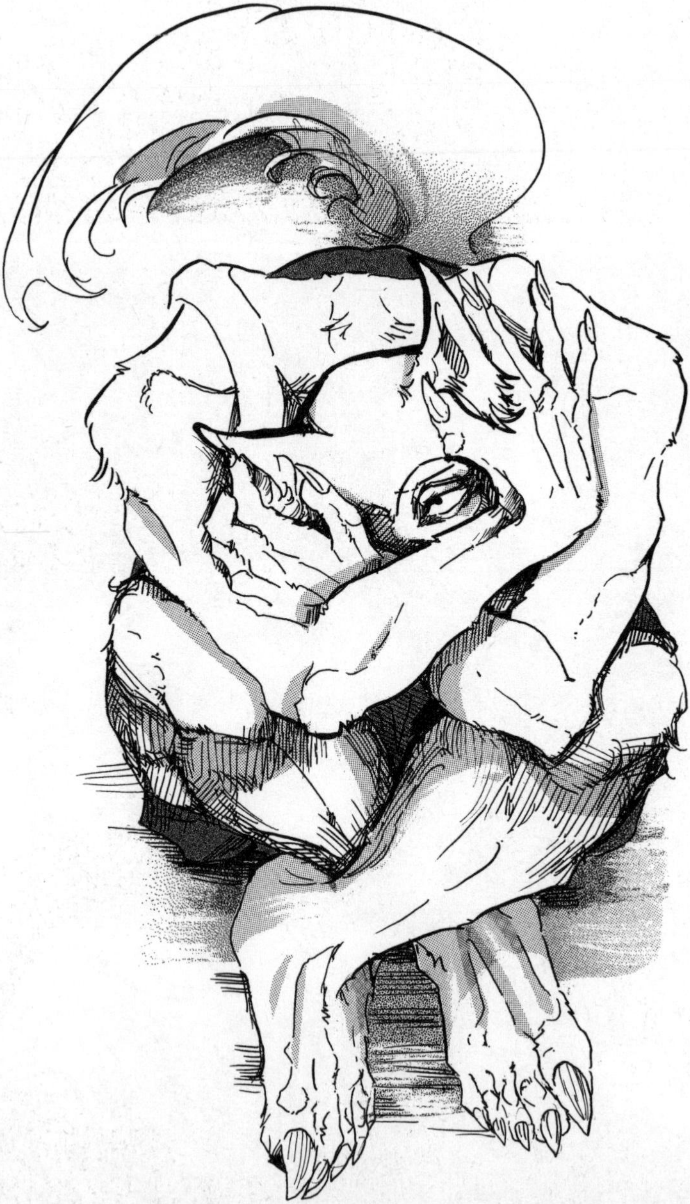

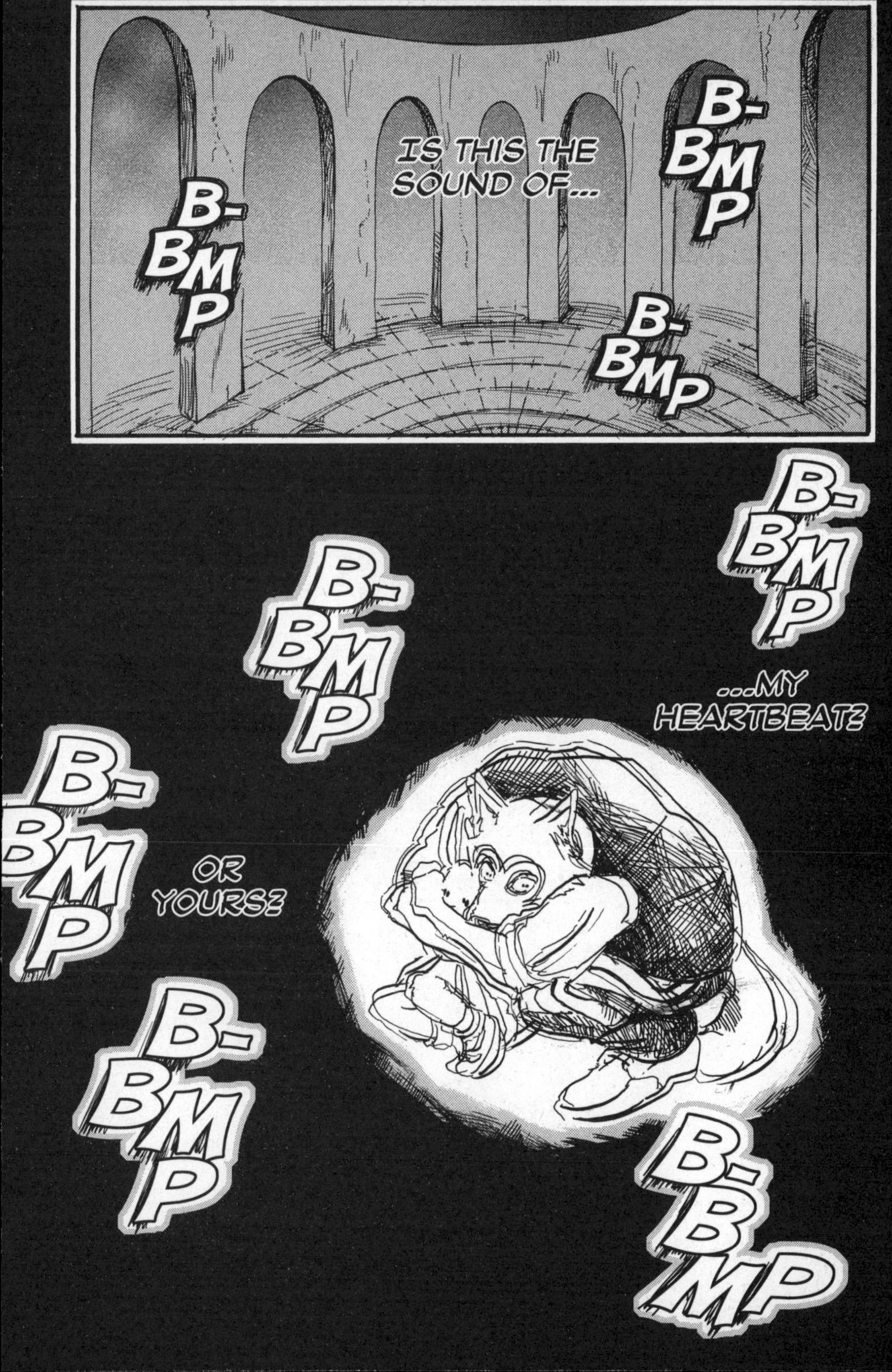
B-BMP
IS THIS THE SOUND OF...
B-BMP
B-BMP
B-BMP
...MY HEARTBEAT?
B-BMP
OR YOURS?
B-BMP
B-BMP
B-BBMP

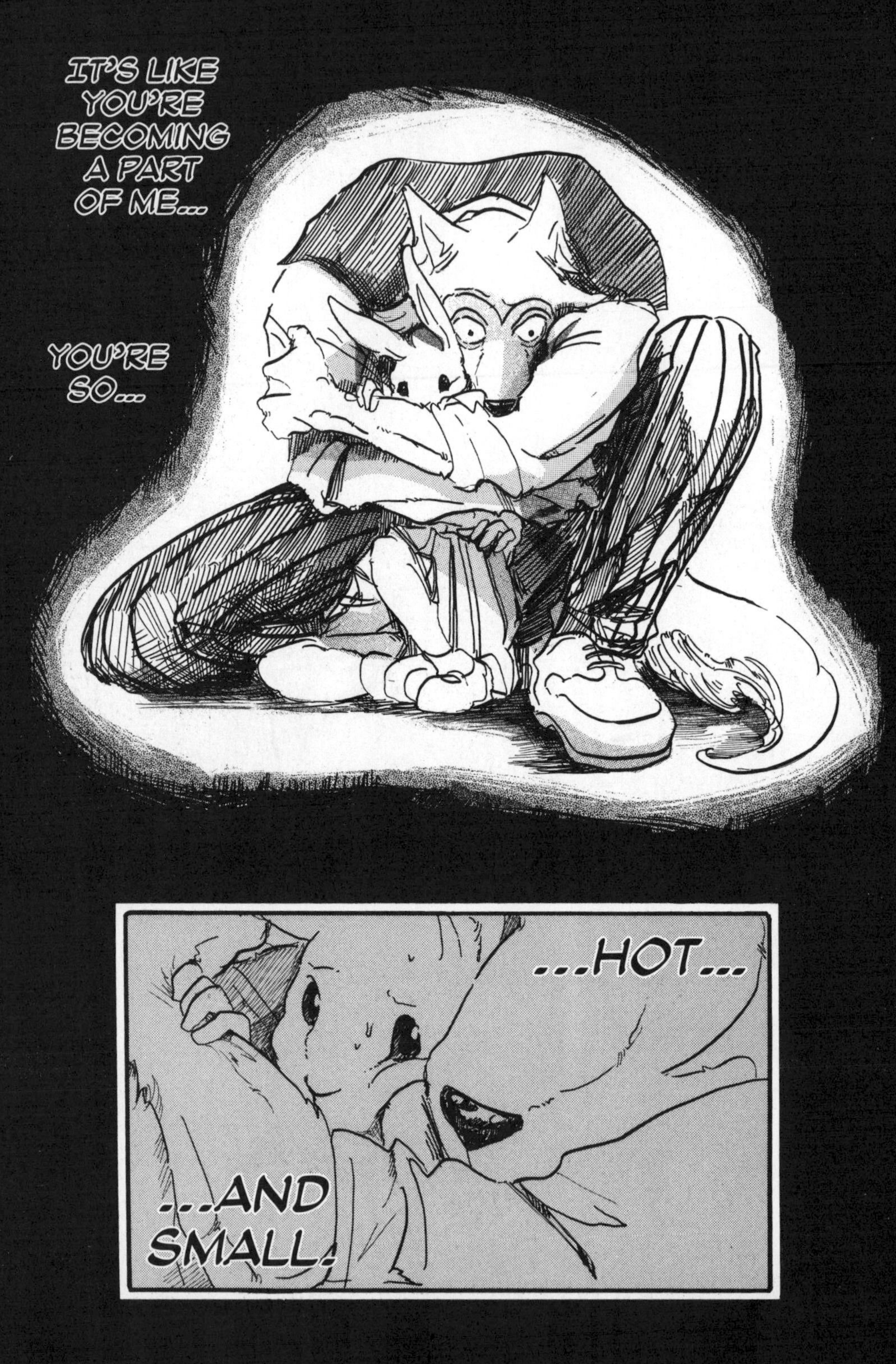
IT'S LIKE YOU'RE BECOMING A PART OF ME...
YOU'RE SO...
...HOT...
...AND SMALL.

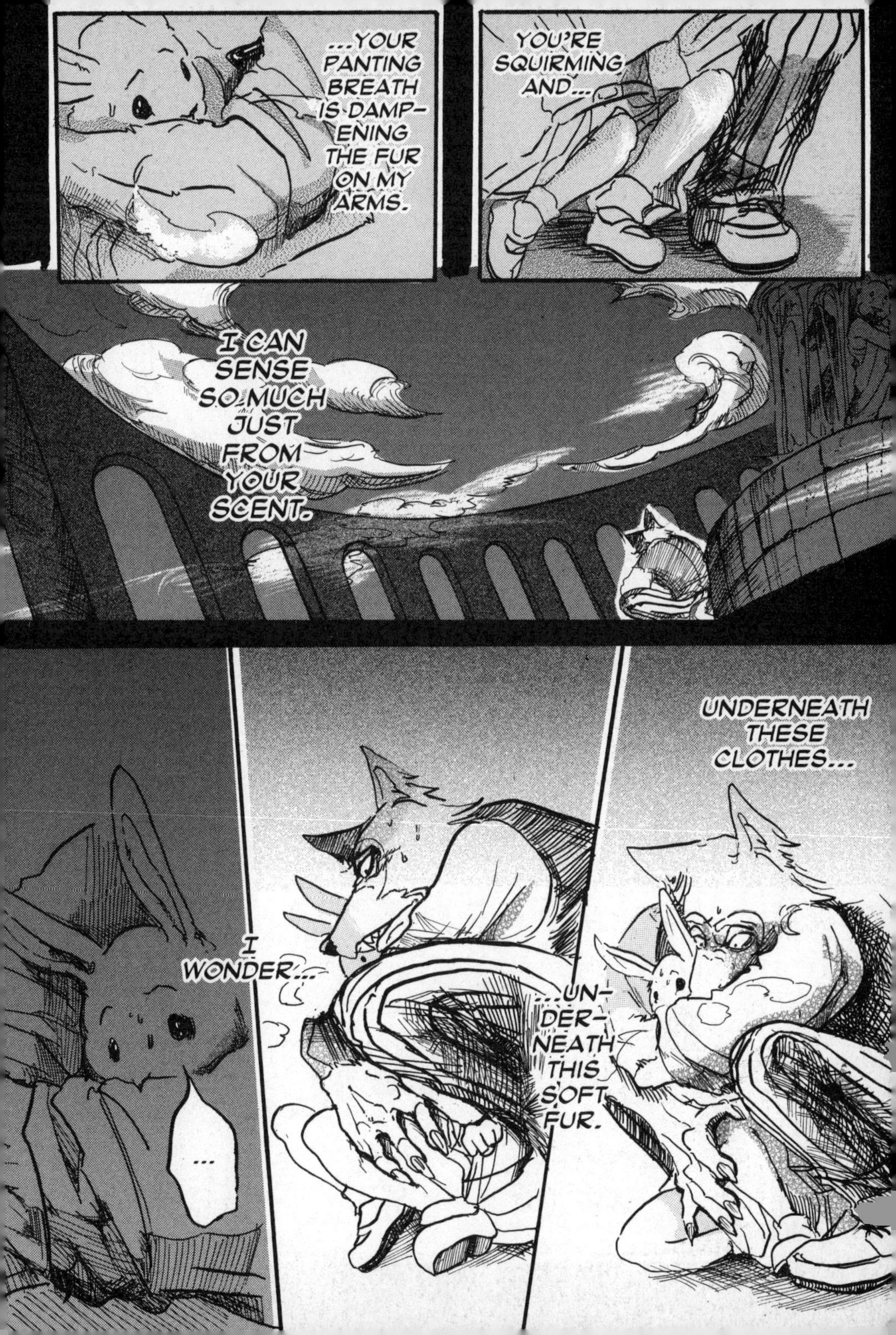
YOU'RE SQUIRMING AND...
...YOUR PANTING BREATH IS DAMPENING THE FUR ON MY ARMS.
I CAN SENSE SO MUCH JUST FROM YOUR SCENT.
UNDERNEATH THESE CLOTHES...
...UNDERNEATH THIS SOFT FUR.
I WONDER...
...

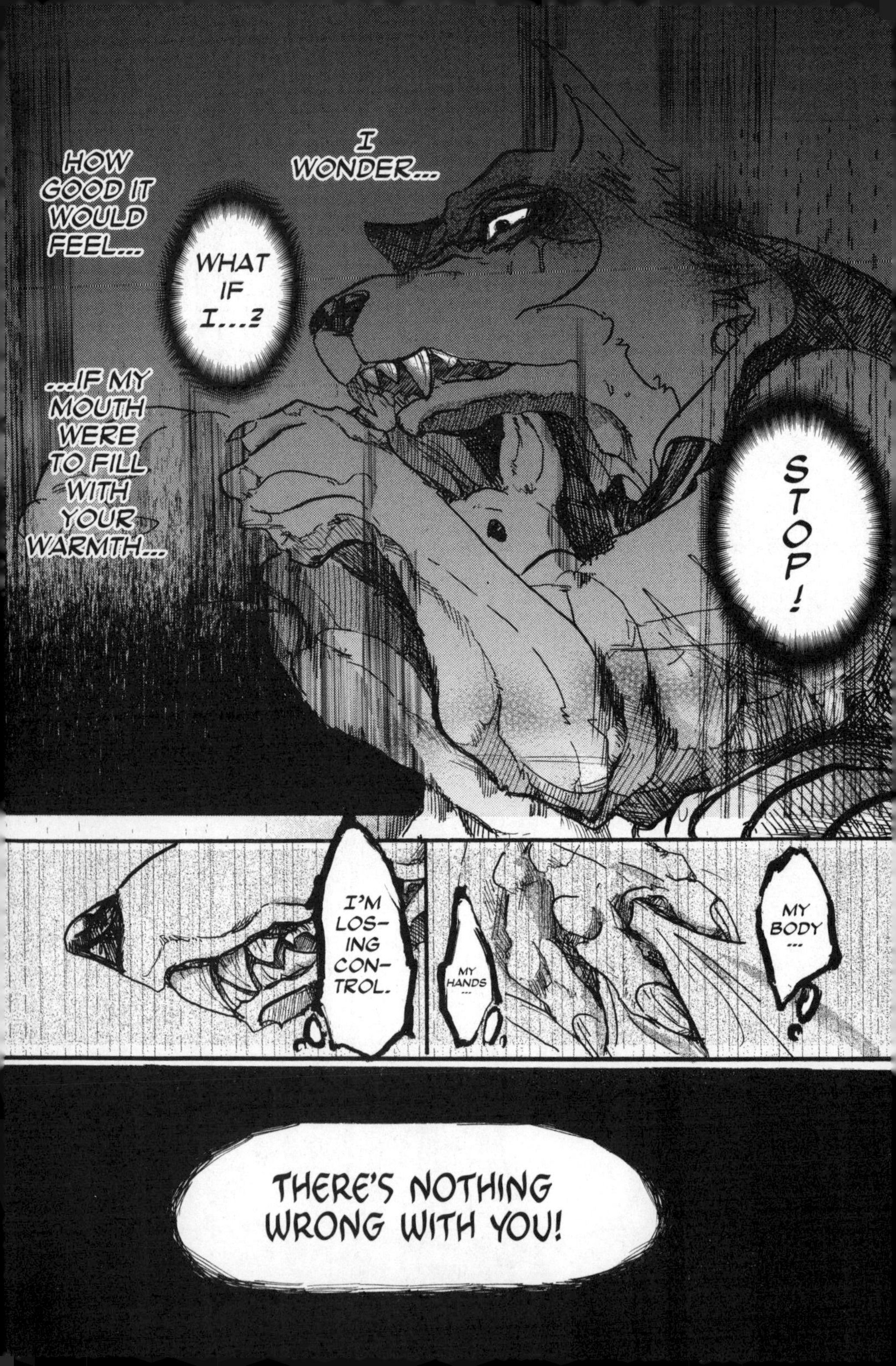
I WONDER...
HOW GOOD IT WOULD FEEL...
WHAT IF I...?
...IF MY MOUTH WERE TO FILL WITH YOUR WARMTH...
STOP!
MY BODY...
MY HANDS...
I'M LOSING CONTROL.
THERE'S NOTHING WRONG WITH YOU!

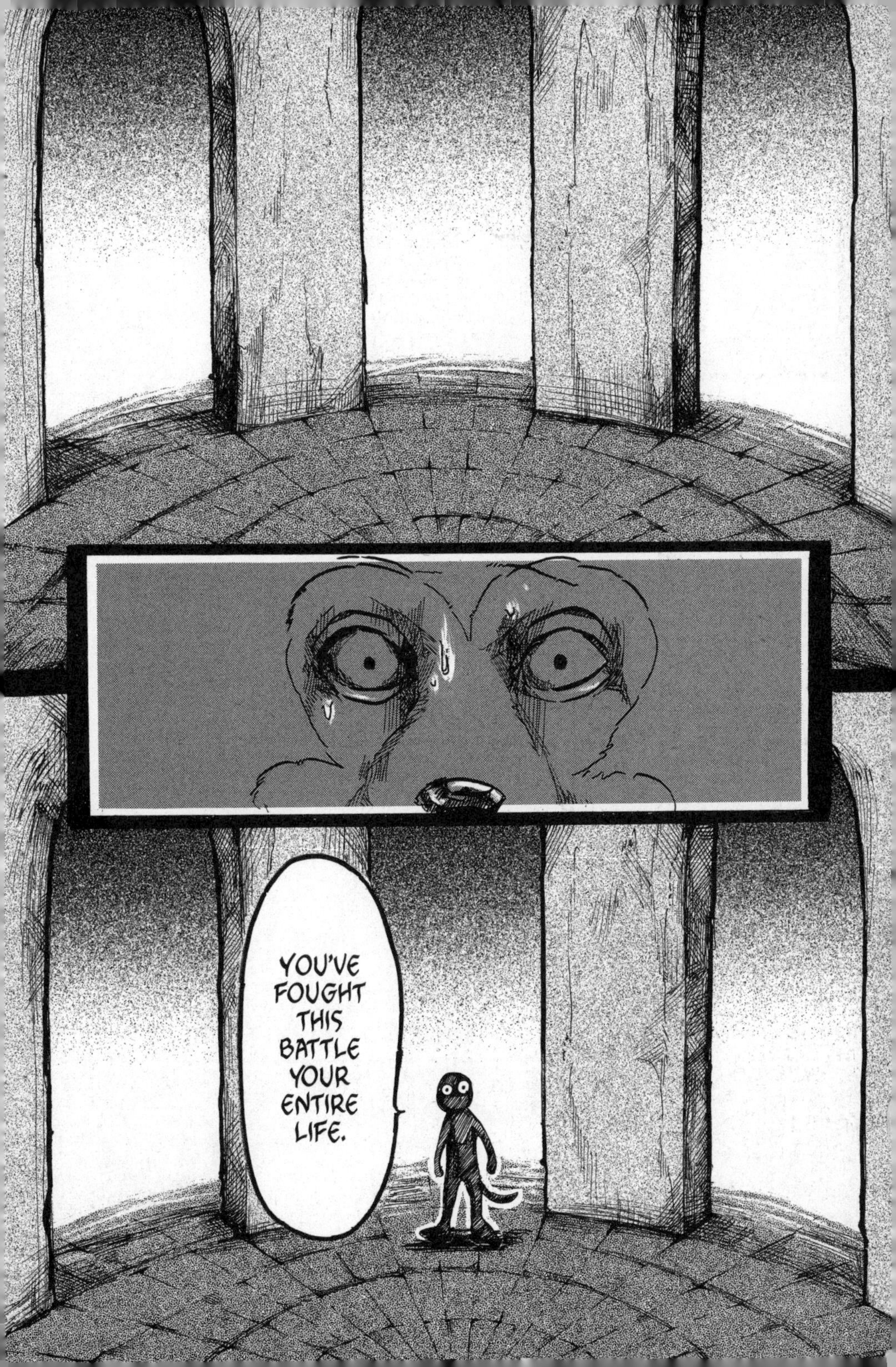
YOU'VE FOUGHT THIS BATTLE YOUR ENTIRE LIFE.

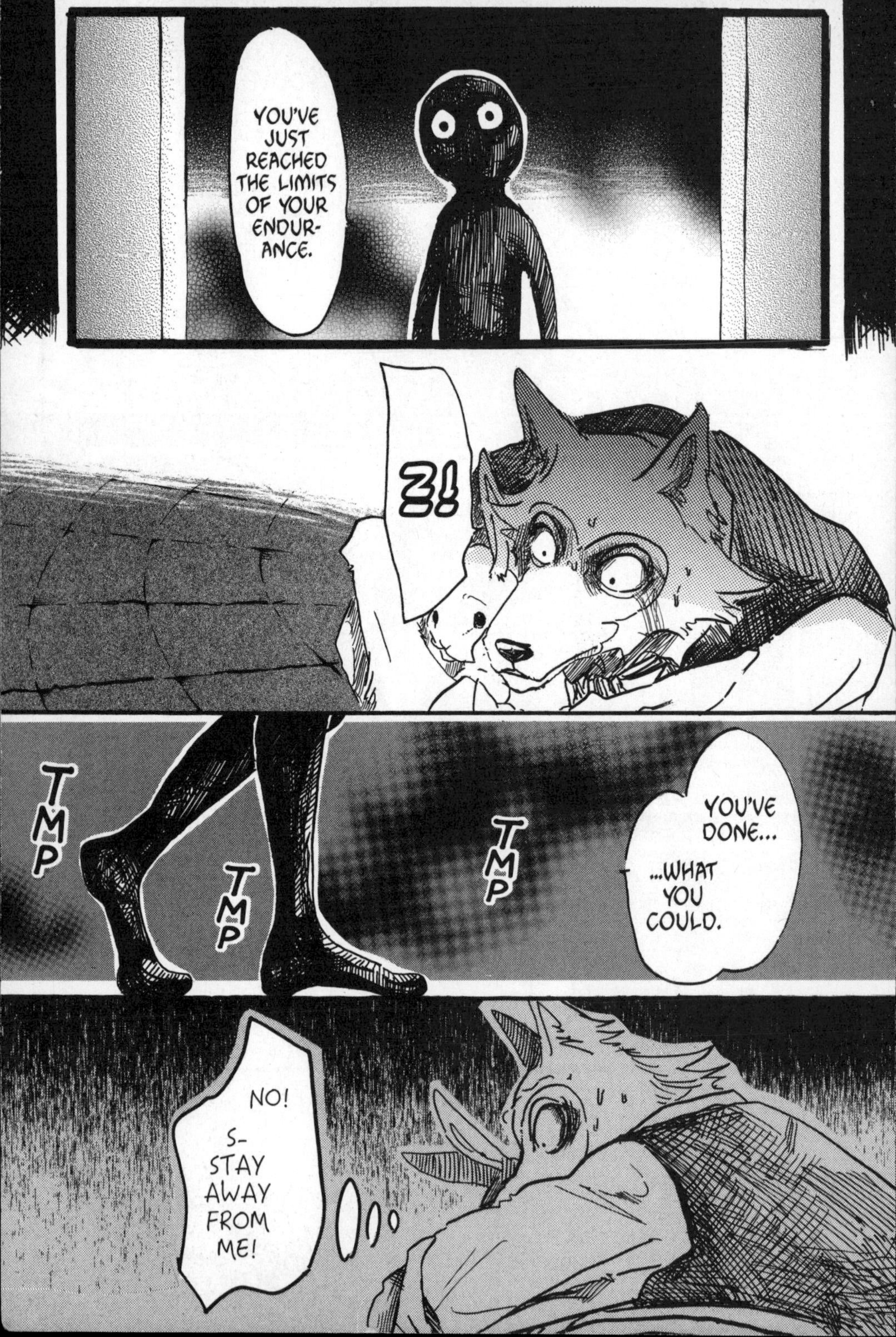
YOU'VE JUST REACHED THE LIMITS OF YOUR ENDUR-ANCE.
!!
YOU'VE DONE...
...WHAT YOU COULD.
TMP
TMP
TMP
NO!
S-STAY AWAY FROM ME!

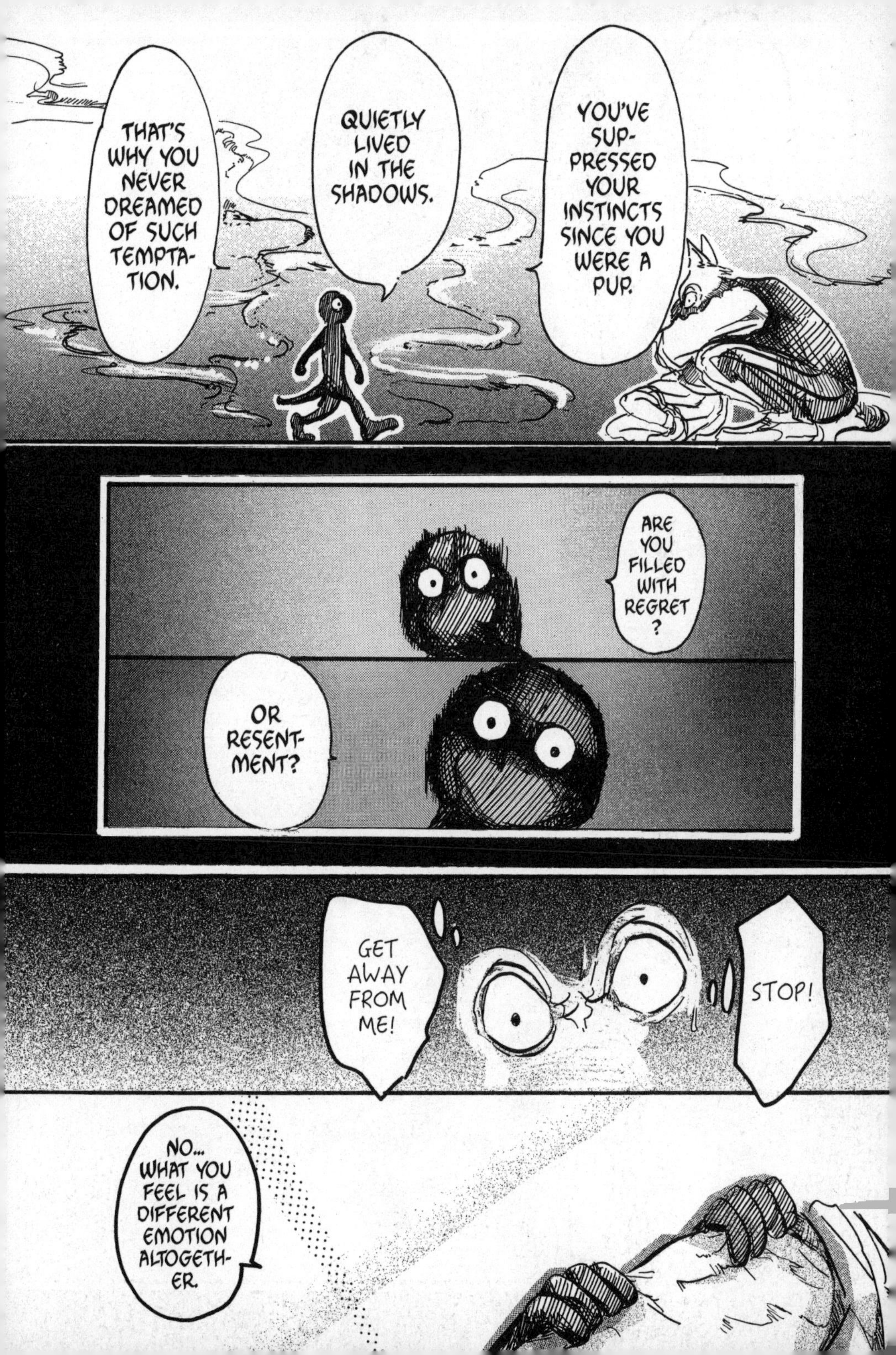
YOU'VE SUPPRESSED YOUR INSTINCTS SINCE YOU WERE A PUP.
QUIETLY LIVED IN THE SHADOWS.
THAT'S WHY YOU NEVER DREAMED OF SUCH TEMPTATION.
ARE YOU FILLED WITH REGRET?
OR RESENTMENT?
STOP!
GET AWAY FROM ME!
NO... WHAT YOU FEEL IS A DIFFERENT EMOTION ALTOGETHER.

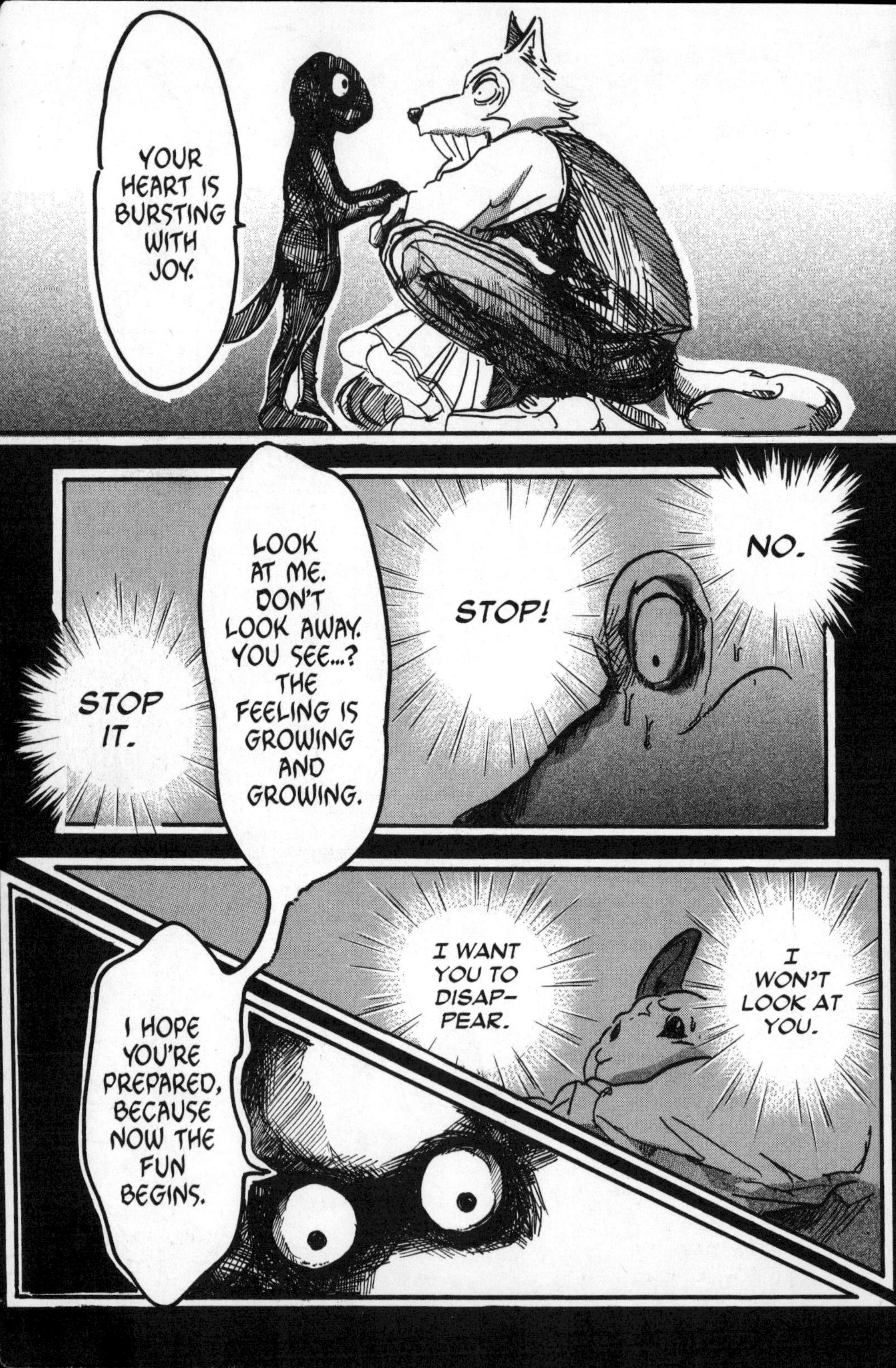
YOUR HEART IS BURSTING WITH JOY.
NO.
STOP!
LOOK AT ME. DON'T LOOK AWAY. YOU SEE...? THE FEELING IS GROWING AND GROWING.
STOP IT.
I WON'T LOOK AT YOU.
I WANT YOU TO DISAP-PEAR.
I HOPE YOU'RE PREPARED, BECAUSE NOW THE FUN BEGINS.

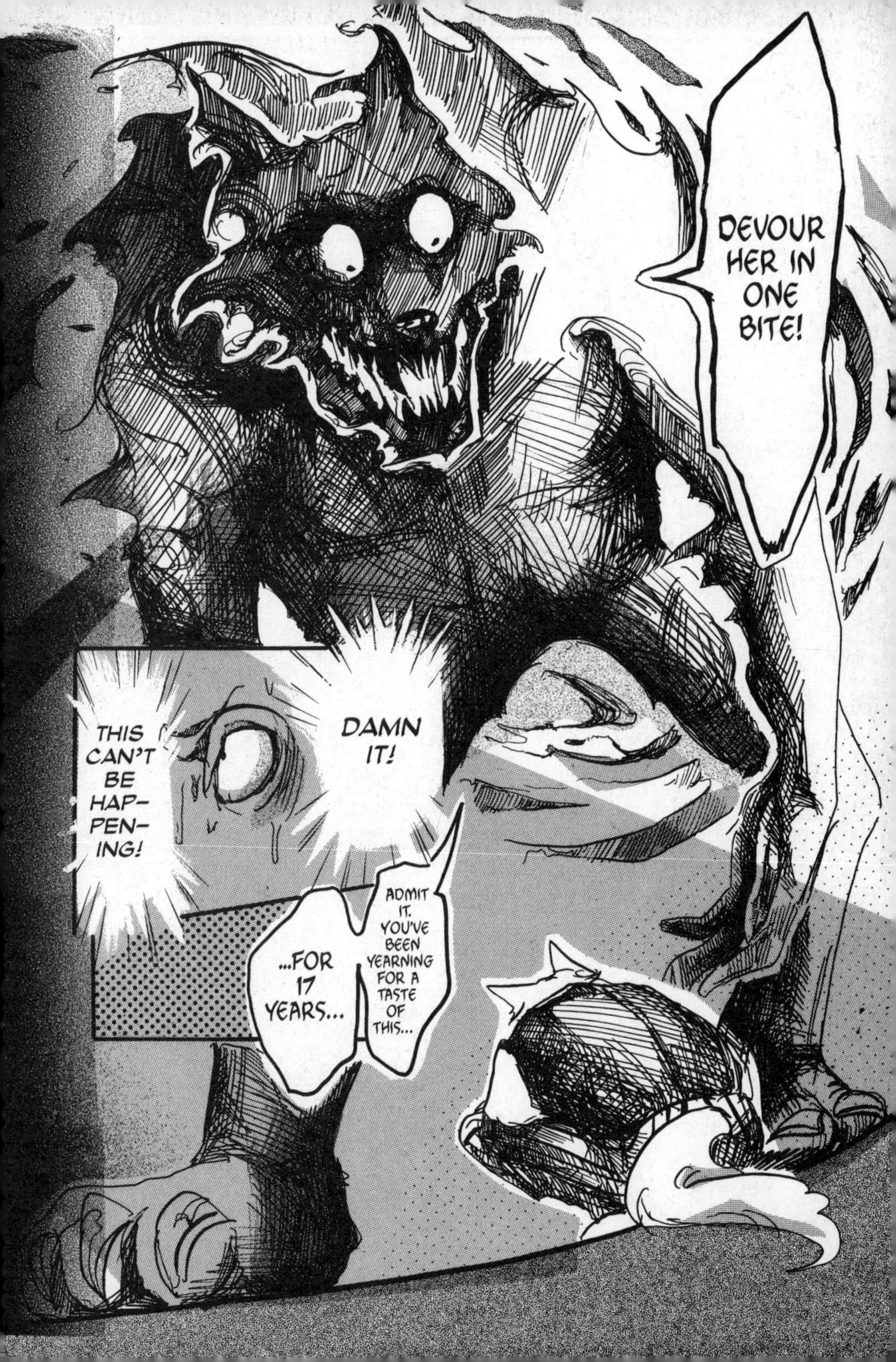
DEVOUR HER IN ONE BITE!
ADMIT IT. YOU'VE BEEN YEARNING FOR A TASTE OF THIS...
...FOR 17 YEARS...
DAMN IT!
THIS CAN'T BE HAP-PEN-ING!

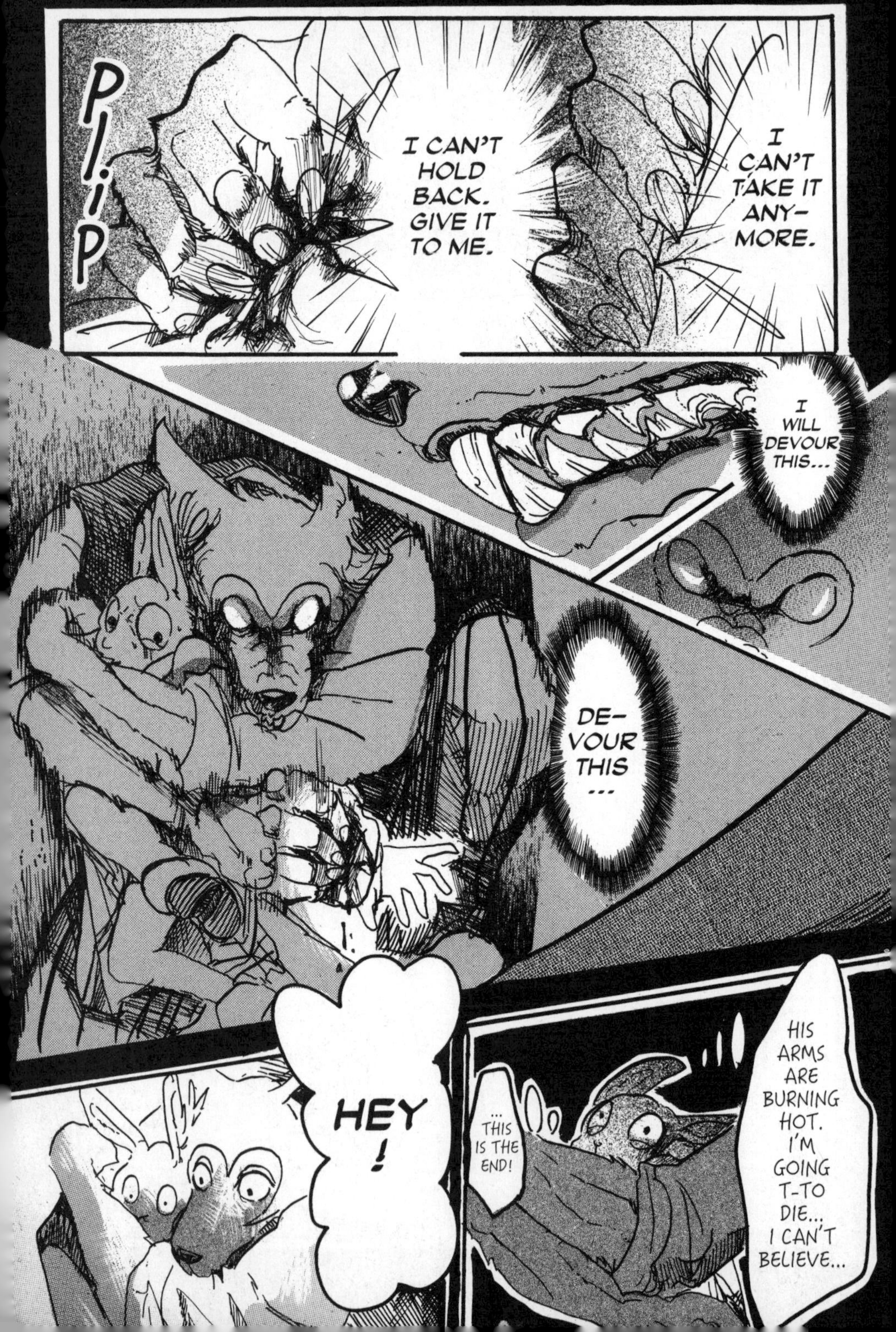
I CAN'T TAKE IT ANY-MORE.
I CAN'T HOLD BACK. GIVE IT TO ME.
PLIP
I WILL DEVOUR THIS...
DE-VOUR THIS ...
HIS ARMS ARE BURNING HOT. I'M GOING T-TO DIE... I CAN'T BELIEVE...
... THIS IS THE END!
HEY!

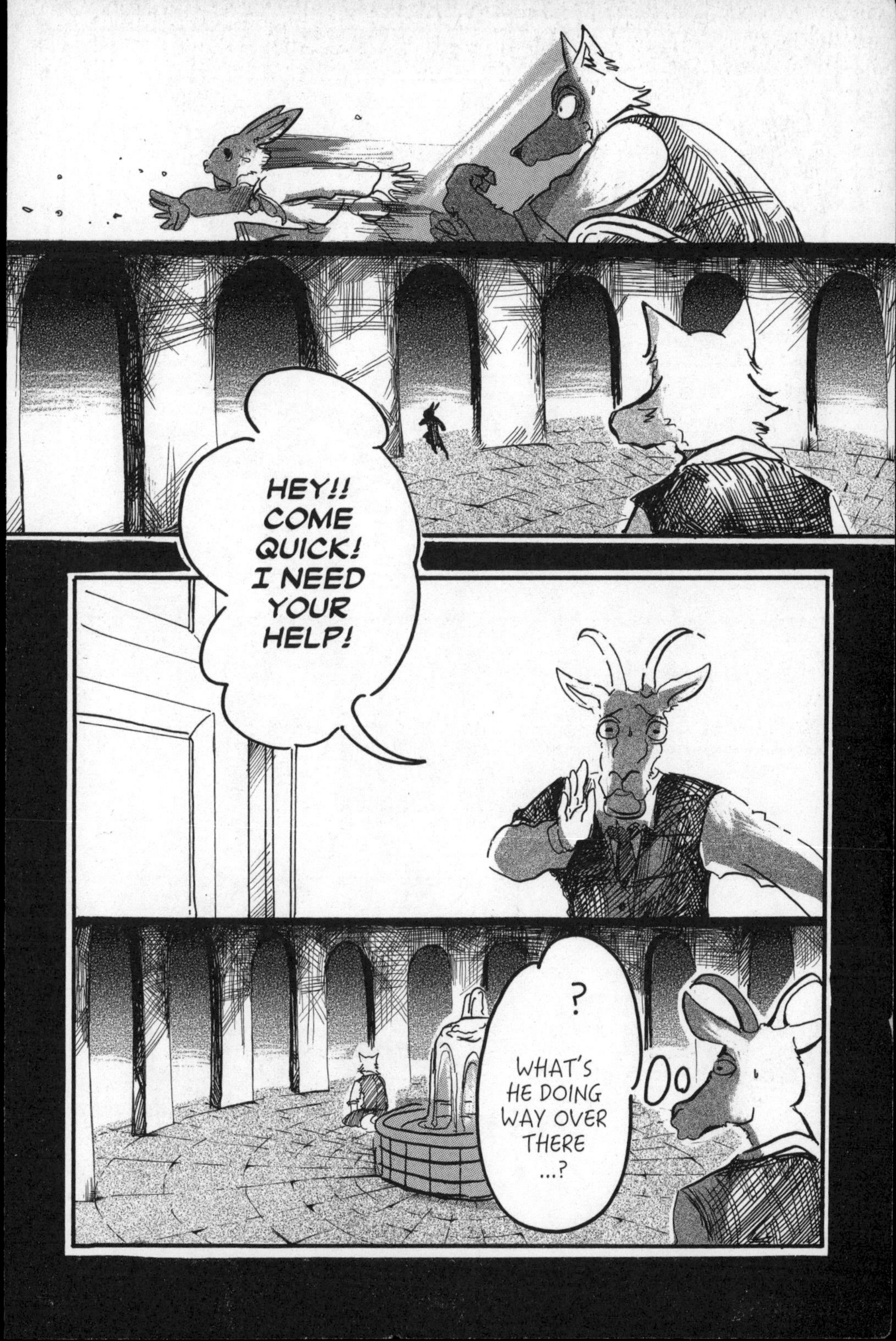
HEY!! COME QUICK! I NEED YOUR HELP!
?
WHAT'S HE DOING WAY OVER THERE ...?

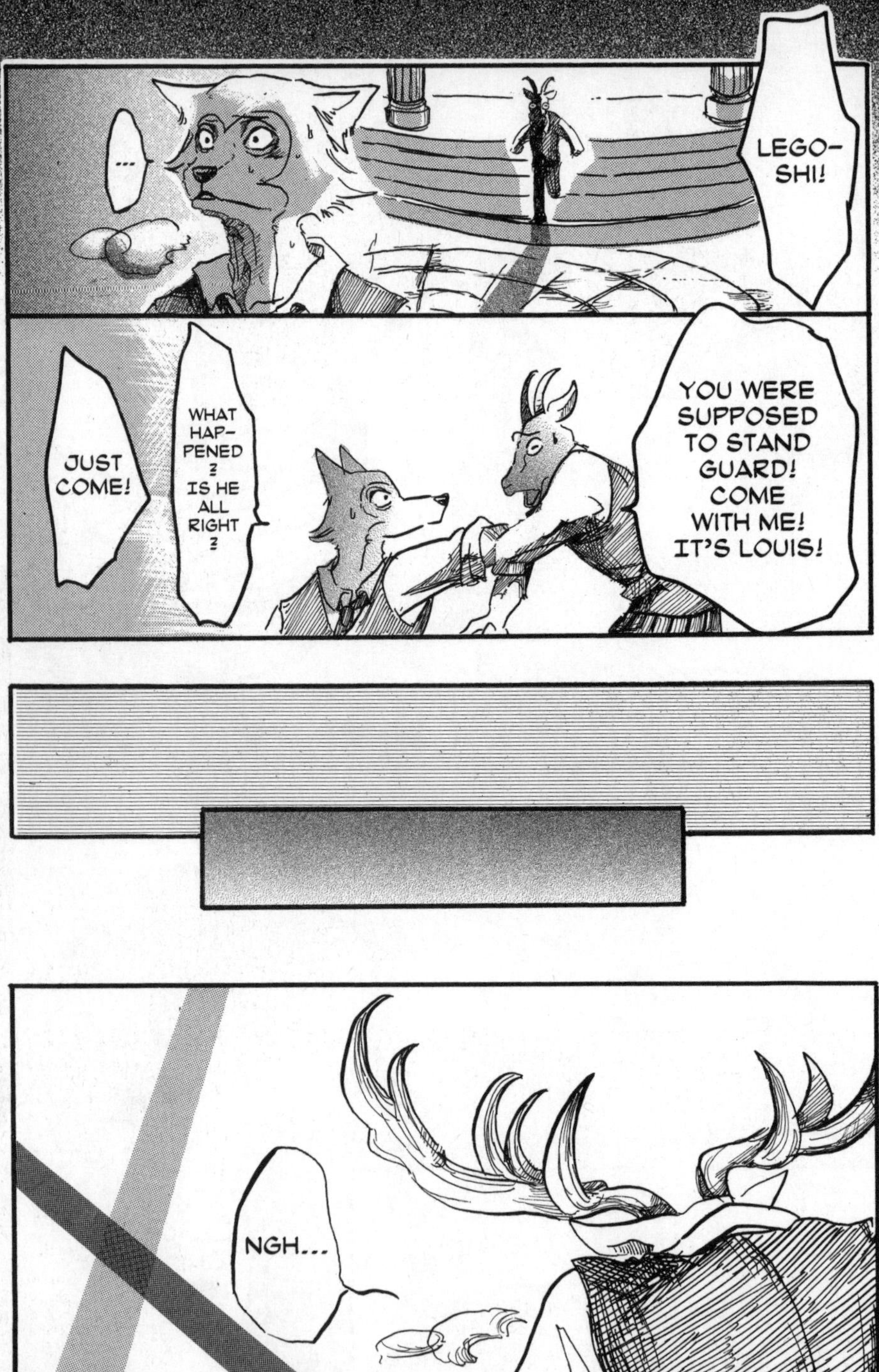
LEGO-SHI!
...
YOU WERE SUPPOSED TO STAND GUARD! COME WITH ME! IT'S LOUIS!
WHAT HAP-PENED? IS HE ALL RIGHT?
JUST COME!
NGH...

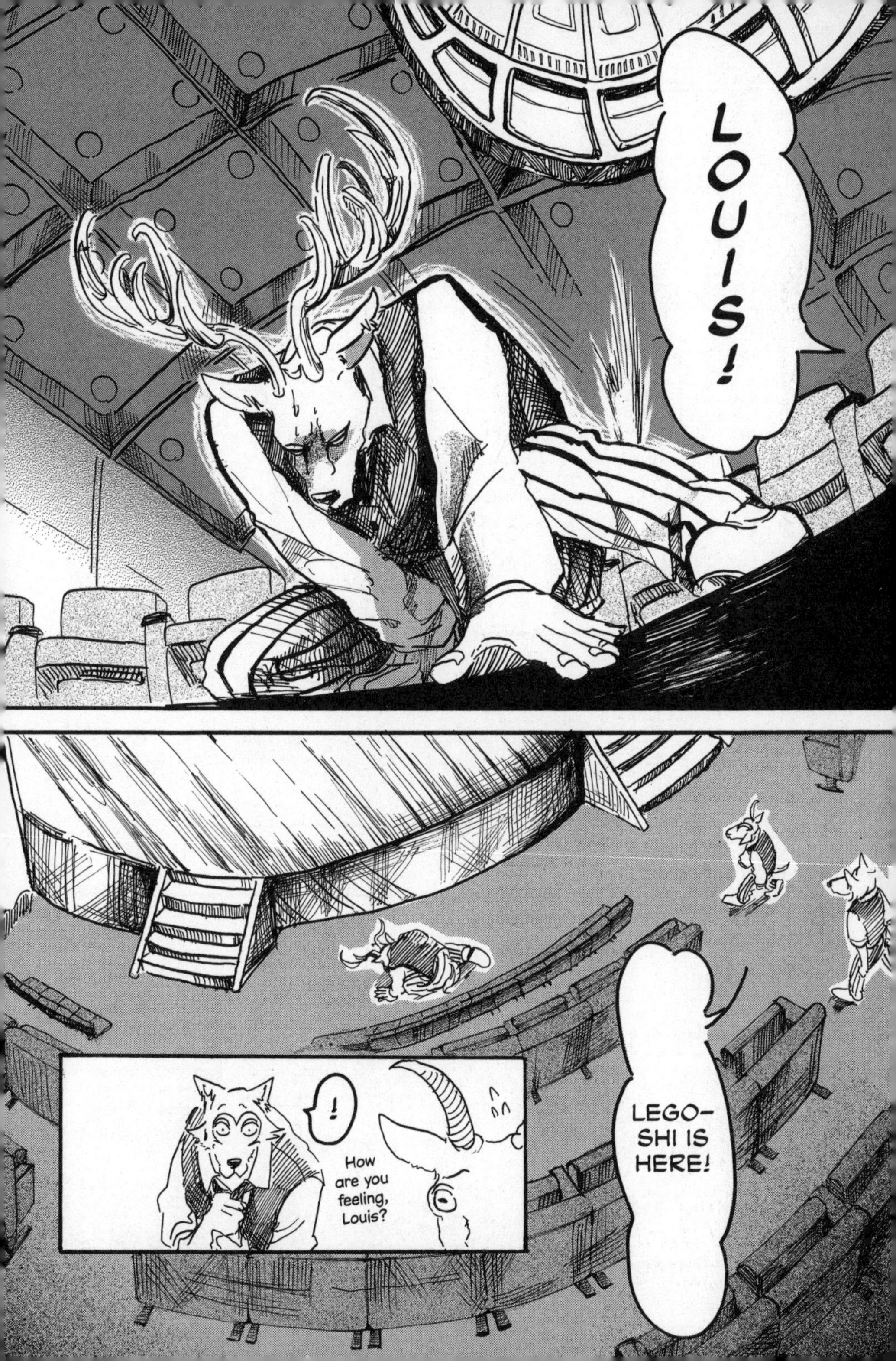
LOUIS!
LEGO-SHI IS HERE!
How are you feeling, Louis?
!

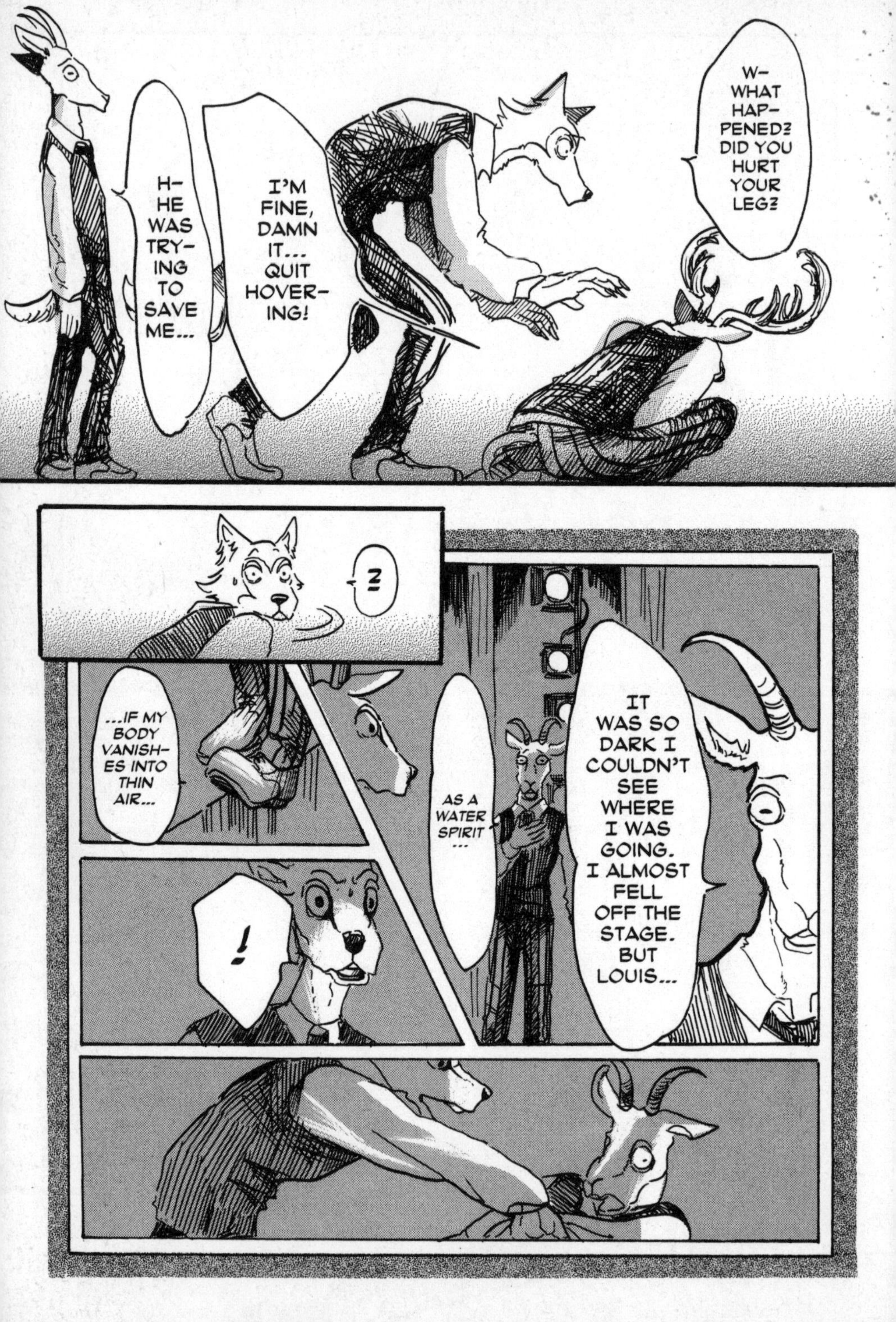
W-WHAT HAPPENED? DID YOU HURT YOUR LEG?
I'M FINE, DAMN IT... QUIT HOVERING!
H-HE WAS TRYING TO SAVE ME...
IT WAS SO DARK I COULDN'T SEE WHERE I WAS GOING. I ALMOST FELL OFF THE STAGE. BUT LOUIS...
AS A WATER SPIRIT...
?
...IF MY BODY VANISHES INTO THIN AIR...
!

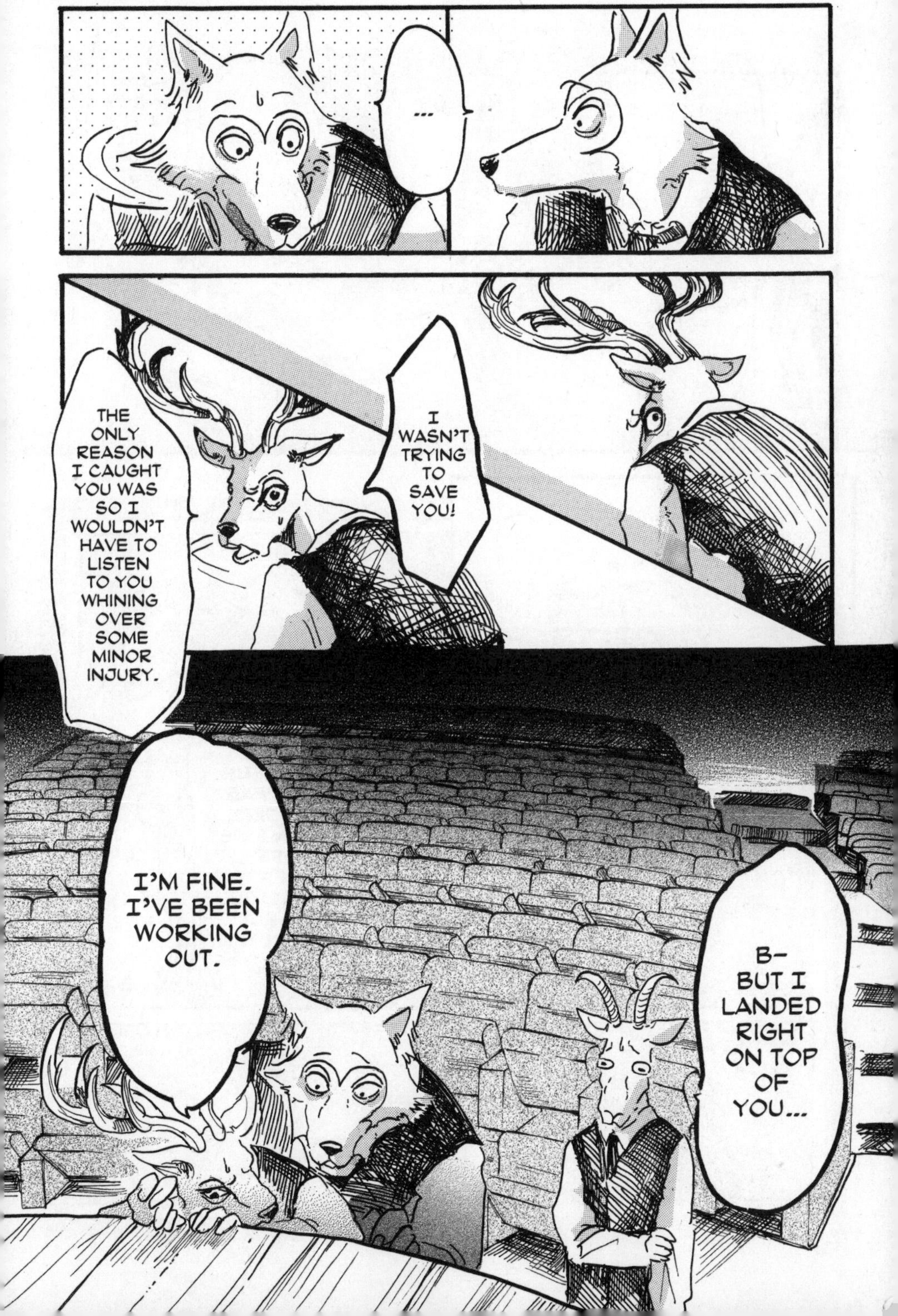
...
I WASN'T TRYING TO SAVE YOU!
THE ONLY REASON I CAUGHT YOU WAS SO I WOULDN'T HAVE TO LISTEN TO YOU WHINING OVER SOME MINOR INJURY.
B- BUT I LANDED RIGHT ON TOP OF YOU...
I'M FINE. I'VE BEEN WORKING OUT.

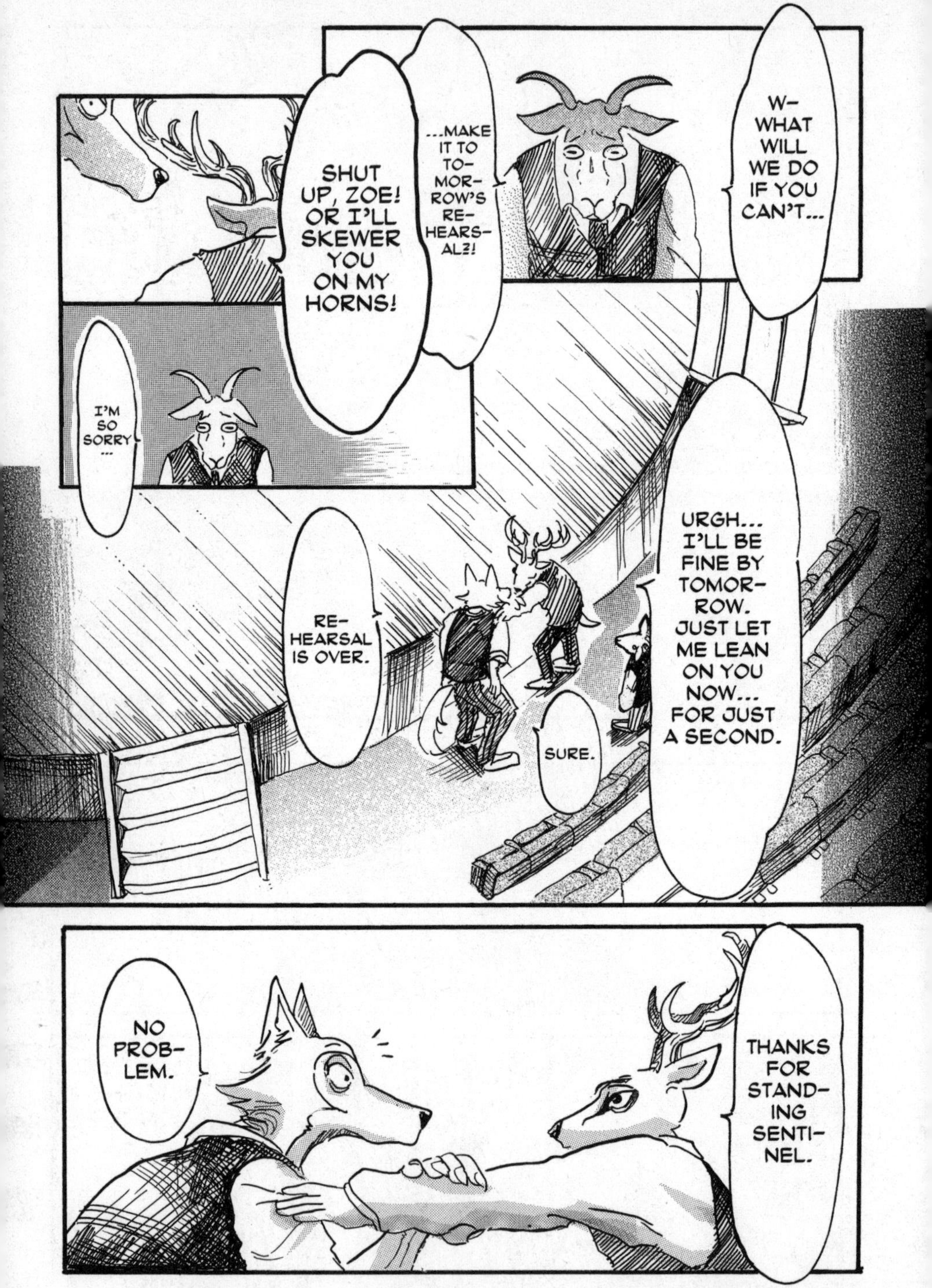
W- WHAT WILL WE DO IF YOU CAN'T...
...MAKE IT TO TOMORROW'S REHEARSAL?!
SHUT UP, ZOE! OR I'LL SKEWER YOU ON MY HORNS!
I'M SO SORRY...
URGH... I'LL BE FINE BY TOMORROW. JUST LET ME LEAN ON YOU NOW... FOR JUST A SECOND.
REHEARSAL IS OVER.
SURE.
THANKS FOR STANDING SENTINEL.
NO PROBLEM.

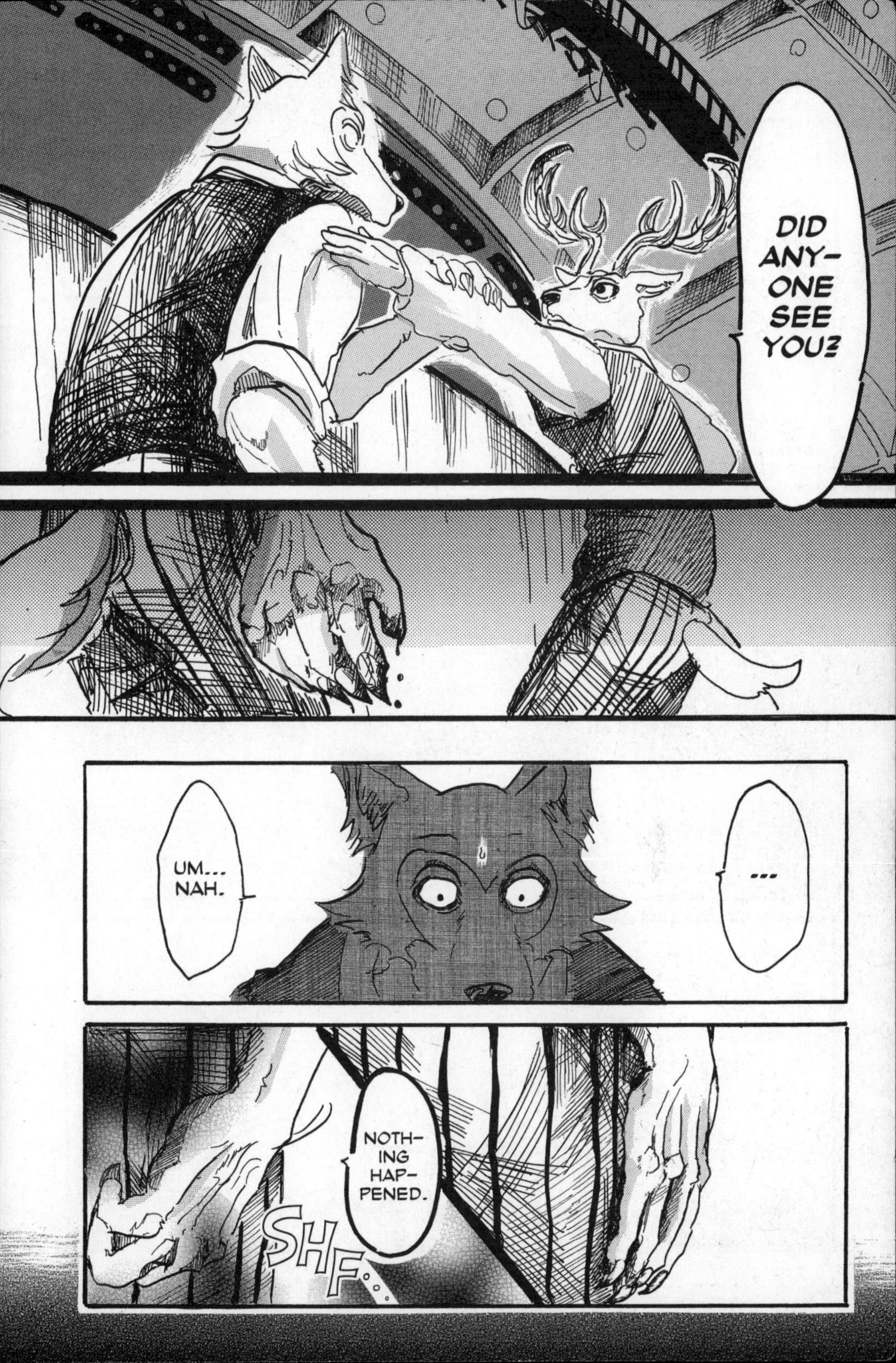

DID ANY-ONE SEE YOU?
...
UM... NAH.
NOTH-ING HAP-PENED.
SHF...

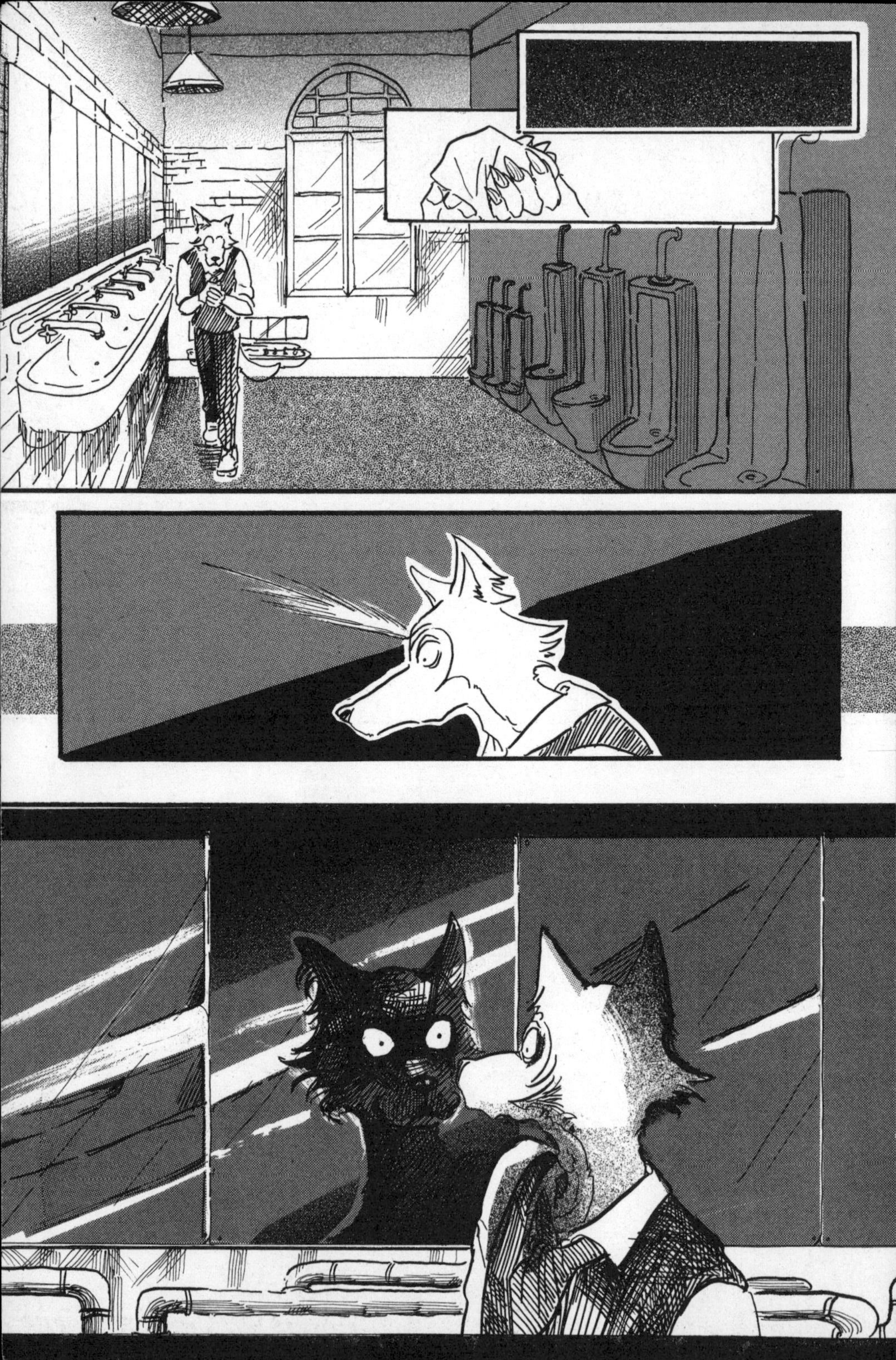

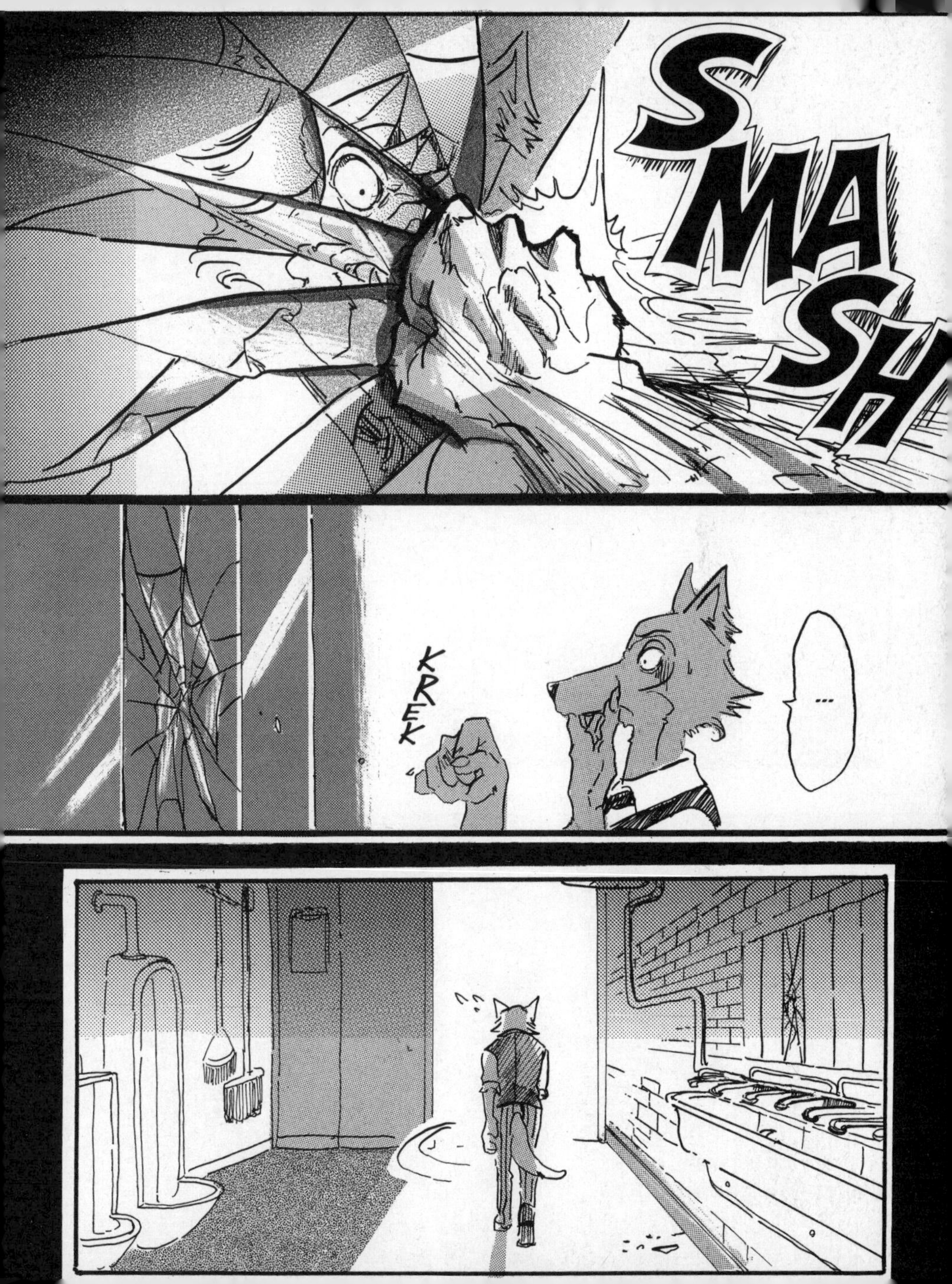
SMASH
…
KREK

Chapter 6: The Beasts' First-Magnitude Star

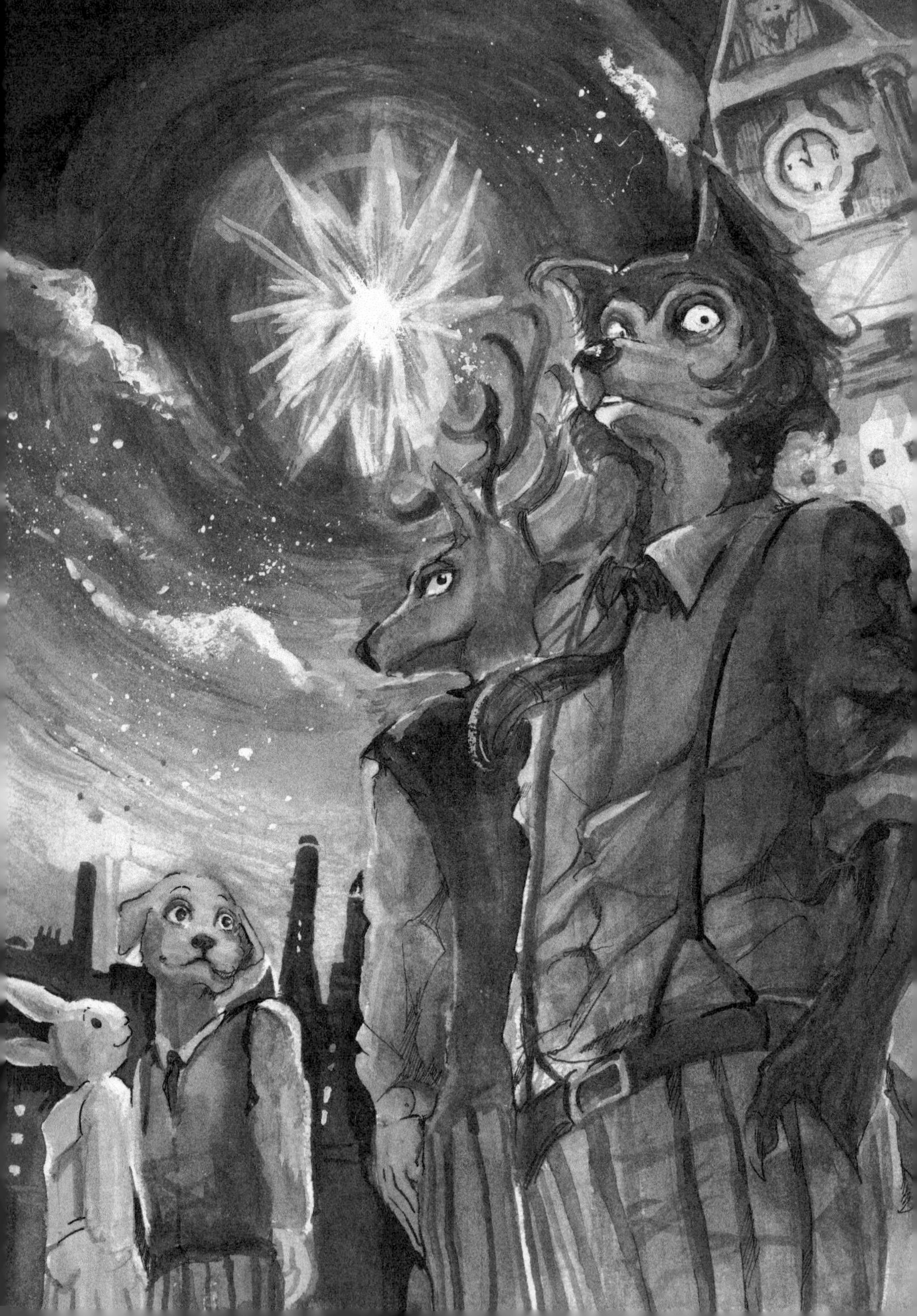

BEASTARS Vol.1

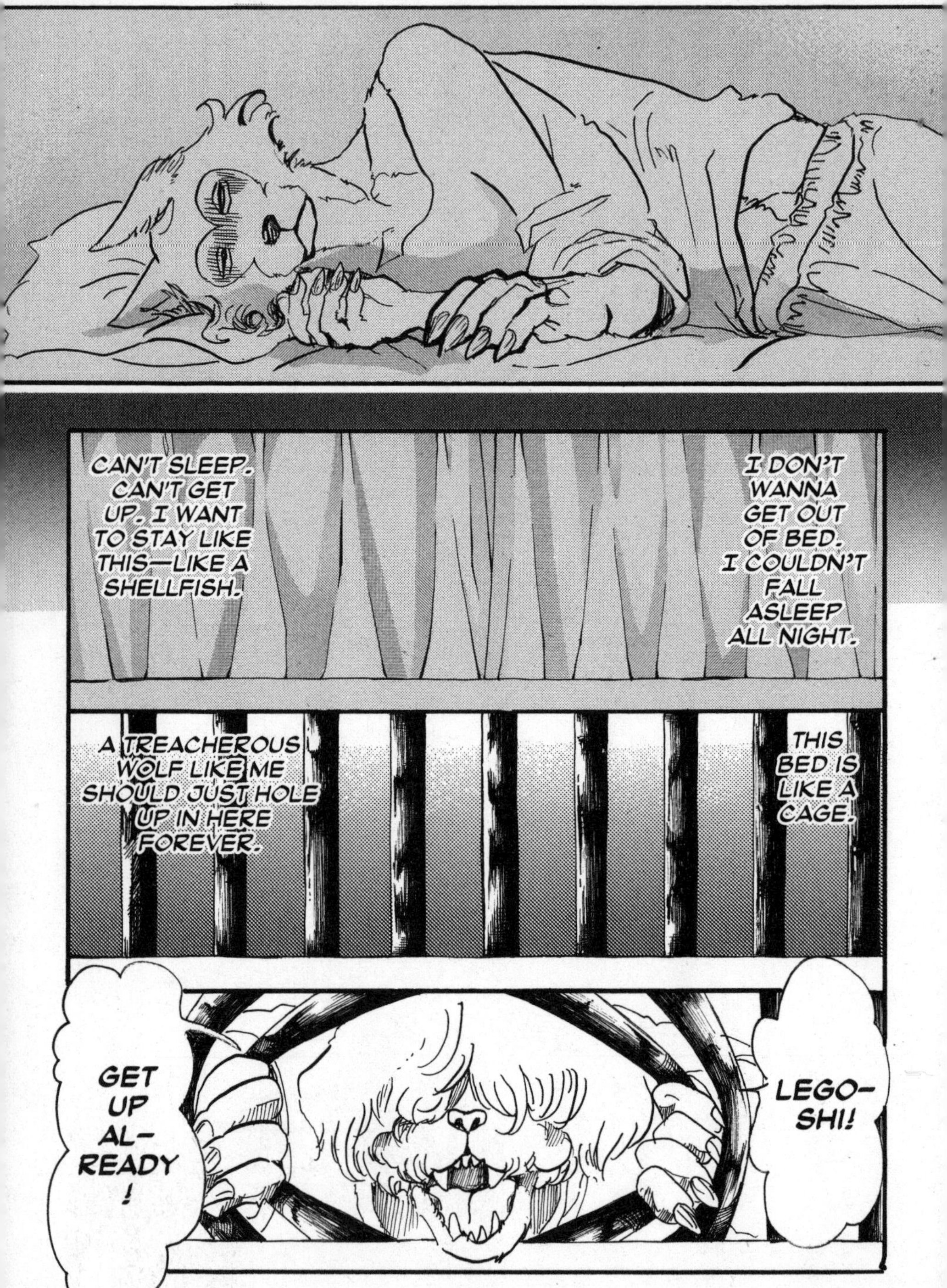
I DON'T WANNA GET OUT OF BED. I COULDN'T FALL ASLEEP ALL NIGHT.
CAN'T SLEEP. CAN'T GET UP. I WANT TO STAY LIKE THIS—LIKE A SHELLFISH.
THIS BED IS LIKE A CAGE.
A TREACHEROUS WOLF LIKE ME SHOULD JUST HOLE UP IN HERE FOREVER.
LEGO-SHI!
GET UP AL-READY!

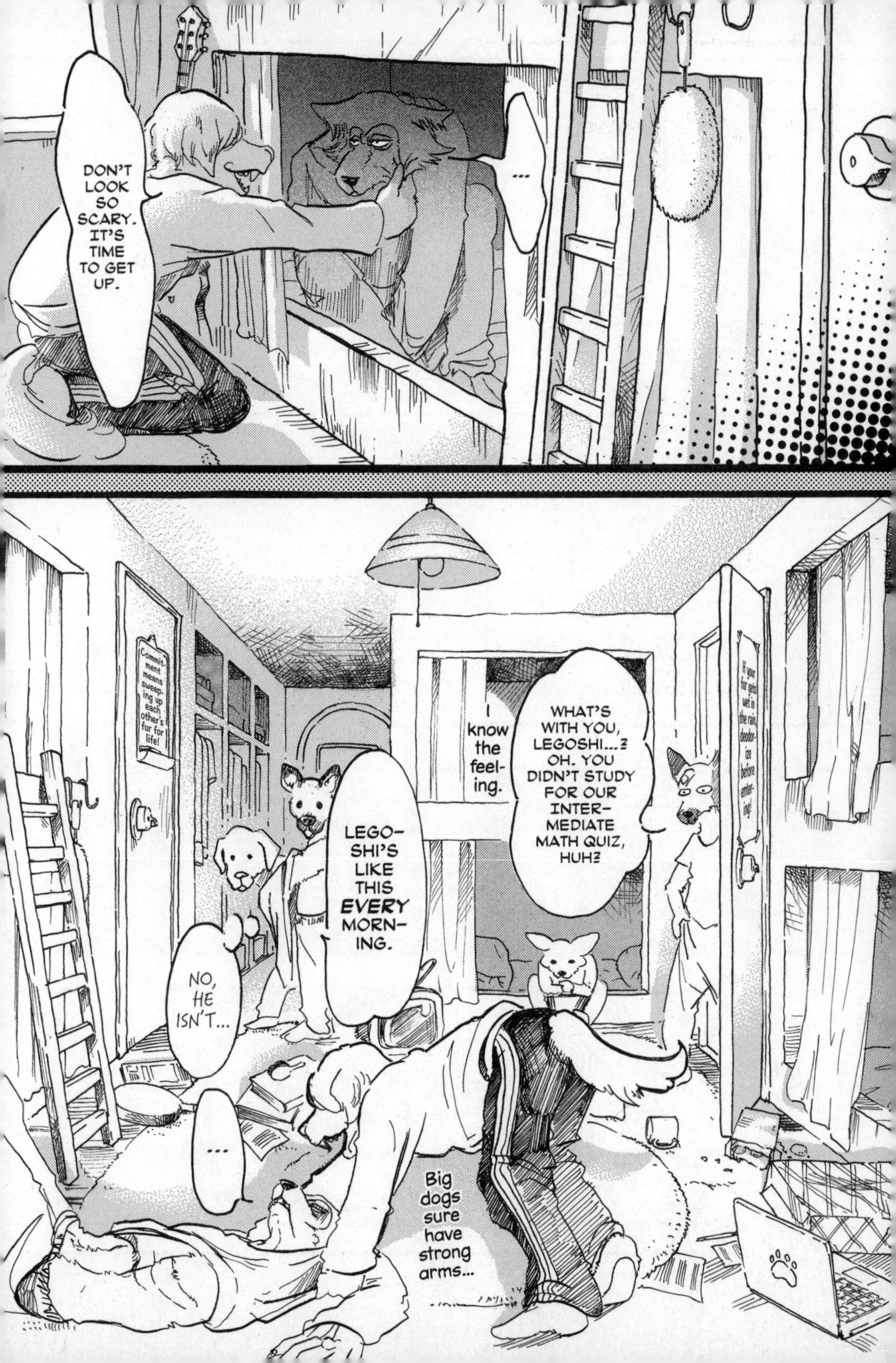
...
DON'T LOOK SO SCARY. IT'S TIME TO GET UP.
If your fur gets wet in the rain, deodorize before entering!
WHAT'S WITH YOU, LEGOSHI...? OH. YOU DIDN'T STUDY FOR OUR INTERMEDIATE MATH QUIZ, HUH?
I know the feeling.
LEGOSHI'S LIKE THIS **EVERY** MORNING.
Commitment means sweeping up each other's fur for life!
NO, HE ISN'T...
Big dogs sure have strong arms...
...

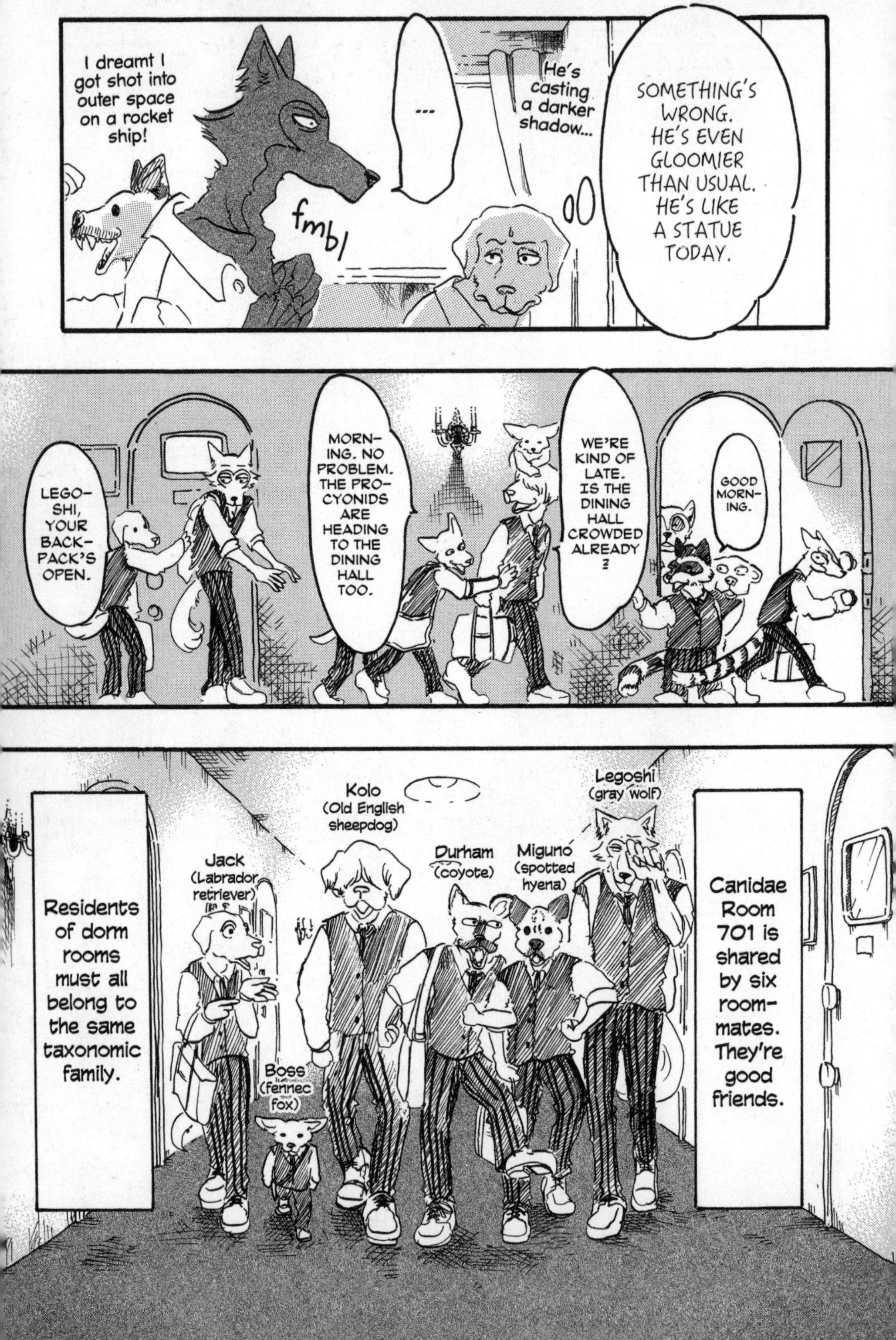
SOMETHING'S WRONG. HE'S EVEN GLOOMIER THAN USUAL. HE'S LIKE A STATUE TODAY.
He's casting a darker shadow...
...
I dreamt I got shot into outer space on a rocket ship!
fmbl
GOOD MORNING.
WE'RE KIND OF LATE. IS THE DINING HALL CROWDED ALREADY?
MORNING. NO PROBLEM. THE PROCYONIDS ARE HEADING TO THE DINING HALL TOO.
LEGOSHI, YOUR BACKPACK'S OPEN.
Canidae Room 701 is shared by six roommates. They're good friends.
Legoshi (gray wolf)
Miguno (spotted hyena)
Durham (coyote)
Kolo (Old English sheepdog)
Jack (Labrador retriever)
Boss (fennec fox)
Residents of dorm rooms must all belong to the same taxonomic family.

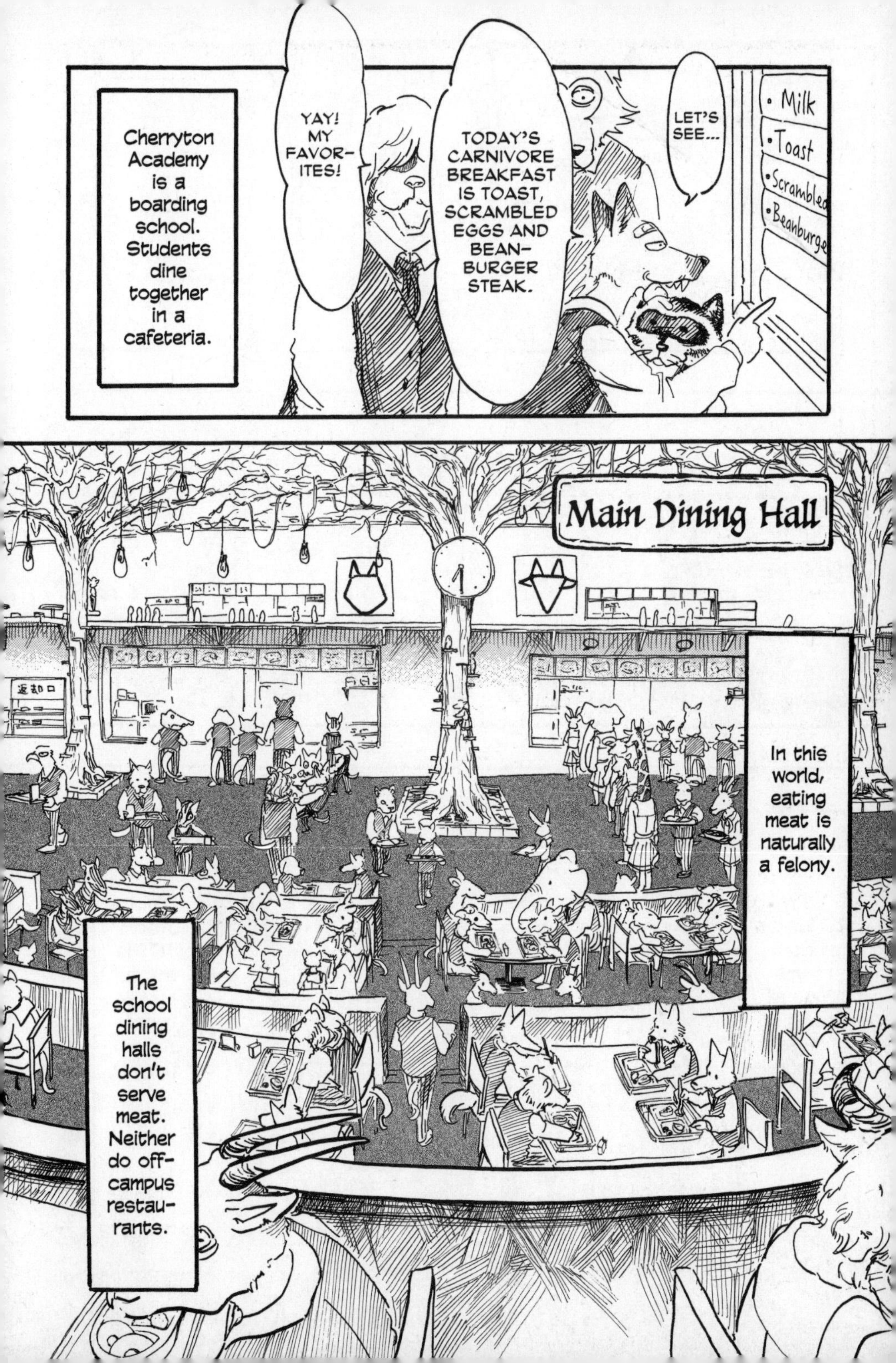

• Milk
• Toast
• Scrambled
• Beanburge
LET'S SEE...
TODAY'S CARNIVORE BREAKFAST IS TOAST, SCRAMBLED EGGS AND BEAN-BURGER STEAK.
YAY! MY FAVOR-ITES!
Cherryton Academy is a boarding school. Students dine together in a cafeteria.
Main Dining Hall
In this world, eating meat is naturally a felony.
返却口
The school dining halls don't serve meat. Neither do off-campus restau-rants.

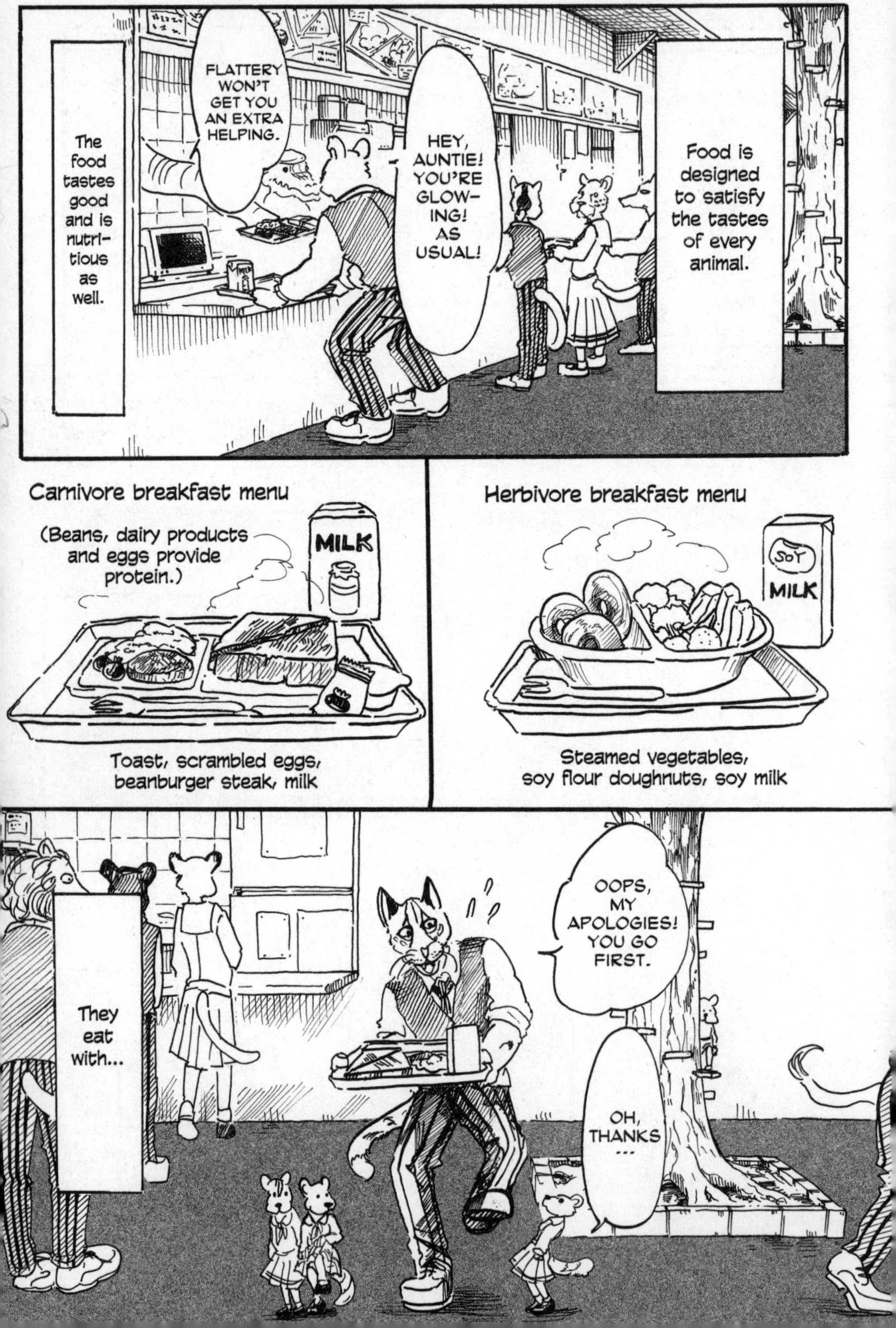

Food is designed to satisfy the tastes of every animal.
HEY, AUNTIE! YOU'RE GLOW-ING! AS USUAL!
FLATTERY WON'T GET YOU AN EXTRA HELPING.
The food tastes good and is nutri-tious as well.
Herbivore breakfast menu
SOY MILK
Steamed vegetables, soy flour doughnuts, soy milk
Carnivore breakfast menu
(Beans, dairy products and eggs provide protein.)
MILK
Toast, scrambled eggs, beanburger steak, milk
OOPS, MY APOLOGIES! YOU GO FIRST.
OH, THANKS...
They eat with...

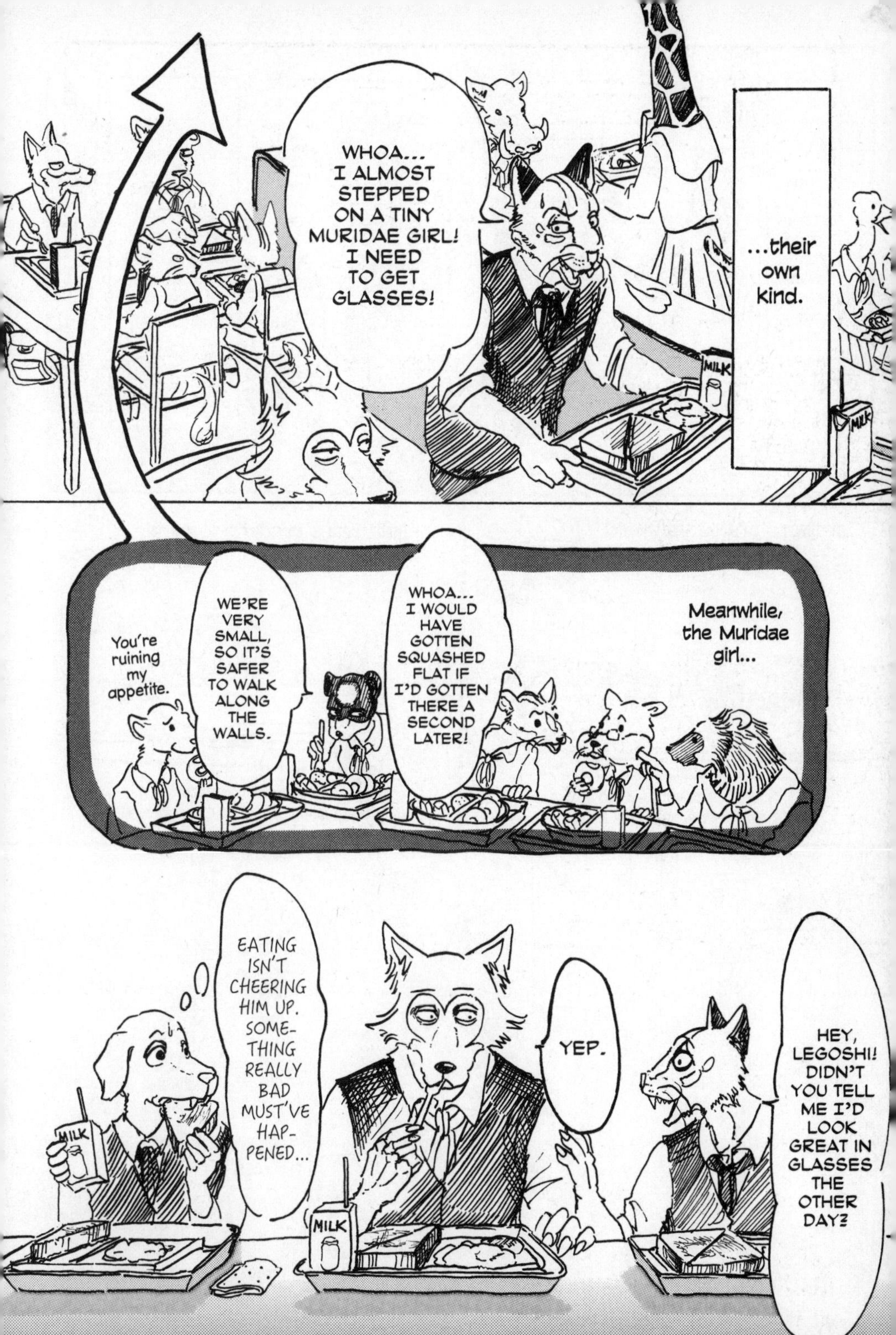
...their own kind.
WHOA... I ALMOST STEPPED ON A TINY MURIDAE GIRL! I NEED TO GET GLASSES!
Meanwhile, the Muridae girl...
WHOA... I WOULD HAVE GOTTEN SQUASHED FLAT IF I'D GOTTEN THERE A SECOND LATER!
WE'RE VERY SMALL, SO IT'S SAFER TO WALK ALONG THE WALLS.
You're ruining my appetite.
HEY, LEGOSHI! DIDN'T YOU TELL ME I'D LOOK GREAT IN GLASSES THE OTHER DAY?
YEP.
EATING ISN'T CHEERING HIM UP. SOME-THING REALLY BAD MUST'VE HAP-PENED...
MILK

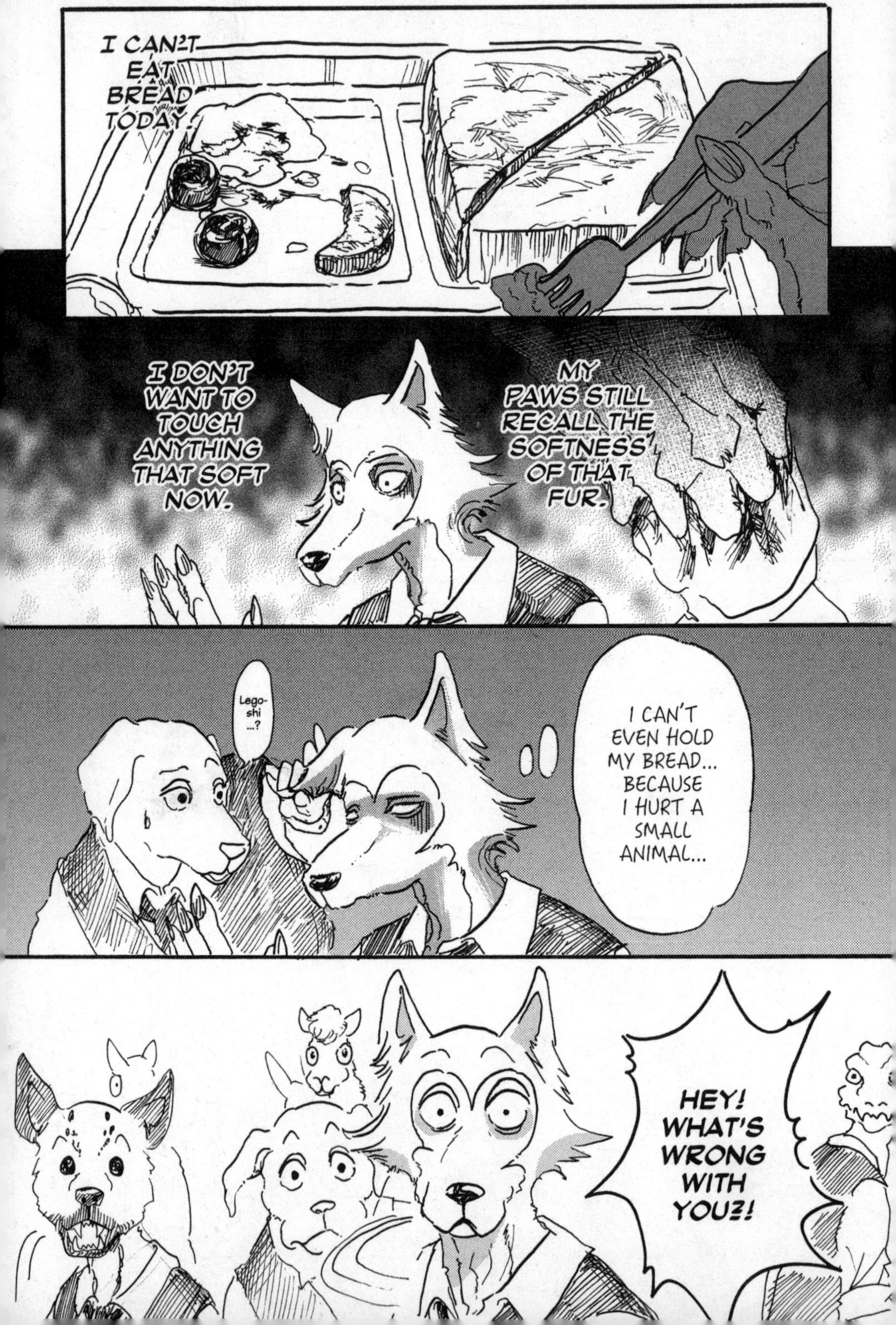
I CAN'T EAT BREAD TODAY.
MY PAWS STILL RECALL THE SOFTNESS OF THAT FUR.
I DON'T WANT TO TOUCH ANYTHING THAT SOFT NOW.
I CAN'T EVEN HOLD MY BREAD... BECAUSE I HURT A SMALL ANIMAL...
Lego-shi ...?
HEY! WHAT'S WRONG WITH YOU?!

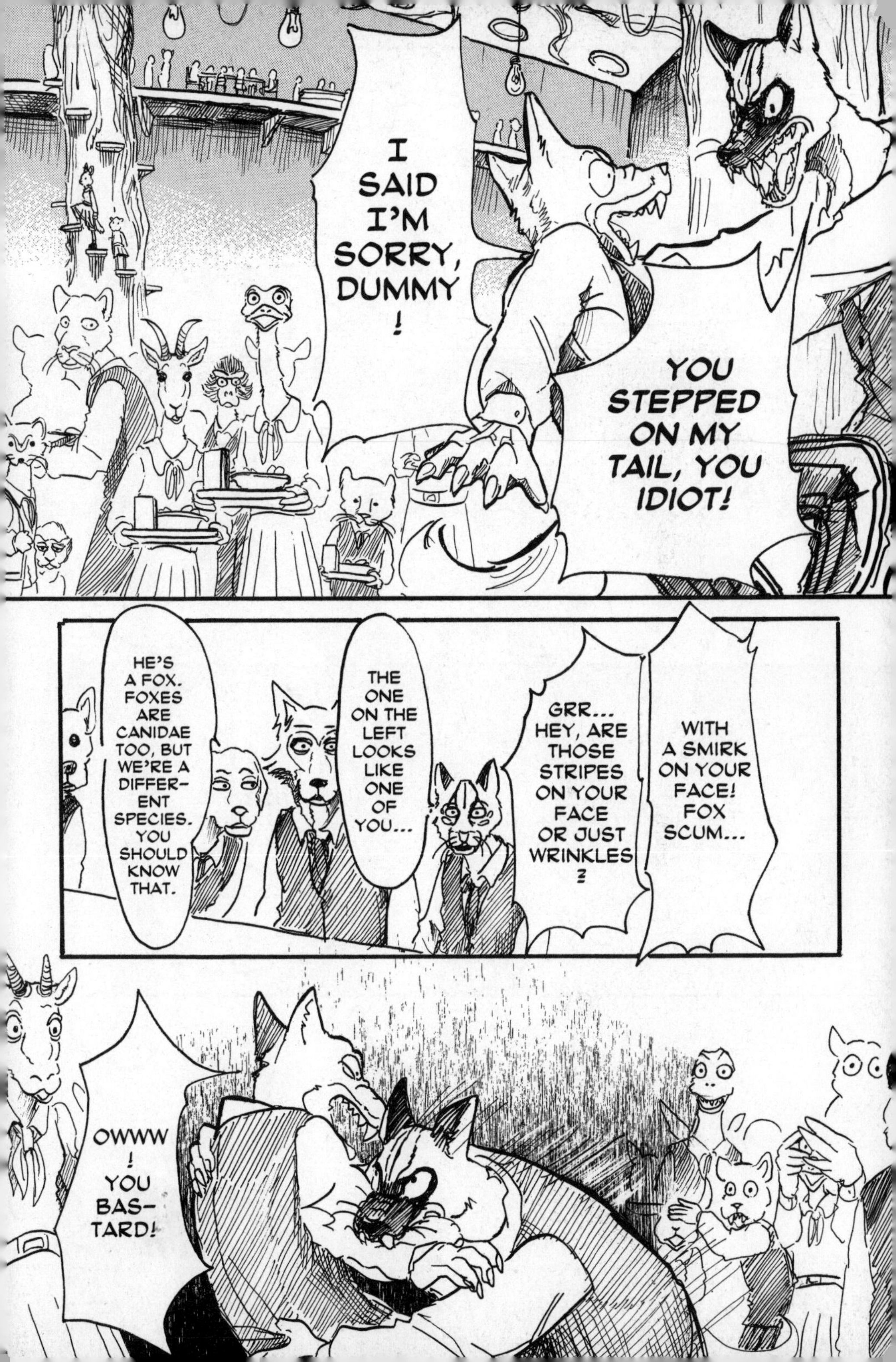
YOU STEPPED ON MY TAIL, YOU IDIOT!
I SAID I'M SORRY, DUMMY!
WITH A SMIRK ON YOUR FACE! FOX SCUM...
GRR... HEY, ARE THOSE STRIPES ON YOUR FACE OR JUST WRINKLES?
THE ONE ON THE LEFT LOOKS LIKE ONE OF YOU...
HE'S A FOX. FOXES ARE CANIDAE TOO, BUT WE'RE A DIFFER-ENT SPECIES. YOU SHOULD KNOW THAT.
OWWW! YOU BAS-TARD!

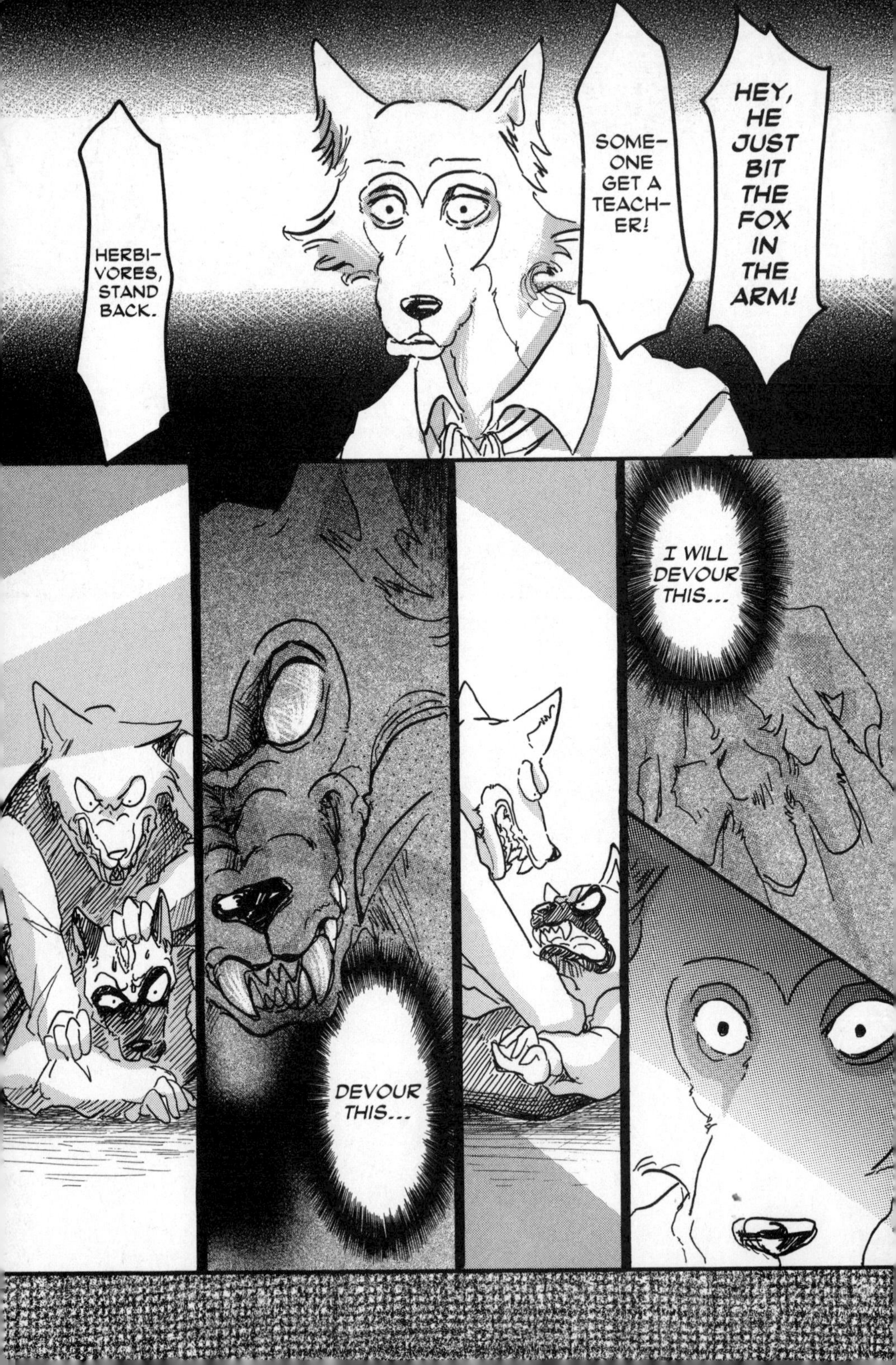
HEY, HE JUST BIT THE FOX IN THE ARM!
SOME-ONE GET A TEACH-ER!
HERBI-VORES, STAND BACK.
I WILL DEVOUR THIS...
DEVOUR THIS...

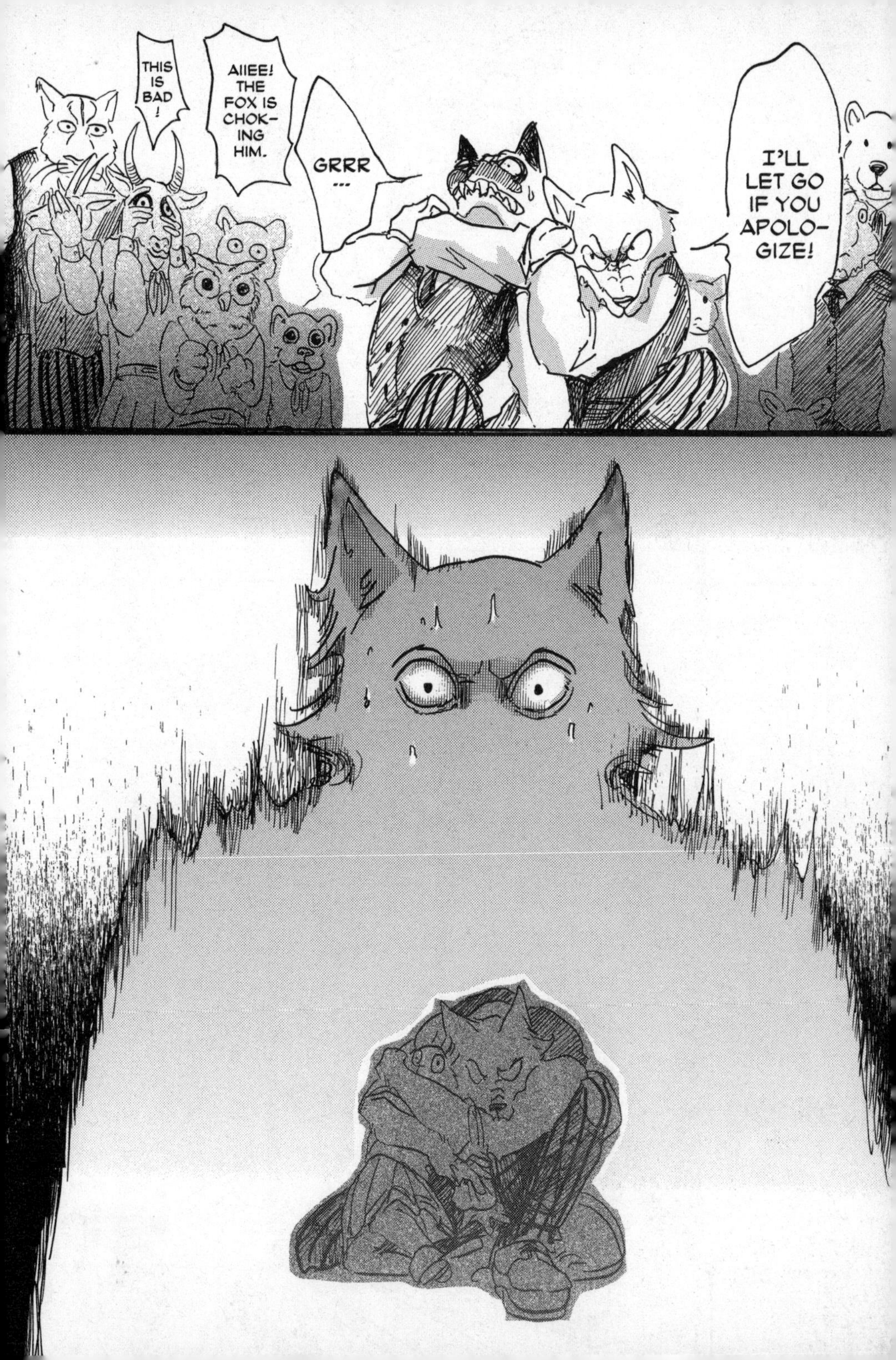
I'LL LET GO IF YOU APOLOGIZE!
GRRR...
AIIEE! THE FOX IS CHOKING HIM.
THIS IS BAD!

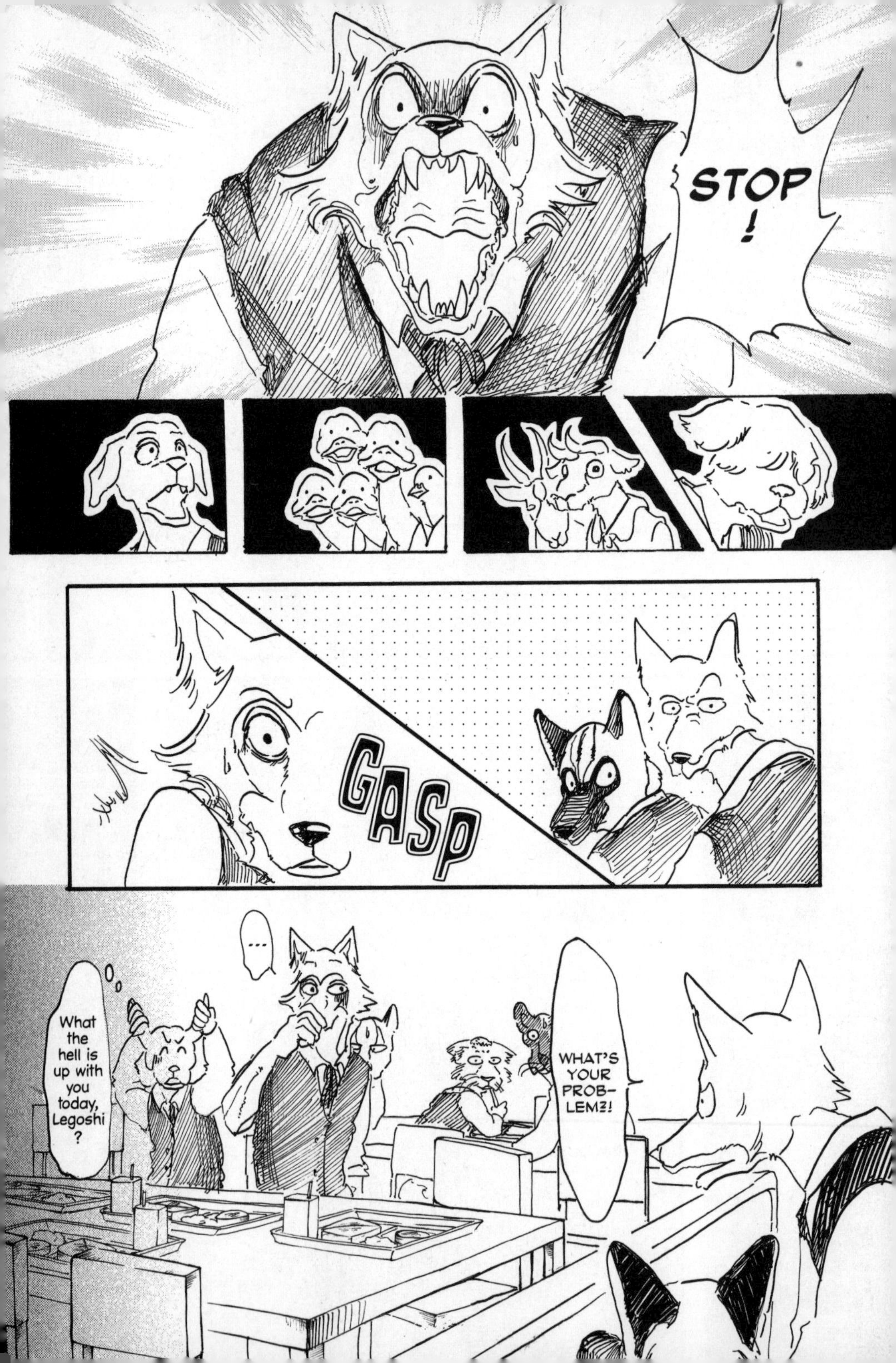
STOP!
GASP
WHAT'S YOUR PROB-LEM?!
...
What the hell is up with you today, Legoshi?

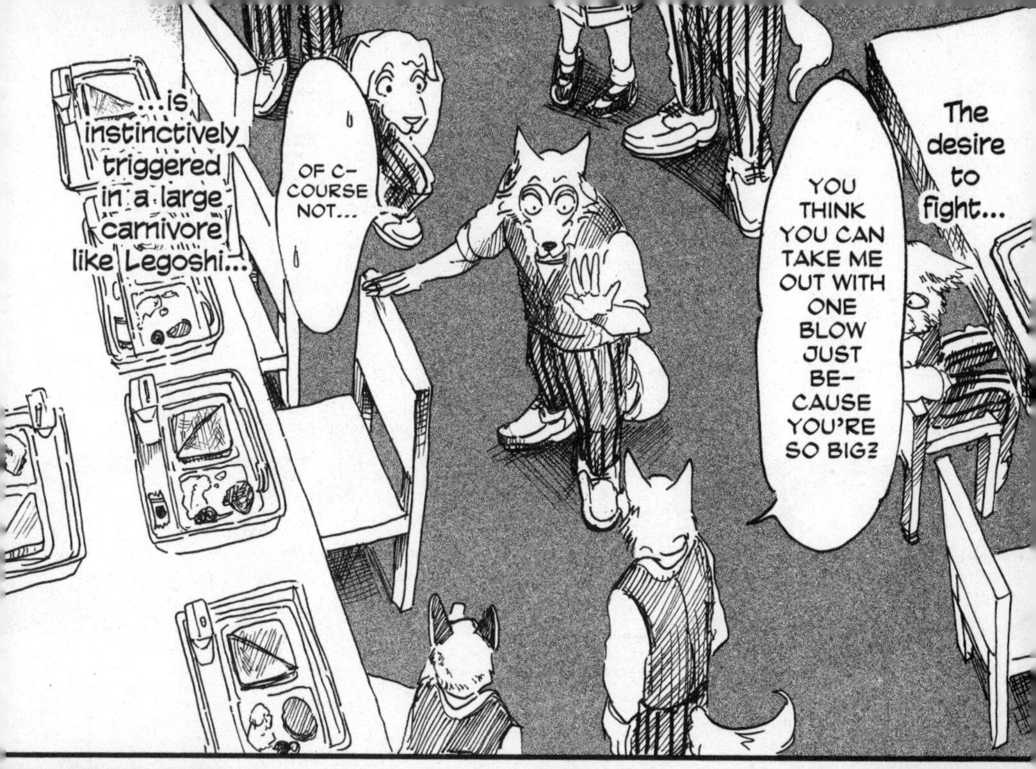
The desire to fight...
YOU THINK YOU CAN TAKE ME OUT WITH ONE BLOW JUST BE-CAUSE YOU'RE SO BIG?
OF C-COURSE NOT...
...is instinctively triggered in a large carnivore like Legoshi...

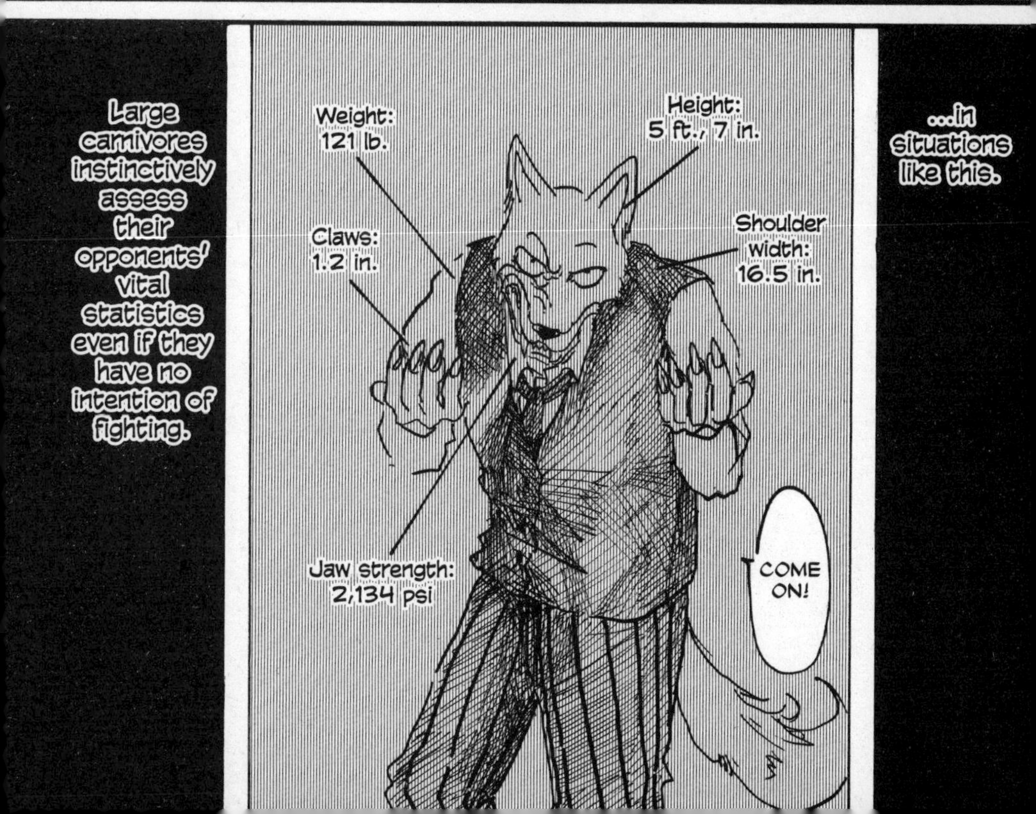
...in situations like this.
Height: 5 ft., 7 in.
Shoulder width: 16.5 in.
Weight: 121 lb.
Claws: 1.2 in.
COME ON!
Jaw strength: 2,134 psi
Large carnivores instinctively assess their opponents' vital statistics even if they have no intention of fighting.

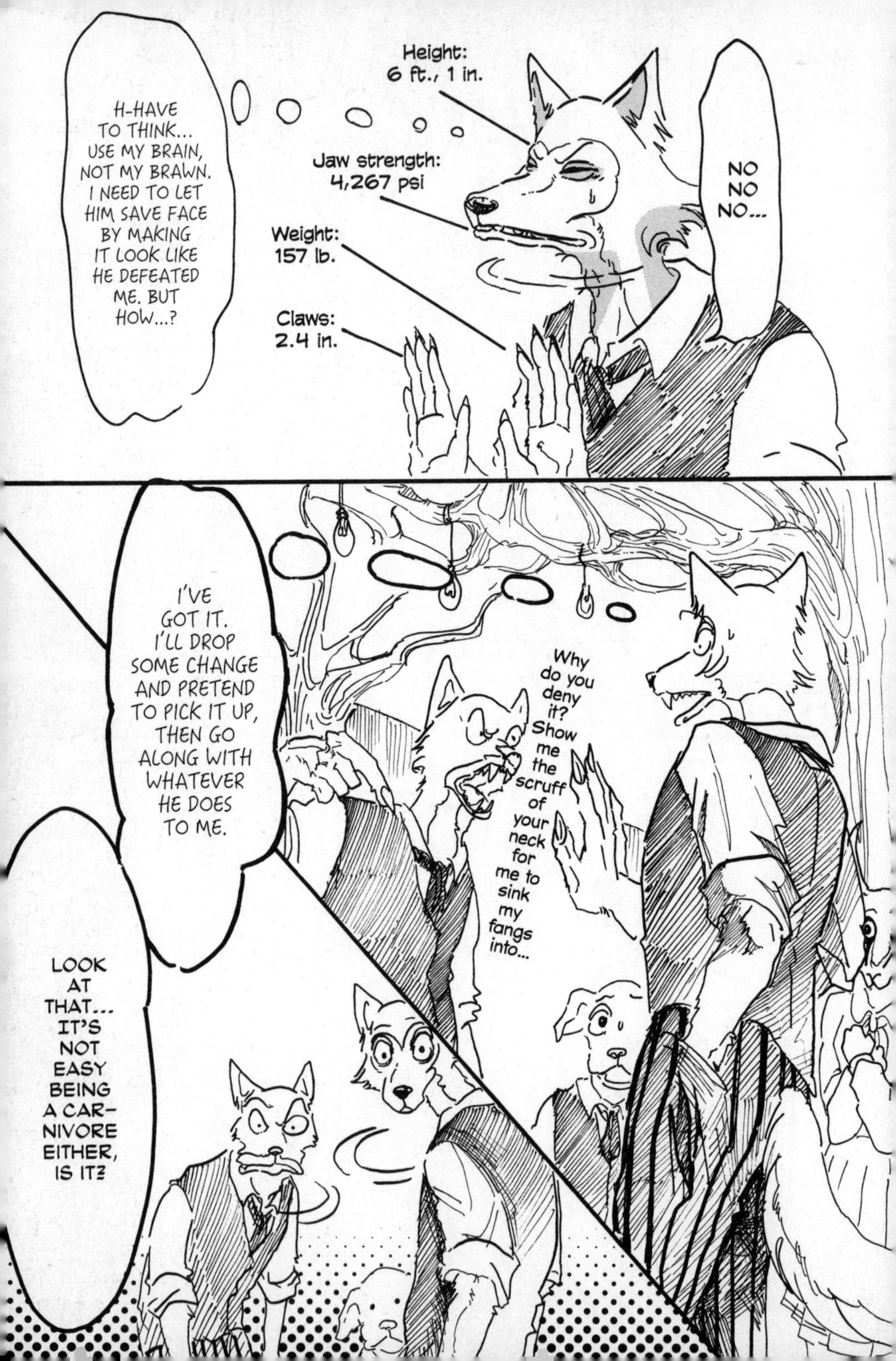
NO NO NO...
Height: 6 ft., 1 in.
Jaw strength: 4,267 psi
Weight: 157 lb.
Claws: 2.4 in.
H-HAVE TO THINK... USE MY BRAIN, NOT MY BRAWN. I NEED TO LET HIM SAVE FACE BY MAKING IT LOOK LIKE HE DEFEATED ME. BUT HOW...?
Why do you deny it? Show me the scruff of your neck for me to sink my fangs into...
I'VE GOT IT. I'LL DROP SOME CHANGE AND PRETEND TO PICK IT UP, THEN GO ALONG WITH WHATEVER HE DOES TO ME.
LOOK AT THAT... IT'S NOT EASY BEING A CAR-NIVORE EITHER, IS IT?

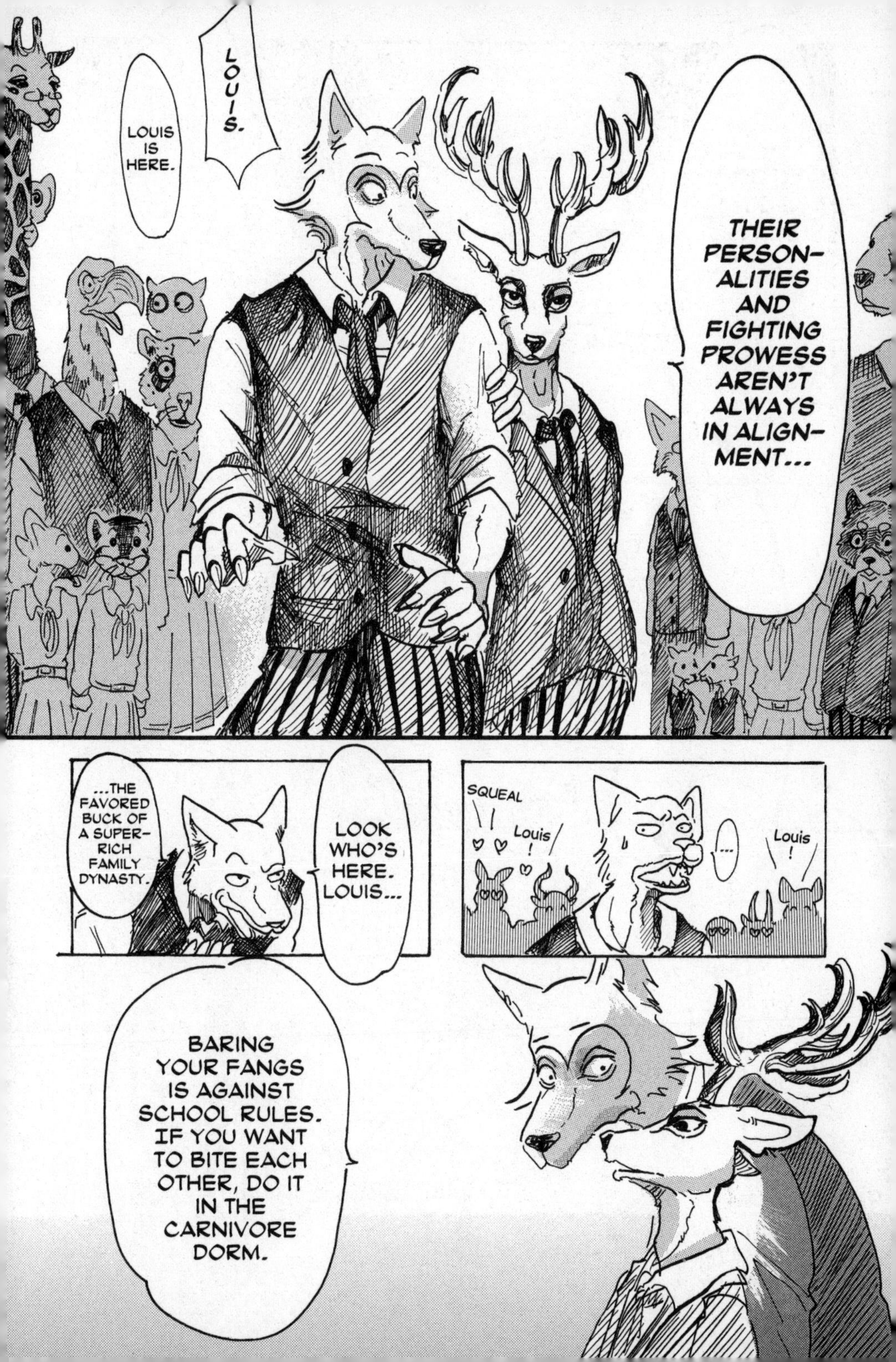
THEIR PERSONALITIES AND FIGHTING PROWESS AREN'T ALWAYS IN ALIGNMENT...
LOUIS.
LOUIS IS HERE.
Louis!
...
SQUEAL
Louis!
LOOK WHO'S HERE. LOUIS...
...THE FAVORED BUCK OF A SUPER-RICH FAMILY DYNASTY.
BARING YOUR FANGS IS AGAINST SCHOOL RULES. IF YOU WANT TO BITE EACH OTHER, DO IT IN THE CARNIVORE DORM.

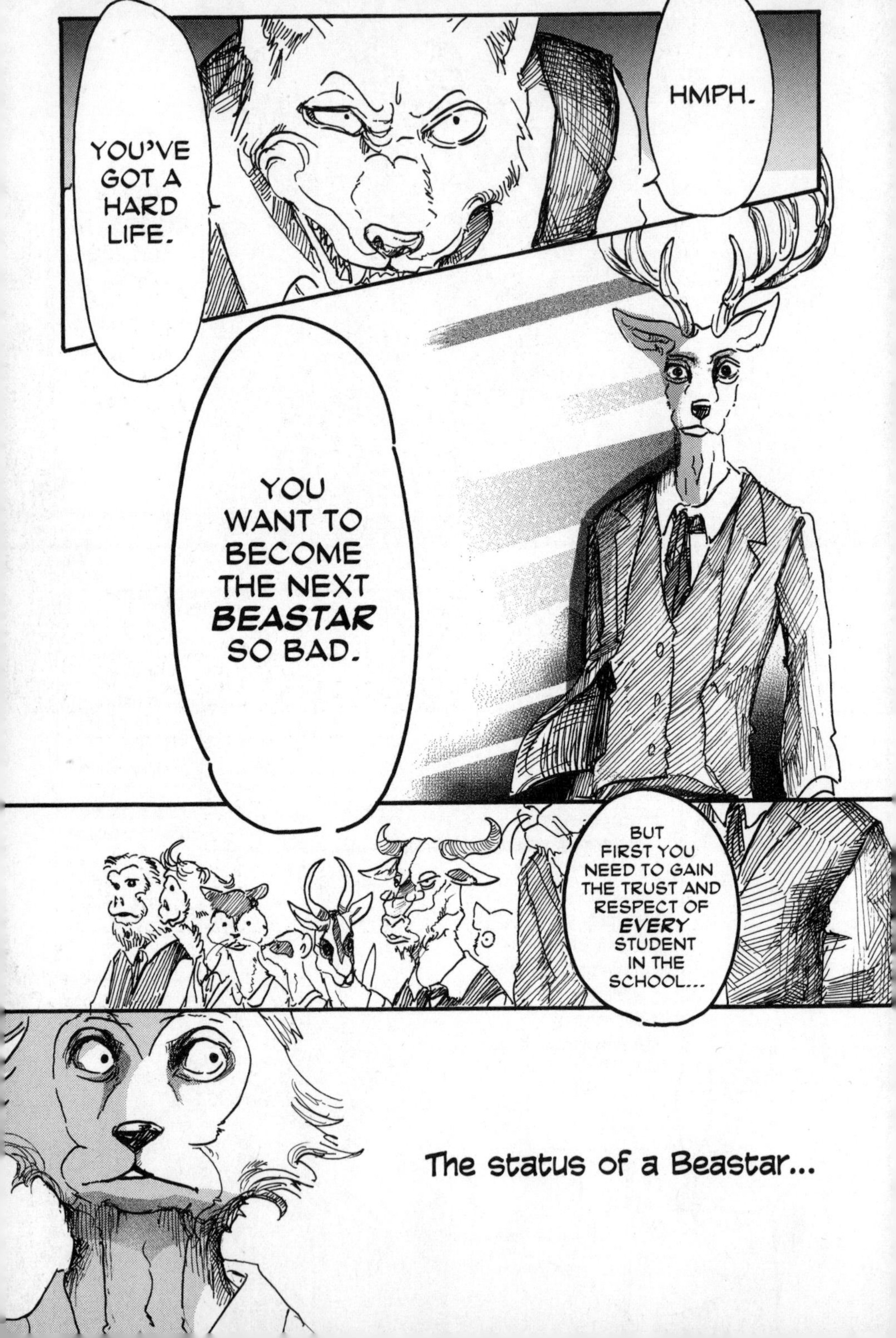
HMPH.
YOU'VE GOT A HARD LIFE.
YOU WANT TO BECOME THE NEXT *BEASTAR* SO BAD.
BUT FIRST YOU NEED TO GAIN THE TRUST AND RESPECT OF *EVERY* STUDENT IN THE SCHOOL...
The status of a Beastar...

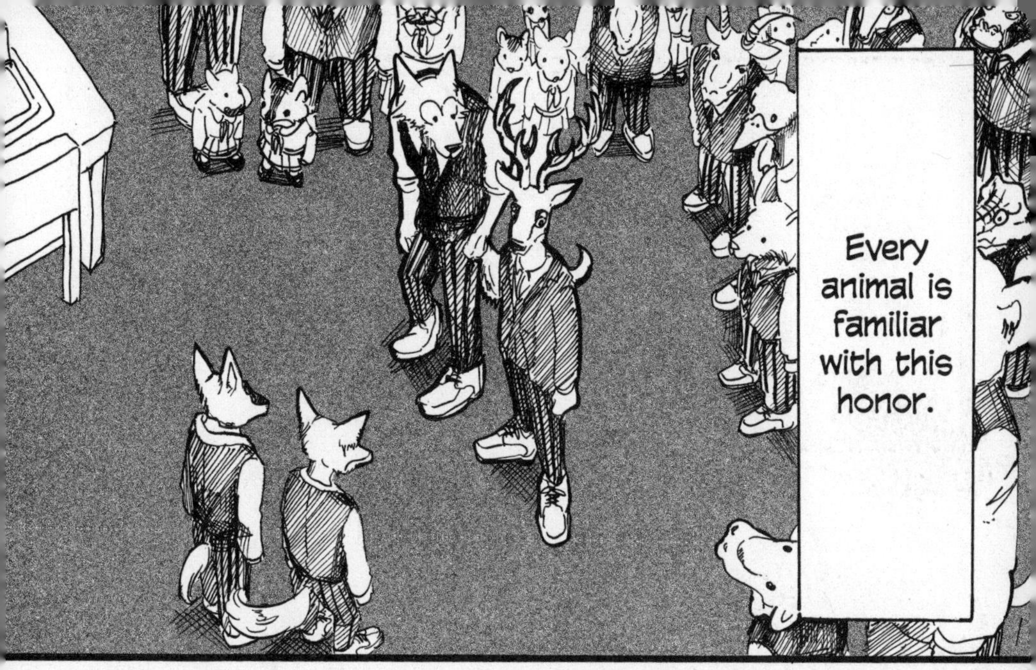
Every animal is familiar with this honor.
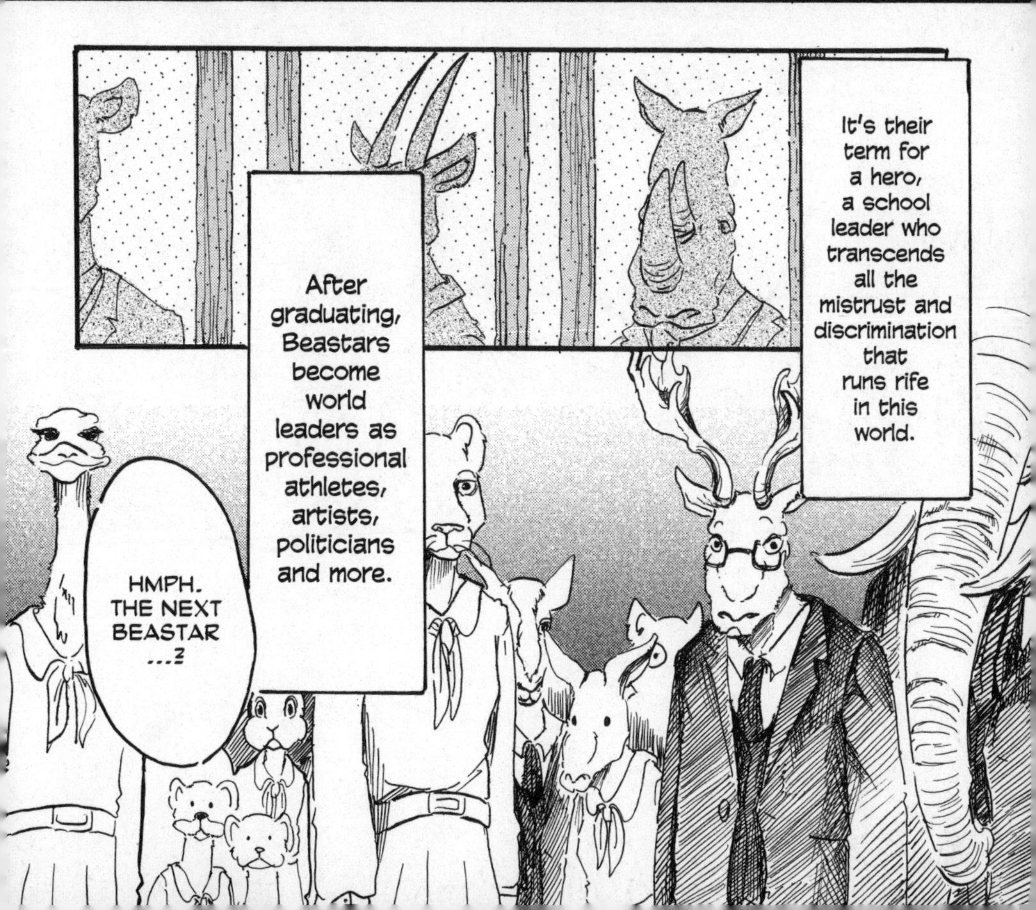
It's their term for a hero, a school leader who transcends all the mistrust and discrimination that runs rife in this world.
After graduating, Beastars become world leaders as professional athletes, artists, politicians and more.
HMPH. THE NEXT BEASTAR...?

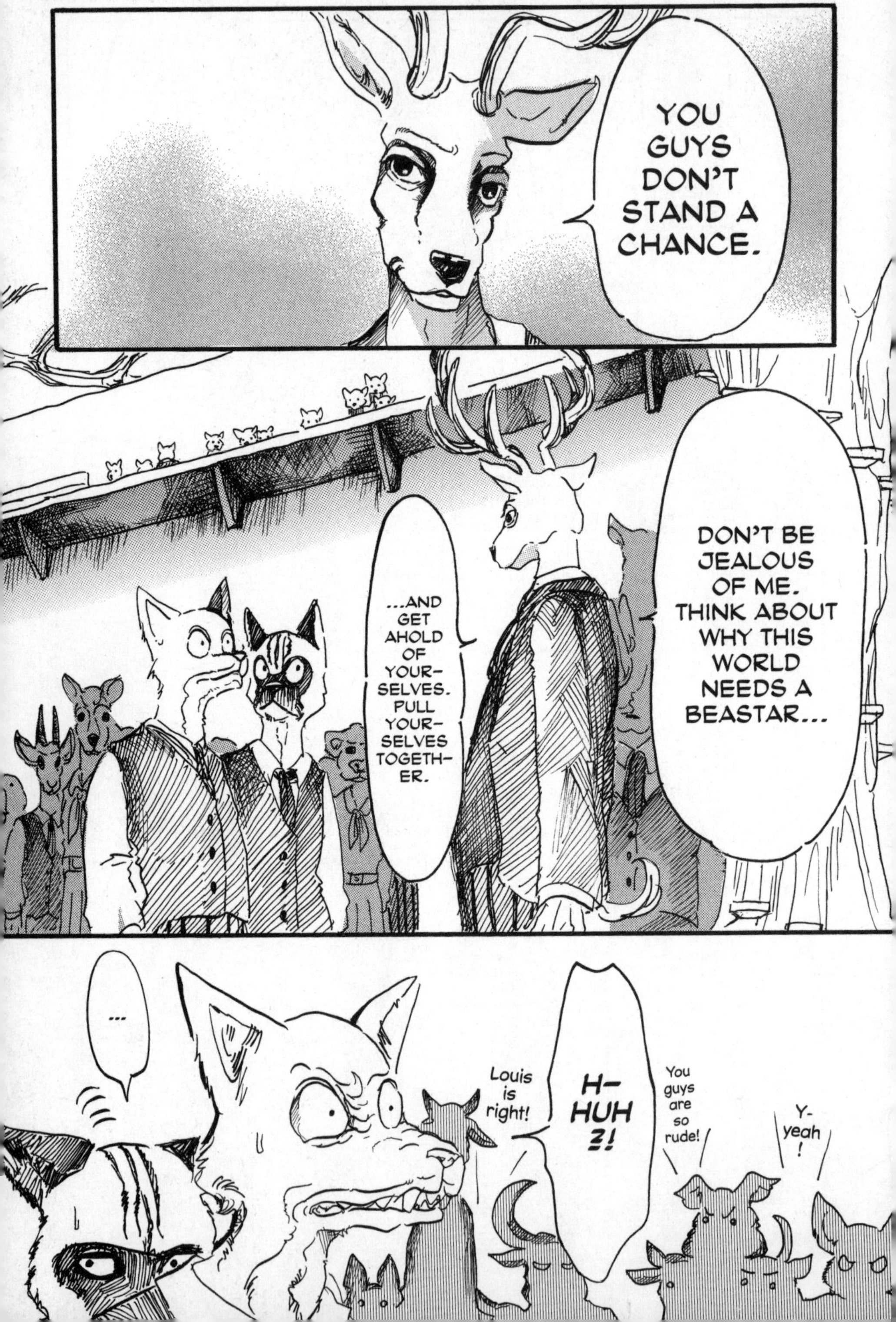
YOU GUYS DON'T STAND A CHANCE.
DON'T BE JEALOUS OF ME. THINK ABOUT WHY THIS WORLD NEEDS A BEASTAR...
...AND GET AHOLD OF YOURSELVES. PULL YOURSELVES TOGETHER.
Y-yeah!
You guys are so rude!
H-HUH?!
Louis is right!
...

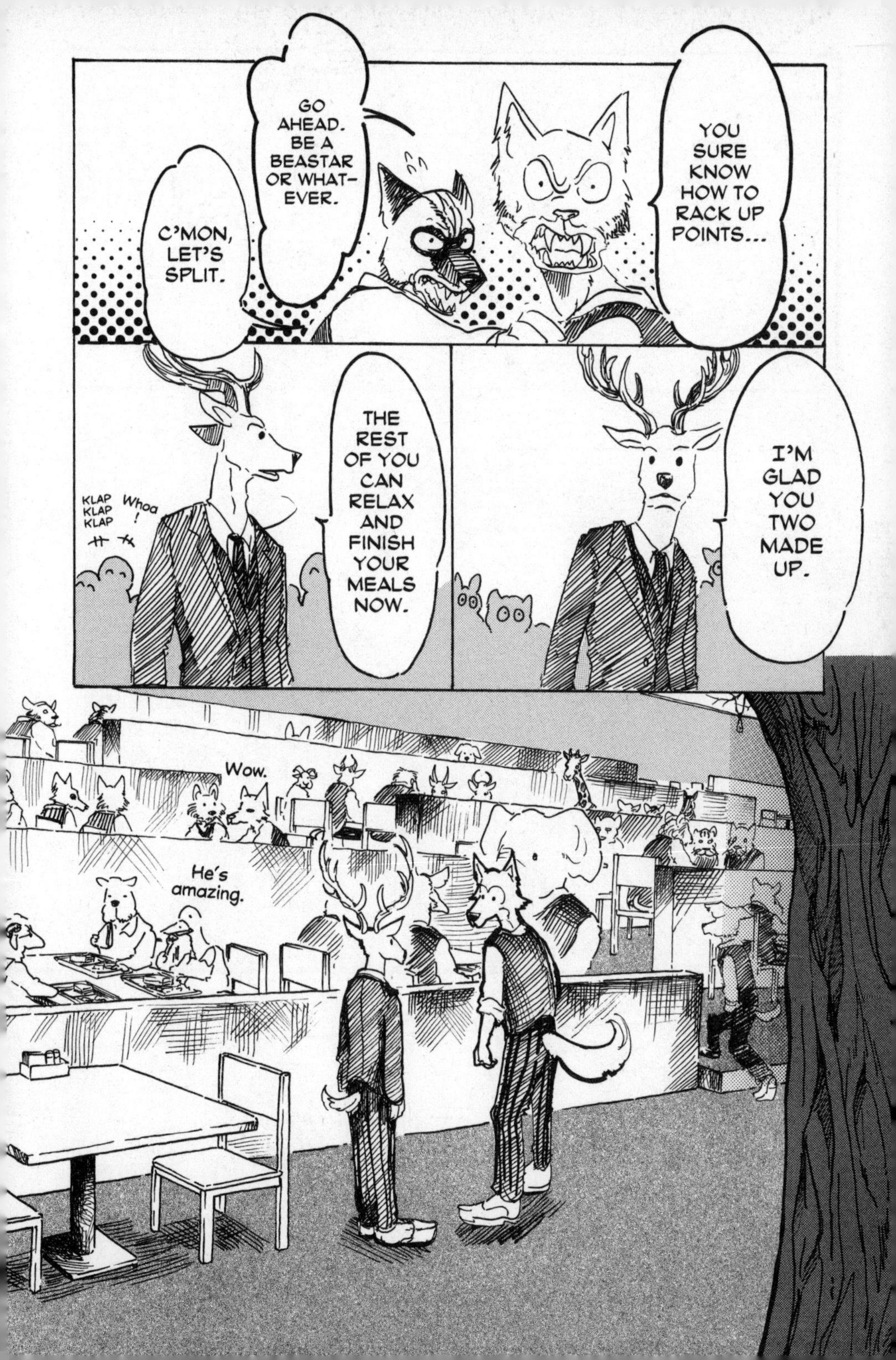
YOU SURE KNOW HOW TO RACK UP POINTS...
GO AHEAD. BE A BEASTAR OR WHAT-EVER.
C'MON, LET'S SPLIT.
I'M GLAD YOU TWO MADE UP.
THE REST OF YOU CAN RELAX AND FINISH YOUR MEALS NOW.
Whoa!
KLAP KLAP KLAP
Wow.
He's amazing.

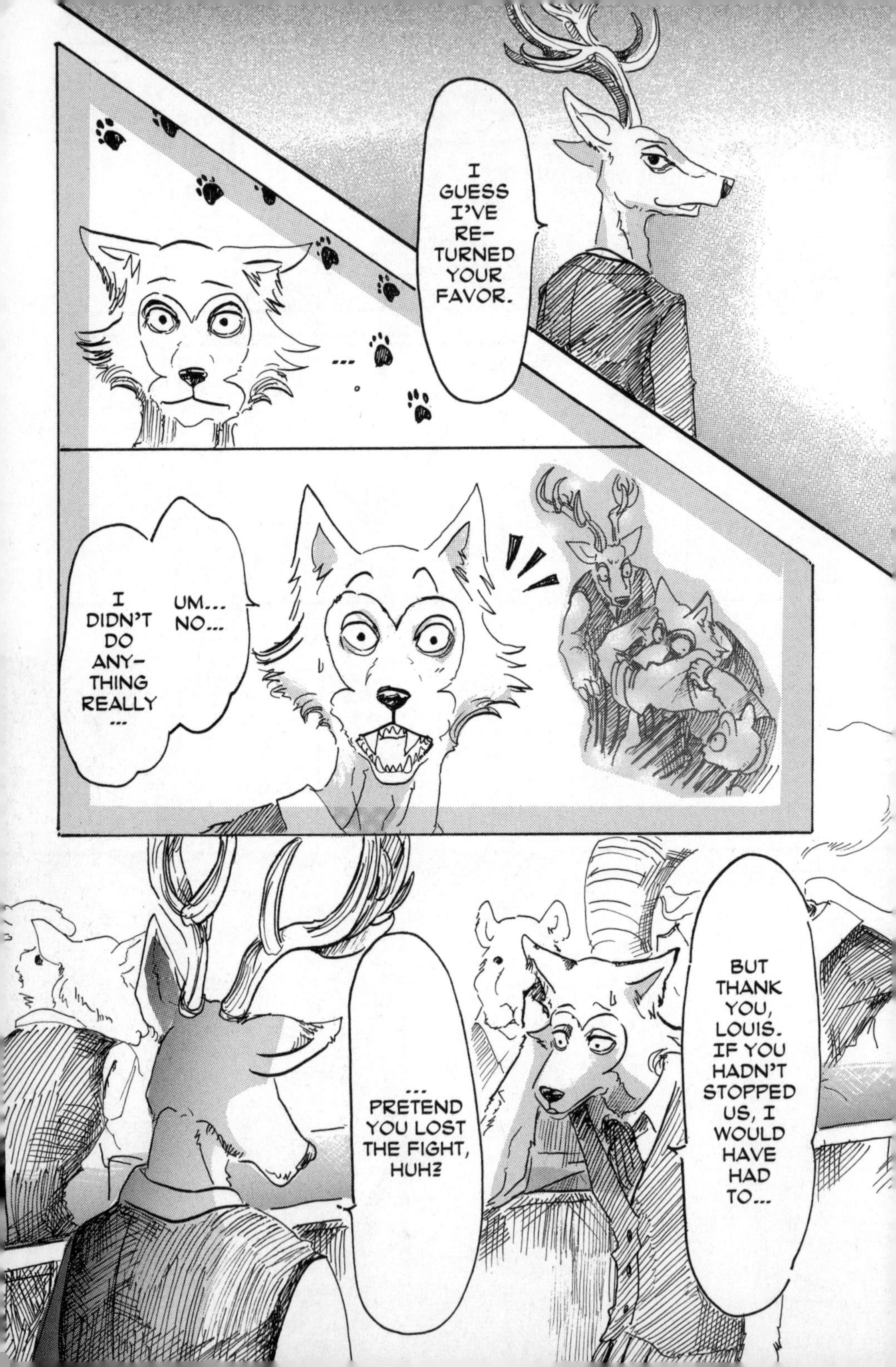
I GUESS I'VE RE-TURNED YOUR FAVOR.
...
UM... NO...
I DIDN'T DO ANY-THING REALLY ...
BUT THANK YOU, LOUIS. IF YOU HADN'T STOPPED US, I WOULD HAVE HAD TO...
... PRETEND YOU LOST THE FIGHT, HUH?

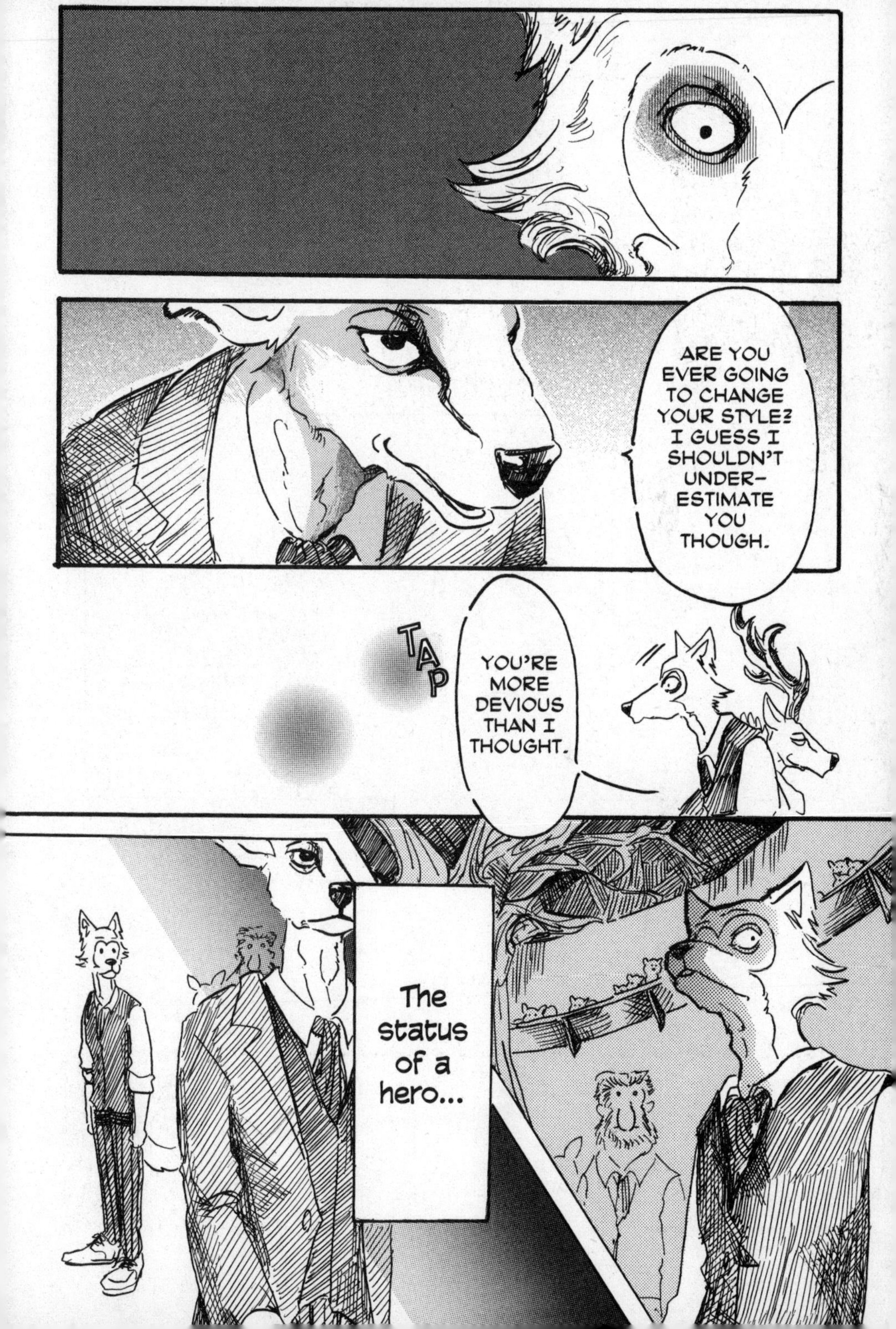
ARE YOU EVER GOING TO CHANGE YOUR STYLE? I GUESS I SHOULDN'T UNDER-ESTIMATE YOU THOUGH.
TAP
YOU'RE MORE DEVIOUS THAN I THOUGHT.
The status of a hero...

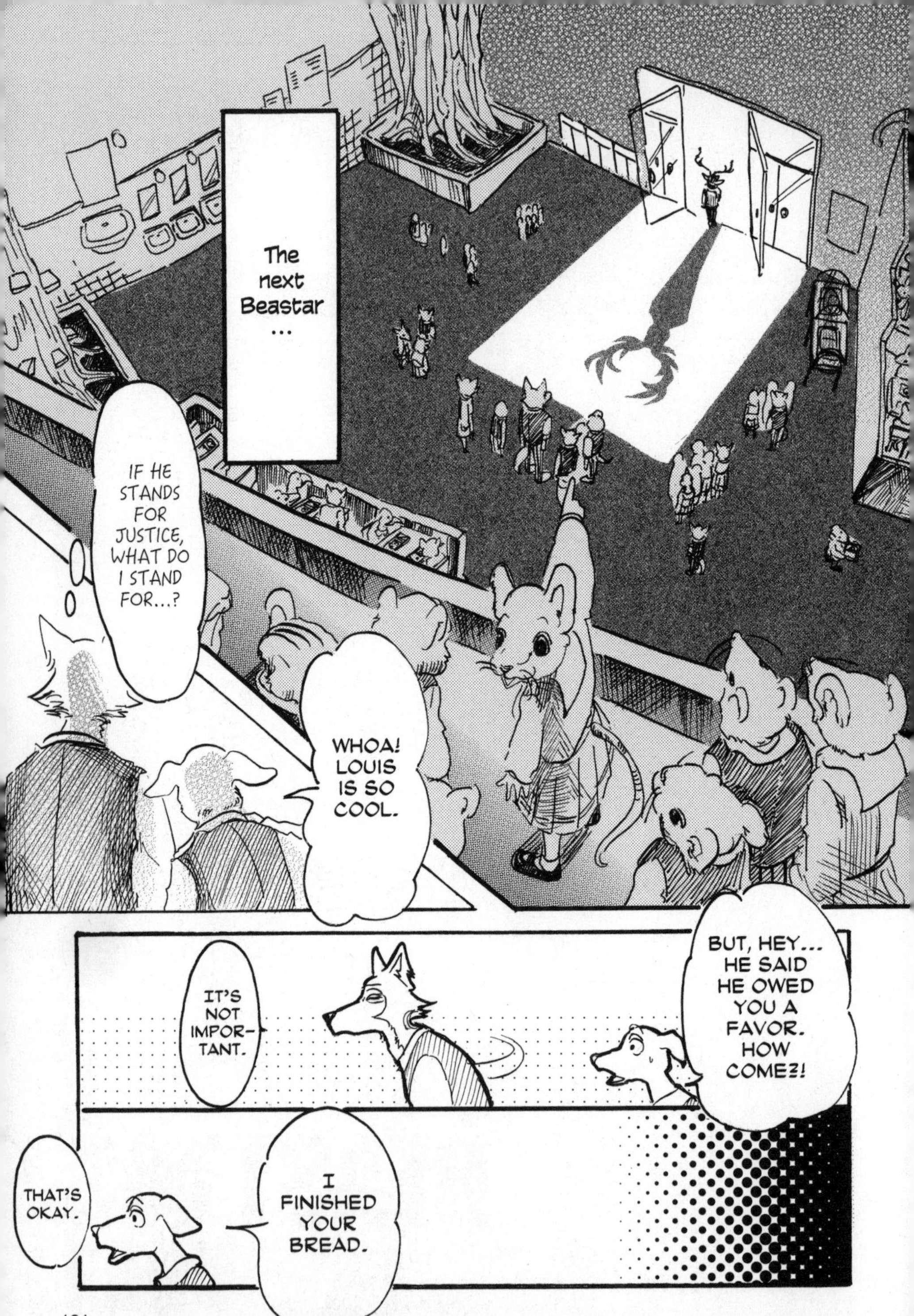
The next Beastar...
WHOA! LOUIS IS SO COOL.
IF HE STANDS FOR JUSTICE, WHAT DO I STAND FOR...?
BUT, HEY... HE SAID HE OWED YOU A FAVOR. HOW COME?!
IT'S NOT IMPOR-TANT.
I FINISHED YOUR BREAD.
THAT'S OKAY.

**BEASTARS
Vol.1**

Chapter 7:
Game Preserve Level 100

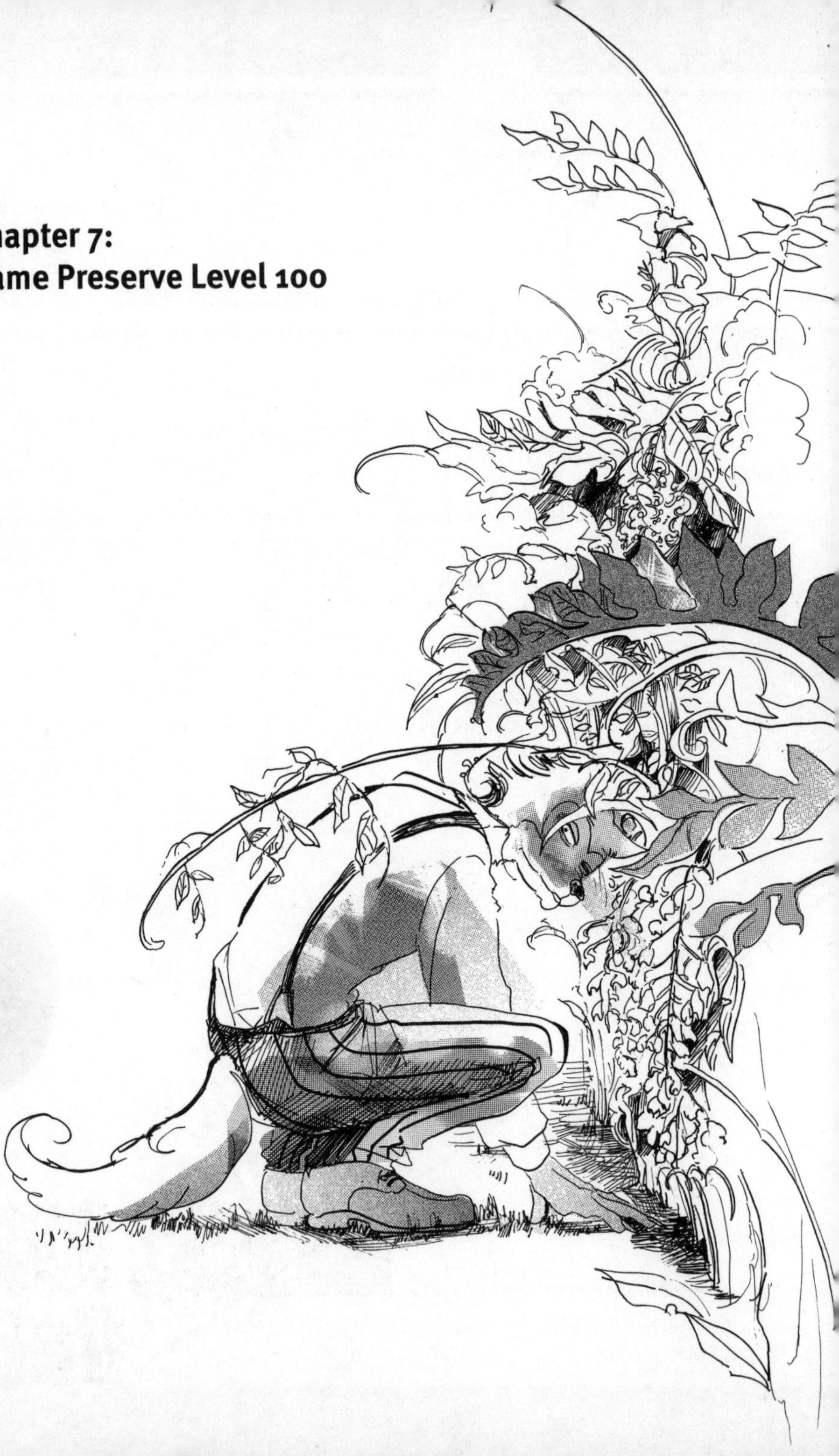

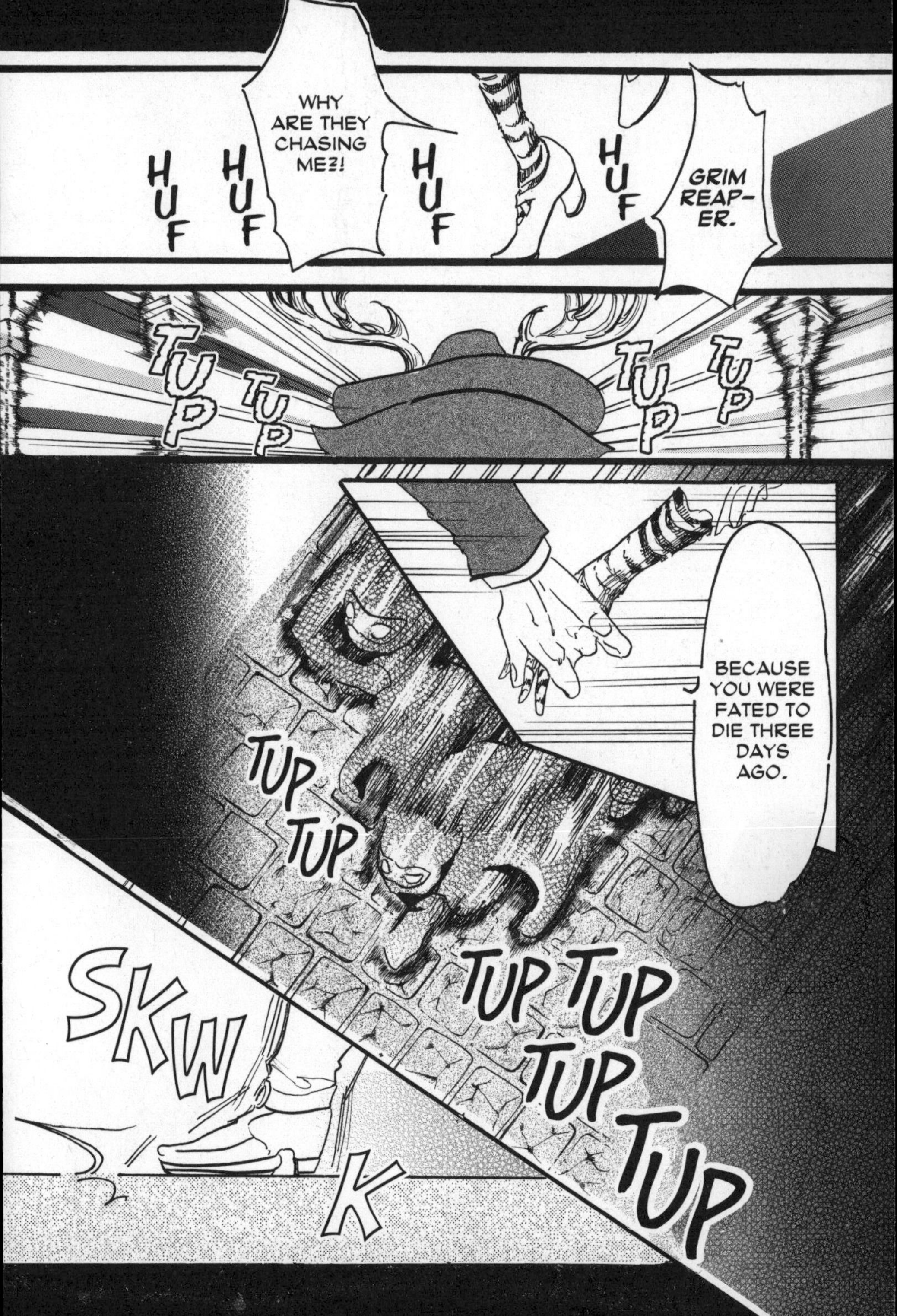

WHY ARE THEY CHASING ME?!
HUF
HUF
HUF
HUF
GRIM REAPER.
TUP
TUP
TUP
TUP
BECAUSE YOU WERE FATED TO DIE THREE DAYS AGO.
TUP TUP
TUP TUP TUP TUP TUP
SKWK

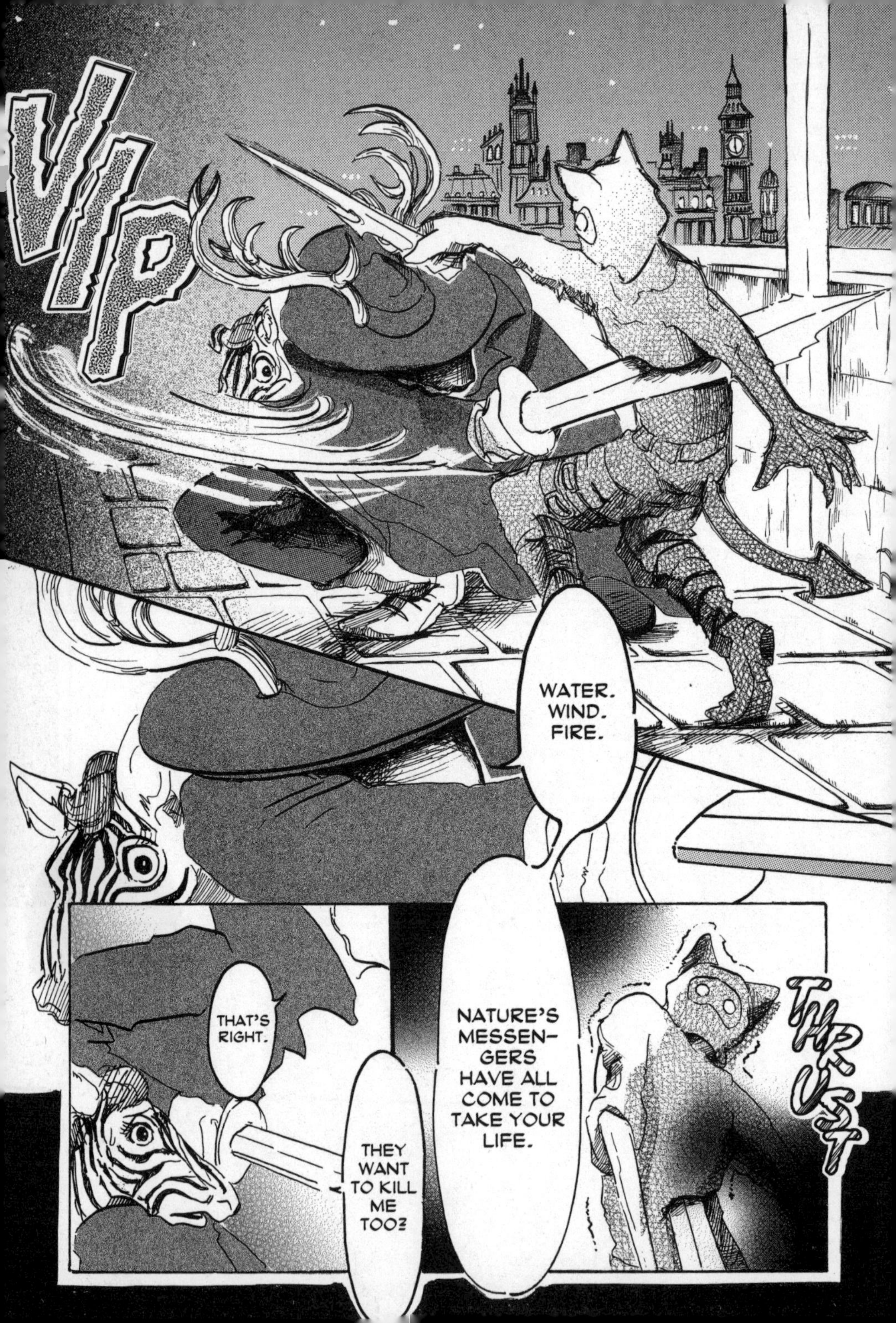
VIP
WATER. WIND. FIRE.
THRUST
NATURE'S MESSEN-GERS HAVE ALL COME TO TAKE YOUR LIFE.
THAT'S RIGHT.
THEY WANT TO KILL ME TOO?!

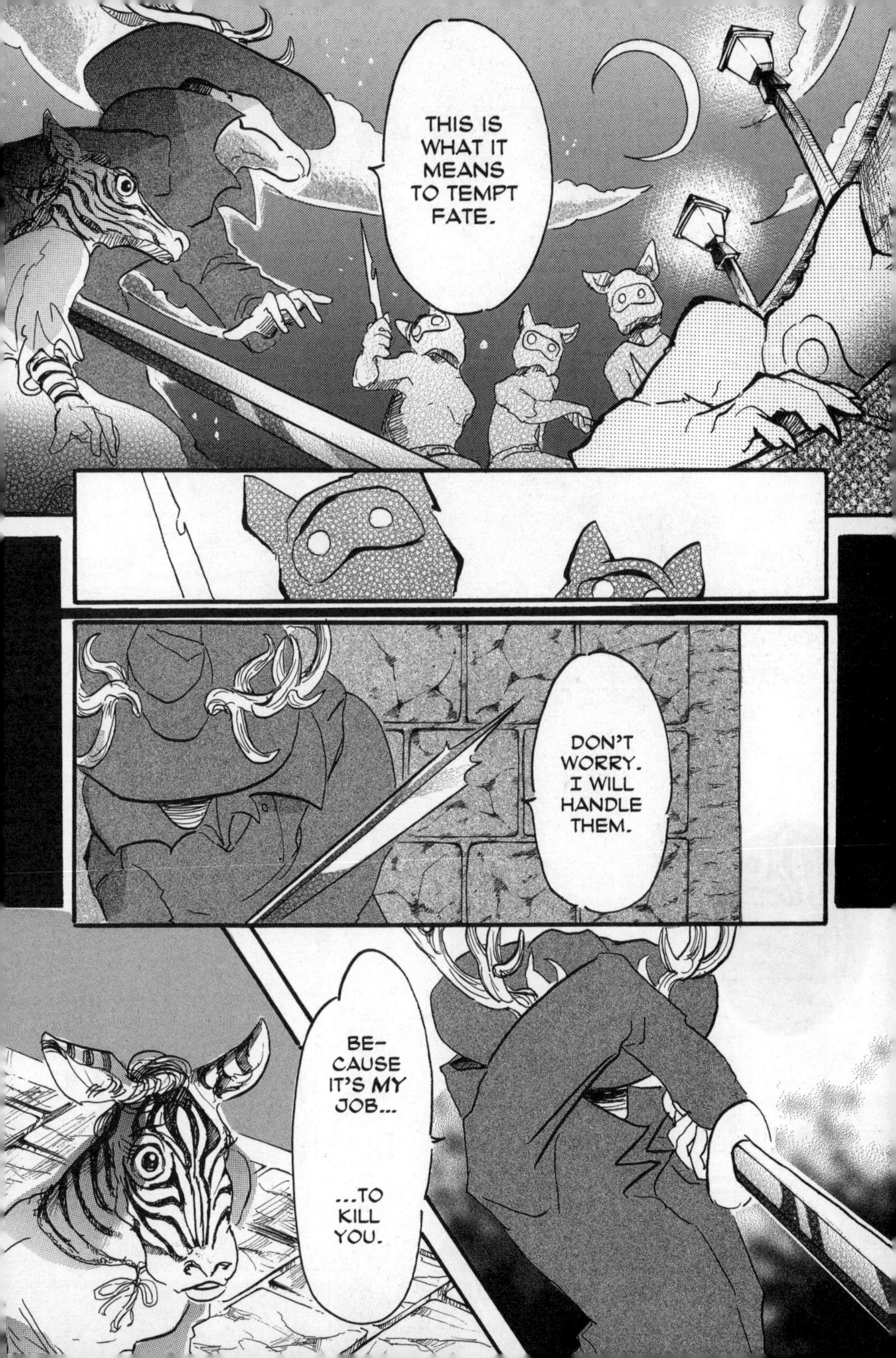
THIS IS WHAT IT MEANS TO TEMPT FATE.
DON'T WORRY. I WILL HANDLE THEM.
BE-CAUSE IT'S MY JOB...
...TO KILL YOU.

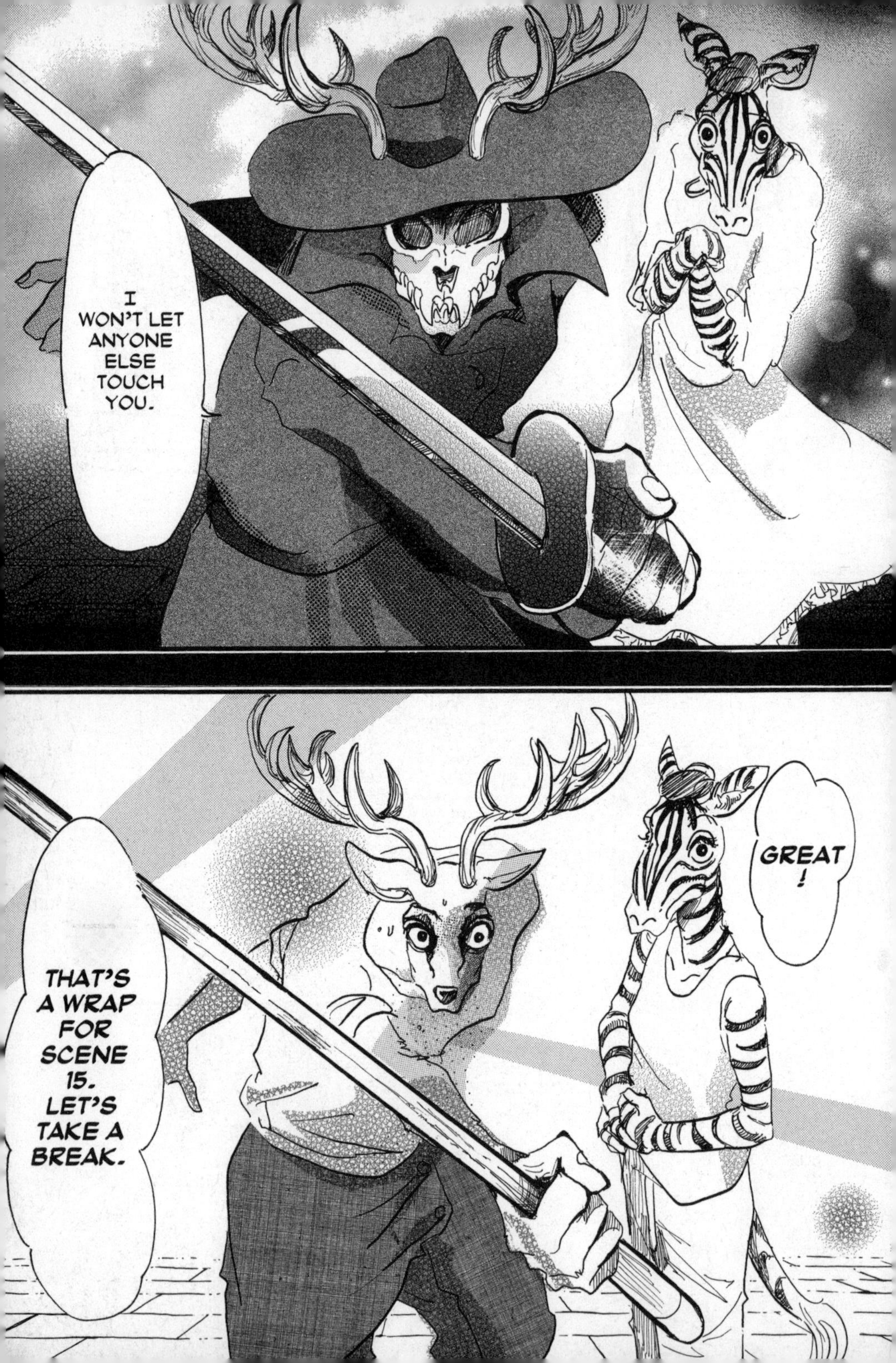
I WON'T LET ANYONE ELSE TOUCH YOU.
GREAT!
THAT'S A WRAP FOR SCENE 15. LET'S TAKE A BREAK.

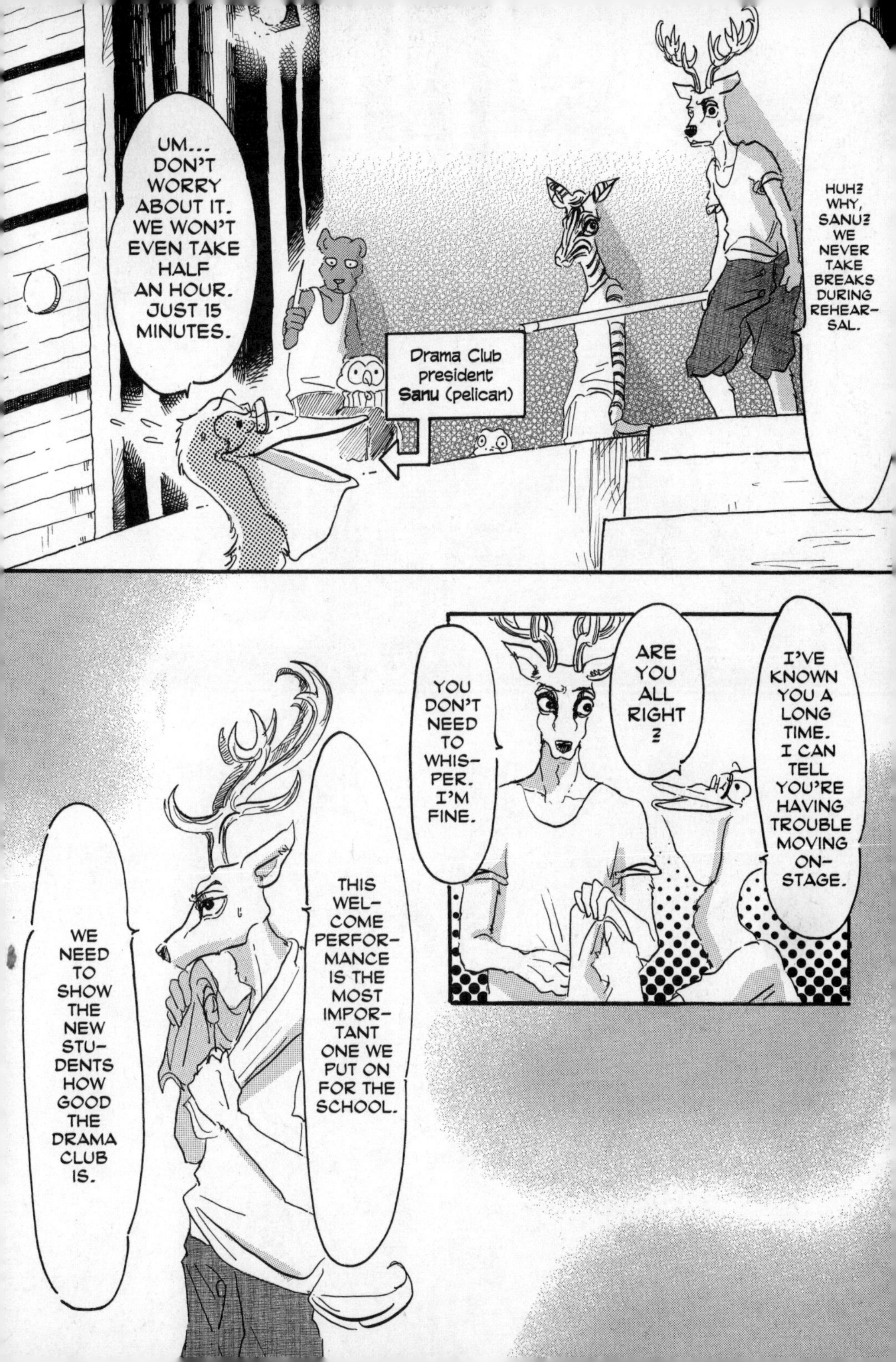
HUH? WHY, SANU? WE NEVER TAKE BREAKS DURING REHEARSAL.
Drama Club president Sanu (pelican)
UM... DON'T WORRY ABOUT IT. WE WON'T EVEN TAKE HALF AN HOUR. JUST 15 MINUTES.
I'VE KNOWN YOU A LONG TIME. I CAN TELL YOU'RE HAVING TROUBLE MOVING ON-STAGE.
ARE YOU ALL RIGHT?
YOU DON'T NEED TO WHISPER. I'M FINE.
THIS WELCOME PERFORMANCE IS THE MOST IMPORTANT ONE WE PUT ON FOR THE SCHOOL.
WE NEED TO SHOW THE NEW STUDENTS HOW GOOD THE DRAMA CLUB IS.

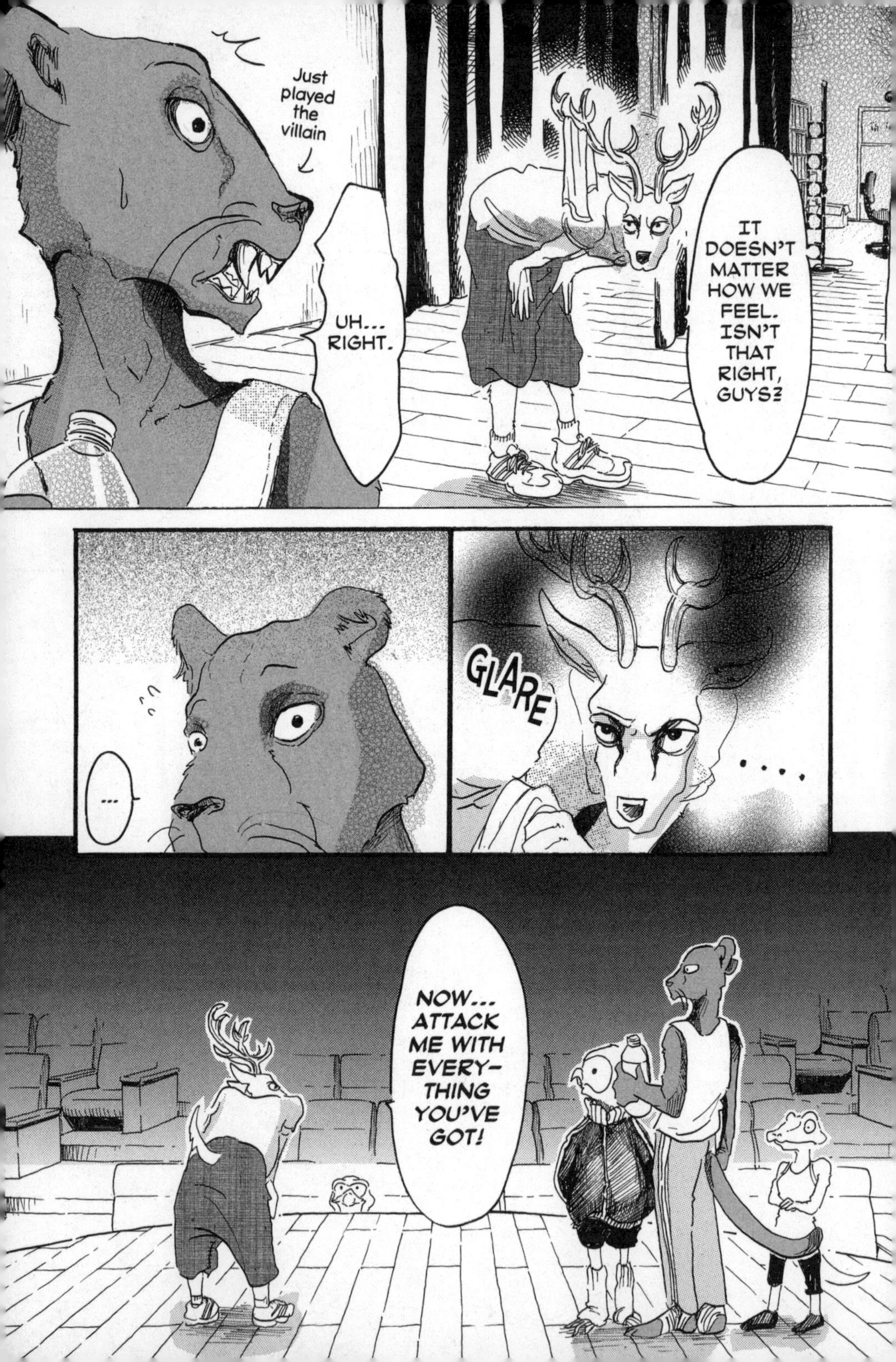
IT DOESN'T MATTER HOW WE FEEL. ISN'T THAT RIGHT, GUYS?
UH... RIGHT.
Just played the villain
GLARE
....
...
NOW... ATTACK ME WITH EVERY-THING YOU'VE GOT!

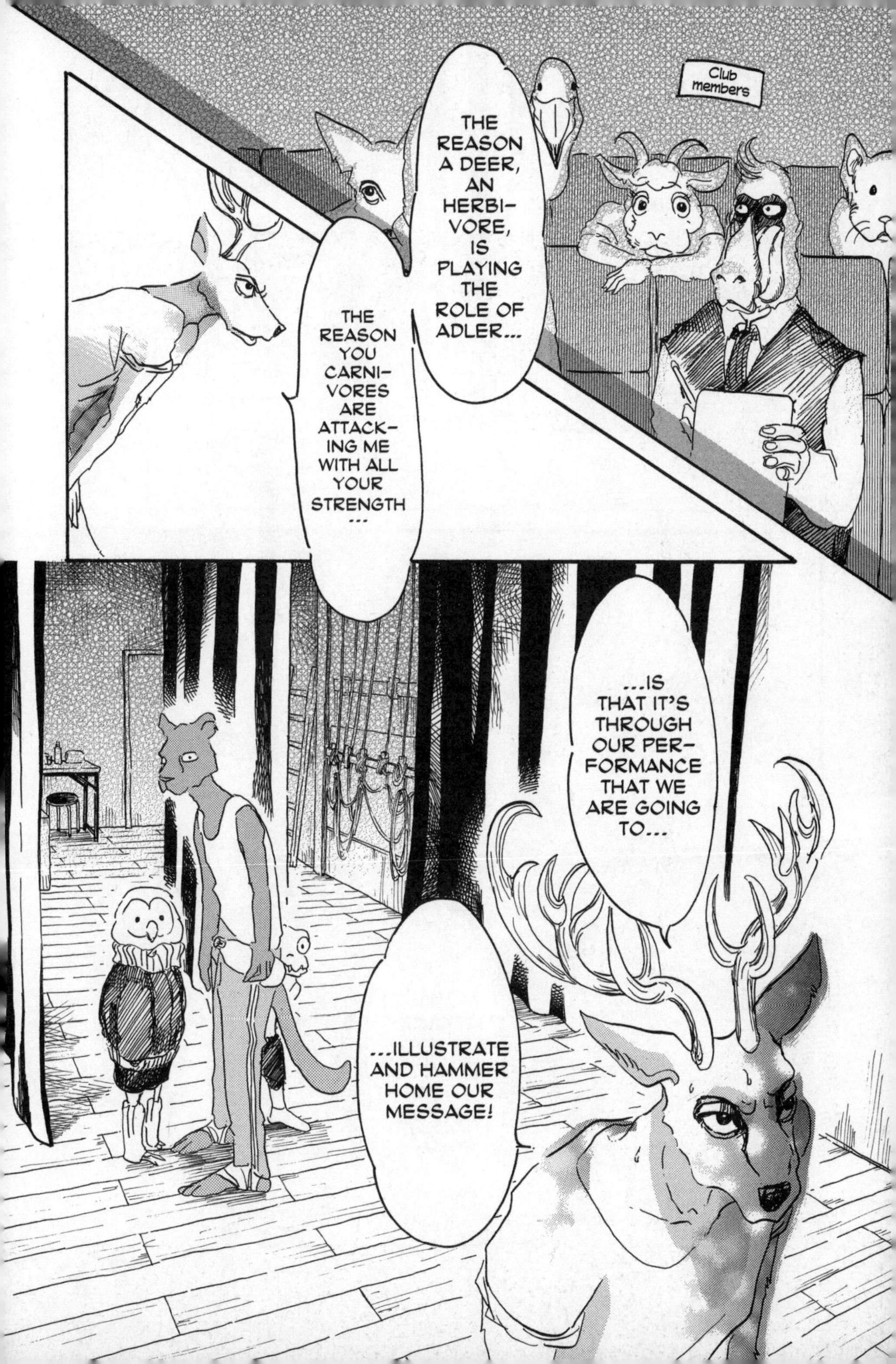
Club members
THE REASON A DEER, AN HERBIVORE, IS PLAYING THE ROLE OF ADLER...
THE REASON YOU CARNIVORES ARE ATTACKING ME WITH ALL YOUR STRENGTH...
...IS THAT IT'S THROUGH OUR PERFORMANCE THAT WE ARE GOING TO...
...ILLUSTRATE AND HAMMER HOME OUR MESSAGE!

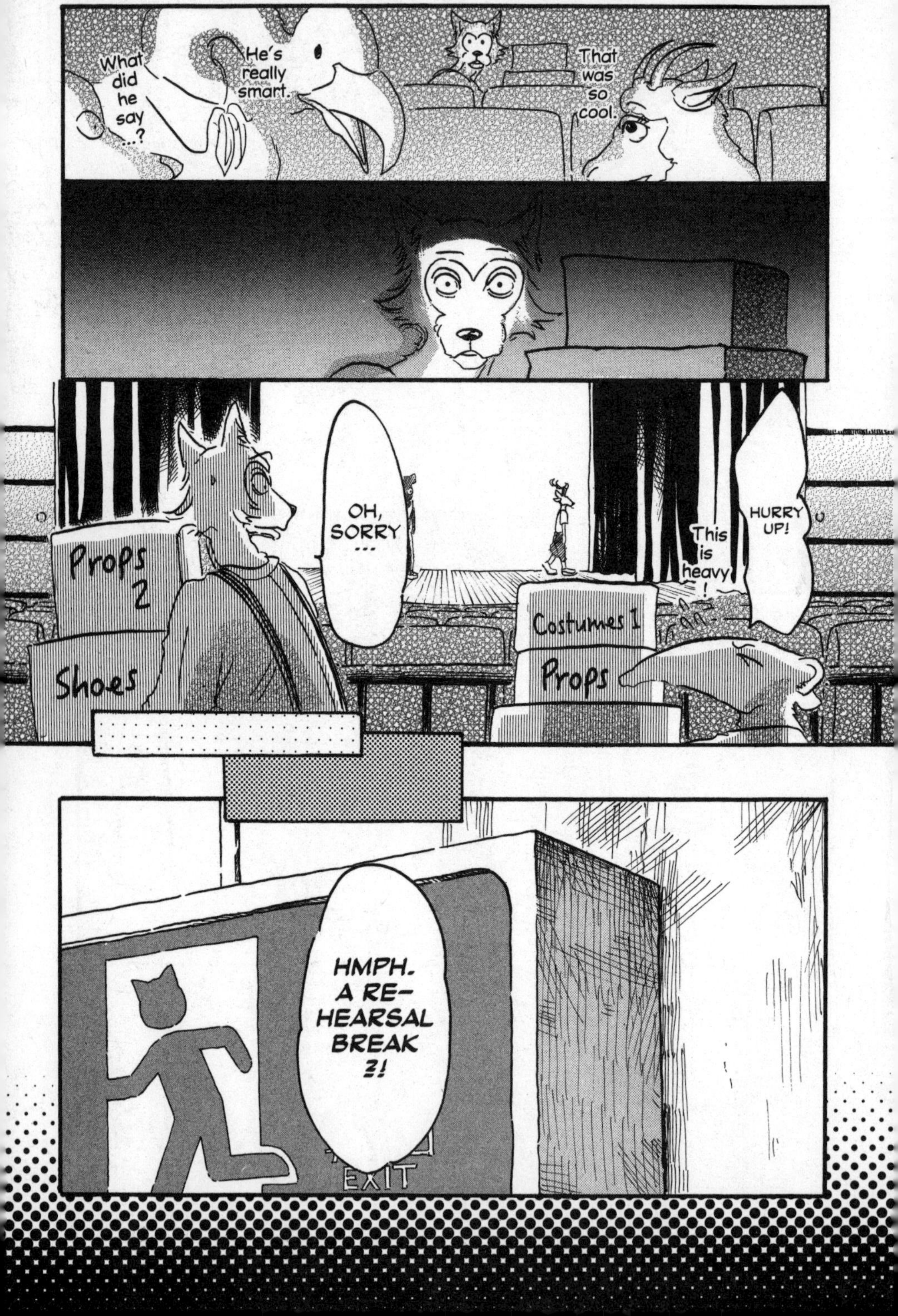
That was so cool.
He's really smart.
What did he say ...?
HURRY UP!
This is heavy!
OH, SORRY ...
Costumes 1
Props
Props 2
Shoes
HMPH. A RE-HEARSAL BREAK ?!
EXIT

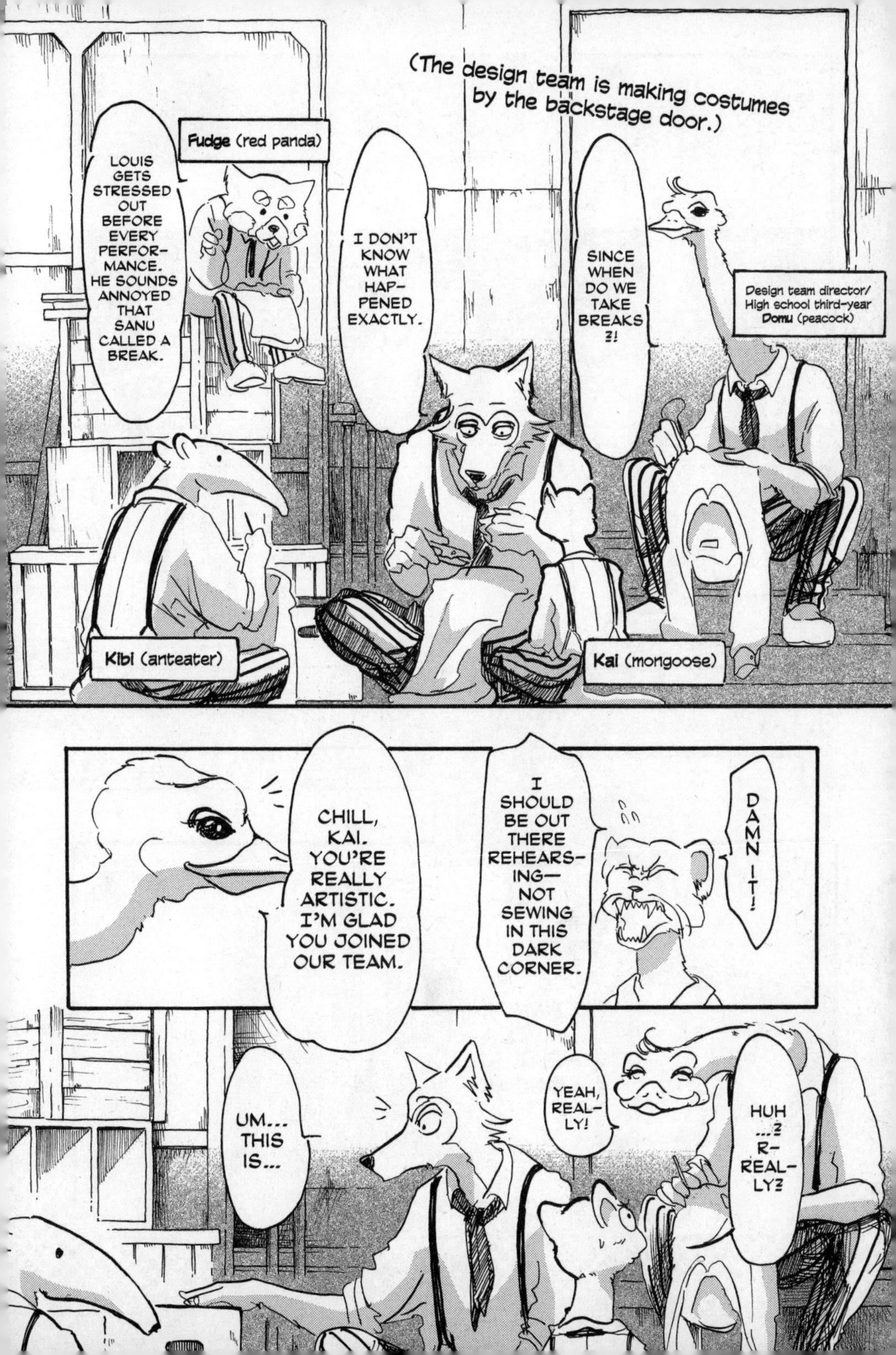
(The design team is making costumes by the backstage door.)
Design team director/ High school third-year Domu (peacock)
SINCE WHEN DO WE TAKE BREAKS?!
I DON'T KNOW WHAT HAPPENED EXACTLY.
Fudge (red panda)
LOUIS GETS STRESSED OUT BEFORE EVERY PERFORMANCE. HE SOUNDS ANNOYED THAT SANU CALLED A BREAK.
Kai (mongoose)
Kibi (anteater)
DAMN IT!
I SHOULD BE OUT THERE REHEARSING—NOT SEWING IN THIS DARK CORNER.
CHILL, KAI. YOU'RE REALLY ARTISTIC. I'M GLAD YOU JOINED OUR TEAM.
HUH...? R-REALLY?
YEAH, REALLY!
UM... THIS IS...

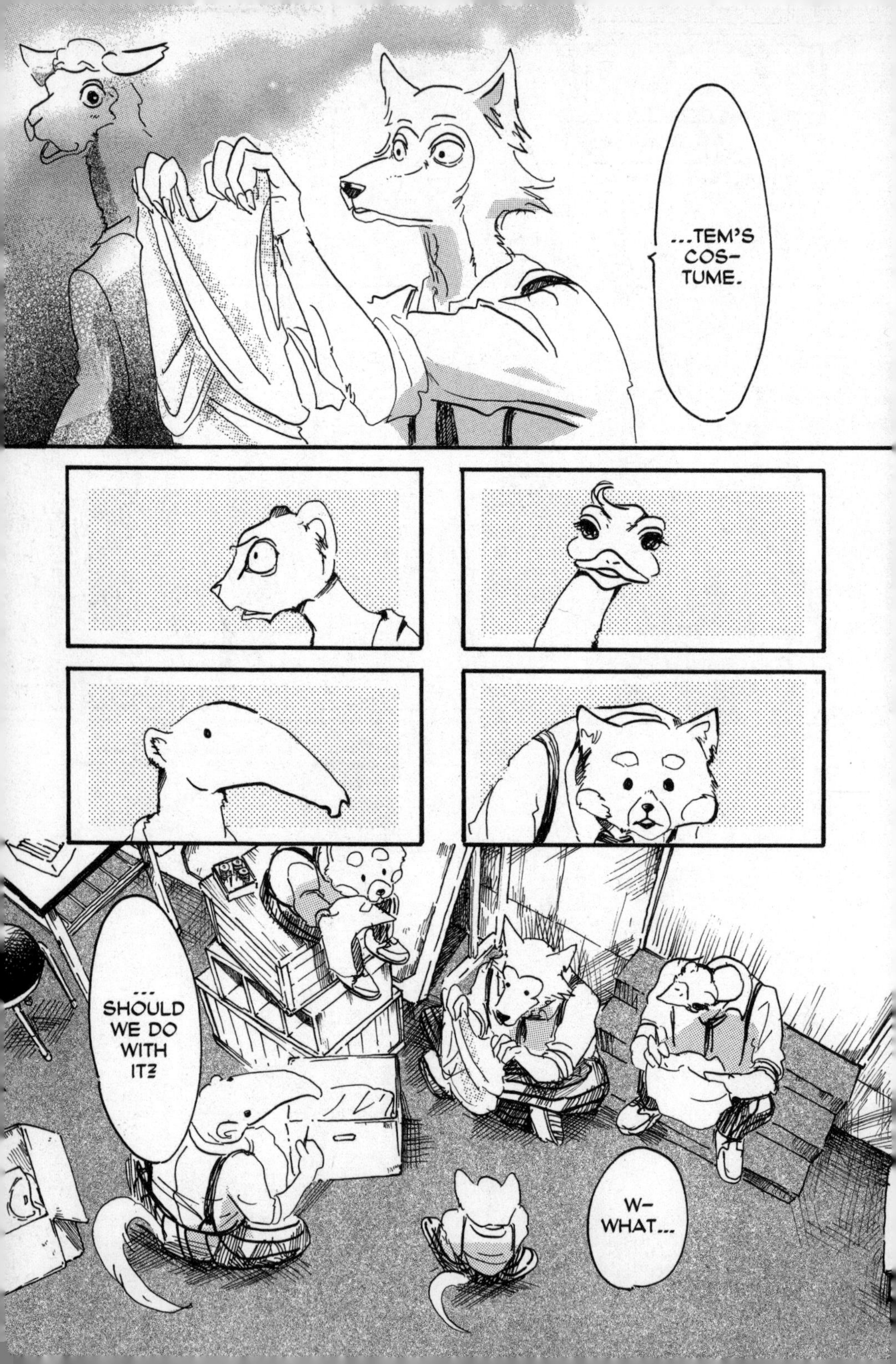
...TEM'S COS-TUME.
W-WHAT...
...SHOULD WE DO WITH IT?

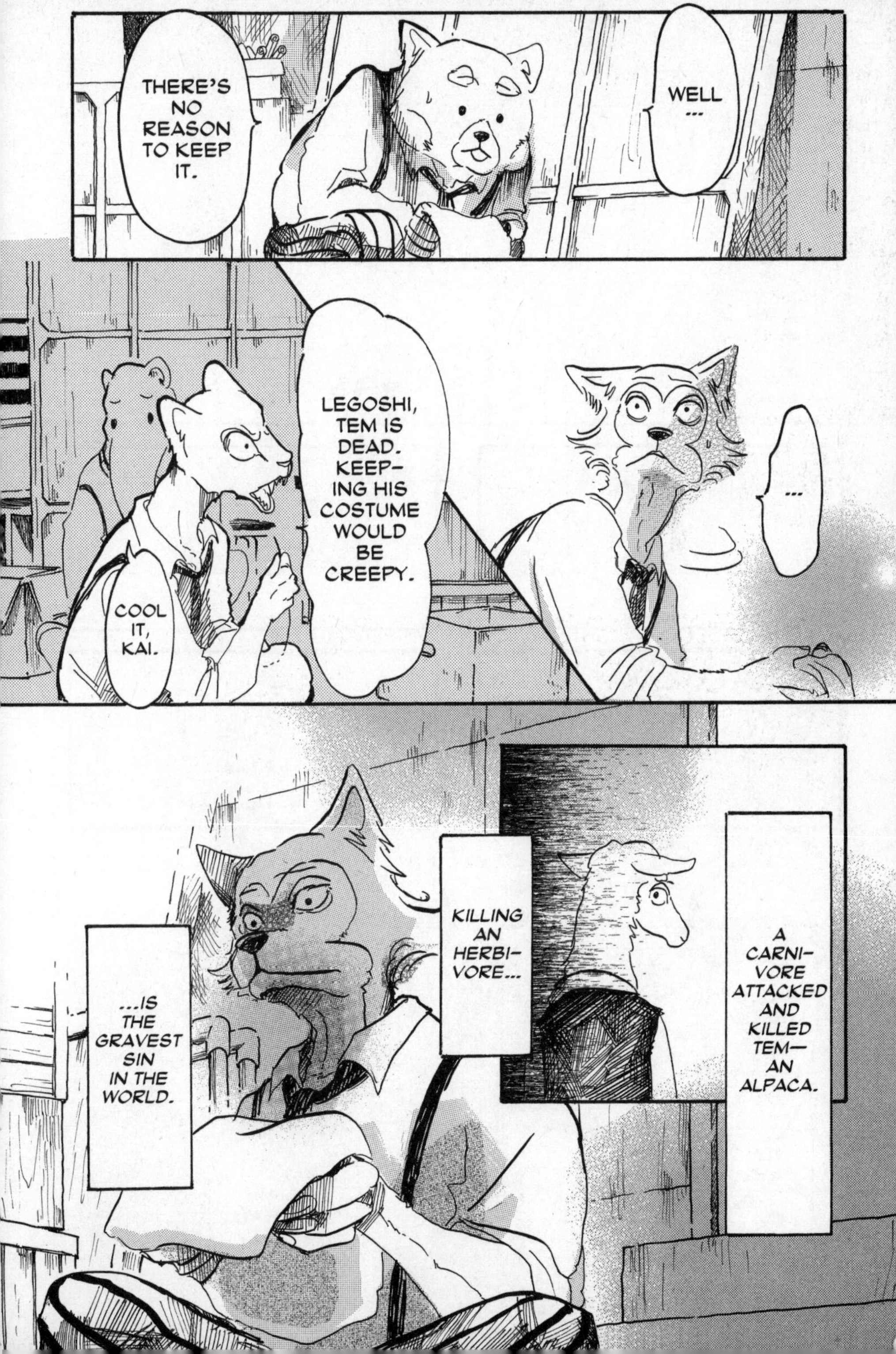
WELL...
THERE'S NO REASON TO KEEP IT.
...
LEGOSHI, TEM IS DEAD. KEEP-ING HIS COSTUME WOULD BE CREEPY.
COOL IT, KAI.
A CARNI-VORE ATTACKED AND KILLED TEM— AN ALPACA.
KILLING AN HERBI-VORE...
...IS THE GRAVEST SIN IN THE WORLD.

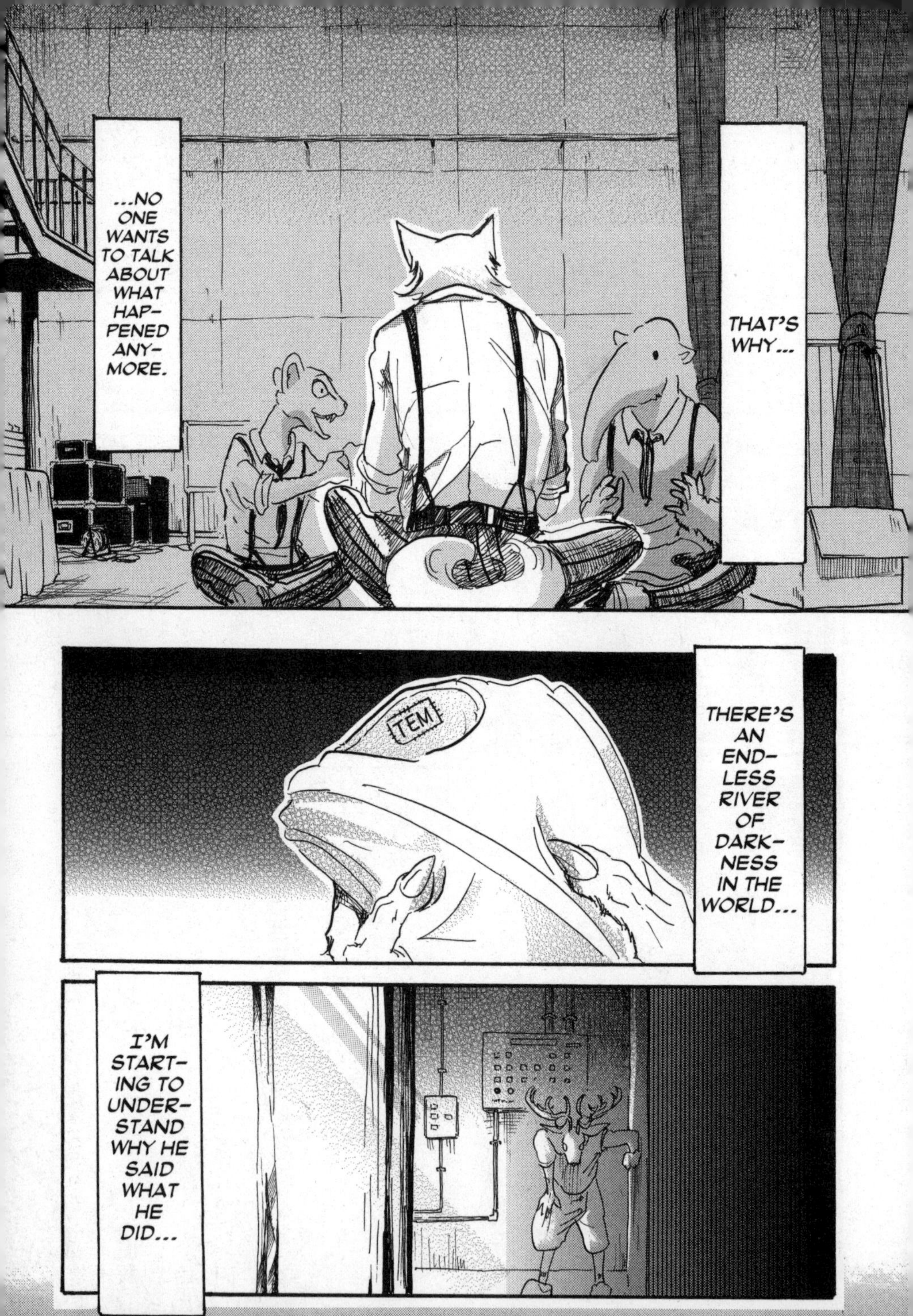
...NO ONE WANTS TO TALK ABOUT WHAT HAPPENED ANYMORE.
THAT'S WHY...
THERE'S AN ENDLESS RIVER OF DARKNESS IN THE WORLD...
TEM
I'M STARTING TO UNDERSTAND WHY HE SAID WHAT HE DID...

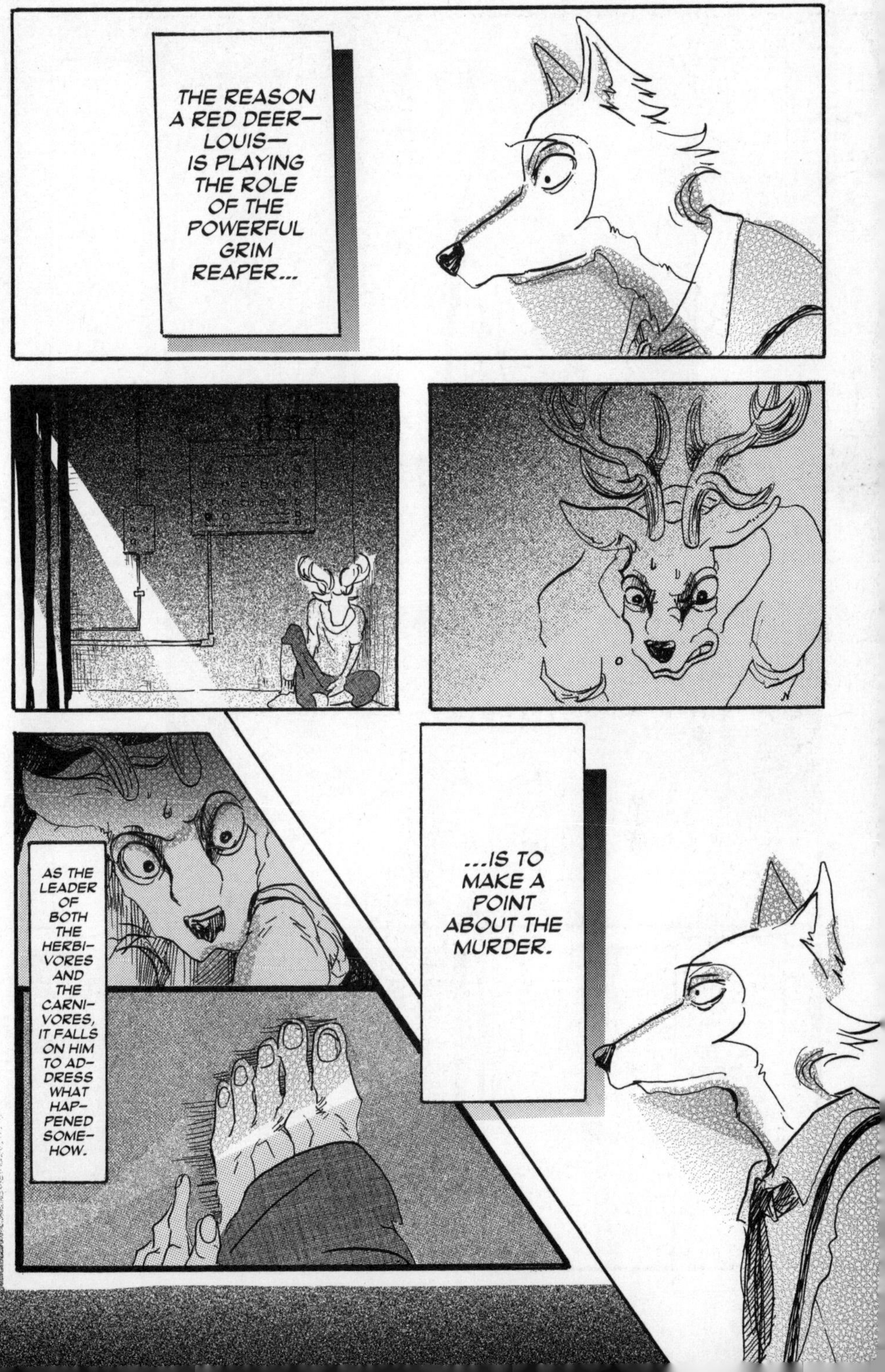
THE REASON A RED DEER—LOUIS—IS PLAYING THE ROLE OF THE POWERFUL GRIM REAPER...
...IS TO MAKE A POINT ABOUT THE MURDER.
AS THE LEADER OF BOTH THE HERBIVORES AND THE CARNIVORES, IT FALLS ON HIM TO ADDRESS WHAT HAPPENED SOMEHOW.

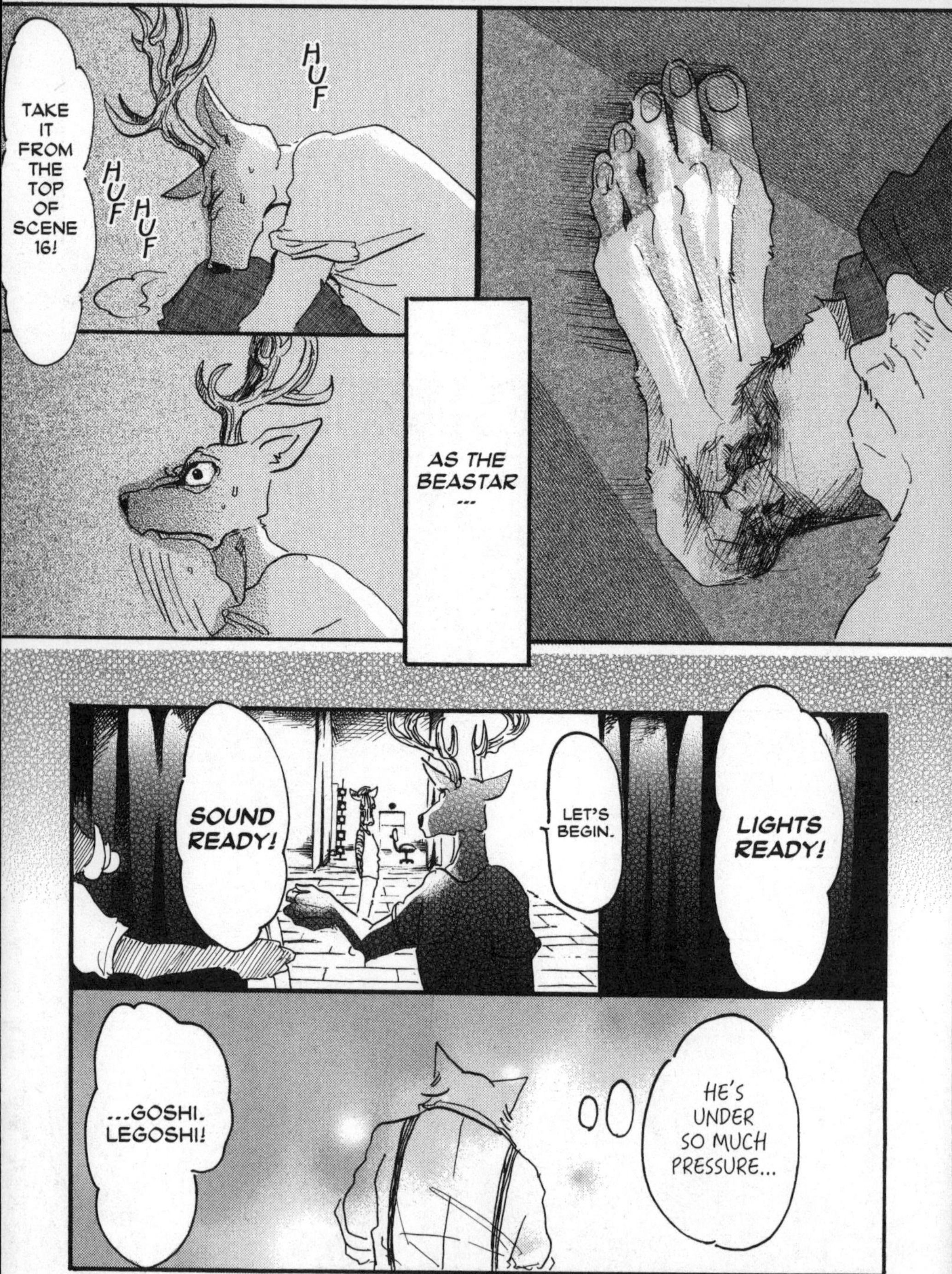
AS THE BEASTAR ...
HUF
TAKE IT FROM THE TOP OF SCENE 16!
HUF HUF
LIGHTS READY!
LET'S BEGIN.
SOUND READY!
HE'S UNDER SO MUCH PRESSURE...
...GOSHI. LEGOSHI!

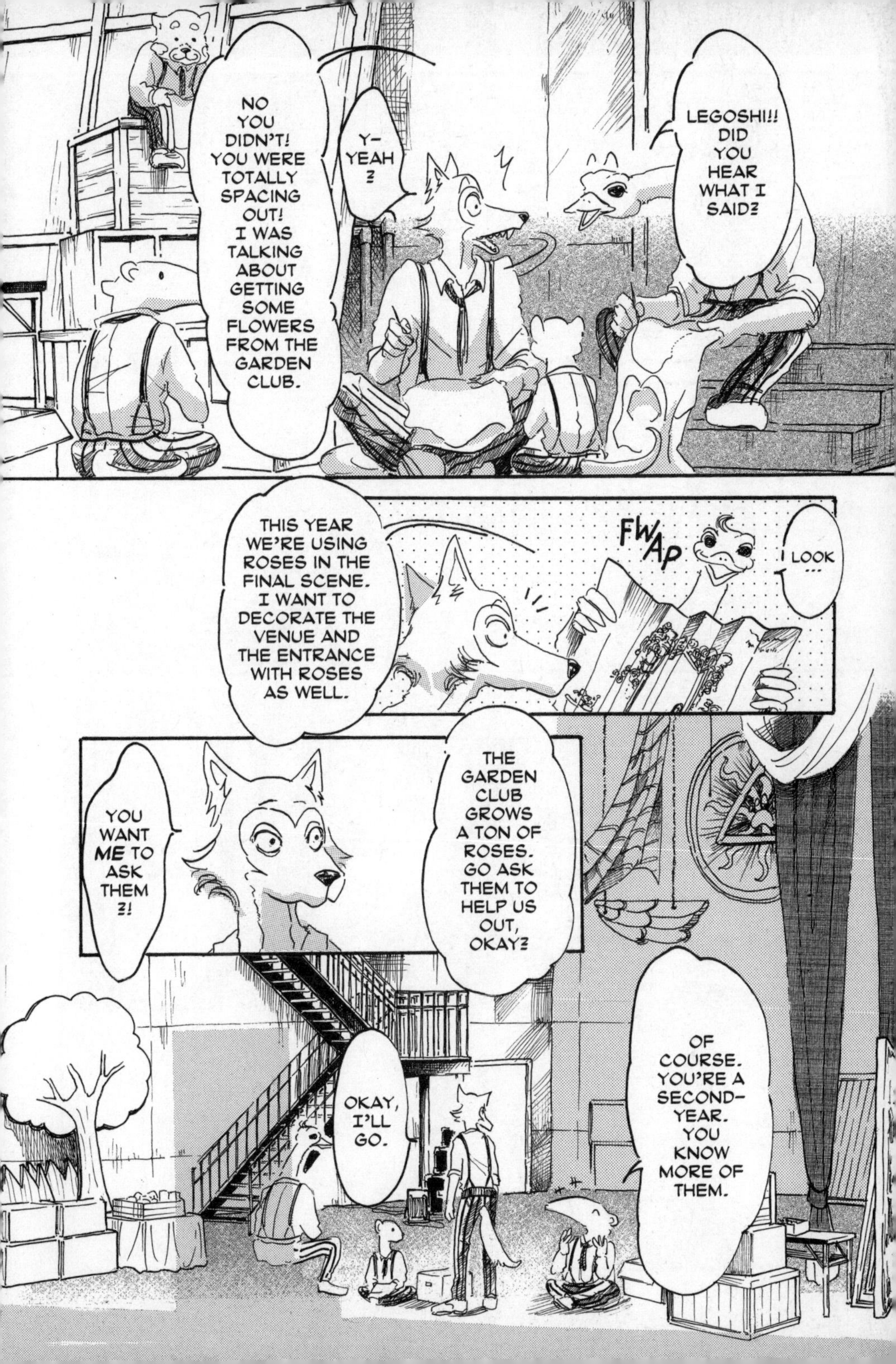

LEGOSHI!!! DID YOU HEAR WHAT I SAID?
Y-YEAH?
NO YOU DIDN'T! YOU WERE TOTALLY SPACING OUT! I WAS TALKING ABOUT GETTING SOME FLOWERS FROM THE GARDEN CLUB.
LOOK...
FWAP
THIS YEAR WE'RE USING ROSES IN THE FINAL SCENE. I WANT TO DECORATE THE VENUE AND THE ENTRANCE WITH ROSES AS WELL.
THE GARDEN CLUB GROWS A TON OF ROSES. GO ASK THEM TO HELP US OUT, OKAY?
YOU WANT ME TO ASK THEM?!
OF COURSE. YOU'RE A SECOND-YEAR. YOU KNOW MORE OF THEM.
OKAY, I'LL GO.

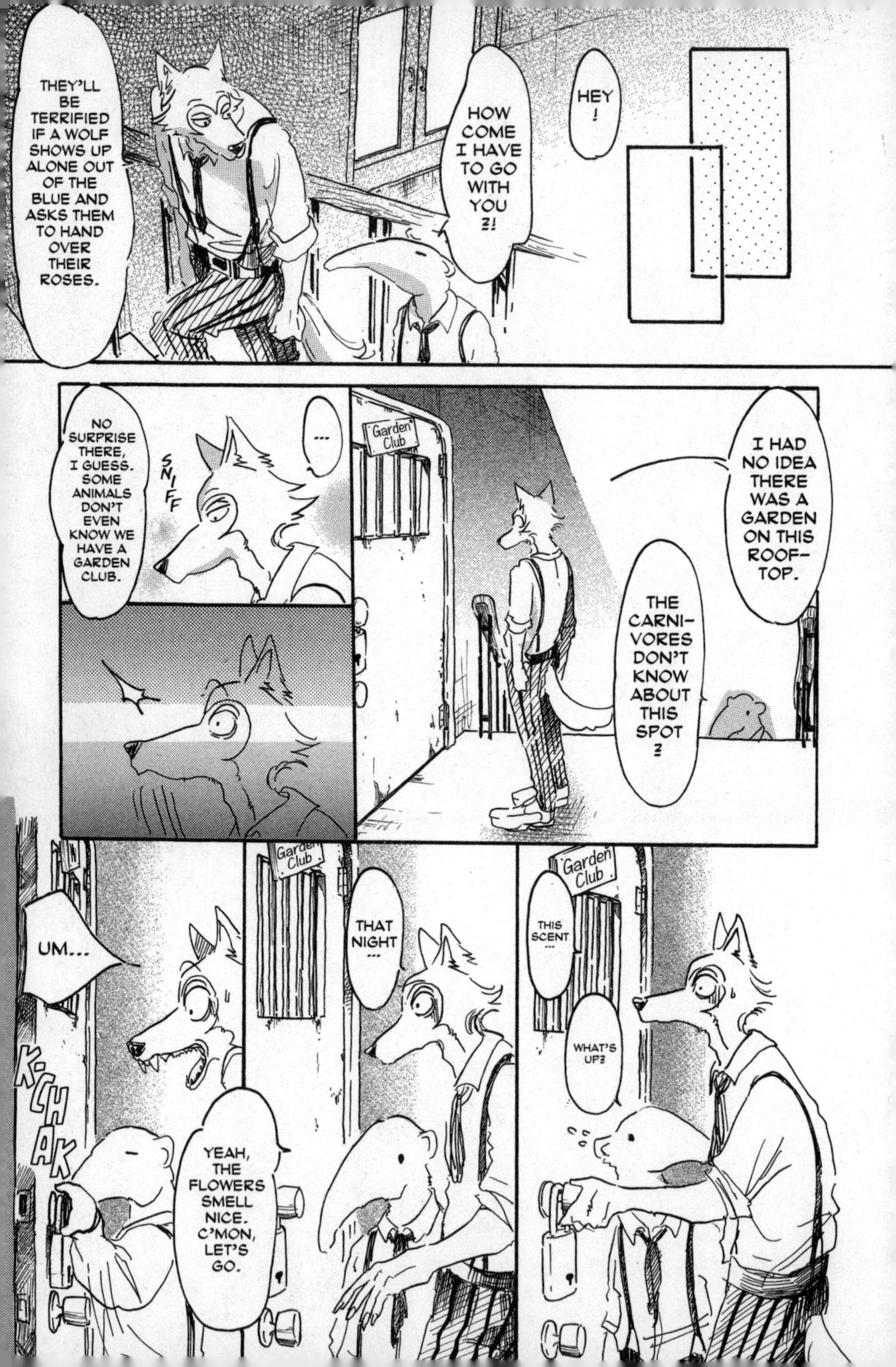
HEY!
HOW COME I HAVE TO GO WITH YOU?!
THEY'LL BE TERRIFIED IF A WOLF SHOWS UP ALONE OUT OF THE BLUE AND ASKS THEM TO HAND OVER THEIR ROSES.
I HAD NO IDEA THERE WAS A GARDEN ON THIS ROOF-TOP.
THE CARNI-VORES DON'T KNOW ABOUT THIS SPOT?
Garden Club
...
SNIFF
NO SURPRISE THERE, I GUESS. SOME ANIMALS DON'T EVEN KNOW WE HAVE A GARDEN CLUB.
Garden Club
THIS SCENT...
WHAT'S UP?
Garden Club
THAT NIGHT...
YEAH, THE FLOWERS SMELL NICE. C'MON, LET'S GO.
UM...
K-CHAK

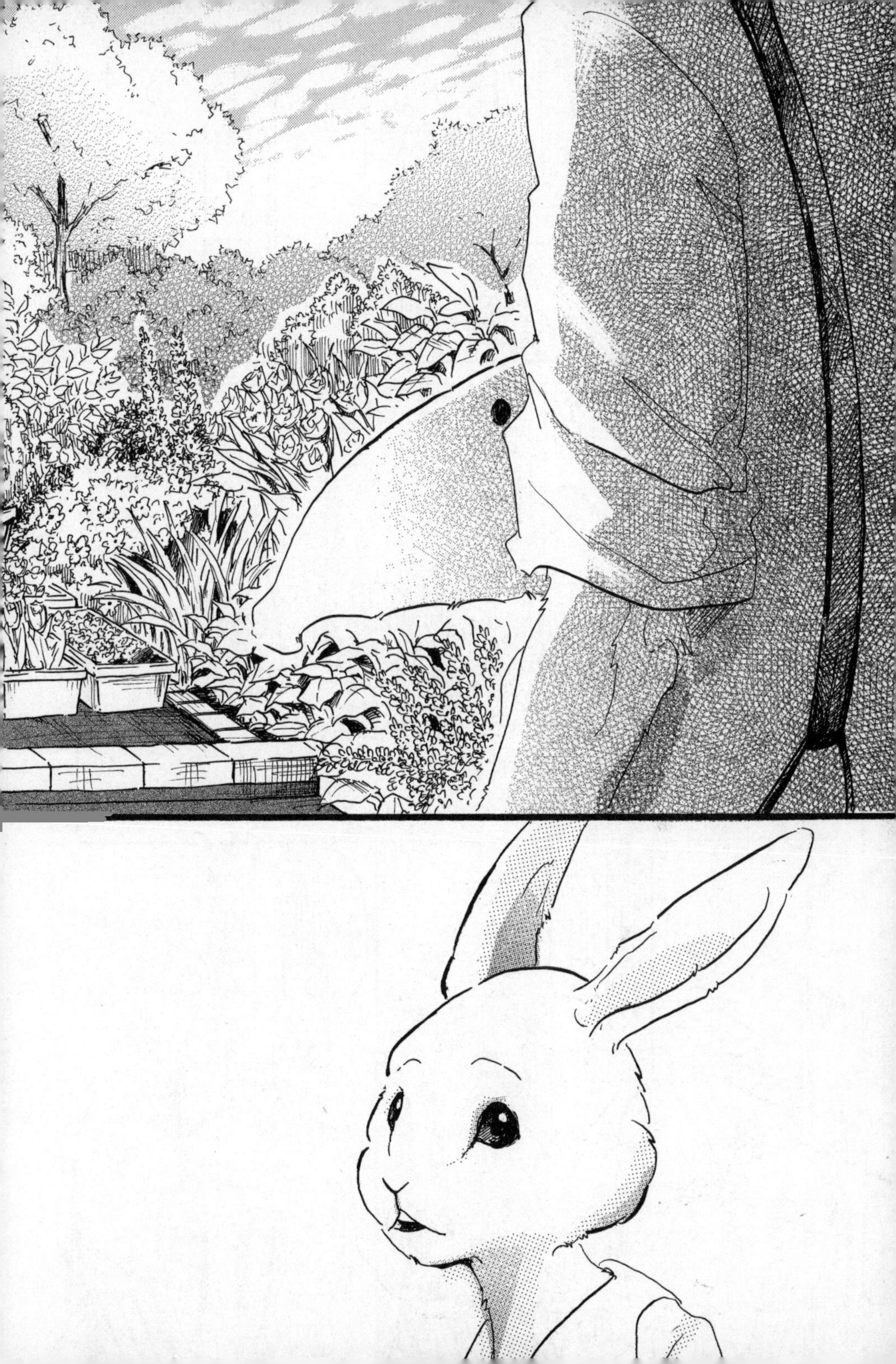

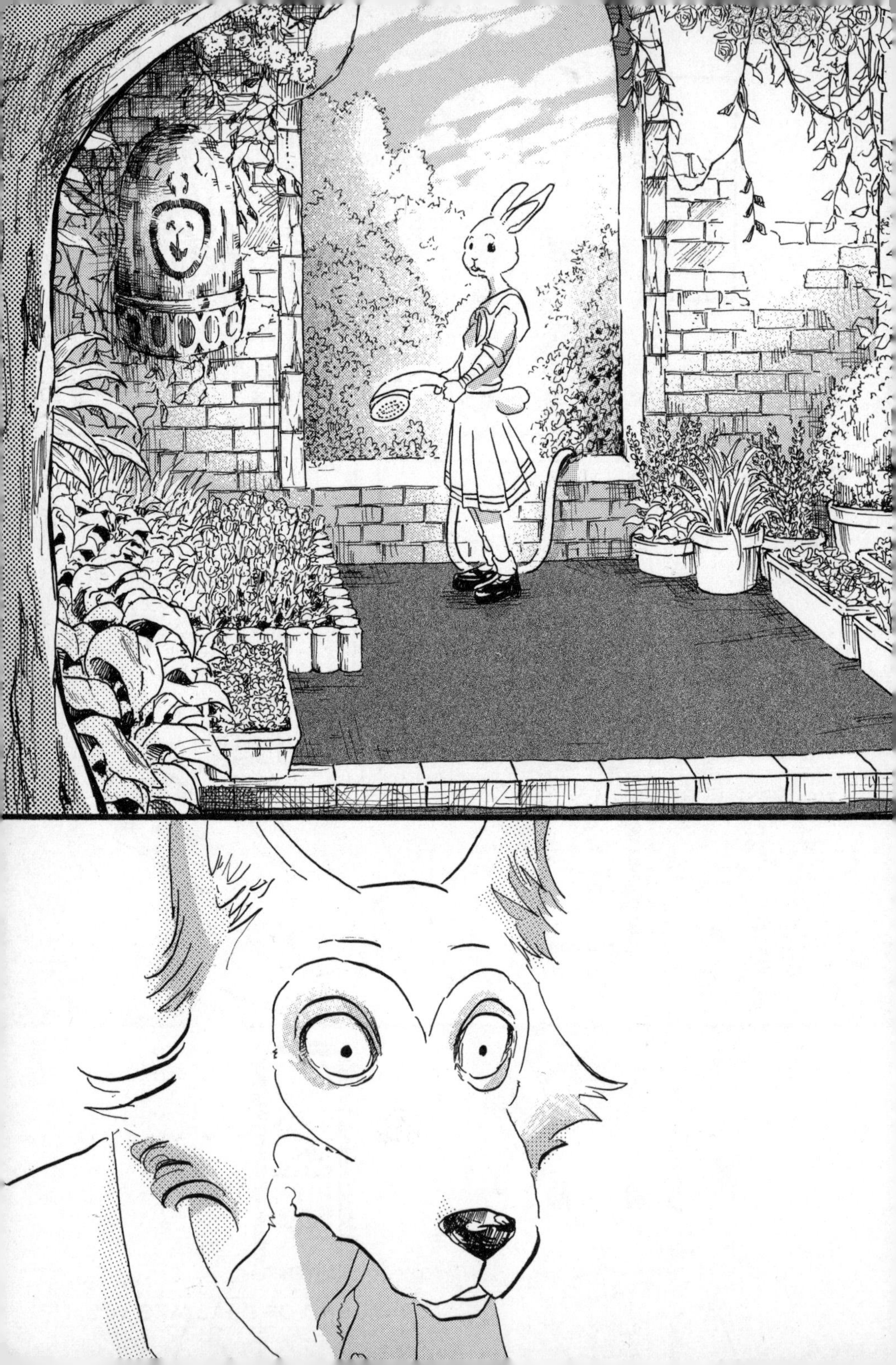

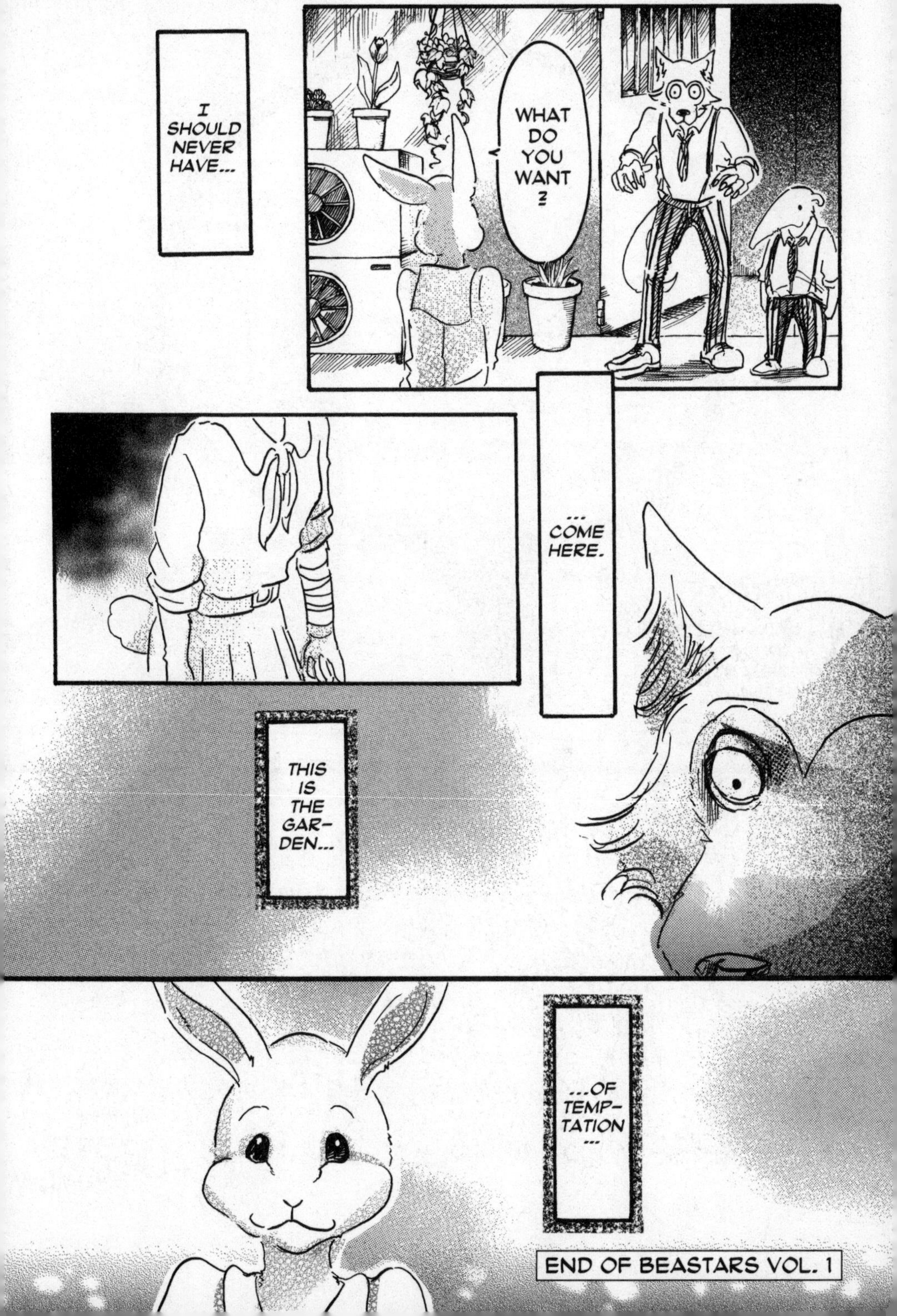
WHAT DO YOU WANT?
I SHOULD NEVER HAVE...
...COME HERE.
THIS IS THE GARDEN...
...OF TEMPTATION...
END OF BEASTARS VOL. 1

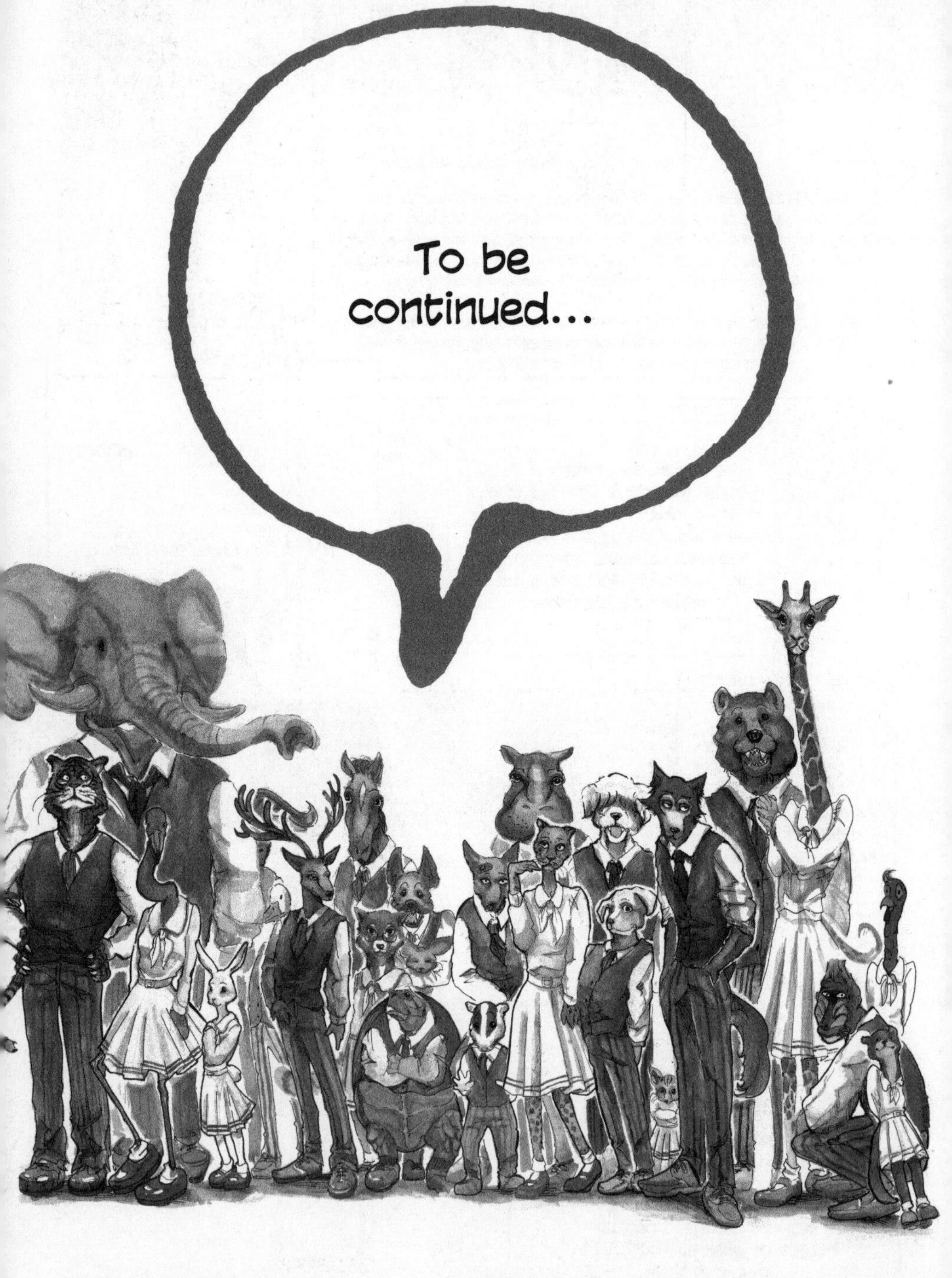
To be continued...

Legoshi Character Design Notes

I'M PARTICULAR ABOUT THESE DETAILS:

- FUR ON THE SIDES OF HIS FACE
- WIDE DOUBLE EYELIDS
- I PAY SPECIAL ATTENTION WHEN I'M DRAWING HIS PAWS.

When did you create this character?

I already had ideas for a wolf character back in junior or senior high. Those were about a much more mature wolf though. He told jokes. In my first concept, he worked as a doctor with a six-year-old assistant. In the next version, I think I made him a stylist who worked in a Paris Collection boutique...

His appearance remained the same, but his backstory was always changing. He's extremely awkward and young in the manga version. I enjoy drawing him.

PROFILE

LEGOSHI (AGE 17)
MALE
CARNIVORE CANIDAE
(GRAY WOLF)
BIRTHDAY: APRIL 9
ASTROLOGICAL SIGN: ARIES
BLOOD TYPE: O
HEIGHT: 6 FT., 1 IN.
WEIGHT: 157 LB.
ENJOYS INSECTS AND WEATHER FORECASTS

How did you come up with his name?

There's an actor named Bela Lugosi who plays Dracula in old movies. When I heard that name as a kid, I thought it sounded incredibly elegant, mysterious and powerful. So I borrowed a little from his name.

Is he modeled after someone?

His face is based on the French movie actor Mathieu Amalric. I sometimes think of Kenichi Matsuyama when I'm drawing his body.

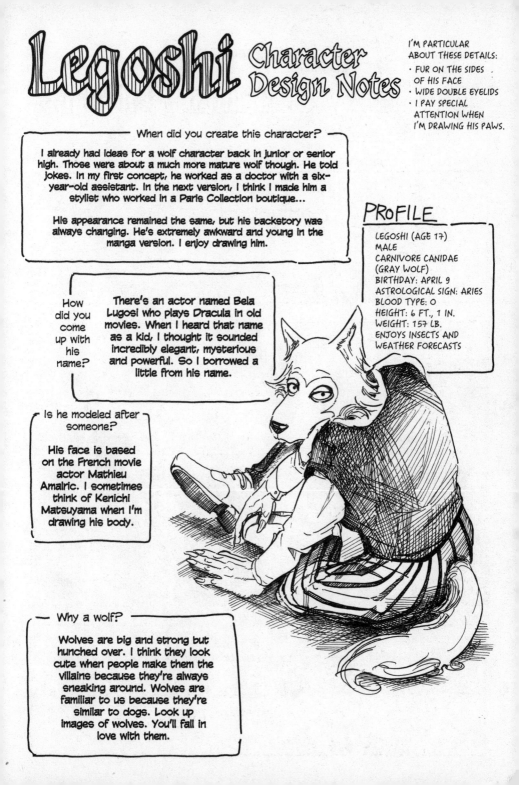

Why a wolf?

Wolves are big and strong but hunched over. I think they look cute when people make them the villains because they're always sneaking around. Wolves are familiar to us because they're similar to dogs. Look up images of wolves. You'll fall in love with them.

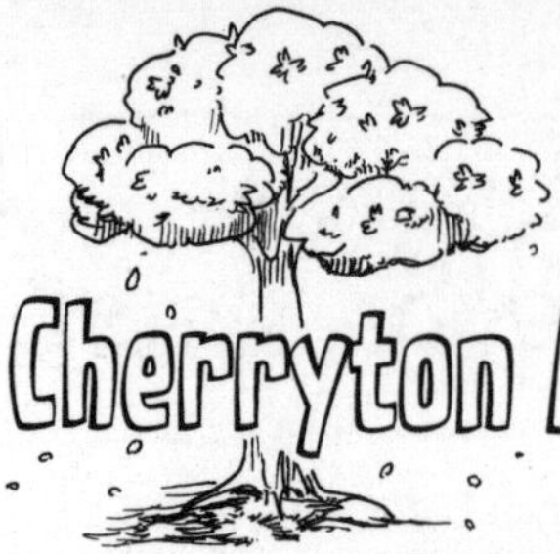

About Cherryton Academy Uniforms

The school uniforms are very formal.
Don't the animals find clothes like that uncomfortable to wear?

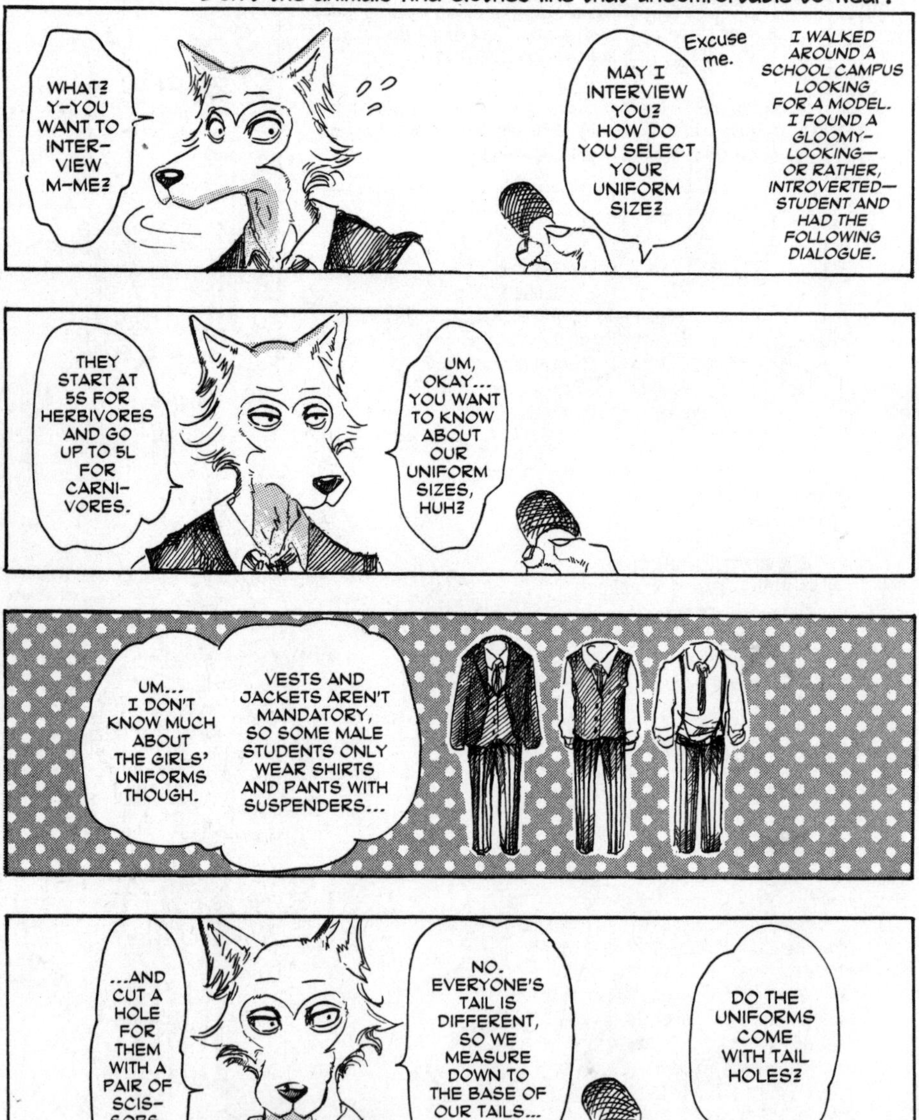
I WALKED AROUND A SCHOOL CAMPUS LOOKING FOR A MODEL. I FOUND A GLOOMY-LOOKING—OR RATHER, INTROVERTED—STUDENT AND HAD THE FOLLOWING DIALOGUE.
Excuse me.
MAY I INTERVIEW YOU? HOW DO YOU SELECT YOUR UNIFORM SIZE?
WHAT? Y-YOU WANT TO INTER-VIEW M-ME?
UM, OKAY... YOU WANT TO KNOW ABOUT OUR UNIFORM SIZES, HUH?
THEY START AT 5S FOR HERBIVORES AND GO UP TO 5L FOR CARNI-VORES.
VESTS AND JACKETS AREN'T MANDATORY, SO SOME MALE STUDENTS ONLY WEAR SHIRTS AND PANTS WITH SUSPENDERS...
UM... I DON'T KNOW MUCH ABOUT THE GIRLS' UNIFORMS THOUGH.
DO THE UNIFORMS COME WITH TAIL HOLES?
NO. EVERYONE'S TAIL IS DIFFERENT, SO WE MEASURE DOWN TO THE BASE OF OUR TAILS...
...AND CUT A HOLE FOR THEM WITH A PAIR OF SCIS-SORS.

Sizes

The basic protocol is that smaller animals have the right of way.

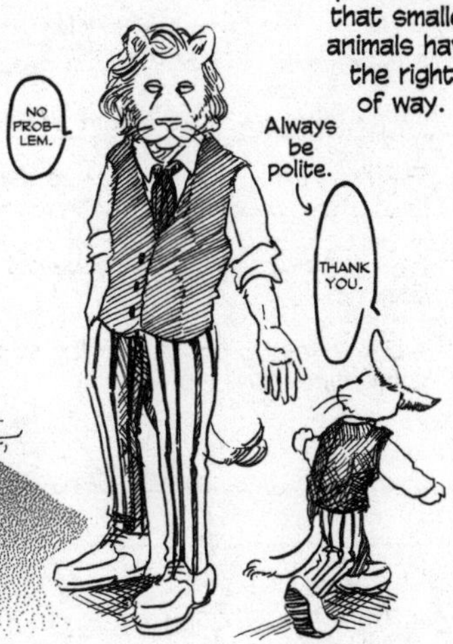
NO PROB-LEM.
Always be polite.
THANK YOU.

Appliances like urinals in the boys' bathrooms don't appear to be different sizes because the perspective is off. They really do come in various heights.

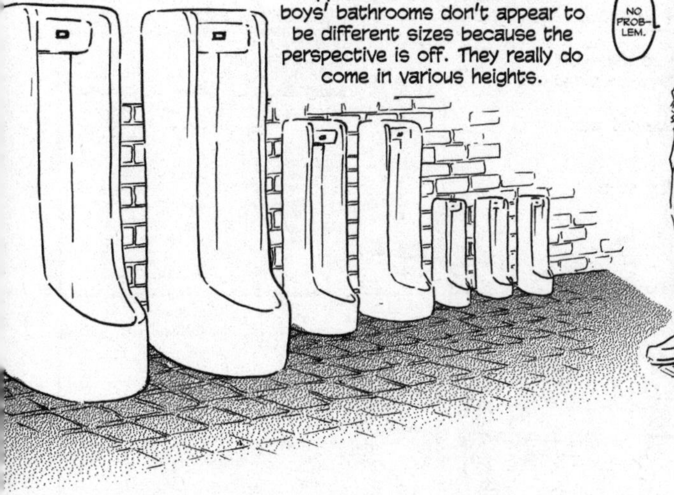

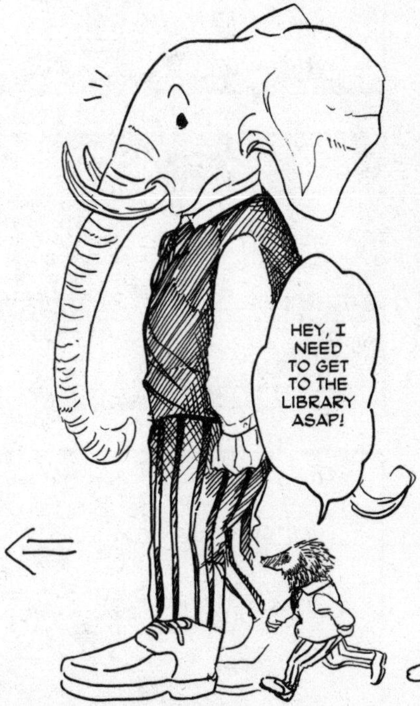
HEY, I NEED TO GET TO THE LIBRARY ASAP!

Big animals, such as elephants, are sometimes used like taxis. They might offer you a ride if they're in a good mood.

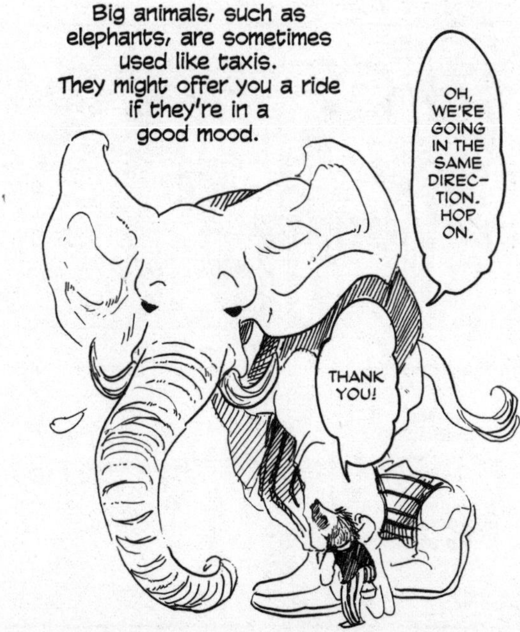
OH, WE'RE GOING IN THE SAME DIREC-TION. HOP ON.
THANK YOU!

Team Paru's Workplace

This is what my workplace looks like.

Two assistants support me.

They're both older than me, so we use honorifics when speaking to each other.

We get along well. It's a pleasant place to work!

And this isn't a promotion for some shady part-time job!

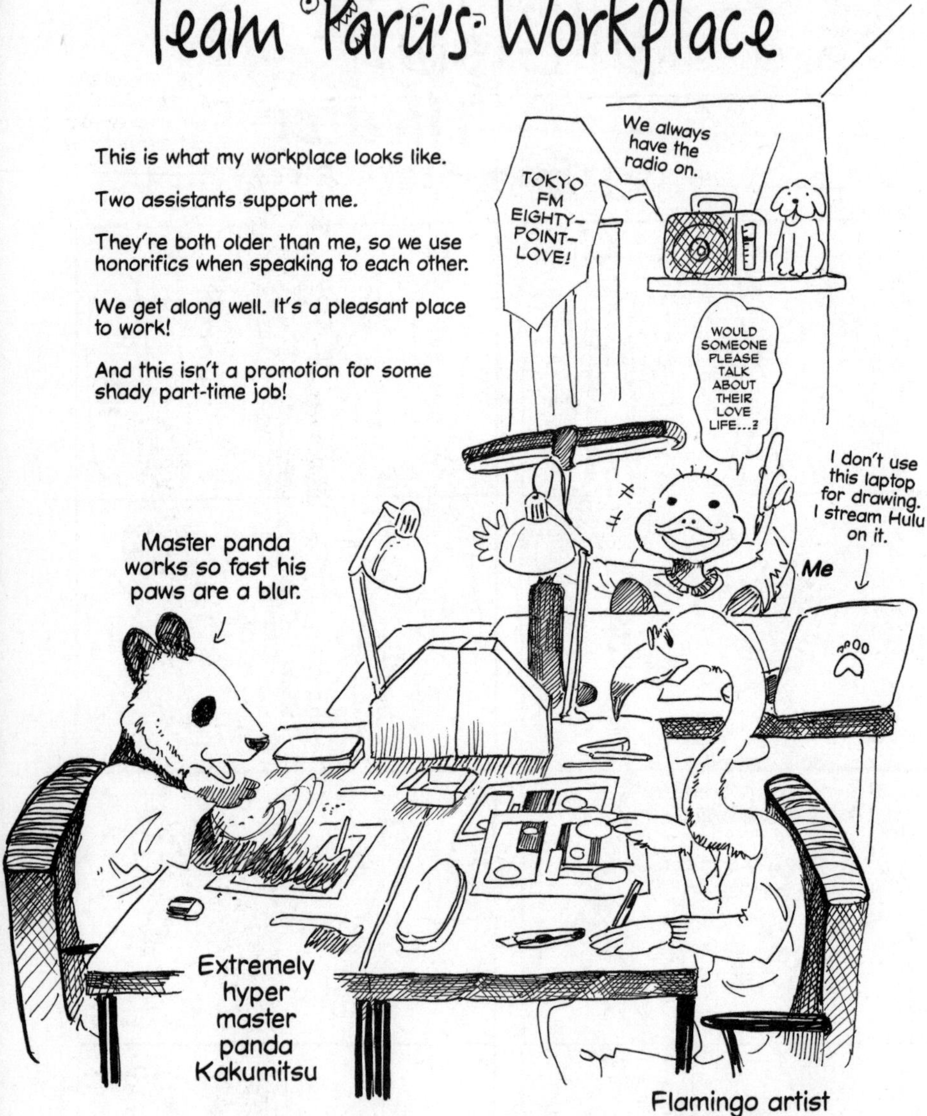
We always have the radio on.
TOKYO FM EIGHTY-POINT-LOVE!
WOULD SOMEONE PLEASE TALK ABOUT THEIR LOVE LIFE...?
I don't use this laptop for drawing. I stream Hulu on it.
Me
Master panda works so fast his paws are a blur.
Extremely hyper master panda Kakumitsu

Flamingo artist Momoya

Sketching and shading screen tones

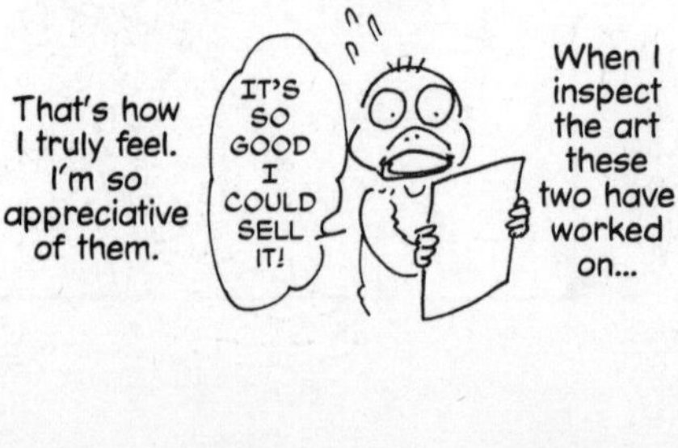
When I inspect the art these two have worked on...
IT'S SO GOOD I COULD SELL IT!
That's how I truly feel. I'm so appreciative of them.

Legoshi's Boo-Hoo Theater

Theme: Static Electricity

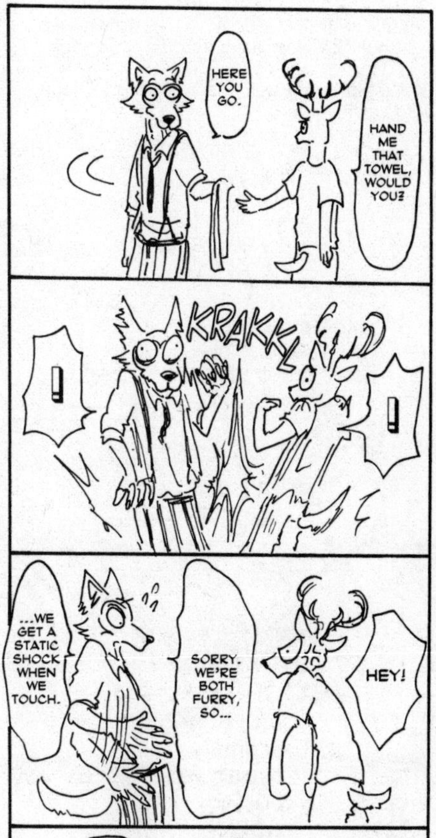
HAND ME THAT TOWEL, WOULD YOU?
HERE YOU GO.
!
KRAKKL
!
HEY!
SORRY. WE'RE BOTH FURRY, SO...
...WE GET A STATIC SHOCK WHEN WE TOUCH.
...
UM... I THINK I CAN SAFELY TOUCH YOU HERE THOUGH...

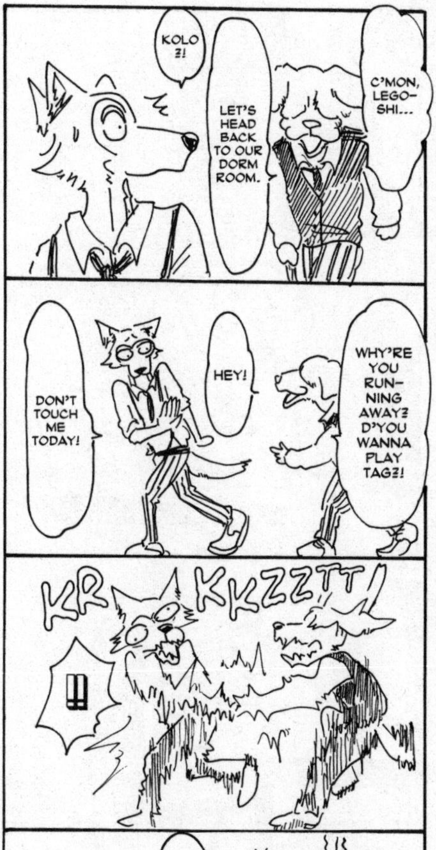
C'MON, LEGOSHI...
LET'S HEAD BACK TO OUR DORM ROOM.
KOLO?!
WHY'RE YOU RUNNING AWAY? D'YOU WANNA PLAY TAG?!
HEY!
DON'T TOUCH ME TODAY!
KR KKZZTT!
!!
AH HA HA HA... I GUESS I SHOULD GO ALONE THEN.
YEP.
HE LOOKS HIPPER NOW THOUGH...

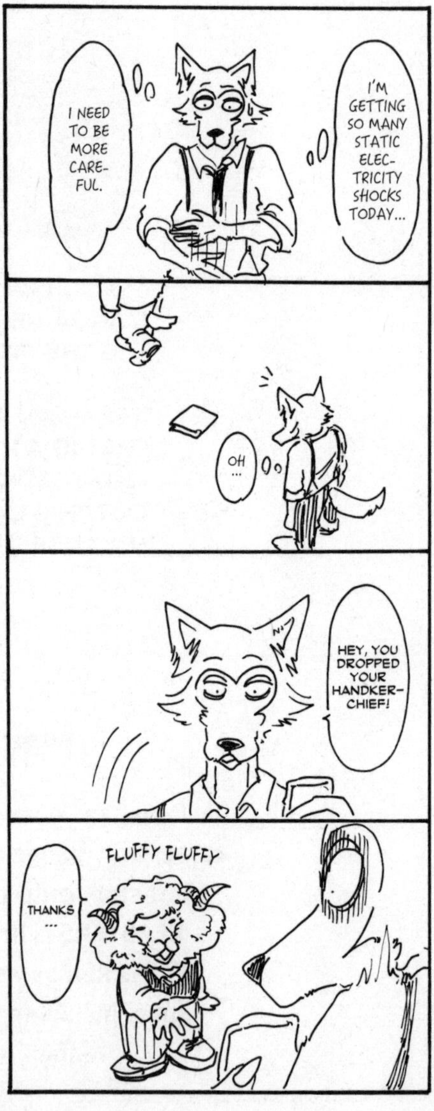
I'M GETTING SO MANY STATIC ELEC-TRICITY SHOCKS TODAY...
I NEED TO BE MORE CARE-FUL.
OH ...
HEY, YOU DROPPED YOUR HANDKER-CHIEF!
FLUFFY FLUFFY
THANKS ...

THANK YOU FOR TAKING THE TIME TO READ THESE BONUS CARTOONS.

I HOPE YOU ENJOYED THIS MANGA.

I'LL TALK ABOUT THE
MANGA HERE, SINCE THIS
IS THE FIRST VOLUME.

THIS IS AN ANIMAL MANGA
THAT IS A HUMAN DRAMA.
AND I DIDN'T JUST BLURT
OUT THIS CONTRADICTION
BECAUSE I'M NERVOUS...

PARU ITAGAKI

Paru Itagaki began her professional
career as a manga author in 2016 with the
short story collection **BEAST COMPLEX**.
BEASTARS is her first serialization.
BEASTARS has won multiple awards in
Japan, including the prestigious 2018
Manga Taisho Award.